3$

Princess Margaret

Princess Margaret

A Biography

THEO ARONSON

MICHAEL O'MARA BOOKS LIMITED

For my sisters
PEGGY MANBY and JEAN PITCHFORD

First published in Great Britain in 1997 by
Michael O'Mara Books Limited
9 Lion Yard, Tremadoc Road
London sw4 7nq

A CIP catalogue record for this book is available from the British Library

ISBN 1-85479-248-2

1 3 5 7 9 10 8 6 4 2

Designed and typeset by Martin Bristow
Printed and bound by Clays Limited, St Ives plc

Contents

Contents

Acknowledgments

ALTHOUGH THIS BOOK is in no way authorized or sanctioned, my chief thanks are to its subject, Princess Margaret. For two of my previous books, *Royal Family: Years of Transition* and *The Royal Family at War*, the Princess has very kindly received me in order to give me her memories, observations and opinions, many of which I have been able to incorporate in this study. I am grateful to Her Royal Highness for her help and hospitality.

Other members of the royal family who have very kindly and on several occasions received me to share their thoughts of the years covered by the span of this book are Queen Elizabeth the Queen Mother, the Prince of Wales, Princess Alice, Duchess of Gloucester and the late Princess Alice, Countess of Athlone.

I am also indebted to members of the various royal households who, to a greater or lesser extent, have given me information and assistance during my research into the recent history of the royal family. Although none of them has been specifically consulted for this book, their contributions have helped me come to a greater understanding of life in the royal households.

This biography has depended, to a considerable extent, on oral evidence. Much of this has been given to me in confidence and, for obvious reasons, I have respected the wishes of those many people who have asked to remain anonymous. I am extremely grateful to them for their co-operation. Others who have very kindly helped me in various ways are, in alphabetical order, Harold Ashwell, the late Stella, Lady Bailey, Toby Barker, Stephen Birmingham, Miriam Bloomberg, Michael Bott, André Bothner, Mervyn Clingan, Aedwyn Darroll, Phyllis Dent-Watson, Jayne Fincher, Lady Grahame, David Griffiths, the late Dowager Viscountess Hambleden, the Earl of Harewood, the late Joan Lascelles, Andrew Lownie, Alan Scales,

Peter Scott-Thompson, Yvone Sterenborg, the late Group Captain Peter Townsend, Hugo Vickers, Denise Wakeford, the late Jock Webster.

I am grateful to the staffs of the British Library, the Newspaper Library at Colindale, the University of Reading Archives, the Bristol Reference Library, the Bath Reference Library and, not least, the Frome Library. I am indebted to the authors and publishers of all the books listed in my Bibliography, especially to those of all previous biographies of Princess Margaret. Three books which have proved especially useful are, in order of publication, *HRH The Princess Margaret* by Nigel Dempster, *Princess Margaret, Countess of Snowdon* by Christopher Warwick, and *Margaret: The Untold Story* by Noel Botham.

As always, my chief thanks are to Brian Roberts for his unfailing help and encouragement.

PROLOGUE

The Last Real Princess

Princess Margaret remains, in many ways, the most interesting member of the British royal family. Part imperious royal figure, part *femme du monde*, she is quite different from the rest of them. She is more sophisticated, more *outré*. Everything – the lavish hats, the long cigarette holder, the drawling voice, the brightly lipsticked mouth, the artfully dyed hair, the frequently replenished whisky glass, the high heels – reinforces the image of a raffish divorcée. Through a family that has often been accused of being too county and conventional, she has swept like a breath of, if not exactly fresh, then certainly scented, air.

The Princess has been described as 'a law unto herself'.[1] Unlike her conscientious sister, Queen Elizabeth II, she will blithely miss important family occasions. She carries out her official engagements in a perfunctory fashion, showing very little of the charm and enthusiasm of the Queen Mother. While her nephews' ex-wives, the Princess of Wales and the Duchess of York, have shamelessly courted the attention of the media, Princess Margaret has treated it with disdain. She has never, unlike her niece Princess Anne, won public acclaim by dedicating herself to some newsworthy charitable cause.

Her style of life has been unorthodox. While the rest of her family move in an unvarying routine between Windsor, Sandringham and Balmoral, she will be sunning herself in Italy, Turkey or the Caribbean. She has none of the horsey, frankly philistine, tastes of so many members of the royal family. Her interests are more worldly; she enjoys travel, ballet, music, the theatre, parties. Seeing herself as something of a bohemian, she has moved in risqué circles, leading what the disapproving Queen calls a 'guttersnipe life'.[2] Among her friends have been actors, dancers, pop singers. Her private life has been racked by scandal; it has been a catalogue of unhappy, unfulfilled and unsuitable relationships. Monarchy, as one observer has put it, 'is a gamble, and in Princess Margaret it has turned up a card'.[3]

Yet she remains dauntingly royal. Princess Margaret is very conscious of the fact that she is the daughter of a king, the sister of a queen. In her youth, only one life stood between her and the succession to the British throne. Her imperiousness is legendary. Any show of over-familiarity, any hint of *lèse-majesté*, will be met by an icy stare. Dare to say 'your sister' instead of 'the Queen' and she will cut you dead. Even her friends are obliged to address her as 'Ma'am' or, if especially close, as 'Ma'am darling'. Those who do not know her well find themselves bewildered by her approachability at one moment, her royal hauteur the next.

Her behaviour and attitudes can be astonishingly high-handed. When faced with a bore, she will cut short the conversation with a sharply expressed 'Quite' and turn her back. On one occasion, when discussing the abolition of the royal presentation parties at which the Season's debutantes would be presented to the monarch, and which, in the more egalitarian atmosphere of post-Second World War Britain, had become an anachronism, she made a wonderfully idiosyncratic remark. 'We had to stop them,' she explained. 'Every *tart* in London was being presented.'[4] In other words, the presentation parties had not been abolished because they had become too exclusive but because they were no longer exclusive enough.

This duality in her nature, this pull between being a rebel and being royal, is compounded by the awkwardness of her status. What, exactly, is a princess supposed to do in the second half of the twentieth century? She was born into an almost Victorian world of pomp, privilege and deference. Governess-educated, cocooned, indulged, she was never expected to do much more than look attractive and act graciously. In some ways, she is like an exile from another era, the last real princess.

Princess Margaret has been variously described as tragic, unresolved, a royal maverick, a woman of conflict, a princess without a cause. And although she is neither the unhappy figure of some imaginings nor the spoiled brat of others, she has been her own worst enemy. Referred to, these days, as 'the Princess Diana of her time', she enjoyed enormous popularity when she was in her twenties. But she has lost it all. Her opinion-poll ratings are embarrassingly low. Her good points – her loyalty to the Queen, her sense of royal obligation, her affection for her friends – have been submerged in an avalanche of criticism. She complains that she has been misreported and misrepresented since the age of seventeen. If this is true, then she has only herself to blame for leading so controversial a life. Rightly or wrongly, Princess Margaret's public image remains firmly that of a selfish, arrogant and capricious personality. Born with all possible advantages – beauty, vivacity, intelligence, wealth and position – she has led a curiously unfulfilled life. 'She had everything,' says one courtier's wife, 'and then she destroyed herself. Her nature was to make everything go wrong.'[5]

But it was not quite as simple as that.

PART ONE

Margaret Rose

CHAPTER I

Glamis Castle

Princess Margaret was born, appropriately enough, during a violent thunderstorm. Equally dramatic was the setting for her birth: Glamis Castle, ancestral home of the Earls of Strathmore and Kinghorne. Her mother, the Duchess of York, had been born Lady Elizabeth Bowes-Lyon, the ninth child of the fourteenth Earl of Strathmore, and it was to her family's Scottish seat, Glamis Castle on Tayside, that the Duchess of York had come to give birth to her second child in the late summer of 1930.

With its turrets, battlements and impregnable red sandstone walls, Glamis is an impressive pile, both romantic and menacing. In its time it has played host to such significant historical figures as Mary, Queen of Scots, James Stuart, the Old Pretender, and Sir Walter Scott. It is for its more blood-curdling associations, however, that Glamis is chiefly remarkable. Its story is one of violent deaths, gruesome murders and terrifying ghosts. Macbeth is said to have slain Duncan in the guardroom: 'Glamis hath murdered sleep, and therefore . . . Macbeth shall sleep no more!' ring Shakespeare's lines. The castle has witnessed other equally grim, and better authenticated, deaths. King Malcolm's Room is where the murdered King Malcolm II of Scotland died; its floor is still stained, it is claimed, with his blood. The Hangman's Chamber takes its name from the two desperate men who had hanged themselves within its dank walls. In the Room of Skulls captured members of the Ogilvy family, bitter enemies of the Lyons, were walled up alive and, despite gnawing at their own flesh, finally died of starvation, their corpses rotting away into a pile of bones.

Among the many ghosts that apparently roam its rooms and corridors is the tormented spirit of Jane Douglas, burned as a witch in the sixteenth century; another, that of Earl Beardie, is doomed to play endless games of cards with the Devil as a penance for having staked his soul in a card game. Most chilling of all is the legend of the famous Monster of Glamis – the hairy, hideously deformed, egg-shaped creature, heir to one Lord Glamis – who was kept hidden under lock and key in some secret part of the castle for decade after decade. The whereabouts of this monster was known only to each succeeding earl, who, as his own death approached, would pass on the secret to his heir, and to one or two trusted retainers whose duty it was to shove food into the creature's prison. It has been said that on one occasion a party of sceptical house guests, determined to disprove the monster's existence by making a methodical search of the entire castle, took advantage of their host's temporary absence to visit every one of its rooms, of which there are more than a hundred. To mark their progress, they hung towels out of each window. When, afterwards, they trooped outside, it was to make the disconcerting discovery that there were seven windows without towels. Many villagers in Glamis firmly believed the rumour that a maid, having stumbled across the monster's place of incarceration, had had her tongue cut out to prevent her from revealing the dreaded family secret. Indeed, as a child, Lady Elizabeth Bowes-Lyon had been warned by a kitchenmaid that 'if she dared look out of the night nursery window late at night, she would see the tongueless woman running across the park, pointing in agony to her bleeding mouth'.[1]

Presumably no such frightening images were being entertained by the Duchess of York as she waited at Glamis for the birth of her second child during that August of 1930. For the thirty-year-old Duchess the castle held happier memories. Her mother, Lady Strathmore, born Cecilia Cavendish-Bentinck, had transformed the rebuilt nineteenth-century wing of the house in which the family now lived into a comfortable and flower-filled home, one to which the Duchess, strongly conscious of her Scottish ancestry, always felt drawn. When, in 1923, she had married the Duke of York, second son of King George V and Queen Mary, the young couple had spent part of their honeymoon at Glamis. And although their first child, Princess Elizabeth, had been born, on 20 April 1926, in the Strathmores' London home, 17 Bruton Street, it was to Glamis that the Duchess decided to come for the birth of her second child. The baby was due to be born during the second week of August.

For this proposed Scottish accouchement, the King's permission had to be sought and granted. The birth of a child to the Duke and Duchess of York was, after all, a matter of national – indeed, inter-national – importance. Because the Heir Apparent, King George V's eldest son, the Prince of Wales, was still unmarried, the Prince's younger brother – the Duke of York – was next in the line of suc-cession, with his daughter, Princess Elizabeth, third. If the baby were a boy, it would replace Princess Elizabeth in the order of suc-cession; if a girl, it would rank fourth. In the event of the thirty-six-year-old Prince of Wales remaining unmarried and childless, there was a strong possibility that one of the children of the Duke and Duchess of York – perhaps even the expected infant – might one day succeed to the throne. Glamis Castle, therefore, might well prove to be the scene of the birth of a future British monarch.

Into these matters of international significance there now entered an element of farce. By tradition, all royal births had to be witnessed by a minister of the Crown, usually the Home Secretary. The cus-tom had its origins in the famous 'warming-pan' plot of 1688, when it was widely – and quite wrongly – believed that Mary of Modena, Queen Consort of King James II, had had another woman's baby smuggled into her bed in a warming-pan; this baby had then been passed off as the legitimate heir to the throne. Ever since then, in order to prevent any uncertainties about the legitimacy of royal off-spring, it was ordered that a government minister should be present at any such birth. To this outdated custom, the Duke and Duchess of York were obliged to agree. (The tradition was finally abolished in 1948 by the Duke of York himself when, as King George VI, he spared his daughter Princess Elizabeth any such indignity while she was giving birth to Prince Charles.) At least, by 1930, the ministeri-al witness no longer had to be present in the very room where the birth was taking place; he could wait outside. 'If there has to be a gentleman waiting outside my bedroom door,' remarked the Duchess of York wryly, 'I hope it's someone we know.'[2]

The gentleman proved, in fact, to be someone whom the Yorks would not, in a social sense, have 'known'. The Home Secretary of the day was J.R. Clynes, a former millworker who was now a minister in Ramsay MacDonald's Labour government. Clynes was to be accompanied by Harry Boyd, the Ceremonial Secretary at the Home Office. It had been suggested that the two men should be accommodated in a hotel in Perth, and that as soon as the Duchess of York went into labour, they could take a train which would get them to Glamis in time for the birth. Although this suggestion did not bother Mr Clynes unduly, it 'horrified' poor Mr Boyd. A fussy, anxious, meticulously neat little man, the Ceremonial Secretary was 'overwhelmed' by the responsibility now thrust upon him. The very fact that the Duchess of York had decided to have her baby at Glamis was deeply disturbing to his bureaucratic mind. He felt sure that the public would suspect that the affair was being conducted in 'an irregular hole-and-corner way'. How risky, then, to rely on the train from Perth to get Clynes and himself to Glamis. 'Just imagine if it should occur in the early hours of the morning, and the Home Secretary could not get to Glamis in time,' wailed Boyd. 'This child will be in direct succession to the Throne and if its birth is not properly witnessed, its legal right might be questioned.'[3]

It was to the Countess of Airlie, one of Queen Mary's ladies-in-waiting, that Harry Boyd poured out these doubts and fears. To quell them, she suggested that he and the Home Secretary stay with her at nearby Cortachy Castle; she assured him that it was close enough to Glamis to prevent any 'calamity'. Boyd agreed, and to make doubly certain of not missing the birth, the two men, without waiting to be summoned to Scotland, left London to arrive at Cortachy on 5 August.

For no fewer than sixteen days they sat cooling their heels while the baby, unpredictable even before birth, kept them waiting. 'I feel sorry for Mr Clynes having to be here so long,' wrote the Duke of York to his mother, Queen Mary, on 10 August. 'I always wanted him to come up when he was sent for, which would have been much simpler.'[4]

But the Duke should have been feeling sorry for Mr Boyd rather than for Mr Clynes. Unlike Boyd, the Home Secretary was a shy though imperturbable man, quite content to be shown round the countryside by Lady Airlie and to be entertained in various great houses in the district. 'I discovered under his homely exterior,' wrote Lady Airlie, 'a deeply sensitive mind, touchingly appreciative

of beauty.' No amount of country-house visiting could distract Mr
Boyd, however. As day after day passed with no news from Glamis,
he became progressively more frantic. Not even the specially
installed telephone line nor the waiting motorcyclist could put his
mind at ease. He began to suspect some sort of plot. By the morning
of 21 August – fifteen days after the baby had originally been due –
looking 'wild-eyed and haggard after sitting up all night', Boyd telephoned Glamis yet again, only to be assured by the admirably long-
suffering Comptroller of the Duke of York's household that there
was still no news.

Finally, as Lady Airlie was dressing for dinner that evening, her
telephone rang. The call was for Mr Boyd. Still in her dressing-
gown, she ran to his room and banged on the door. 'A telephone call
for you from Glamis,' she shouted. She heard, she reports, a tremendous opening and shutting of wardrobes and then a wail of anguish.
'I can't go downstairs,' cried Boyd, I'm not dressed and I can't find
my suit.' 'Then put on your dressing-gown and take the call in my
room,' Lady Airlie yelled back. 'I'm not dressed either but it does-
n't matter.' Boyd dashed out of his bedroom wearing a dark blue
kimono and, snatching up Lady Airlie's bedroom telephone,
exclaimed, 'What! In an hour? You haven't given us much time. We
must start at once.'

While the anguished Boyd scrambled into his clothes, Clynes
was 'calmly waiting at the door in his big coat and Homburg hat'. As
Boyd hurried him out to the waiting car, Clynes paused to look up at
the dramatically stormy sunset sky. 'Just look at that Boyd,' he
mused. '"In such a night did Dido from the walls of Carthage. . . ."'
This was too much for Boyd. Cutting Clynes short, he bundled him
into the car and the two of them went racing off through the night
towards Glamis.[5]

They arrived with half an hour to spare. By that time a violent
storm had broken. With Shakespearian theatricality, the thunder
rumbled, the lightning flashed, the wind howled and the rain lashed
down. The Duchess of York had been prepared for delivery in the
Tapestry Room by her three physicians, Sir Henry Simpson, Dr
Neon Reynolds and Dr David Myles. At 9.22 pm on 21 August
1930, the Duchess gave birth to a daughter weighing 6 pounds 11
ounces. Only after this weighing was Home Secretary Clynes
allowed into the room to verify the birth. 'I found crowded round

the baby's cot the Duke of York, Lord and Lady Strathmore and Lady Rose Leveson-Gower, the Duchess's sister,' he wrote. 'They at once made way for me, and I went to the cot and peeping in saw a fine chubby-faced little girl lying wide awake.'[6]

'Yesterday evening at twenty-two minutes after nine o'clock,' read the official announcement on 22 August 1930, 'Her Royal Highness the Duchess of York was safely delivered of a Princess.'[7] The birth of another grandchild to the sovereign was greeted with due honours. Gun salutes thudded out from Hyde Park and the Tower of London and the bells of St Paul's Cathedral and Westminster Abbey pealed out in celebration. Congratulatory cables flooded in from all over the British Empire.

It was not until the night after the birth, however, when the storm had died down, that the event could be celebrated by the villagers and tenants at Glamis. To the skirl of bagpipes, they surged up Hunter's Hill where three specially chosen young girls set fire to the brushwood beacon. The celebrations were considerably enlivened by the barrels of free beer supplied by the baby's grandfather, Lord Strathmore. The blazing bonfire, visible for miles around, was watched from a window set high in one of the castle's towers by the newborn's four-year-old sister, Princess Elizabeth.

Particularly gratifying to the local people was the fact that the baby had been born in Scotland. Because of this Scottish birth, Princess Margaret was often to be described, in the years ahead, as being typically 'Stuart', in contrast to what was regarded, in the same journalistic shorthand, as Princess Elizabeth's stolid, more 'Hanoverian' appearance. And indeed, for a while, the younger princess's looks did seem to reflect something of the elegance and romance of the ill-starred Stuart dynasty. Only in the face of Princess Margaret's increasingly Hanoverian appetites did such references begin to die.

Not until two weeks after the baby's birth was her name decided upon. This was undoubtedly due to the fact that the parents had been hoping for a boy. So, apparently, had the King and Queen, though that royal couple seemed pleased enough with the arrival of a second granddaughter. Not long after they had arrived at Balmoral for their annual autumn stay, they visited Glamis. Queen Mary pronounced, 'E looking very well and the baby a darling.' As the child's name was still undecided, the Duchess later wrote to Queen Mary to say, 'I am very anxious to call her Ann Margaret as I think that Ann of York sounds pretty, and Elizabeth and Ann go so well together. I wonder what you think? Lots of people have suggested Margaret [as a first name] but it has no family links really on either side.'

This was not quite accurate. Although there may have been no immediate family links to the name, Margaret had been a royal name for centuries, particularly popular in Scotland. (It had been the name of the eleventh-century queen of Malcolm III of Scotland, who had been canonized as Saint Margaret.) It was not, however, to Margaret but to Ann that King George V objected, and the couple therefore had to bow to the King's wishes. But when next the Duchess wrote to her mother-in-law on the subject, it was with an unmistakable firmness. We 'have decided now to call our little daughter "Margaret Rose", instead of Margaret Ann, as Papa [the King] does not like Ann – I hope that you like it. I think that it is very pretty together.'[8] It undoubtedly was: 'Margaret Rose of York' had a decidedly mellifluous ring.

According to Scots law, Princess Margaret's birth should have been registered within twenty-one days. But the Duke of York, although no more superstitious than the next man, delayed the registration because the birth certificate would have been numbered 13. Not until 2 October did he present himself at the Glamis post office-cum-sweetshop to register the birth. By then, there had been another birth in the village and the delay ensured that the Princess's number in the register was 14.

Princess Margaret's religious, as opposed to her civil, naming was a far more splendid affair. She was christened in the private chapel at Buckingham Palace on 30 October 1930 by Cosmo Gordon Lang, Archbishop of Canterbury. Dressed in the cream-coloured silk and Honiton-lace robe first worn by Queen Victoria's eldest child, Victoria (later the German Empress Frederick), she was carried to the gold, lily-shaped font which had been filled with water from the River Jordan. Her five sponsors, or godparents, were Edward, Prince of Wales, for whom his brother Prince George, later Duke of Kent, stood proxy; the future Queen Ingrid of Denmark, for whom her aunt, Lady Patricia Ramsay, stood proxy; Princess Victoria, the second of King George V's three sisters; Lady Rose Leveson-Gower, one of the Duchess of York's sisters; and the Honourable David Bowes-Lyon, the Duchess's adored younger brother.

Although, throughout her childhood, the Princess was to be known as Margaret Rose in public, in the family she was called simply Margaret. Unlike her sister, Princess Elizabeth, whose nickname was Lilibet, Princess Margaret had no family version of her name; not, that is, until a younger generation began to call her Aunt Margot. Even as a child, she hated the double forename. 'You gave Lilibet three names,' she once complained to her mother. 'Why didn't you give me three instead of only two? Margaret Rose!'[9]

The four-year-old Princess Elizabeth produced her own version of her new sister's name. 'I shall call her Bud,' she announced to Lady Cynthia Asquith. 'Why Bud?' asked the bemused Lady Cynthia. 'Well,' explained the Princess, 'she's not a real rose yet, is she? She's only a bud.'[10]

To understand the private and public conflicts that were to bedevil Princess Margaret's life, one needs to appreciate the grandiose world into which she was born.

In 1930, the year of her birth, the British royal family, in terms of status and prestige, was the most important family in the world. Her grandfather, King George V, held what his grandmother Queen Victoria had once blandly and justifiably described as 'the greatest position there is'.[11] He was King-Emperor of the largest empire the world had ever known; holding sway over a quarter of the world's landmass and a quarter of the world's population. In fact, not until three years after Princess Margaret's birth would the British Empire – or Commonwealth as it was coming to be called – reach its geographical zenith, with an area of almost 14 million square miles and a population of 493 million. London, the heart of this great imperial conglomeration, was the world's largest city, boasting a population of almost eight million. To many an Eastern or African subject, the British monarch, enthroned in this fabled, faraway capital, seemed more like a deity than a mortal.

To all outward appearances, Great Britain remained the mightiest nation on earth; not until after the Second World War, with the rise of the new superpowers, the United States and the USSR, was it to lose its position of global pre-eminence. And although, as a constitutional monarch, King George V wielded very little personal power, he remained the world's most recognizable, respected and impressive figurehead: the symbol of an empire on which the sun never set.

In purely dynastic terms, too, King George V was the world's leading sovereign. A mere dozen years before Princess Margaret's birth, Europe's other great imperial monarchies had been swept away. Those sovereigns who, before the First World War, had vied with King George V in stature – Tsar Nicholas II of Russia, the German Kaiser Wilhelm II, the Emperor Franz-Josef of Austria-Hungary – had all disappeared from the scene, leaving the British king as the world's only truly important monarch. The House of Windsor remained the one royal family of any consequence; beside it, Europe's other royal houses seemed either lacklustre or Ruritanian.

Although, personally, George V was a man of modest tastes and limited intelligence, his court was run on the most magnificent lines. 'Nothing,' wrote one visiting Continental princess,

is more irreproachably perfect in every detail than the King of England's Court and Household, a sort of staid luxury without ostentation, a placid, aristocratic ease and opulence which has nothing showy about it. Everything is run on silent wheels that have been perfectly greased; everything fits in, there are no spaces between, no false note. From the polite, handsome and superlatively groomed gentleman-in-waiting who receives you in the hall, to the magnificently solemn and yet welcoming footman who walks before you down the corridor, everything pleases the eye, satisfies one's fastidiousness. . . .'[12]

The great ceremonial and social occasions were brilliantly stagemanaged affairs, conducted with the utmost punctiliousness. The Opening of Parliament, Trooping the Colour, the Ascot processions, the courts, balls, banquets, investitures and garden parties were as notable for their solemnity as their splendour. 'My goodness it was stiff,' remembered one lady-in-waiting. 'You can't imagine how stiff it was.'[13] Presiding over these formal functions, George V and Queen Mary were like figures out of another age. The King, neatly bearded and ruddy-cheeked, stubbornly adhered to the fashions of his youth: in top hat, frock coat, side-creased trousers and spats, he always looked immaculate. Queen Mary, too, remained faithful to the pre-First World War opulence approved of by her husband. Whatever else might change, one could always be sure of Queen Mary's toques, ankle-length skirts, lace parasols and long, pointed shoes. On state occasions, with the King in gold-braided and bemedalled uniform and the Queen in some shimmering dress ablaze with jewellery ('No one could wear jewellery like Queen Mary, and so much of it,' claimed one member of the Court [14]) they looked the very quintessence of old-fashioned majesty.

In stately and unvarying rotation, the Court moved from one magnificent royal residence to the next. The monarch's official homes, Buckingham Palace, Windsor Castle and St James's Palace, were treasure houses, crammed with priceless paintings, furniture and objets d'art; his private homes, Balmoral Castle and Sandringham House, were hardly less expensively, if somewhat more tastelessly, appointed. Other London properties were Kensington Palace, Marlborough House and Clarence House. As the sovereigns moved from one royal seat to another, so were they attended by a team of secretaries, equerries, ladies-in-waiting, police officers and personal servants, while every royal home had, of course, its own resident indoor and outdoor staffs. The number of employees ran into thousands.

The King's private, and preferred, life was that of a country squire. In cultural or intellectual pursuits he had no interest whatsoever; he loathed travel. George V was never happier than when shooting at Balmoral or at Sandringham. Yet even here his life ran with all the precision of a regularly oiled clock. 'My father's life was a masterpiece in the art of well-ordered, unostentatious, elegant living,' claimed his eldest son, the Prince of Wales, afterwards Duke of Windsor.

No matter the place, no matter the occasion, perfection pervaded every detail. The shooting lunches served in a tent in the field at Sandringham were prepared with the same expert care by the chef as the fine banquets set before crowned heads at Windsor Castle or Buckingham Palace. And the approach of the head gamekeeper with the game card to my father's seat at table, after the morning's bag was counted, was as solemn and grave as that of an ambassador presenting his letters of credence. Nothing ever seemed to be forgotten; nothing ever seemed to go wrong. The secret of all this smooth perfection, an old courtier once explained to me, was the system of having the equivalent of a man and a half for every job. [15]

Surrounded by exaggerated deference, cheered whenever they appeared in public, treated with an almost religious reverence, the royal family could hardly be blamed for imagining themselves as a breed apart. 'The important thing to remember,' the grandest of British grandees once explained, 'is that in the eyes of the royal family, we're all glorified footmen and ladies' maids.'[16]

The same almost unreal qualities marked the royal couple's outlook and attitudes. They were conservative, conventional and virtuous to an extraordinary degree; and if the Queen's tastes were not quite as philistine as the King's, she had long ago learned to adjust her more imaginative mind to his. Both were obsessed, above all, with upholding the dignity and integrity of the monarchy. To them, the institution was sacrosanct. A sense of royal duty, of royal self-sacrifice, of royal industry, overrode all other considerations. The royal family, noted one of its members, 'did not talk of love and affection and what we meant to each other, but rather – and even about that not easily – of duty and behaviour and what we ought to do. . . .'[17]

It was into this formal, rarefied, stultified, tradition-bound and duty-driven institution that Princess Margaret was now launched. She was to spend the greater part of her life torn between trying to meet its exacting standards and flouting its long-established conventions.

CHAPTER 2

The Yorks

IN THE YEAR OF PRINCESS MARGARET'S BIRTH, her father, Prince Albert, Duke of York, turned thirty-five. Whatever his virtues, he could hardly have been described as an impressive-looking man. Although princes need not necessarily be intelligent, it is essential that they have some sort of public presence. The Duke of York had none. Fine-boned and slightly built, he looked frail, seemed lacking in physical stamina. His air was tense, hesitant, ill-at-ease. An observer had only to notice the incessant working of his jaw muscles to appreciate that he was under severe strain. The truth was that the Duke of York was sadly ill equipped for his role in public life: intensely shy, he lacked small talk, and was incapable of making a spontaneous gesture. The most debilitating handicap of all was his speech impediment. Although, by the time of his second daughter's birth, the Duke had overcome the worst of his stammer, it tended to re-emerge under pressure; his public delivery remained slow and monotonous. All in all, he looked very largely what he was – a well-meaning man, but ill educated, self-doubting, unresolved.

Born on 14 December 1895, the Duke of York had endured a singularly cheerless childhood. King George V and Queen Mary had been inadequate parents. Both were shy, inhibited, inarticulate people, not given to displays of emotion or affection. The relationship between the King and Queen and their four surviving sons had lacked warmth and intimacy (with their only daughter, Princess Mary, things had been slightly better), with the result that the sons had never been able to relax with, let alone confide in, their parents. The King was a short-tempered man, critical and exacting. The nearest he would come to a show of paternal friendliness was to indulge in a sort of chaffing banter. Queen Mary, naturally reserved and with very little understanding of a child's mind, had been curiously detached and unemotional. Her first loyalty was to her husband: as monarch and as man, and in that order. 'I have always to remember,' she once explained, 'that their father is also their King.'[1]

Prince Albert, or Bertie, as he was known in the family (his full names were Albert Frederick Arthur George), had been raised by nurses and tutors. His mother had played so little part in his upbringing that only after his nurse had suffered a nervous breakdown did she discover that the woman had not had a day off in over three years. Meanwhile, the nurse's haphazard method of feeding him had left Prince Albert with chronic stomach trouble. In time, when a rather more satisfactory nurse had to be replaced by a tutor, the King chose the most upright, humourless and uninspired man imaginable: in the course of his dreary educational routine, the young prince learned almost nothing. In contrast to his older brother, Prince Edward, later Prince of Wales and always known in the family as David, Prince Albert developed into a highly strung youngster, given to moods which swung between deep depression and almost hysterical excitement. He had, and would always retain, an explosive temper.

Making life still more difficult for this sensitive boy were two physical defects: his knock knees and his stammer. The first was remedied by the wearing of painful splints, which he was obliged to keep on even in bed. At times they hurt him so badly that he burst into tears. Occasionally his manservant, Finch, one of the few kind-hearted people about him, would take pity and allow him to sleep without them. His speech defect, which began to manifest itself when he was seven, almost certainly resulted from this naturally left-handed boy being forced to use his right hand, and led to his being mercilessly teased by his brothers and sister. This teasing, unchecked by his parents, merely ensured that his stammer became worse. It was at its worst, significantly, in the presence of his intimidating father.

Prince Albert's years of private tutoring in the cloistered, artificial and privileged atmosphere of the various royal homes were followed by a sudden exposure to the rough-and-tumble of the naval colleges of first Osborne, and then Dartmouth. The boy was forced to cope not only with the harsh regimes and the unfamiliar communal living, but with homesickness, shyness, slowness and, of course, that embarrassing stammer. By no means clever, his stammer made him appear more stupid still. Not unnaturally, he hesitated to speak up in class. As a result, he was subjected to his father's hectoring letters, and to frightening scenes in his father's library. In his final examinations at Osborne, in December 1910, the fourteen-year-old Prince Albert was placed 68 out of 68.

His subsequent career in the Royal Navy was hardly more illustrious. In September 1913, with his training at Dartmouth completed, the Prince joined HMS *Collingwood* as an ordinary midshipman. But a duodenal ulcer obliged him to absent himself from his duties for long periods, and although he managed to see action at the Battle of Jutland during the First World War, soon after that his ulcer forced him to leave the navy. He left it, it must be admitted, with a reputation as an unaffected and likeable young man who had borne his long periods of pain and frustration with considerable fortitude.

Something more than this, though, was necessary for the part he was now expected to play in public life. With the popular Prince of Wales (the 'cock pheasant' to Albert's 'ugly duckling'[2]) often away on extended tours of the Empire, Prince Albert, created Duke of York in 1920, found himself increasingly in the spotlight. It was a position he loathed. For him, public appearances and, worse still, public speaking, were forms of torture.

His many failings were, however, compensated for by a certain doggedness; a resolve to do whatever had to be done to the best of his abilities. It was in an area not hitherto associated with the monarchy that he was able to make a mark. Created President of the Boys' Welfare Association – an organization dedicated to promoting better working conditions, and which was afterwards given the more impressive-sounding title of the Industrial Welfare Society – the Duke of York took his position very seriously. For this interest in the workers, and for the knowledge he gained of their jobs, he earned the nickname 'The Industrial Prince'; his brothers referred to him, less reverently, as 'the Foreman'. Out of these activities grew the celebrated Duke of York's Camp. For almost two decades from 1921, these summer camps to which, in the interests of inter-class contact, working boys and public schoolboys were brought together, became an institution. In the uncritical, undemanding company of these lads, Prince Albert blossomed. Year after year the slight figure of the Duke of York, in his open-necked shirt, baggy shorts and long socks, would be seen sitting happily among a crowd of youngsters, all bellowing the famous camp song, 'Under the Spreading Chestnut Tree'.

But not even achievements such as these could earn him any parental approval. On the contrary, the King remained as critical as always. He once sent his son, then away on an official tour, a press photograph. 'I send you a picture of you inspecting Guard of Honour (I don't think much of their dressing) with your equerry walking on your right side next to the Guard, and ignoring the officer entirely,' complained the King. 'Your equerry should be outside and behind, it certainly does not look well.'[3] Resignedly, the Prince wrote back to explain that the photograph had been taken after, and not during, the inspection.

Queen Mary remained as remote from her sons as adults as she had from them as children. 'They were strangers to her emotionally,' wrote her Lady-in-Waiting, Lady Airlie, 'a nest of wild birds already spreading their wings and soaring beyond her horizon.'[4] The Queen could never bring herself to discuss anything really serious or intimate with them. 'David dined with me this evening,' reads a typical report from the Queen to the King. 'We talked a lot but of nothing very intimate.'[5] 'She really is far too reserved,' commented Prince Albert to the Prince of Wales on one occasion, 'she keeps too much locked up inside herself.'[6]

In short, the three things the Duke of York's nature most ardently craved – affection, approval and encouragement – were conspicuously lacking in his home circle. He found these qualities, as princes, past and present, have so often found them, in the world of the theatre. During his early twenties, the Duke of York enjoyed a relationship with a musical-comedy star called Phyllis Monkman. Small, shapely, with an easy manner and an effervescent sense of humour, Phyllis Monkman was exactly the type of woman to give the young Prince reassurance. She was enough of a lady, however, never to reveal the full extent of their romance. When she died in 1976, at the age of eighty-four, a treasured photograph of the young man who was later to become King George VI was found among her effects.

Another of the Duke's romances was with a rather more 'suitable' candidate: Lady Maureen Vane-Tempest-Stewart, daughter of the seventh Marquess of Londonderry. She, too, was the sort of vivacious, self-confident woman to whom the diffident young man found himself attracted. But Lady Maureen apparently preferred a younger son of the seventeenth Earl of Derby and, by marrying him in 1920, had only herself to blame for not becoming the next Queen of England.

In that same summer of 1920, when the Duke of York was twenty-five, he met and fell passionately in love with the nineteen-year-old Lady Elizabeth Bowes-Lyon.

Unlike the Duke of York, Elizabeth Bowes-Lyon had enjoyed a blissful childhood. Born on 4 August 1900, she had been raised in an atmosphere quite different from that of the royal family. 'I have nothing but wonderfully happy memories of childhood days at home,' she once admitted to a friend, 'fun, kindness, and a marvellous sense of security.'[7] The Strathmores were not only very grand (they could trace their descent back to King Robert the Bruce of Scotland), but also very rich. Lady Elizabeth's childhood had been divided between the ancient Scottish castle of Glamis, the elegant Queen Anne mansion of St Paul's Walden Bury in Hertfordshire, and an impressive town house in St James's Square in London. While her father, the fourteenth Earl of Strathmore, was a quiet, courteous man, her mother – a member of the equally aristocratic, if not quite as long established, Cavendish-Bentinck family – was a much livelier figure: artistic, cheerful, interested in everything. It was chiefly from her mother that Lady Elizabeth, the ninth in a family of ten children, inherited her personality.

From this warm and secure background, Lady Elizabeth Bowes-Lyon grew into a gay, vital, unaffected and kind-hearted young woman. Already, at the age of nineteen in the summer of 1920, she was showing signs of a remarkable inner serenity and an exceptional strength of character. She was also a beauty. Small and graceful (she was only 5 feet 2 inches tall), Lady Elizabeth was blessed with typically Celtic looks: black hair, blue eyes and a skin like cream.

That the Duke of York should fall in love with this enchanting young woman was hardly surprising. Nor was he the only one. Several highly eligible young men, including Prince Albert's equerry, the dashing James Stuart, were in love with Lady Elizabeth. There can be no doubt that she, who was in the most decorous way possible something of a flirt, enjoyed all this male attention. But she also enjoyed her independence, so that when, in the spring of 1921, the besotted Duke of York asked her to marry him, she refused. She was apparently reluctant to exchange her free-and-easy existence for the restrictions of life as a member of the royal family. The Strathmores, so wealthy and long-established themselves, were not unduly impressed by the prospect of a marriage into the monarchy. 'No, I was very used to that sort of life,' explained Lady Alice Montagu-Douglas-Scott, the equally aristocratic bride of the Duke of York's younger brother, Prince Henry, on once being asked if marriage into the royal family had meant a considerable adjustment on her part.[8]

But the Duke of York, whose chief characteristic was perseverance, persevered. Although Lady Elizabeth turned down a second proposal, he refused to give up. In this venture, at least, the young man had his parents' unqualified support. The King, normally so censorious, had been thoroughly disarmed by the fact that this young woman, far from being afraid of him, treated him with great directness. He pronounced her to be 'charming, so pretty and engagingly natural'. He conceded that his son would be 'a lucky fellow' if Lady Elizabeth accepted him.[9] Queen Mary claimed that she was 'the one girl who could make Bertie happy'.[10]

Still Lady Elizabeth hesitated. Not, apparently, until Lady Airlie confessed to her, over the teacups, how much she had hated the idea of giving up her freedom to marry a soldier and of how she had come to love army life, did the young woman make up her mind. When, on 13 January 1923, Prince Albert proposed for a third time, she accepted. 'All right. Bertie,' read the prearranged wording of the telegram announcing the glad news to his parents. 'We are delighted and he looks beaming,' recorded the Queen two days later.[11]

Why, in the end, had Lady Elizabeth Bowes-Lyon agreed to marry the Duke of York? He was, in spite of his hesitant manner, a good-looking man with a natural elegance. Although, when compared with the socially accomplished Prince of Wales, he appeared slow and stupid, he improved upon knowing: he was kind, sincere, dependable, and had the sort of knockabout sense of humour that Lady Elizabeth found diverting. With her innate self-confidence, she may well have been drawn to his very lack of it. Always so ready to help, to encourage and to give pleasure, she might not have been able to resist the opportunity of being the one to provide what was so badly needed; needed, moreover, by so highly placed a figure in national, and international, life. Marriage was the only possible destiny for women of Elizabeth Bowes-Lyon's class and generation, and not every woman gets the chance to marry the King of England's son. She cannot, as Frances Donaldson has put it in her shrewd analysis of Lady Elizabeth's possible motives, 'have been entirely cold to her opportunity'.[12]

The couple were married in Westminster Abbey on 26 April 1923. There was much public approval of the fact that into the decidedly Germanic, somewhat inbred royal family, the blood of a Scottish 'commoner' was being introduced. The couple themselves, as they drove through the acclaiming streets in the fitful spring sunshine, appeared so strikingly good-looking, so charmingly fresh. 'I am very, very happy,' admitted the normally inarticulate Duke of York to his mother, 'and I can only hope that Elizabeth feels the same as I do. I know I am very lucky to have won her over at last.'[13]

'He is a man,' wrote Lady Strathmore to Lady Airlie of the Duke of York, 'who will be made or marred by his wife.'[14]

In later life, Queen Elizabeth the Queen Mother would go to great lengths to play down her own role in the moulding of her husband's career. In her determination to present him as an important monarch, she would always insist that he was the stronger character, the maker of decisions, the originator of ideas. 'Before coming to any decision or even before accepting an invitation,' claimed one of her ladies-in-waiting, 'she would always say, "I'll have to ask the King."'[15] It is said that when the historian John Wheeler-Bennett came to write the official biography of King George VI, the Queen Mother asked him to tone down the many references to her influence on her husband.

There is no denying that influence, however. Beneath the Duchess of York's melting charm and invincible *joie de vivre* was a certain steeliness. Although never aggressive or domineering, she was an astute and strong-willed young woman. From the outset of the marriage, she set out, with great tact, subtlety and good humour, to build up her husband's self-confidence. Their characters were wonderfully complementary. Where he was hesitant, she was assured; where he was given to worrying, she was serene; where he was introspective, she was outgoing; where he was short-tempered, she was long-suffering; where he shunned the limelight, she basked in it. She was always ready with the spontaneous gesture, the warm smile, the appropriate word.

The Yorks' marriage was extremely happy. It was quite obvious that the couple were devoted to each other. 'They reminded me of us,' wrote Alfred Duff Cooper (later Lord Norwich) to his wife after an evening at the theatre, 'sitting together in a box having private jokes, and in the interval when we were all sitting in the room behind the box they slipped out, and I found them standing together in a dark corner of the passage talking happily as we might. She affects no shadow of airs and graces.'[16]

Another factor in the building-up of the Duke of York's self-esteem was his partial mastery of his stammer. Encouraged by his wife, he agreed to consult the celebrated Australian-born speech therapist, Lionel Logue. From the time of his very first visit, the Duke showed an improvement. Logue's method of treatment was both psychological and physical: he built up his patient's confidence, and taught him how to breathe correctly. Although the Duke was never to speak really fluently, he was largely cured of his frustrating impediment. In private conversation, among his family, friends and members of his household, his defect was hardly noticeable. 'With others,' wrote one of his equerries, 'he stammered occasionally but the stammer was not a "stutter" with visible movements of the head and lips. It took the form of silence during which he tried to emit, pronounce, the offending word or a synonym. . . .'[17]

Socially, the Yorks tended to live a quiet life. Together with his father's sense of duty and high moral code, the Duke of York had inherited the King's preference for a familiar routine and his distrust of the smart world. 'The pattern of their lives was much the same,' claimed the Prince of Wales, 'with the steady swing of habit taking them both year after year to the same places at the same time and with the same associates. Strongly rooted each in his own existence, they tended to be withdrawn from the hurly-burly of the life I relished.'[18] The couple were certainly not part of the brittle café society that made up the Prince of Wales's circle. The Duke of York, with his conventional tastes, was considered too stolid; the Duchess, with her unfashionable clothes and old-fashioned graces, too unsophisticated. The Duke's interests were the usual ones of his breed:

hunting, shooting, riding, tennis. He never opened a book. The Duchess, if not an intellectual, was more cultured: she enjoyed reading, paintings and the theatre. Their social life was largely confined to country-house visiting, where indoor recreation invariably took the form of such naive activities as parlour games and the wearing of fancy dress. They carried out their public duties, which included a long tour of Australia and New Zealand in 1927, with considerable success ('the Duchess leaves . . . a continent in love with her,' declared the gallant Governor of South Australia[19]) but were always delighted to get back to their tranquil domestic life.

The happiness of the Yorks' marriage was greatly enhanced by the birth of their first daughter on 21 April 1926. Because the couple had, as yet, no real home of their own and were obliged to live in various rented houses, the baby was born, by Caesarean section, in one of the Strathmores' London houses. 'Such a relief and joy,' wrote Queen Mary in her diary, 'at 2.30 we went to London to 17 Bruton Street to congratulate Bertie and . . . saw the baby who is a little darling with a lovely complexion and pretty fair hair.'

The Duke of York was ecstatic. 'You don't know what a tremendous joy it is to Elizabeth and me to have our little girl,' he afterwards wrote to Queen Mary. 'We always wanted a child to make our happiness complete, and now that it has at last happened, it seems so wonderful and strange. . . .'[20]

The baby was christened Elizabeth Alexandra Mary after her mother, her great-grandmother (Queen Alexandra, wife of Edward VII) and her grandmother. The name Victoria, which had been obligatory in previous generations, was apparently not even considered.

It was into this little family circle – this island of domestic contentment amid the overwhelming grandeur and formality of the British monarchy – that Princess Margaret was born in the summer of 1930. The ethos of the Yorks' cosy household was precisely captured by a remark allegedly made by the four-year-old Princess Elizabeth on the birth of her baby sister. 'We've always played Three Bears,' she said to her parents. 'Now we can play Four Bears!'[21] The anecdote, for all its appositeness, is apocryphal. It probably belongs to King George VI's compilation of 'Things my daughters never said'.

CHAPTER 3

'Golden Age'

T HE INFANT PRINCESS MARGARET grew up in two homes. At
the time of her birth, the Yorks' London home was No. 145
Piccadilly; a year later King George V presented them with Royal
Lodge in Windsor Great Park. The much trumpeted simplicity of
the Yorks' private life was, of course, relative. Both 145 Piccadilly
and Royal Lodge were substantial homes; the family was also able
to spend holidays on the royal family's private estates at Balmoral in
Scotland (where they occupied Birkhall) and Sandringham in Norfolk; and in the Strathmore homes of Glamis Castle and St Paul's
Walden Bury. They travelled in royal trains and were chauffeured in
royal cars; they were attended by private secretaries, equerries,
ladies-in-waiting, detectives, and were served by butlers, house-
keepers, valets, ladies' maids, footmen and a considerable body of
lesser servants.

The Duke and Duchess of York had moved into 145 Piccadilly
on their return from their tour of Australia, in 1928, two years before
Princess Margaret's birth. It was an imposing, five-storied nineteenth-century house faced in Portland stone, situated near Hyde
Park Corner. Nearby stood Apsley House, the grandiose London
home of the Dukes of Wellington; four doors away was the Roth-
schild mansion. The house boasted a handsome drawing room, dining room, library, study, various sitting rooms, a conservatory, several
bedrooms, kitchens, and quarters for the sizeable staff. There was
an impressive central staircase, crowned by an elegant glass dome,
and there was also a lift. 'There were enormous oil paintings in
heavy gilt frames . . .' was how one guest described the entrance

hall. 'Two immense elephant tusks hung on the walls and there was a life-sized statue of a black boy . . . clothed in courtly style. An ornate clock ticked away the passing minutes on an elaborate chest of drawers, and on an ornamental table, the visitors' book lay open.'[1]

The nursery rooms, on the top floor, were furnished in a less overwhelming fashion. Flooded with light, they were decorated in pale colours. From their front windows there was a view across the traffic to St George's Hospital opposite; its lighted windows used to shine out all through the night. Beyond and to the left was the great wall surrounding the grounds of Buckingham Palace. From the back windows the view was across Hyde Park. As the small garden behind the house was overlooked by its neighbours, there was rather more privacy to be had in the enclosed space beyond, known as Hamilton Gardens.

No. 145 Piccadilly was bombed during the Second World War. All traces of the house have long since disappeared. Of that once impressive row of houses, only Apsley House remains, marooned amidst the surging traffic.

Royal Lodge in Windsor Great Park was an altogether different proposition. Converted by one of the few members of the House of Hanover with any artistic taste – the Prince Regent, afterwards King George IV – into a charming cottage *ornée*, it had since fallen into disrepair. By 1930, its rooms sub-divided, its paint peeling and its roof caving in, the house was in a shabby state. But the Yorks appreciated its potential, and gradually, the house was restored and enlarged, and the grounds redesigned and replanted. The Duchess, with her appreciation of its essentially light-hearted character and her penchant for pastel colours, insisted that it be painted a pale rose pink; she described its new appearance as 'strawberries and cream'.[2] The Duke, discovering an enthusiasm for gardening, became an expert on azaleas and rhododendrons. For decades the Duchess of York, later as Queen and then as Queen Mother, used this delightful house as her weekend residence. It is also the only weekend retreat that Princess Margaret has been able to call home.

Remembering his own bleak childhood, the Duke of York was determined that 'come what might, Princess Elizabeth and Princess Margaret should look upon their early years as a golden age'.[3] 'Come what might', in this instance, turned out to be the Duke's own unexpected accession to the throne in 1936 but, in the six years that

lay between Princess Margaret's birth and this momentous event, his daughters enjoyed an almost idyllic childhood. Although they were brought up, as was still customary for children in their position, by nurses and a governess, they were able to see their parents as often as possible and not only at set times (usually the hour after tea), as was the case in so many aristocratic homes. No matter how busy the day, or how early the start, wrote one member of the household, each morning began with high jinks in their parents' bedroom. And each day ended in the parents overseeing baths and bedtime. 'Hilarious sounds of splashing could be heard coming from the bathroom. Later, pillow fights would set [the nanny] begging them [the Duke and Duchess] not to get the children too excited.' Afterwards, arm in arm, the young parents would go downstairs, heated, dishevelled and damp. Down the stairwell would float the sounds of 'Goodnight, Mummy. Goodnight, Papa!'[4]

The nursery was presided over by the nanny, Mrs Clara Knight, known as 'Allah'; apparently a childish mispronunciation of Clara. Mrs Knight (the Mrs was an honorary title) was the daughter of a tenant farmer on the Strathmores' Hertfordshire estate, and had been nanny first to the infant Lady Elizabeth Bowes-Lyon, and then to the children of Lady Elizabeth's eldest sister, Mary, who became Lady Elphinstone. She was an old-fashioned nanny in the best sense: upright, kind, conscientious, devoted to her charges. Because of her height, her calm features and the fact that she was seldom seen out of her pristine uniform, Allah struck at least one observer as noble looking.

Allah was assisted by two nursery maids, red-haired, Scottish-born sisters, Margaret and Ruby MacDonald. The elder, Margaret, known as 'Bobo' to her charges, devoted herself to Princess Elizabeth. In time, as the Princess's personal maid and dresser, Bobo became her friend and confidante; it would later be claimed that no one was closer to Queen Elizabeth II than Bobo MacDonald. Her position was strengthened by the fact that Allah was now obliged to devote her time to the new baby, Princess Margaret.

The Duchess of York, no less than her husband, was determined that her daughters should enjoy as untroubled a childhood as possible. It was still reasonable to believe, in the early 1930s, that the pre-ordained, privileged way of life of the aristocracy would last for ever, and that well-born young girls, and certainly princesses, need not be subjected to too exacting an education. The Duchess, writes one chronicler approvingly, 'had a definite idea of the sort of training she wished her daughters to receive, and pursued her course untroubled by other people's doubts'. What girls needed, she maintained, was plenty of fresh country air, the ability to dance and draw and appreciate music, good manners, perfect deportment, and feminine grace. The Duchess was one of those 'whose natural instinct is to emphasize the contrast between the sexes rather than to assimilate them to one another'. As for 'book-learning', it should be 'kept in proper proportion with the rest and in subordination to the whole'.[5] This, maintained the Duchess, was how she and her sisters had been brought up, and they had all married well. One of them, she added roguishly, very well.

With these considerations in mind, the Duchess began looking about for a governess, for there had never been any question of the princesses attending school with other children. So, when Princess Elizabeth was six and Princess Margaret two, the Duchess of York appointed a young Scotswoman, Marion Crawford, as their governess. It is from the new governess, known inevitably as 'Crawfie', that one gets a first real glimpse of the infant Princess Margaret. She 'was an enchanting, doll-like child, still in the nursery,' she writes. 'She was Allah's sole charge, and I saw little of her at first. She was the baby everyone loves at sight, but from the very beginning I had a feeling about Lilibet that she was "special". I had met many children of all sorts in my time, but never one with so much character at so young an age. . . .'[6]

Thus, from the very outset, and in typically effusive fashion, did Marion Crawford set out the thesis that characterizes her celebrated, indeed notorious, book, *The Little Princesses*. By contrasting the sterling qualities of the future Queen with her younger sister's more capricious personality, Crawfie gave authority to what – by the time of the book's publication in 1950 – many people already believed. To Princess Margaret's apologists, and to the Princess herself, *The Little Princesses* – for all its author's sycophancy – is in the nature of a poisoned well.

Marion Crawford had come to the attention of the Duke and Duchess of York while she had been giving private lessons to various aristocratic children living near her home in Dunfermline in

Scotland. She had attended the Moray House Training College in Edinburgh and had ambitions to train as a child psychologist. Among her pupils was a daughter of Lady Rose Leveson-Gower, sister of the Duchess of York and, just two weeks after Marion Crawford had been presented to the visiting Duke and Duchess, they asked her to undertake the education of their two daughters. She agreed to a trial period and, in the spring of 1932, when she was twenty-two, she arrived at Royal Lodge to start her duties.

Taking up her position permanently in September 1932, Marion Crawford remained with the family for over fifteen years. Abandoning her hopes of a further career and postponing, time and again, her plans for marriage (her employers always had a pressing reason for her to stay), Crawfie devoted herself to her royal charges. Her salary was hardly princely, with most of it going, she complained, on clothes suitable for such a household. She left royal service for marriage to the patient George Buthlay, who worked for Drummonds Bank in Scotland, only after the two princesses were fully grown up. As a reward for her years of service, she was given Nottingham Cottage, a grace-and-favour house in the grounds of Kensington Palace.

Marion Crawford then committed what was, in royal eyes, a cardinal sin: in 1950 she published *The Little Princesses*, her syrupy but sharply observed account of her life as a royal governess. The way she handled the publication was less than honest. Only after an American publisher had accepted the manuscript did Crawfie approach the little princesses' mother, by then Queen, for permission. This was refused. But by that stage it was too late. Proofs were sent to the Queen's friend Lady Astor by the editors of the American *Ladies' Home Journal*, which was due to serialize the book. Nancy Astor, appreciating the delicacy of the situation, sent them on to the Queen. Her Majesty was extremely put out, not only by Crawfie's duplicity and betrayal of trust, but by the tone and bias of the book. The parents were depicted as being not really interested in their daughters' education, and Princess Margaret was portrayed as spoilt, wayward and jealous of her saintly, if decidedly priggish, elder sister. The whole thing, wrote the Queen in a six-page letter to Lady Astor, had been 'a great shock to us'. It was essential that the royal family be able to trust 'those about us'; she could only imagine that 'our late and completely trusted governess' had 'gone off her head'.[7] The Queen's letter was followed by one from her

Private Secretary, asking for various cuts to be made in the text of
The Little Princesses. Certainly, when the book was published in
Britain in 1950 (after serialization in *Woman's Own*) several passages
which appeared in the American edition had been omitted.

Royal reaction to the British publication of the book was dracon-
ian. Crawfie had to leave her grace-and-favour cottage; her entry in
Who's Who was withdrawn; her name was not even mentioned in
officially authorized biographies such as John Wheeler-Bennett's
King George VI or Dorothy Laird's *Queen Elizabeth the Queen Mother*.
She retired to Aberdeen from where, with extraordinary insensitiv-
ity, she pestered the family with frequent requests. All were
refused. Nor did Crawfie's literary outpourings end with *The Little
Princesses*. She wrote, as well as several more books on the royal family, weekly columns on their doings for British and American magazines. Her reporting career ended ignominiously when her gushing
descriptions of Queen Elizabeth II's appearance at Trooping the
Colour and Royal Ascot in 1955 were published just before the first
ceremony was cancelled and the second event postponed.

A rumour that Princess Margaret secretly kept in touch with her
former governess was hotly denied. And there is a story that the
writer, Peter Fleming (brother of the creator of James Bond, Ian
Fleming), attending a royal luncheon party one day and imagining
that Queen Elizabeth II had mentioned the word 'Crawfie', brightly asked, 'Oh, Ma'am, how is she?' The puzzled Queen repeated
the word 'Porchy' – the nickname of her stud manager, Lord Porchester. In all innocence, Fleming pressed on. 'I thought you said
Crawfie,' he explained. His remark was met by an icy royal silence.[8]

When Marion Crawford died in 1987 no member of the royal
family attended her funeral or even sent a wreath. She bequeathed
to her former pupil, Queen Elizabeth II, a small box of personal
mementoes which was promptly placed in the Royal Archives at
Windsor Castle. And she left another legacy – to her other pupil,
Princess Margaret, the expression 'doing a Crawfie' is synonymous
with an act of betrayal. Yet her portrayal of Princess Margaret cannot
be dismissed out of hand. There is a great deal of truth in what she
wrote. Knowing that the Princess would read what she had written,
the governess would have employed considerable discretion. Even
so, the picture that emerges is one of an over-indulged and ill-disci-
plined personality, only too ready to mock and mimic.

Marion Crawford played an important part in Princess Margaret's upbringing. It was Crawfie who coaxed her away from the possessive Allah, who wanted to keep the child in her pram and feed her by hand long after she was capable of doing things for herself. It was Crawfie, too, who got the little girl out of the ribbons, bows and frills which Allah thought fitting for a princess, and into simple cotton print dresses. Crawfie, by encouraging her to join in the games in Hamilton Gardens, put paid to the persistent rumours that the younger princess had been born deaf and dumb. 'Wait for me, Lilibet. . . . Wait for me!' Princess Margaret's cries would ring out for everyone – lined up at the railings to see the King's granddaughters – to hear. The idea that the Princess could possibly have been deaf and dumb caused great amusement in the household. In later life Princess Margaret drily described herself as having been, in infancy, 'rather chatty'.[9]

In time, and to Allah's consternation, Crawfie took her charges beyond the confines of Hamilton Gardens and into Hyde Park itself. From then on, the expeditions became more adventurous. Accompanied by one of the Duchess of York's ladies-in-waiting and shadowed by a detective, Crawfie took the princesses walking through the streets, travelling by bus and Underground ('It's so handy for the Underground,' the adult Princess Margaret would joke when living in Buckingham Palace[10]) and to public swimming baths. Their greatest treat was the annual visit to a pantomime. Obliged always to sit in the royal box, with its restricted view, the children longed to be allowed to sit in the stalls or the dress circle. On the young Princess Margaret, the colour and excitement of these pantomimes made an indelible impression. As soon as she could talk at all, she would re-enact most of the parts in a corner of the nursery.

In fact, from an early age, Princess Margaret revealed herself to be an imaginative child. She had several make-believe friends; among them were 'Pinkle Ponkle', 'Inderbombanks' and, most important of all, 'Cousin Halifax'. She was quick to blame Cousin Halifax for whatever she might have done wrong or whatever she had left undone. 'I was busy with Cousin Halifax,' she would reply haughtily.[11] 'Hoosh-mi' was her word for a typically nursery mash of meat, potato and gravy – all 'hoosh-mied' together and fed to the protesting child. Clambering on to her father's knee, she would demand 'Windy water', which was what she called soda water. 'You can't like it!' the Duke would protest. 'Oh yes I do,' she would insist. 'It crackles my nose.'[12] To postpone the start of a lesson, she would cannily regale her governess with recitals of her 'appalling' dreams. 'Crawfie, I must tell you an amazing dream I had last night,' she would exclaim, and her sister and governess would listen enthralled to her accounts of 'green horses, wild-elephant stampedes, talking cats and other remarkable manifestations'. Her talent for acting, and for the sort of mimicry for which she was to become renowned, indeed notorious, was remarkable. At charades she always shone. 'The gift of fun-poking – and very clever fun-poking' kept her listeners in fits of slightly uneasy laughter.[13]

Another of her talents was for music. This was, perhaps, hardly surprising in someone who, at the age of only nine months, had astounded her grandmother, Lady Strathmore, by humming the waltz from *The Merry Widow*. She started music lessons – singing and piano – at the age of seven with a Miss Mabel Lander and quickly revealed what has been described as 'a real gift'. If she had been trained, it is often said, Princess Margaret would have become a very good singer.

A source of endless amusement for both princesses was 'Y Bwthyn Bach' – The Little House – the child-scale cottage in the grounds of Royal Lodge which had been presented to Princess Elizabeth by the 'people of Wales'. Only at one spot, the stairwell, could an adult stand upright. Within its cosy, chintzy interior, fitted with every modern convenience including plumbing and electricity (but not, complained Princess Margaret, a telephone), the two princesses practised the sort of housewifely skills – dusting, cleaning and cooking – which they would never ever be called upon to use. Their cooking efforts were apparently abysmal. 'The things I had to eat!' remembered their mother in old age. 'Rock-hard scones!'[14]

The princesses also gardened in their own small plots. Princess Elizabeth grew flowers, Princess Margaret potatoes; 'King Edwards were the best,' she announced.[15] Identically dressed, usually in tartan skirts, jerseys, little jackets, white socks and lace-up shoes, and trailed by a pack of the soon-to-be-famous corgis, the princesses would set off with spades, hoes and wheelbarrows to work in their gardens. The fact that they were always dressed alike ensured that they were often treated as though they were the same age, something which greatly encouraged the younger sister's precocity.

But all was not, as Crawfie puts it, 'always sweetness and light' between the sisters. There were the inevitable taunts, arguments and fights. Where the elder sister would slap, the younger would bite. Shrill cries of 'You brute! You beast!' would ring out as they viciously snapped each other's hat elastics. 'Margaret always wants what I want,' Princess Elizabeth would grumble. 'Margaret was often naughty,' complains Crawfie, 'but she had a gay bouncing way with her which was hard to deal with.'[16]

Princess Margaret started her schooling at the age of five. The schoolroom at 145 Piccadilly was one of the Duchess's sitting rooms, leading off the main drawing room. As far as education was concerned, claimed Crawfie in one of those passages which was to infuriate the royal family, the parents had great confidence in her, leaving much to her own judgment. 'No one ever had employers who interfered so little. . . . I had often the feeling that the Duke and Duchess, most happy in their own married life, were not over concerned with the higher education of their daughters.'[17]

The set programme of lessons, devised by the governess, was made up of religious instruction, arithmetic, history, grammar, geography, literature and writing. Two Frenchwomen came in to teach French grammar and conversation. In addition there were lessons in dancing, music, singing and drawing. On wet afternoons, when the princesses could not play in Hamilton Gardens, they would be read to by Crawfie: the Lambs' *Tales from Shakespeare*, *Winnie the Pooh* by A.A. Milne, and Thackeray's *The Rose and the Ring* were regulars. Horses were among their favourite toys. On the landing beneath the great glass dome of 145 Piccadilly were ranged over thirty toy horses, some on wheels, some over two feet high. These the two princesses would attend to assiduously: feeding them, watering them, grooming them, harnessing them. This obsession for toy horses lasted until real horses became important. When they were old enough, the princesses were taught to ride by Mr Owen, a groom at Windsor.

In the afternoons, after tea, the children would join their parents for rowdy games of snap, happy families and racing demon. Sometimes, if their mother was reading to them, their father would work on his tapestry. An expert with the needle, the Duke of York once embroidered a dozen chair covers in petit point for Royal Lodge;

only when it came to the tedious stitching of the backgrounds did he ask for help.

Rightly or wrongly, Princess Margaret emerges from Marion Crawford's pages as a talented and amusing little girl, but one who was also wilful, untidy and impetuous. It is she who rips the wrapping paper off presents while her more orderly sister preserves it and folds it away. Princess Margaret crams coffee crystals into her mouth while Princess Elizabeth sorts them into sizes before eating them. The younger princess leaves her clothes all over the place, the elder packs hers neatly away. 'You don't look very angelic, Margaret!' the Duchess once said to her daughter, about to set off for a fancy-dress party dressed as an angel. 'That's all right,' quipped the girl. 'I'll be a Holy Terror.'[18]

Yet every now and then one gets a more sympathetic glimpse: an indication of an affectionate and generous nature. Once, when the celebrated creator of Peter Pan, J.M. Barrie, was sitting beside Princess Margaret at her birthday party at Glamis, he asked her if the present beside her plate was her very own. Imagining him to be envious, she immediately placed the present between them. 'It is yours *and* mine,' she said.[19]

'She was a plaything,' writes Crawfie. 'She was warm and demonstrative, made to be cuddled and played with.' Her undemonstrative father would be 'almost embarrassed, yet at the same time most touched and pleased, when she wound her arms round his neck, nestled against him and cuddled and caressed him.'[20]

CHAPTER 4

The Dynasty

Princess Margaret's memories of her grandfather, King George V, are characteristically forthright: 'He was the most objectionable old man,' she says.[1] Her opinion is understandable. To a girl who was only five when he died, George V must have been something of an ogre. With his scratchy beard, bulging eyes and bluff, quarterdeck manner, he was not the sort of man to endear himself to a child. The Princess denies that she ever called him 'Grandpapa England', as fondly reported by Crawfie. 'We were much too frightened of him to call him anything but Grandpapa,' she says.[2]

On the other hand, Princess Elizabeth was very fond of her grandfather; indeed, one of her earliest recorded quips concerned him. One Christmas at Sandringham, while listening to the carol 'While Shepherds Watched Their Flocks by Night', the attention of the three-and-a-half-year-old Princess was caught by the phrase 'to you and all mankind'. 'I know that old man kind,' she announced afterwards. 'That's you, Grandpapa. You are old, and you are very very kind.'[3] And Archbishop Lang was once astonished, on being ushered into the Sovereign's presence, to see him playing 'horse' to the Princess's 'groom'. The King-Emperor was shuffling about the carpet on all fours while his little granddaughter led him about the room by his beard.

The King's interest in his granddaughters' education was minimal; he was himself singularly ill educated. The best that even the most sympathetic of George V's biographers can say is that he was 'below the educational and perhaps intellectual standards of the

ordinary public-school-educated country squire.'⁴ On first meeting
his granddaughters' governess, the King had only one instruction.
'For goodness' sake,' he said in his booming voice, 'teach Margaret
and Lilibet to write a decent hand, that's all I ask you. Not one of
my children can write properly. They all do it exactly the same way.
I like a hand with some character in it.'⁵ In fact, he was in no position
to pontificate about handwriting, for his own was like a schoolboy's
(Lord Clark claimed that he had never seen an adult man write so
slowly and laboriously); nor could he spell. But Crawfie was able to
fulfil the King's instructions: both princesses developed firm, legi-
ble handwriting, full of character.

Princess Margaret's opinion of her grandmother, Queen Mary, is
equally frank. 'She was absolutely terrifying,' she says. 'She didn't
really like children and made no sort of effort with them.'⁶ The sum-
mons to visit this straight-backed, unsmiling, inarticulate old
Queen, seated stiffly in a sitting room crowded with *objets* of varying
aesthetic value, always left the Princess with a 'hollow, empty feeling' in the pit of her stomach. 'We always felt that we were going to
be hauled over the coals for something we had done.' The fact that
they seldom were made the prospect no easier.⁷ Nor were Queen
Mary's visits to 145 Piccadilly any less formal. On her arrival, she
would be greeted by the Duchess of York and her two daughters,
first with the regulation curtsy, then with a kiss on her right hand
and finally with a kiss on both cheeks. The process was repeated
when she took her leave.

In later life Princess Margaret is supposed to have told Gore
Vidal that she had detested her grandmother, and that Queen Mary
had had an inferiority complex about her granddaughters because
they were 'royal' and she was not. This is nonsense. Queen Mary's
father, the Duke of Teck, might have been a member of a minor
branch of a Continental royal family but her mother – like Queen
Victoria – had been a granddaughter of King George III. In any case,
Queen Mary was certainly more 'royal' than Princess Margaret's
own mother.

Unlike the King, Queen Mary took considerable interest in her
granddaughters' education. Although Crawfie might well have exaggerated the old Queen's influence, there can be no doubt that she
made certain suggestions. On being shown the governess's proposed
curriculum, she advocated more Bible reading, history, geography

and poetry. Having herself a deep interest in family history, the Queen felt sure that historical and dynastic genealogies were interesting to children, and for these particular children, very important.

The Queen influenced her granddaughters in other ways as well. She not only took them on cultural outings – to concerts, museums and art galleries – but gave them lessons in what it meant to be born royal. Two stories concerning Princess Elizabeth might just as well have applied to Princess Margaret. 'Good morning, little lady,' the Lord Chamberlain once said to the older princess. 'I'm not a little lady. I'm Princess Elizabeth,' answered the child tartly. Later that day, dragging her granddaughter behind her, Queen Mary entered the Lord Chamberlain's office. 'This is Princess Elizabeth,' she announced, 'who hopes one day to be a lady.'[8] On another occasion, at a concert in the Queen's Hall, the young Princess was fidgeting to such an extent that Queen Mary asked if she would prefer to go home. 'Oh, no, Granny,' came the answer. 'We can't leave before the end. Think of all the people who'll be waiting to see us outside.' The Queen immediately instructed a lady-in-waiting to hustle the child out by a back way and take her home in an inconspicuous taxi.[9]

In ways like this were both princesses made aware of their obligations. Being royal was no excuse for bad behaviour; nor was it a means of ensuring instant and gratifying acclamation. Public approval was something to be earned, not expected as an automatic right. Queen Mary was teaching her granddaughters how not to behave when blessed, or encumbered, with royal birth.

'I didn't really know him,' says Princess Margaret of her Uncle David, who was, by turns, styled as Prince of Wales, then King Edward VIII, and finally Duke of Windsor.[10] The truth is that by the time the Princess was old enough to register her uncle's presence, he had all but disappeared from her family circle. On the other hand, the Princess's claim might be defensive, an attempt to distance herself from the one member of the family to whom she is invariably compared. Time and again Princess Margaret has been accused of 'taking after' her Uncle David; both have been represented as black sheep, as rogue elements in the otherwise dutiful circle of royalty.

Born on 23 June 1894, the Prince of Wales was in his late thirties during Princess Margaret's infancy. No longer quite the Prince

Charming of his earlier days, he remained a popular figure: hand-some, debonair, informal. Considering himself to be in tune with the more democratic spirit of the times, he constantly railed against the stuffy traditionalism of his father's Court; his professed dream was to see the monarchy modernized. All in all, the Prince of Wales was regarded as forward-looking, innovative, unconventional. The King and Queen, critical enough of his public attitudes, were in despair about their eldest son's private life. They were deeply upset by his drinking, nightclubbing and womanizing. Above all, they felt that his reckless behaviour was doing the monarchy incalculable harm.

The Duke and Duchess of York were less censorious. They were prepared to put up with, if not exactly approve of, the Prince's rack-ety way of life. They could only hope that in spite of his succession of married mistresses, he would one day settle down and marry. During the early years of their own marriage, the Prince of Wales would frequently visit the family at 145 Piccadilly or Royal Lodge. His own weekend retreat, Fort Belvedere, known simply as the Fort, was not far from Royal Lodge. He would often take part in the children's after-tea games – snap and happy families. 'He gave Lili-bet all the A. A. Milne children's books. ... . Both little girls knew most of the poems by heart and, needless to say, their favourite one was "Changing Guard at Buckingham Palace".'[1]

But it was not so much at Buckingham Palace that the 'guard' was being changed, as at the Prince's London home, St James's Palace. For in 1930, the year of Princess Margaret's birth, the Prince of Wales met Wallis Warfield Simpson. This, in turn, led to a distinct strain in the relationship between the Prince of Wales and the Duke and Duchess of York. Within a very few years, the couple had come to appreciate that the new woman in the Prince's life posed more of a threat than his previous mistresses had ever done. For there could be no doubt that this most eligible bachelor – the most eligible in the world – had fallen deeply and abjectly in love with a highly unsuitable woman: a divorced and remarried American without beauty, youth, wealth or, by European aristocratic standards, birth.

By the summer of 1934, Mrs Ernest Simpson was thirty-eight to the Prince's forty. Having led a distinctly louche life, she had by now developed into a sophisticated *femme du monde*: a small, sharp, gravel-voiced figure with a chic that was a shade too metallic and a vivacity that was a shade too assertive. In the eyes of the royal family, however, Wallis Simpson was something more sinister than this. They saw her as a dangerous adventuress who, somehow or other, had managed to entrap the Prince. They resented not only her domination of her lover, but the fact that he was loading her with expensive jewellery and parading her in society – even, on one occasion, presenting her to the King and Queen at a ball at Buckingham Palace. They feared that sooner or later this unseemly love affair with a woman who had two husbands living would seriously damage the prestige of the Crown. They could only hope that, in time, the Prince of Wales's obsession with Mrs Simpson would pass.

On the household at 145 Piccadilly the affair was beginning to cast long shadows. The longest and deepest shadow of all was to fall upon Princess Margaret.

The four-year-old Princess Margaret made a memorable public appearance in November 1934 at the wedding of another of her father's brothers, her uncle Prince George, Duke of Kent. Unbeknown to the little princess, her Uncle George had been giving his family almost as much trouble as her Uncle David.

Born on 20 December 1902, Prince George was exceptionally good-looking: tall and slim, with dark blue eyes and a flashing smile. Among the somewhat philistine members of the royal family, he was very much the odd man out. Where even the Prince of Wales shared the hunting, shooting and fishing tastes of his breed, Prince George's interests were more cultured and sophisticated. Ready enough to fly planes and drive fast cars, he was just as happy visiting art galleries, listening to records and playing Cole Porter songs on the piano. He loved the cinema, the theatre and the ballet; among his many artistic interests were interior decorating, collecting antiques and arranging flowers. While the other men of the family would be shooting at Sandringham or Balmoral, he would be sunbathing on the Riviera. In fact, Prince George had many of the tastes and traits that were to reappear in his niece, Princess Margaret.

But the Prince's nature had its darker side. Society was full of stories about his sexual exploits and his drug-taking. At one stage, he became so badly addicted to drugs that the Prince of Wales, to whom he was very close, was obliged to take him in hand. The two brothers retired to the country where the younger one was kept under strict surveillance. By the following year, his addiction seems to have been conquered. Even the King, who seldom had a good word to say for his eldest son, was moved to thank him for all that he had done for Prince George.

Equally scandalous were Prince George's unorthodox sexual tastes, for he was apparently bisexual. Noël Coward is said to have been one of his many male lovers, and Randolph Churchill told the diplomat and writer, Sir Robert Bruce Lockhart, that the Prince had once been obliged to pay a large sum for the recovery of certain love letters to a young man in Paris. On one occasion he was arrested, together with a well-known homosexual, in a notorious gay club, and only after his identity was discovered was he released from the police cells.

It was with a mixture of pleasure and relief that the King and Queen heard the news, in August 1934, of Prince George's engagement. His choice of bride was what might have been expected of him: not for Prince George some pretty little English debutante, but instead the twenty-seven-year-old Princess Marina of Greece and Denmark. Very much part of the complicated network of interrelated European royal families (her paternal grandfather had been the King of the Hellenes; her maternal grandfather a brother of the Tsar of Russia), Princess Marina brought a breath of Continental air and a transcendent chic into the House of Windsor.

The couple were married in Westminster Abbey on 29 November 1934. Prince George, created Duke of Kent a few days before the ceremony, was resplendent in the full-dress uniform of the Royal Navy – in which he had once served reluctantly and ingloriously – while Princess Marina, in a Molyneux dress, looked like a fashion plate. It was the four-year-old Princess Margaret, however, who provided the ceremony with some of its more hilarious moments. Seated in full view of the congregation on a small footstool, upholstered in red plush, which had been brought specially from Buckingham Palace for the occasion, she was clearly bored by the long service. Although she tried to sit up as primly as possible, 'her little knees', remembers one guest, 'would gradually relax until the royal panties were exposed, whereupon her mother and her grave elder sister hurriedly called her to decorum.'[12]

In later life, Princess Margaret would refer to the Kents as 'beautiful people'.[13] If the Duke of Kent had not been killed during the

Second World War, the adult Princess Margaret might well have developed a close relationship with this most artistic and hedonistic of her uncles. As it was, she was at one time very close to the Duke's widow, Princess Marina. But relations between the two women cooled when the Duchess of Kent, extremely conscious of her own royal lineage, made it clear that she felt that Princess Margaret was not nearly conscious enough of hers.

In the spring of 1935, Princess Margaret took part in one of those great royal pageants by which the monarchy re-establishes its hold on the public imagination. On 6 May 1935, King George V and Queen Mary drove in state to St Paul's Cathedral to attend the Silver Jubilee Thanksgiving Service to mark the twenty-fifth anniversary of George V's accession.

'Masses of troops,' wrote the diarist 'Chips' (Sir Henry) Channon on Jubilee Day,

magnificent and virile, resplendent in grand uniforms, with the sun glistening on their helmets. The thunderous applause for the royal carriages. The Yorks in a large landau with two tiny pink children [Princess Elizabeth and Princess Margaret, identically dressed, as always]. The Duchess of York was charming and gracious, the baby princesses much interested in the proceedings and waving. The next landau carried the Kents, that dazzling pair; Princess Marina wore an enormous platter hat, chic but slightly unsuitable. She was much cheered. . . . So it passed. Finally the Prince of Wales smiling his dentist smile and waving to his friends, but he still has his old spell for the crowds . . . then more troops and suddenly, the coach with Their Majesties. All eyes were on the Queen in her white and silvery splendour. Never has she looked so serene, so regally majestic, even so attractive. Suddenly she has become the best-dressed woman in the world.[14]

Not only on the day of the Thanksgiving Service but for days afterwards, the celebrations continued. Wherever the King and Queen appeared they were vociferously cheered; each night they were obliged to come out on to the central balcony of Buckingham Palace to wave to the roaring crowds. 'I'd no idea they felt like that about me,' exclaimed the King. 'I am beginning to think they must really like me for myself.'[15] Indeed, the King was being hailed not only as a monarch but as a person. He was being hailed, too, as a family man. In those days, the general public would have known almost nothing about the various tensions within the royal family. To them, King George V was the head of a close-knit, harmonious and attractive clan; an ageing man surrounded by his children and grandchildren. By the mid-1930s, the royal family had come to be regarded as a grander, more colourful version of the average British household.

Of these momentous events Princess Margaret, not yet five at the time, has no recollections whatsoever.

This sense of family (in the public perception, at least), was further enhanced, later that year, when the King's third son, Prince Henry, Duke of Gloucester, married Lady Alice Montagu-Douglas-Scott, a daughter of the Duke of Buccleuch. Born on 31 March 1900, Prince Henry was the most oafish of the King's four surviving sons. Bluff and convivial, his ruling passion, after sport, was for soldiering. Only on the assurance that his military career would in no way be jeopardized did Prince Henry agree, at the relatively late age of thirty-five, to marry. His choice of bride, however, could hardly have been better. Lady Alice, in spite of being a member of one of the most illustrious families in the land, was a modest-mannered, country-loving young woman, behind whose quiet façade lay great reserves of strength. She was to earn much respect, not only for putting up with a difficult husband, but also for the doggedness with which she devoted herself to her royal duties.

Both Princess Elizabeth and Princess Margaret were to be bridesmaids at the wedding, which was set for 6 November 1935 in Westminster Abbey. The up-and-coming couturier, Norman Hartnell, who designed the bride's dress, also designed Empire-style dresses for the bridesmaids, though these had to be shortened, on George V's instructions, because he wanted to see his granddaughters' 'pretty little knees'.[16] The death of the bride's father, the Duke of Buccleuch, three weeks before the wedding day, meant a scrapping of the planned Westminster Abbey ceremony. Much to Queen Mary's annoyance (but to the ailing King's relief) the venue had to be switched to the chapel of Buckingham Palace. 'Anyhow,' wrote Queen Mary to the Duke of Gloucester, 'Alice will wear her wedding dress and the bridesmaids theirs and we shall all wear the dresses we have chosen.'[17]

'Now,' wrote the King in his diary that evening, 'all the children are married but David.'[18]

And it was the future of David, the Prince of Wales – and consequently the future of the monarchy – which chiefly preoccupied King George V during the few months of life that were left to him. 'After I am dead,' the King said to his new Prime Minister, Stanley Baldwin, 'the boy will ruin himself in twelve months,'[19] for he knew that his son's affair with Mrs Simpson was more serious than his other love-affairs had been. 'I pray to God,' the King once exclaimed, 'that my eldest son will never marry and have children, and that nothing will come between Bertie [the Duke of York] and Lilibet [his elder daughter] and the throne.'[20]

The Yorks were equally anxious. The usual family Christmas at Sandringham that year was a doleful affair, with the King looking ill and the Prince of Wales clearly longing to get back to Wallis Simpson. Only the children seemed oblivious to the strained atmosphere. For Princess Elizabeth and Princess Margaret, Christmas was the usual flurry of list-making, letters to Santa Claus, present-buying (mostly from Woolworths), parcelling-up, stocking-hanging, and the giving and receiving of gifts. But the princesses were back at Royal Lodge when, on the evening of 20 January 1936, King George V died. Crawfie, summoned from her holiday in Scotland, arrived at Royal Lodge to find that the Duke had flown up to Norfolk with the Prince of Wales in the Prince's private plane, and that the Duchess, although recovering from pneumonia, had gone up to their London house. She had left the governess a message. 'Don't let all this depress them more than is absolutely necessary, Crawfie,' she wrote. 'They are so young.'

Not until all the funeral arrangements had been made did Crawfie take her charges back to 145 Piccadilly. The nine-year-old Princess Elizabeth, aware of what had happened, tried to behave with due decorum. 'Oh, Crawfie,' she once asked, midway through grooming one of her toy horses, 'ought we to play?' The five-year-old Princess Margaret, on the other hand, remained oblivious; merely curious as to why Allah should keep bursting into tears.

Dressed in a black coat and beret, Princess Elizabeth was taken by her parents to the King's lying-in-state in Westminster Hall. Although she was considered too young to attend the funeral, she was accompanied by her governess to Paddington Station to see the King's coffin being transferred from the gun-carriage on to the train to Windsor. For her, the day's most vivid moment came when one of the sailors, marching behind the gun-carriage, fainted and the men on either side of him immediately closed in, holding him up and marching him along with the rest. This skilful manoeuvre 'enchanted' the Princess.[21]

But it was Princess Margaret, kept at home with Allah, who made one of the day's most memorable remarks. 'Grandpapa has gone to Heaven,' she explained, 'and I am sure that God is finding him very useful.'[22]

CHAPTER 5

Love versus Duty

AT FIRST, THE ACCESSION OF UNCLE DAVID as King Edward VIII made very little difference on the top floor of 145 Piccadilly. The Duke and Duchess of York, increasingly uneasy about the future, were anxious that none of this unease should be relayed to their two daughters. In fact, the governess was kept in ignorance of unfolding events; her employers never discussed such matters with her. 'But it was impossible,' wrote Crawfie, 'not to notice the change in Uncle David. He had been so youthful and gay. Now he looked distraught, and seemed not to be listening to what was said to him. He made plans with the children, and then forgot them.'[1]

The truth was that by now King Edward VIII was interested in very little other than Wallis Simpson. All his boasting about modernizing the monarchy had resulted in almost nothing. He made a few trivial changes, but that was all. In any case, the new King seems to have had no clear idea of how he was going to change things; or even what exactly it was that he was planning to change. He was no political radical. On the contrary, his views on most political issues of the day were conservative, almost reactionary. It was just that he was against what he called 'George the Fifth men': anyone whom he considered stiff, stuffy, hidebound. So the widespread belief that Edward VIII was a reforming monarch whose democratic intentions were being thwarted by reactionary Court, Church and government interests is without foundation. His cavalier attitudes might have rubbed some in those circles up the wrong way, but there was never even the suggestion of an Establishment 'plot' against him.

Chief among the 'old-fashioned' attitudes to which Edward VIII objected was, not unnaturally, what he considered to be the 'hypocritical' attitude towards divorced persons: or rather, towards one particular divorced, remarried and soon-to-be-divorced person. 'It was scarcely realised at this early stage,' wrote Major the Hon. Alexander Hardinge, the new King's long-suffering Private Secretary, 'how overwhelming and inexorable was the influence exerted on the King by the lady of the moment. As time went on it became clearer that every decision, big or small, was subordinated to her will . . . It was she who filled his thoughts at all times, she alone who mattered, before her the affairs of state sank into insignificance.'[2] Hardinge's opinion was echoed by Edward VIII's Assistant Private Secretary, Alan (Tommy) Lascelles. He complained that the King would shut himself away with Mrs Simpson at the Fort from Thursday to Tuesday, and that when he did come back to Buckingham Palace he would again be closeted with her. 'The Lady is still there,' the footmen would say to the exasperated Private Secretaries. When, finally, the King did agree to receive them on state business, he would be 'too bored to listen' to what they had to say.[3]

Seventeen years later, this same Tommy Lascelles (by then Sir Alan Lascelles) was to find himself embroiled in another royal conflict between love and duty when King Edward VIII's niece, Princess Margaret, was showing an equal determination to marry a divorced person.

In spite of the King's obvious infatuation, only gradually did it dawn on his entourage that he actually intended to marry Mrs Simpson – and not only to marry her, but possibly to make her his Queen. Coronation Day had been set for 12 May 1937; if the King did indeed hope to have Mrs Simpson crowned as Queen Wallis beside him, he would have to have married her before then. For her part, she would have to have been a free woman for what was considered a decent interval before that. The first move, therefore, would be for Wallis Simpson to divorce her husband. (Ernest Simpson, who had long since turned a blind eye to his wife's affair, had conveniently fallen in love with someone else.) Since there was, in those days, a delay of six months between the granting of a decree nisi and a decree absolute, her petition would have to be filed by the autumn of 1936.

In the meantime, the King was anxious for people in official circles to get used to the idea of Wallis Simpson as his future wife, and to this end he therefore held a couple of formal dinners at St James's Palace. Far from keeping Mrs Simpson under cover, he insisted that her name be published in the Court Circular when announcing his guest list. To the second of these dinners, the King invited the Duke and Duchess of York. The Duchess, resenting the fact that the King should make use of people like herself to give respectability to Mrs Simpson, remained resolutely impervious to what a fellow guest called 'the lady's sparkling talk'.

This dinner was also the setting for a famous exchange between the Duchess of York and Winston Churchill. With characteristic mischievousness, Churchill introduced the subject of an earlier marriage scandal in the royal family, that of King George IV and Mrs Fitzherbert. The Duchess was not prepared to discuss it. 'Well,' she said crisply, 'that was a long time ago.' Undeterred, Churchill pressed on. He turned the conversation to the Wars of the Roses, the civil war between the royal Houses of Lancaster and York. The fact that Edward VIII planned to use the title of Duke of Lancaster as an incognito was not lost on the Duchess of York.

'That was a very, very long time ago,' she snapped.[4]

The two princesses met Mrs Simpson only once during this turbulent year, when the King drove over to Royal Lodge from nearby Fort Belvedere to show his brother his newly acquired station wagon. Turning into the entrance of Royal Lodge, the King made a complete swing around the circular driveway and drew up at the front door. The Duke and Duchess of York came out to greet him, and he insisted that they inspect the station wagon. 'It was amusing to observe the contrast between the two brothers,' wrote the Duchess of Windsor in her memoirs,

David all enthusiasm and volubility as he explained the fine points of the machine, the Duke of York quiet, shy, obviously dubious of this new-fangled American contrivance. It was not until David pointed out its advantages as a shooting brake that his younger brother showed any real interest. 'Come on, Bertie,' David urged, 'Let's drive around a little, I'll show you how easy it is to handle. . . .'

After a few minutes they returned, and we all walked through the garden. I had seen the Duchess of York before on several occasions at the Fort and at York House [St James's Palace]. Her justly famous charm was highly evident. I was also aware of the beauty of her complexion and the almost startling blueness of her eyes. Our conversation, I remember, was largely a discussion on the merits of the garden at the Fort and that at Royal Lodge. We returned to the house for tea, which was served in the drawing room. In a few minutes the two little princesses joined us. Princess Elizabeth, now Queen, was then ten, and Princess Margaret Rose was nearly six. They were both so blonde, so beautifully mannered, so brightly scrubbed, that they might have stepped straight from the pages of a picture book. Along with the tea things on a large table was a big jug of orange juice for the little girls. David and his sister-in-law carried on the conversation with his brother throwing in only an occasional word.[5]

The princesses had been brought into the room by their governess, and her observations on Mrs Simpson, some of which were omitted from the British edition of *The Little Princesses*, are telling. 'I looked at her with some interest,' Crawfie writes of the visitor. 'She was a smart, attractive woman, with that immediate friendliness American women have. She appeared entirely at her ease; if anything, far too much so . . . she had a distinctly proprietary way of speaking to the new King. I remember she drew him to the window and suggested how certain trees might be moved, and a part of the hill taken away to improve the view.'[6] As the view which Wallis Simpson was planning to improve was the Yorks' view, her effrontery was astonishing.

The visit had been, the Duchess of Windsor continued serenely, very pleasant. 'But I left with the impression that while the Duke of York was sold on the American station wagon, the Duchess was not sold on David's other American interest.'[7] According to Crawfie – again, only in the American edition of her book – Princess Elizabeth afterwards asked, 'Who is she?' thereby indicating that she realized that Uncle David's companion must be someone special. Today, however, Princess Margaret denies that the question was ever asked. This seems likely, since Crawfie also says that 'No one alluded to that visit when we met again later that evening. . . . Maybe the general hope was that if nothing was said, the whole business would blow over.'[8]

To distract the princesses during this increasingly troubled period, their governess suggested that they learn to swim. The Duke and

Duchess agreed. It was decided that they should take lessons at the Bath Club, a well-known gentleman's club. For this, the children acquired the club's regulation swimsuits, dark blue with initials in white, and white caps. 'Lilibet looked so pretty in hers. She was a long, slender child with beautiful legs,' enthused Crawfie, adding, inevitably, that 'Margaret looked like a plump navy-blue fish.' The lessons went very well once their instructress, Miss Amy Daly, had overcome her consternation at having to teach two royal children. The five-year-old Princess Margaret was naturally more apprehensive than her sister, and tended either to linger on the top step or cling to the side. 'Don't be a limpet, Margaret!' or 'Keep steady, Margaret!' Princess Elizabeth would shout encouragingly.

The Duke and Duchess often came to watch their daughters splashing about among the other children. The Duke was amazed at the ease and openness with which his daughters accomplished things. 'I don't know how they do it,' he exclaimed. 'We were always so terribly shy and self-conscious as children. These two don't seem to care.' Both his daughters ended by taking life-saving certificates, with Princess Elizabeth having to jump into the water, fully dressed, to 'save' her sister. 'The outings to the swimming club were the high spots of the week during those rather uneasy times,' writes Crawfie, 'and they helped a lot to take our minds off the clouds that were gathering about us all.'[9]

That summer the Yorks went, as always, to Birkhall near Balmoral Castle. The princesses loved their annual Scottish holiday; indeed, it was the chief landmark in their calendar, and they tended to date events by 'before we went to Scotland' or 'when we got back from Scotland'. Birkhall was a small, early eighteenth-century house standing on the banks of the River Muick. Within, its atmosphere was entirely Victorian: its furniture dark and heavy, its walls crammed with Landseer paintings and Spy cartoons. It was still lit by oil lamps and heated by foul-smelling oil stoves, while in each bathroom there were three basins: one marked 'teeth', one 'hands', and the third 'face'. In the Duke's bathroom there was also a sign bearing the hectoring text: 'Cleanliness is next to Godliness'.

While the Yorks were enjoying themselves in their usual way – the Duke shooting, the Duchess reading and writing letters, the princesses dividing their time between schoolwork and play – the

King was spending his holiday in a much less conventional fashion, taking a party, which included Mrs Simpson, on a cruise along the Dalmatian coast on the borrowed yacht *Nahlin*. If the world had not known about his love-affair before then, it certainly came to know about it during this well-publicized voyage. Only the British press, demonstrating a discretion and loyalty which seems astonishing today, played down Mrs Simpson's role in this Balkan jamboree. It even went so far as to cut her out of those photographs in which she appeared beside the King.

On their return, Wallis Simpson joined the King's house party at Balmoral where, to the increasing irritation of the Duchess of York, she acted the royal hostess (she even slept in the bed which Queen Mary had occupied for over twenty-five years). In October she formally petitioned for divorce, Ernest Simpson having provided evidence of theoretical adultery with the engagingly named Miss Buttercup Kennedy, and the decree nisi was awarded on 27 October 1936. The press barons, in deference to the King's wishes, remained silent. In six months' time the decree would become absolute. 'With my Coronation fixed for May 12,' wrote the King, 'this seemed to allow ample time for me to work things out.'[10]

By 'to work things out', Edward VIII presumably meant a scheme whereby he could marry Wallis Simpson and hang on to his crown. Never for a moment, though, did he consider giving her up. No pleas, arguments or calls to honour and duty could change his mind on this. When, eventually, Stanley Baldwin, the Prime Minister, forced himself to tackle the King on the question of Mrs Simpson, only one solid fact emerged from their conversations: the King was determined to marry Mrs Simpson, even if it meant abdicating his throne. This stark fact became clear to the Duke of York only after he had returned to 145 Piccadilly from Birkhall early in November. He was visited by Hardinge, the King's Private Secretary, who had come to tell the Duke about the Prime Minister's discussions with the King and to explain that if the King insisted on marrying Mrs Simpson, he would have to go. The crown would then pass to the Duke of York. 'A nightmare web,' as King George VI's official biographer puts it, 'began slowly enmeshing him.'[11]

During the following weeks, the crisis hurtled towards its inevitable climax. On 2 December the press broke its long silence, the virulence of its tone astonishing the two principal players in the drama. Wallis Simpson fled to friends in the South of France. From there, on a crackling telephone line, she kept in touch with the King, sometimes urging him to fight for his rights, at others offering to give him up. One by one the various schemes for a way out of his dilemma collapsed. Neither the British nor the Dominion governments would hear of a morganatic marriage. The Cabinet turned down the King's request – inspired by Mrs Simpson – to broadcast directly to the nation. Wisely, he would have nothing to do with the formation of a so-called 'King's Party'. Nor would he agree to postpone the marriage until after his Coronation.

Throughout all these negotiations, there was a constant coming and going at 145 Piccadilly as the increasingly anguished Duke of York was obliged to receive various political and ecclesiastical figures. Hanging over the banisters, the two princesses watched the stream of callers, which included, of course, the Prime Minister, Stanley Baldwin. The Duke and Duchess never spoke to the children about what was happening.

But something must have been said. When the bemused Princess Margaret asked her sister what all the unaccustomed fuss was about, Princess Elizabeth had an answer. 'I think Uncle David wants to marry Mrs Baldwin,' she explained, 'and Mr Baldwin doesn't like it.'[12]

On Sunday, 6 December 1936, King Edward VIII finally made up his mind to abdicate. Not until the following evening, however, did he tell the Duke of York of his decision. The Duke, who was already describing himself as 'the proverbial sheep being led to the slaughter', was, according to one member of his family, 'absolutely appalled' at the prospect of becoming King.[13] He, better than anyone, knew how sadly ill equipped he was for the role; he later admitted that, on finally realizing that nothing could save him from his fate, he broke down, 'and sobbed like a child'.[14] Making things even worse, at this time of terrible ordeal the Duke was deprived of the presence of his chief comfort and support, for the Duchess of York was in bed with influenza. 'One afternoon,' reports Crawfie, 'the Duchess sent for me to go and see her. She was occupied when I reached her room, and I stood outside in an alcove by the landing window, waiting, and watching the crowds gathered below, who, like myself, were wondering what the next move was to be. And then something happened that told me that the abdication had taken place. The bedroom door opened. Queen Mary came out of the Duchess's room. She who was always so upright, so alert, looked suddenly old and tired.'[15]

To Queen Mary, the whole business was inexplicable. She could appreciate that her son was in love with Mrs Simpson and, as a woman of experience, would have been able to understand if he had wanted to keep her as his mistress. What the Queen could not understand was that the King could contemplate marrying a divorced woman with, as she head-shakingly put it, 'two husbands living'.[16] And as for his giving up the throne in order to marry her, this was quite beyond her comprehension. 'To my mother,' as the Duke of Windsor afterwards wrote, 'the Monarchy was something sacred and the Sovereign a personage apart.'[17]

Once Queen Mary had left the Duchess of York's sickroom, the governess entered. The Duchess was in bed, propped up among pillows. 'I'm afraid there are going to be great changes in our lives, Crawfie,' she said. 'We talked for a little while as to how we were going to break the news to the children, and what differences it would make. The break was bound to be a painful one. We had all been so happy in our life at 145.' 'We must take what is coming to us,' the Duchess added, 'and make the best of it.'

When Crawfie told her charges that they were going to live in Buckingham Palace, they were horrified. 'What!' exclaimed Princess Elizabeth, 'You mean for ever?' Princess Margaret's reaction was more practical. 'But I've only just learned to write "York",' she wailed.[18]

On 10 December 1936, in the presence of his three brothers – the Dukes of York, Gloucester and Kent – King Edward VIII sat down at his desk at the Fort to sign the Instrument of Abdication. Princess Elizabeth, who by now understood the situation better, was able to explain it to her younger sister. Uncle David, she said, was going away and never coming back, and their Papa was going to be King. 'Does that mean that you will have to be the next queen?' asked Princess Margaret. 'Yes, some day,' replied her sister. 'Poor you,' said the younger girl. And that, in spite of claims to the contrary, was to remain Princess Margaret's attitude. At no stage did she ever wish to be queen. 'However numerous and severe might be the difficulties that beset her,' writes Lady Longford diplomatically, 'she was not to forget that she had been spared that one thing.'[19]

How differently, one wonders, would the course of Princess Margaret's life have run if she had succeeded to the throne? The responsibilities of her office would have anchored her more securely; her life would have been more fulfilled and her personality might have developed along different lines; marriage to a suitable consort would have given her stability. Queen Margaret would undoubtedly have been a livelier, more elegant and more culturally active figure than Queen Elizabeth II, while the demands of her position might well have tempered the imperiousness and capriciousness for which she was to become notorious. She could have been immensely popular. Such speculation is not really fanciful: for twelve years, from 1936 until the birth of Prince Charles in 1948, only one life stood between Princess Margaret and an eventual succession to the throne.

On 11 December 1936, with the Instrument of Abdication having been ratified by Parliament, the Duke of York succeeded to the throne as King George VI. Lady Cynthia Asquith, visiting 145 Piccadilly that day, reports that Princess Elizabeth, seeing a letter on the hall table addressed to 'Her Majesty the Queen', said wonderingly, 'That's Mummy now, isn't it?' But Princess Margaret was still wrestling with the problem of her new title. 'I have only just learned how to spell York – YORK –' she again grumbled, 'and now I am not to use it any more. I am now to sign myself Margaret all alone.'[20]

Two other names had to be changed as well. Reassuringly, if unimaginatively, the Duke of York had chosen to be styled as King George VI, and it was also decided that the abdicated King would in future use the style 'His Royal Highness the Duke of Windsor'. The 'Royal Highness' prefix was, however, to be denied to his wife and any descendants, an edict which was to rankle with the new duke until the end of his life.

There was one last scene to be played out: the ex-King's farewell broadcast to the nation. In a moving and dignified address that same day, he gave his reason, and his justification, for abdicating the throne. 'I have found it impossible to carry the heavy burden of responsibility and to discharge my duties as King as I would wish to do without the help and support of the woman I love.' Then, having taken leave of his family, all of whom had assembled for a final dinner at Royal Lodge, the Duke of Windsor was driven away to

Portsmouth, where the destroyer HMS *Fury* was waiting to carry him off to France and a life of exile.

On the following morning the new King, ashen-faced and numb with nerves, left 145 Piccadilly to attend his Accession Council at St James's Palace. Crawfie explained to the princesses that on their father's return from the Accession Council, they would have to curtsy to him as King; in the past, they had always curtsied to their grandfather, King George V. 'And now you mean we must do it to Papa and Mummy?' asked Princess Elizabeth. 'Margaret too?' 'Margaret also,' replied Crawfie, 'and try not to topple over.' When the King returned, both children greeted him with deep curtsies. 'I think perhaps nothing that had occurred had brought the change in his condition to him as clearly as this did,' writes the governess. 'He stood for a moment touched and taken aback. Then he stooped and kissed them both warmly.'[21]

This story, however, like so many of Crawfie's anecdotes, has since been dismissed by the family. And certainly, even if it is true that the princesses did make obeisance to their father on that day, they never again curtsied to their parents, only to Queen Mary.

The royal family never forgave the Duke of Windsor for what they regarded as his shameful jettisoning of duty for love. Many years later, Princess Margaret, who had by then faced a similar dilemma, was asked if she had seen much of her uncle after he had gone into exile.

'Only at funerals,' she drawled.[22]

PART TWO

The King's Daughter

CHAPTER 6

'A Family Life at Court'

THE DUKE AND DUCHESS OF YORK, claimed the Prime Minister, Stanley Baldwin, when faced with the prospect of Edward VIII's abdication, would fill the vacant throne very well. Not everyone shared the Prime Minister's opinion. Indeed, in private, Baldwin himself expressed his reservations about George VI's qualifications for the task. 'There's a lot of prejudice against him,' he admitted. 'He's had no chance to capture the popular imagination as his brother did. I'm afraid he won't find it easy for the first year or two.'[1]

To the general public, the forty-one-year-old King George VI was an almost unknown figure. He had none of the gravitas of his formidable father, King George V, or the charm of his popular brother, King Edward VIII. The former had been widely respected; the latter idolized. The little that the public did know about the new King was hardly reassuring. He appeared to have no taste for kingship. Lacking any sense of royal showmanship, he neither looked nor acted like a monarch. It was rumoured that he suffered from 'falling fits' (epilepsy), and that he would be unable to stand the strain of his position. The fact that the sovereign's customary Christmas broadcast was cancelled that first year, and the proposed Durbar in India postponed, merely strengthened suspicions about his lack of physical stamina. Nor were matters helped by the Archbishop of Canterbury's well-intentioned but tactless reference, in his Abdication broadcast, to the new King's stammer. The 'occasional momentary hesitation' in the monarch's speech, intoned His Grace, 'need cause no sort of embarrassment, for it causes none to him who speaks'.[2]

Unhappily, the new King himself shared all these reservations. He was acutely conscious of lacking the presence, personality and experience for the role into which he had suddenly been thrust. During the first few months of his reign he felt overwhelmed by the magnitude of his task: by the relentless publicity; the strain of public appearances; the necessity of public speaking; the volume of work in the parliamentary boxes. 'I've never even seen a State paper,' he wailed to his cousin, Lord Louis Mountbatten.[3] Under the pressures of his new position, his short temper became shorter still; the King was often incoherent with rage.

There were reservations, too, about the thirty-six-year-old Queen Elizabeth's ability to fulfil her great destiny. She might have proved successful enough in a minor role, but what sort of queen would she make? She certainly had nothing of Queen Mary's commanding presence. For years, she had been known as 'the little Duchess'; might she not, with her small stature, wispy fringe, ready smile and uncertain taste in clothes, prove too 'little', too lacking in majesty? The fashionable set who had surrounded King Edward VIII considered her woefully unsmart, and he himself is said to have referred to her as 'that common little woman'.[4]

On the other hand, the couple were able to bring certain easily recognizable qualities to their job: a sense of monarchal continuity and stability and, equally important, a reassuring respectability. The fact that there was now a young, attractive family at the centre of national life proved to be of inestimable value to the monarchy as an institution. 'I know the people of this country,' declared the socialist politician J.H. Thomas at the time of the Abdication, 'I know them. They 'ate 'aving no family life at Court.'[5] The two little princesses, in other words, were proving to be trump cards in the royal hand. So it was with considerable enthusiasm that the crowds who gathered outside 145 Piccadilly and then Buckingham Palace greeted the comings and goings of the new King and his family. Princess Margaret remembers 'battling through enormous, loving crowds' to reach the Palace.[6] The King and Queen had moved in almost immediately, but it was not until mid-February 1937, over two months after their father's accession, that the princesses arrived to live permanently in their new home.

Buckingham Palace, known originally as Buckingham House, had come into royal ownership when it was bought by the young

King George III in 1762. The house had been virtually rebuilt, in the shape of an open square, by John Nash on the orders of King George IV, and the square then closed by the erection, during Queen Victoria's reign, of the east front facing the Mall. Not until 1913 – a mere twenty-three years before King George VI took up residence – was the Palace given its now familiar Portland stone façade. Within, the building was a rambling arrangement of grandiose state apartments, draughty corridors, wide staircases and numberless high-ceilinged rooms of varying sizes. By 1937, its decoration tended to mirror the taste of the most recent royal showman, King Edward VII; some of the public rooms, commented one member of the household, resembled the stage settings of a luxurious pantomime. Some bedroom lights could be switched off only in the corridor outside, and dressing-gowned female household members on the way to the bathroom were quite likely to bump into the Palace postman trudging round the interminable passages to deliver letters. Another full-time employee was the 'vermin man', whose mice-killing methods are said to have both fascinated and horrified the princesses. It was a brisk, five-minute walk from the nursery wing to the gardens.

But in spite of all this, Princess Margaret remembers Buckingham Palace as 'cosy'. The royal family's private suite was on part of the first floor, on the Green Park side of the Palace. The nurseries were on the floor above, looking bright and cheerful in a new coat of paint; from their front windows the girls could watch the ceaseless activity in the Mall. Princess Elizabeth shared her bedroom with Bobo MacDonald; Princess Margaret shared hers with Allah. Far from being daunted or depressed by the endless corridors (by now lined with their toy horses) the princesses delighted in careering along them. Princess Margaret could be seen frantically pedalling her kiddy-car, with the familiar cry of 'Wait for me, Lilibet. Wait for me!' To the Palace staff, accustomed to the funereal formality of King George V's day, it was as though the place had suddenly come alive.

At first, the matter of a schoolroom presented something of a problem. The traditional schoolroom was one of the darkest and gloomiest rooms in the Palace, for the heavy stone balustrading outside the windows gave the impression of prison bars and kept out the light. For the King, one look into this depressing room filled, no doubt, with painful childhood memories, was enough. No, he said firmly to the governess, it simply would not do. Instead, the princesses took their lessons in a small, sunny room overlooking the gardens. 'It was not very easy to teach, at the same time,' complains Marion Crawford, 'two children of such different ages, character and development.' Princess Margaret, 'a born comic', tended to be disruptive. Yet her charm was irresistible. 'Margaret had a way, when she knew I was cross with her, of fixing me with those beautiful blue eyes of hers, and saying persuasively, "Crawfie! Laugh!" So, often, alas, I had to laugh.'[7]

If the weather was fine, an out-of-doors schoolroom would be set up in the little summer house in the Palace grounds. The gardens were one of the chief delights of the princesses' new home. After cramped, sooty Hamilton Gardens, they were vast. Princess Margaret, eyeing the lake, asked the governess if the Mediterranean – about which she had just learned in a geography lesson – was as big. Their favourite spot was a little mound at the end of the gardens, from which they could watch the traffic in Buckingham Palace Road. One day they spotted the Queen being driven by. 'It's Mummy!' shrieked Princess Margaret, waving ecstatically.

The princesses were, in fact, now seeing a great deal less of their parents. Only first thing in the morning, and possibly at lunch and teatime, was the family together. The King would now have to spend much of the morning in his study, attending to state business with his secretaries and receiving ministers and ambassadors. In the afternoon there would be official functions or more visitors, and after tea he would have to work on the boxes. In the evenings there would be receptions, dinners or command performances. The Queen, too, had a busy schedule. She had to cope with a mountain of correspondence, receive ambassadors' wives and other visitors, and attend various official functions. Occasionally she would be seen, in the middle of the morning, wearing full evening dress, tiara and jewels, on her way to a portrait sitting.

Sometimes the two little girls, dressed in their matching quilted, rosebud-patterned dressing-gowns, would be allowed to watch their parents leading the procession of other members of the royal family into the Throne Room on the occasion of an evening court. These were the occasions at which debutantes, wearing the obligatory full evening dress with five-foot trains and with three curled ostrich feathers in their hair, were presented to the King and Queen. The royal couple would sit side by side on their thrones, with other members of the family, all with their equerries and ladies-in-waiting, grouped behind. While soft music was played by the band of one of the Guards regiments in the gallery above, the debutantes would be called up, one by one, to be presented and make their obeisance to the sovereigns. The princesses were always interested in seeing what their superlatively elegant aunt, Princess Marina, Duchess of Kent, would be wearing. When she was grown up, Princess Margaret once said, she would dress like Aunt Marina.

Once the first numbing shock of his accession had worn off, George VI began to impress those about him by his common sense, dedication, integrity and moral courage. He might not have been quick, clever or original, but he had about him a reassuring dependability, coupled with an unbounded sense of duty. Unlike his flashier elder brother, he was extremely conscientious. He was determined, as he put it, 'to make amends' for the abdicated King's selfish and disruptive behaviour.[8]

Even more quickly, and a great deal more impressively, did Queen Elizabeth prove her worth. On this vastly increased stage, the somewhat 'actressy' qualities which had always marked her proved to be exactly what was needed. Under the expert guidance of the couturier Norman Hartnell, her clothes became more elegant and more romantic. She adopted those pastel colours by day, and glittering crinolines by night, which were to become, both for her and later for her daughters, obligatory royal fashion for the following quarter-century. Even more important than this, however, she developed a persona which, while undeniably regal and dignified, was also warm, spontaneous and crowd-pleasing. She exuded, in short, a certain 'star quality'. The King's frequent public allusions to his wife's help in carrying out his duties were far from conventional tributes. They were made in heartfelt appreciation of her constant support, encouragement and inspiration.

Before many months had passed, even the abdicated Edward VIII's supporters had to admit that the new monarchs were proving surprisingly successful. 'The King and Queen have gained greatly in presence and dignity,' wrote Chips Channon; he admitted, too, that at their first Opening of Parliament, 'the King seemed quite at ease and so did the Queen'.[9]

* * *

The first great state occasion which Princess Margaret is able to remember in any detail is the coronation of her parents on 12 May 1937, when she was not yet seven, her sister eleven. They had been preparing for the great day for months. Queen Mary had unearthed a thirty-foot-long full-colour panorama of King George IV's coronation, and was thus able to explain to her granddaughters all the roles, rituals and symbols of the ceremony. The princesses were fitted out in identical dresses, designed for the occasion, of white lace with silver bows, while on their heads they were to wear specially made lightweight golden coronets. (The effect of their silver slippers was, however, somewhat spoiled by the short white school-girl socks that were considered appropriate.) A scene was only narrowly avoided when Princess Margaret was assured that the only reason why her purple velvet, ermine-trimmed mantle was shorter than her sister's was because she herself was shorter.

Sitting on a specially built-up seat so as to allow her to be seen by the crowds, Princess Margaret drove with her sister to Westminster Abbey in the Irish State Coach, accompanied by their Aunt Mary, the Princess Royal, and her eldest son, George, Viscount Lascelles. It was the two little princesses who headed the procession of British royalty into the Abbey. The last royal figure to enter before the King and Queen was Queen Mary, magnificent in a dress of gold tissue, a velvet mantle supported by four pages, a diamond tiara, and no less than seven rows of diamonds about her throat. A queen-dowager does not usually attend the coronation of her husband's successor, but Queen Mary appreciated that her presence would be seen as a gesture of monarchal and family solidarity after the upheavals of the Abdication. She took her place in the royal gallery beside her two granddaughters. 'They looked too sweet,' she afterwards wrote, 'in their lace dresses and robes, especially when they put on their coronets.'[10]

Princess Elizabeth's fear that her sister would disgrace them all by falling asleep in the middle of the long ceremony ('After all, she is very young for a coronation, isn't she?') proved unfounded. Throughout all the splendours of the occasion – the blaring trumpets, the swelling anthems, the richly embroidered copes and vestments, the costumed pages, the glittering crowns, the King in satin and velvet and ermine, the Queen in a white gown all shimmering with gold thread – Princess Margaret remained awake, if somewhat bemused. 'Well, did Margaret behave nicely?' asked the governess when the princesses arrived back at the Palace. 'She was wonderful, Crawfie,' answered Princess Elizabeth. 'I only had to nudge her once or twice when she played with her prayer book too loudly.'[11] Princess Margaret denies this. 'I wouldn't have dared . . .' she protests. 'I was sitting between Granny and Aunt Mary!'[12]

It was from about this time onwards that the difference in status between the two sisters began to become more pronounced. After all, Princess Elizabeth would one day be the reigning sovereign. Yet she was only the Heir Presumptive, and not the Heir Apparent, to the throne. There was still a chance that her thirty-six-year-old mother could give birth to a son; in that case the new male baby would become the Heir Apparent – the undisputed future monarch. So Princess Elizabeth remained merely an heir presumptive throughout her father's life, which allowed Princess Margaret to refer to herself, in her sharp fashion, as 'heir apparent to the heir presumptive'.

If Marion Crawford is to be believed, the elder sister now began to take a somewhat bossier tone towards the younger. She did not know what they were going to do with Margaret, she would say if her sister had done something naughty. She would also instruct Princess Margaret, as they set out for a Palace garden party, that if she did see someone in a funny hat, she was not to point at it and laugh. But the younger girl was quite capable of giving as good as she got. She once hopped out of bed in order to imitate the obsessively neat way in which Princess Elizabeth arranged her clothes before getting into bed. It was not the only occasion, says Crawfie, on which Margaret's talent for caricature came in handy.

Possessed of a highly developed dynastic sense, Queen Mary began to take an even closer interest in Princess Elizabeth's upbringing and education. She took both grandchildren on ever more ambitious cultural tours: to the palaces of Hampton Court, Greenwich and Kew, and to the Royal Mint, the Bank of England and the Tower of London. For the eight-year-old Princess Margaret, these marathon tours were a considerable ordeal. 'My grandmother would rush on ahead, surrounded by whoever accompanied her on these expeditions,' she complains, 'while we two would hurry along behind. I was absolutely exhausted by hours on end of walking and standing in museums and galleries.'[13] When, in the spring of 1939, the King and Queen paid a state visit to North America, there was talk of the princesses moving to Queen Mary's home, Marlborough House, so that the old Queen could keep an even closer eye on their progress. Much to the relief of the governess and her pupils, the scheme came to nothing.

Further emphasizing the difference between the future destinies of the princesses, the elder, on turning thirteen, began to take lessons in constitutional history, given to her by Henry (later Sir Henry) Marten, the Vice-Provost of Eton. 'Lilibet,' writes Marion Crawford in one of those passages which no doubt annoyed Princess Margaret,

was far more disciplined than Margaret ever was. Margaret was having quite a lot of social life from the age of ten onward. But the King set a very high standard for Lilibet, perhaps because she is heir to the throne. Margaret was a great joy and a diversion but Lilibet had a kind of natural grace all her own. The King had a great pride in her, and she in turn had an inborn desire to do what was expected of her.[14]

It is hardly surprising, therefore, that the younger sister, admittedly more indulged, should develop an extrovert personality, and that she should try to compensate for her elder sister's more favoured position by behaving in a less responsible, less serious, and often less well-mannered fashion. 'What a good job,' the members of the household would mutter, 'that Margaret is the younger one.'[15] Yet in spite of this gradual divergence in their upbringing, as well as the contrast in their personalities, the sisters remained close. And although, in the years ahead, Princess Margaret's behaviour would often place a severe strain on the relationship, this closeness survived. The very artificiality of their situation ensured that the two sisters should stick together; ensured, too, that they should be regarded, and regard themselves, as set apart from their contemporaries.

The King and Queen did what they could to counteract this atmosphere of exclusiveness. At Glamis, when they visited the Queen's large family, life tended to be easier. Here there were masses of cousins – Elphinstones, Leveson-Gowers, Strathmores – to bring a certain knockabout realism into the princesses' lives. Princess Margaret was especially friendly with her Elphinstone relations. There were dressing-up chests full of old-fashioned clothes, and room after room in which to play hide-and-seek or sardines. It was a fascinating place for children.

At Buckingham Palace, meanwhile, it was decided that the formation of a Girl Guide company might help encourage natural contact with other children. But how could this ever work, exclaimed Miss Violet Synge (later Guide Commissioner for England) when she was approached about the idea; 'Guides must all treat one another like sisters'. On realizing that the princesses were relatively natural little girls, Miss Synge agreed. Since Princess Margaret was too young to be a Guide, however, a Brownie pack was started as well. In the end there were to be twenty Guides and fourteen Brownies, drawn from the children of court officials and Palace employees. The King made only one stipulation. He would not allow his daughters to wear the hideous long black stockings. They reminded him too much of his youth. So the Palace Guides and Brownies were allowed to wear knee-length beige stockings with their uniforms. But, as an exercise in egalitarianism, the formation of these Guide and Brownie troops was not, at first, entirely successful: many of the delighted children turned up at the Palace in party dresses and white gloves, proudly attended by nannies and governesses. And Princess Margaret was astonished to discover – during a game in which the girls, having taken off their shoes and piled them all together, had to find their own, put them on, and race to a finishing line – half the children did not know their own shoes. She always knew.

Another royal home which provided a setting for Princess Margaret's life at this time was Balmoral. On his accession, King George VI had been obliged to forsake 'small, comfortable Birkhall' for the more impressive Balmoral Castle, and it was here that the royal family would spend several weeks each year, from early August until early October. This royal Deeside retreat had been built in the 1850s under the direction of Queen Victoria's husband, Prince Albert, and even in the late 1930s it still retained much of its Victorian atmosphere. With its pale-coloured granite walls, pepper-pot turrets, battlements and stepped gables, Balmoral is a mixture of German *Schloss* and Scottish baronial hall. Inside, it remained in those days a riot of tartan: tartan wallpaper, tartan curtains, tartan carpets, tartan upholstery; as to pictures, Landseers, as one member of the household drily put it, predominated.

For the princesses there were endless delights: riding their ponies across the heather-covered hillsides; the thrilling roaring of stags and the plaintive 'go-back, go-back' of grouse calling from the heather; the enormous teas with shrimps and scones, baps and bannocks; and, most exciting of all, the seven pipers who would march around the dining room after dinner. The princesses would be allowed to watch this nightly ceremony, peering over the banisters from a landing high above the kilted, marching men. One annual event was the Gillies' Ball, given for the staff and their families, and which the King and Queen always opened by dancing with the senior members of the party. From the age of twelve, Princess Elizabeth was allowed to come down for a little while to take part in some of the reels.

However idyllic the place, the Balmoral holiday of 1939 was a seriously disturbed one. The princesses – then aged thirteen and nine – would have known almost nothing about the political events in Europe which had for some time been threatening their cloistered and well-ordered lives. Ever since his accession, George VI had been facing an increasingly ominous world situation. His coronation had coincided with the resignation of Stanley Baldwin and the succession of Neville Chamberlain as Prime Minister. In his efforts to contain the growing aggression of the Axis powers – Hitler's Germany and Mussolini's Italy – by appeasing them, Chamberlain had the King's wholehearted support. A peace-loving man, and one who had lived through the horrors and heartbreaks of one world war and the hardships and disillusionments of the subsequent peace, King George VI was by no means alone in imagining that another war could, and should, be avoided. When in 1938, Chamberlain's demeaning negotiations with Hitler over the Nazi takeover of Czechoslovakia ended in the apparent triumph of the Munich agreement, a relieved King, with the Queen beside him, had led the Prime Minister out on to the Palace balcony to receive the cheers of the no less relieved crowds below.

But the triumph of Munich proved ephemeral. By the summer of 1939 it was becoming clear that war was inevitable; if, as seemed likely, Hitler were to invade Poland, then Britain and France were bound by treaty to defend her. In fact, a Nazi incursion into Poland seemed so imminent that there was even a suggestion that the King's Balmoral visit be postponed. In the end, the royal family travelled up to Scotland as usual; with them in their private train went, as always, their dogs.

The family had been at Balmoral for just over a fortnight when the deteriorating situation in Europe obliged the King to hurry back to London. He had been informed on 21 August of the signing of the non-aggression pact between Nazi Germany and Soviet Russia; since this pact would allow Hitler to move against Poland without fear of Russian intervention, the prospect of war with Nazi Germany was brought much closer. On 23 August the King took the night express from Perth to London, followed, a week later, by the Queen. Balmoral Castle emptied and the two princesses were taken to Birkhall. Marion Crawford was ordered to cut short her own Scottish holiday and to join her charges at Birkhall as soon as possible. On 1 September Hitler invaded Poland. Two days later, with Hitler having failed to reply to an Anglo-French ultimatum demanding the immediate withdrawal of the German forces from Poland, Britain was at war.

At six o'clock that evening the King broadcast to the Empire. He called upon 'my people at home and my people across the seas' to stand firm and united in the 'dark days ahead'.[16] But how did he really feel as he faced not only the prospect of having to assume the demanding role of king-at-war, but also the hardships and horrors that a war was bound to bring? 'We were stunned,' admitted the Queen in later years. 'Sorrowful, of course, but mainly stunned.'[17]

The reaction of the nine-year-old Princess Margaret was trenchant. 'Who is this Hitler,' she demanded, 'spoiling everything?'[18]

CHAPTER 7

Wartime Windsor

'STICK TO THE USUAL PROGRAMME as far as you can, Crawfie,' said Queen Elizabeth over the telephone from London to the children's governess at Birkhall. 'We don't know what is coming, of course, but carry on as long as possible, just as usual.'

And that is what the governess did. She followed the established routine of lessons, homework and recreation but, because she was beginning to find the teaching of two children, 'both of different ages, both extremely bright', increasingly difficult, a Mrs Montaudon-Smith (known, inevitably, as 'Monty') was brought in to take over French classes. For Princess Elizabeth, Henry Marten's lessons in constitutional history continued, though now by post. For relaxation there were walks and rides on the wine-red, heathery hillsides, or old Charlie Chaplin and Laurel and Hardy films and various radio shows. Records were played on an old-fashioned horn gramophone that blared so loudly that half-a-dozen scarves had to be crammed into the horn to muffle the sound. Princess Margaret's favourite record was of the tenor Beniamino Gigli singing the aria 'Your Tiny Hand is Frozen' from Puccini's *La Bohème*. It was an especially apt choice, for the cold at Birkhall was intense. Often the princesses would wake up to find their windows patterned with frost, the water frozen solid in their jugs and their sponges and faceflannels rock hard. They never grumbled about such things. However, getting Princess Margaret to go to bed at night was always a problem, or so her governess complained. Only by marching her to the door, fixing her with a stern look and barking 'Go to bed!' could Crawfie get the girl upstairs.[1]

At this stage, the war touched their daily lives very little. For one thing, the Scottish Highlands seemed very remote from the centre of things; for another, these were the months of the so-called 'phoney war' – that static, six-month-long period between Hitler's conquest of Poland and his attack on Norway. The most that the princesses were called upon to do was to hand round tea and cake to the women who gathered at Birkhall to sew work for the war effort, and to greet, somewhat self-consciously, the evacuee children from the Glasgow slums who were being accommodated on the Balmoral estate. Most of these city-bred children hated life in the country. 'They were terrified by the strange sounds,' remembered the Queen, 'by things like the wind in the trees at night.'[2]

No one knew when the princesses would be reunited with their parents. The high point of their day was the evening telephone call from the King and Queen. With Christmas approaching – by which time they would have been away from their mother and father for over three months – the princesses were taken shopping in Aberdeen where, at Woolworths, they bought most of their presents. On 18 December, the Queen telephoned to say that they would all be spending Christmas together at Sandringham. Although the Norfolk coastline was one of the areas most vulnerable to a German invasion, the curious inactivity of the phoney war allowed the King to be at his beloved Sandringham for Christmas as usual.

The royal family's reunion was tempered – as always for the King – by the prospect of his traditional Christmas Day broadcast; not until that was over, he always said, could he enjoy the day. And absent from the family circle this Christmas was Queen Mary. Under protest, the seventy-two-year-old Queen had agreed to sit out the war at Badminton House in Gloucestershire, the home of her niece Mary, Duchess of Beaufort. Queen Mary had left Sandringham in September, heading a cavalcade of cars carrying her staff of sixty-three, plus their dependants, and over seventy pieces of personal luggage. For the duration of the war, this most formal and metropolitan of queens was to be subjected to all the unfamiliarities of life in the country.

With Christmas over, the princesses were moved from Sandringham to Royal Lodge. Although the King and Queen spent the weekdays at Buckingham Palace, their daughters did not return to live in London. From February until May 1940 they remained at

Royal Lodge, their place of residence being officially described, with deliberate vagueness, as somewhere 'in the country'.

The situation in Europe changed with dramatic suddenness when, on 9 April 1940, Hitler invaded Denmark and Norway; a month later the Germans invaded the Low Countries. To most people, there seemed to be very little doubt that Britain would be next, or that, at the very least, squads of Nazi paratroopers would land in England in order to kill or carry off certain prominent individuals. The princesses were clearly vulnerable to such dangers, as well as to the risks, shared by the whole population, of German air raids. It was therefore suggested that they should be sent to the safety of Canada, for not only many British children, but also many members of Continental royal families, were being sent across the Atlantic. Should not the heir to the British throne be similarly safeguarded? To this suggestion the Queen had a succinct answer: 'The children could not go without me,' she said, 'and I could not possibly leave the King.'³ But nor, quite obviously, could the princesses remain at Royal Lodge, even though it had been camouflaged with paint the colour of mud. On 12 May 1940 the Queen telephoned Marion Crawford. 'Crawfie, I think you had better go at once to Windsor Castle, anyway for the rest of the week.'⁴

They remained there for almost exactly five years.

If any one royal residence can be said to symbolize the British monarchy, it must be Windsor Castle. For almost a thousand years it has been associated with the kings and queens of England. Rising high above the Thames, it is a massive, complex and highly romantic fortress-palace, its central keep dominating a confusion of walls, towers, battlements, gates, courts and residences. Since Hitler, at least according to Princess Margaret in later life, had decided 'that he would use Windsor Castle as his headquarters once Britain had been conquered', the castle was very well guarded, not only defended by troops, but also ringed with slit trenches and barbed-wire entanglements. Today, the Princess is dismissive of these precautions. 'They would never have kept the Germans out,' she says, 'but they certainly kept us in.'⁵

By the time the princesses took up residence in the castle, almost all traces of its pre-war grandeur had been obliterated. Pictures had been removed, chandeliers taken down, carpets rolled up, glass-fronted cabinets turned to the wall and the furniture in the state apartments shrouded in dust sheets. Sculpture, china, silver and other precious possessions had been taken away for safe keeping. Some valuables remained, however. One day the King's Librarian, Sir Owen Morshead, led the princesses into the vaults where he showed them a pile of ordinary leather hatboxes which seemed, at first sight, to be stuffed with old newspaper. Only on closer inspection did the princesses discover that the boxes were crammed with the Crown Jewels.

Wartime life in the castle was full of inconveniences. The number of boilers in operation having been reduced, there were days when hot water had to be lugged up from the distant kitchens to the bedrooms. The nightly blackout of hundreds of windows presented a considerable problem. By the time they had blacked out all the windows, grumbled one servant, it was morning again. More than fifteen hundred acres of once beautiful parkland had been ploughed up and given over to the cultivation of cereal crops. The huge herd of deer had been dramatically reduced. Even horses from the Royal Mews – the famous Windsor Greys – were now being used for such ignoble tasks as drawing ploughs and mowers.

The princesses were accommodated in Lancaster Tower, which dates from the reign of Henry VII. The nursery was a converted sitting room, and each child had a bedroom and bathroom; as always, Princess Elizabeth shared her room with Bobo MacDonald, and Princess Margaret hers with Allah. Because of fuel cuts, the electric fires had a way of going out at the coldest times of the day. There were, too, other inconveniences of wartime. An underground dungeon had been converted into a makeshift bomb shelter (it was to be many months before a more permanent, properly equipped shelter was constructed). Within two nights of their arrival, an air-raid alarm was sounded, and Marion Crawford, dashing down to the shelter, was astonished to see no sign of the princesses, their absence causing Sir Hill Child, the normally impassive Master of the Household, to become considerably fussed. Crawfie rushed upstairs to find out what was wrong. There she discovered Allah who, having first put on her own cap and uniform, was carefully dressing the children. 'We're dressing, Crawfie,' explained Princess Elizabeth in answer to the governess's frantic questioning. 'We must dress.'

'Nonsense!' shouted Crawfie. 'You are not to dress. Put a coat over your nightclothes, at once!' Much to Allah's disapproval, this was done and the girls were hustled down to the shelter. By this time, says Crawfie, Sir Hill Child was 'a nervous wreck'. 'You must understand the princesses must come down at once,' he spluttered. 'They must come down whatever they are wearing.' By the time the all-clear sounded, many hours later, he had regained his composure. Bowing 'ceremoniously' to Princess Elizabeth, he announced gravely, 'You may go to bed, Ma'am.'[6] In time, things became better organized. As soon as the warning sounded, the princesses would scramble into their siren suits, pick up their gas masks and ready-packed suitcases, and hurry along the dark, damp passageways to the shelter.

War or no war, lessons continued as before, with Mrs Montaudon-Smith (whom Crawfie obscurely describes as having a liking for the Bohemian life) still teaching both girls French and Henry Marten coming from Eton to tutor Princess Elizabeth. When, later, Princess Margaret asked whether she, too, could attend history tutorials with Henry Marten, she was deflatingly informed that for her it was 'not necessary'.[7] Much of the rest of their time was dominated by the war. Like children all over the country, the princesses cultivated their vegetable gardens, collected tinfoil, rolled bandages and knitted scarves and socks for the troops. They were subjected to rationing of food and clothing, and were issued with their own clothes coupons. The Queen once told a member of the family that many of her dresses were altered for Princess Elizabeth; 'Margaret gets Lilibet's clothes then, so with the three of us we manage in relays.'[8] The girls looked forward to their Sunday morning egg, the ration being one a week. Although it would be an exaggeration to claim that the royal family actually suffered any privations at table, Princess Margaret does claim that, in years to come, she could not bear to see her children 'plastering their bread with butter'.[9]

The princesses continued their activities as Girl Guides and, later, as Sea Rangers. In the summer, they would camp out overnight near one of Queen Victoria's many little pavilions in the castle grounds. Although Princess Elizabeth did not really enjoy sleeping under canvas ('She was getting older . . .' says the governess, 'and did not want to undress before a lot of other children'), no such inhibitions spoiled Princess Margaret's enjoyment.

She was a menace to the Guides officer in charge. Every evening I would watch the same performance. From the tent that housed Margaret there would burst forth storms of giggles. The Guides officer would appear, say a few well-chosen words, and retreat. The ensuing silence would reign for a minute or two, then a fresh outburst probably meant Margaret was giving her companions an imitation of the Guides officer's lecture.[10]

In October 1940, the ten-year-old Princess Margaret made a small contribution to her sister's wireless broadcast to 'the children of the Empire' during the *Children's Hour* programme on the BBC. At the end of her message, Princess Elizabeth suddenly said, 'My sister is by my side, and we are both going to say goodnight to you. Come on, Margaret.' At this Princess Margaret piped up with a confident 'Goodnight and good luck to you all.'[11]

The princesses lived for the weekends, when their parents would arrive from their week up in London. The autumn of 1940 saw the worst of the Blitz, during which many British cities – and London most of all – were subjected to massive bombing raids. Thousands were killed and injured, and the destruction was on a tremendous scale. It was during this period that King George VI and Queen Elizabeth won the hearts of the nation by their close identification with the suffering of the people. Day after day, as soon as a raid was over, the royal couple were to be found moving among the crowds, questioning, listening, encouraging, sympathizing. This identification was considerably strengthened when Buckingham Palace was bombed and damaged in September 1940. Almost before the wreckage had cooled off, noted one member of the household, the two of them were calmly making their way about the rubble like people crossing a river on stepping stones.

Whatever the casualties or the damage, the Queen, claims Marion Crawford, never let the children see that she was worried about the progress of the war. 'One evening,' remembered a young guardsman who served at Windsor Castle, 'she returned late from London after a dreadful day. Hundreds of houses down, streets up, people crying. The lot. But she came down to see us . . . as she always did, and laughed and joked with the children. And what she was like with the King! For ever loving and soothing. . . .'[12]

In spite of the royal couple's often-expressed determination not to leave Britain ('It just never occurred to us,' claimed the Queen many years later[13]) the Government had made plans to prevent them from falling into enemy hands in the event of a successful German invasion. Two armoured cars were converted to passenger use, and kept ready for a rapid spiriting away of the family. Even before the war, Madresfield in Worcestershire had been rented as a possible place of royal refuge, though it was merely the first of a number of houses selected because of their relative accessibility to Liverpool. 'There was a line of them,' says Princess Margaret, who knew nothing about this until long after the war; 'we were to be shunted from one to the other until we reached Liverpool.' From there, if necessary, the family would be evacuated to Canada. But although the King and Queen must have known of these plans, their daughters, claimed Princess Margaret, were 'never told anything'.[14]

It was at 'Fortress Windsor' that Princess Margaret's theatrical enthusiasms first flowered. For Christmas 1940, Marion Crawford organized a nativity play, *The Christmas Child*, with Princess Elizabeth as one of the Three Kings and Princess Margaret as the Little Child, heading a cast of local schoolboys. Dressed in a simple white dress and rocking a cradle, Princess Margaret sang 'Gentle Jesus, Meek and Mild'. The King, an emotional man, was deeply moved. 'I wept through most of it,' he noted in his diary that evening.[15]

This success encouraged Marion Crawford to think of staging a pantomime. From then on Princess Margaret gave her no peace; 'Crawfie, you did say . . .', she would nag. She produced drawings, arranged parts, designed costumes, and spoke of little else. And so, each Christmas from 1941 onwards, a pantomime was staged in the Waterloo Chamber. They presented *Cinderella*, *The Sleeping Beauty*, *Aladdin* and *Old Mother Red Riding Boots*, with Princess Elizabeth usually appearing in stockings and tunic as the Principal Boy, and Princess Margaret, in wig and long skirts, as the leading lady. 'It was all very heady and madly exciting,' wrote one of the girls conscripted into the cast.

Nonetheless, no one was entirely comfortable once we were into rehearsals. Mr Tanner [the director] had insisted we call the princesses 'Ma'am' and that we curtsy whenever we greeted them. We – well, I at least – were always conscious of who they were and found it difficult to carry on a normal conversation. . . .

I, for one, admired Princess Margaret. I thought her a very good actress. She was the best in our little company. The star, I guess you would say. It had nothing to do with being who she was. Princess Elizabeth was rather stiff. She was never bossy with the other children, but she was quick to correct her sister if she did not approve of her behaviour. Princess Margaret liked doing little pranks – moving props, things like that, and she giggled a lot.[16]

Once, for instance, Princess Margaret smuggled a corgi on stage under her crinoline. When her more conscientious sister carried the bewildered dog off, the Princess 'maintained a perfectly straight face and a look of surprised interrogation. The whole company went into fits of laughter.'[17]

Because these pantomimes were staged for the public, with the proceeds going to the Queen's Wool Fund, an entrance fee had to be decided upon. Princess Elizabeth thought that the suggested ticket price of seven and sixpence (nominally, thirty-seven and a half pence today, but in practice a great deal more than that) would be too much. 'No one will pay that to look at us!' she protested. 'Nonsense,' countered her sister. 'They'll pay anything to see us. . . .'

Significantly, on the morning of these performances, Princess Margaret would be ill. 'Miss Crawford,' Allah would announce, 'Princess Margaret is absolutely pea-green.'[18] But Crawfie knew her pupil well enough to appreciate that she would always be up and ready for the performance. As she reached puberty, so the Princess – like so many sensitive people – began to suffer migraine headaches. For many years she had to cope with these sudden attacks, which start with a kind of flashing blurring of the vision and end in severe headaches and nausea. She was later to become Patron of the Migraine Trust.

The Windsor pantomimes gave Princess Margaret the idea of enlivening the bare walls of the castle's great picture galleries by inserting the pantomime posters into the ornate but now empty gilt frames which had, until the war, once held famous portraits of Britain's kings and queens. 'There was Dick Whittington with his cat gazing down from a frame marked Charles I,' noted the governess. 'Mother Goose appeared as Queen Henrietta Maria and so on all round the room.' Crawfie wondered whether the King would mind this *lèse-majesté*. She had no need to feel apprehensive, however; far from being annoyed at his daughter's inventiveness, George VI was highly amused. 'What do you think,' he once asked a guest, 'of my ancestors?'[19]

Indeed, there were times when the diffident King could hardly believe that this vivacious, talented and already socially accomplished girl was his daughter. There was nothing like one of her pert imitations to bring a smile to his often careworn face. His mother, Queen Mary, coming up from Badminton to Windsor for Princess Elizabeth's confirmation in March 1942, was similarly struck by her granddaughter's sparkle. 'Margaret very short, intelligent face, but not really pretty,' reported the old Queen to her sister-in-law, Princess Alice, Countess of Athlone, in Canada.[20] (Queen Mary's judgment must have been clouded by her determination to find no fault with the elder sister, for there was no denying that Princess Margaret, whatever her failings, was the prettier of the two.) She went on to describe Princess Margaret as *espiègle* – mischievous, roguish – but admitted that 'all the same she is so outrageously amusing that one can't help encouraging her'.[21]

'I was brought up among men,' Princess Margaret robustly maintains and certainly throughout the war, from the ages of ten to fifteen, the Princess spent a great deal of her time in male company.[22]

Windsor Castle in wartime was never the melancholy prison that Marion Crawford would have had her readers believe. For one thing, as the threat of invasion receded and the tide of war gradually turned, the princesses were able to get away. They would go up to London, or to Appleton House on the Sandringham Estate (the big house had been closed 'for the duration'), and even to Balmoral. On the other hand, Windsor Castle itself was full of people, not least young army officers. A company of Grenadier Guards was stationed in the castle and several young officers used to take their meals with the household. Altogether, reckons Crawfie, about seventy officers came and went during these war years at Windsor. They were charming, she says, 'and loved to meet the two girls and talk to them'. The princesses often gave tea parties at which they played hostess to groups of soldiers. With the 'male element' around, says Crawfie, 'Margaret began to develop into a real personality. She kept everyone in fits of laughter, and she had a gay little way with her that won everybody's heart. . . .'[23] 'If you sat at Princess Margaret's end of the table,' remembered one officer, 'the conversation never lapsed for a moment. She was amazingly self-assured, without being embarrassingly so.'[24] She had a way, young as she was, of putting gauche young servicemen at their ease. 'Slipping her small hand into a large one,' she would say, 'Come and look at the gardens', or 'Have you seen our horses?'[25]

This almost festive atmosphere was confirmed by Vicomtesse de Bellaigue, a highly cultured Belgian woman who had been brought in to augment Crawfie's somewhat limited educational abilities. (Princess Margaret would afterwards acknowledge Madame de Bellaigue as 'one of the greatest cultural influences in her life'.)[26] The princesses' lives, maintains Madame de Bellaigue, 'did not seem secluded to me'. There was 'plenty of mixed company – all great fun. There were games, all over the castle, involving many amusing incidents.'[27] There were frequent tea parties for visiting American and Commonwealth airmen, and every day the princesses would chat to the young officers of the so-called 'Windsor Body Guard'. There would be charades and parlour games and uproarious sing-songs, often with Princess Margaret at the piano.

One visiting entertainer, taking part in one of the many variety concerts to be staged at Windsor during the war (the King had a taste for salty, slapstick humour), remarked on Princess Margaret's 'insistence' on being considered more adult than she actually was. The fourteen-year-old girl was wearing 'grown-up shoes with pointed toes and Louis heels'.[28] It is clear that 'The King spoiled Princess Margaret dreadfully,' as one courtier's daughter noted. 'She was his pet . . . she was always allowed to stay up to dinner at the age of thirteen and to grow up too quickly. The courtiers didn't like her much – they found her amusing but. . . . She used to keep her parents and everyone waiting for dinner because she wanted to listen to the end of a programme on the radio.'[29]

Something of Princess Margaret's dawning imperiousness and nascent sexuality – the latter already hinted at by Marion Crawford – was discerned by a somewhat more perceptive observer during these war years. The feminist writer and journalist Rebecca West, commissioned by the *New York Times* to write an article to mark Princess Elizabeth's eighteenth birthday in the spring of 1944, was invited to interview her at Buckingham Palace. There she met both princesses, describing them in her diary as 'very short and not particularly well-dressed'. Princess Elizabeth she found 'sweetly dutiful, possibly with her father's obstinacy', but about Princess Margaret the writer sensed what she called 'a shrewd egotism'. 'When she grows up,' Rebecca West added, 'people will fall in love with her as if she were not royal. The other one is too good, too sexless. . . .'[30]

It was at about this time that two men destined to play, in their different ways, significant roles in Princess Margaret's life, appeared on the scene.

The first of these, Prince Philip of Greece, was distantly related to the princesses. His father was Prince Andrew of Greece and his mother, born Princess Alice of Battenberg, was one of the many granddaughters of Queen Victoria. Prince Philip's family had been tossed about on the tempestuous tides of Greek politics, and he had been educated mainly in Paris and at the two experimental schools of Salem in Bavaria and Gordonstoun in Scotland. From Gordonstoun he had entered the Royal Naval College at Dartmouth, and it had been there, just before the outbreak of war, that the eighteen-year-old cadet had first met the two British princesses. The young Princess Elizabeth had been immensely taken by the blond, handsome and extrovert Prince Philip. Encouraged by his dynastically ambitious uncle – his mother's brother, Lord Louis Mountbatten – this penniless Greek prince gradually began paying court to the future Queen of England.

Throughout the war, in which he served with distinction in the Royal Navy, Prince Philip kept in touch with Princess Elizabeth. He would occasionally be invited to stay at Windsor and was once in the audience at a Christmas pantomime. The fact that he was in the front row, looking just like a Viking, is said to have caused Princess Elizabeth to sparkle. Another picture – that of the young naval officer rolling in the aisle at the dreadful jokes and puns – is no doubt equally accurate.

'I like Philip,' wrote the King to Queen Mary in March 1944. 'He is intelligent, has a good sense of humour and thinks about things the right way.' The Prince was very much the sort of chaffing, honest, outdoors kind of man of whom the King approved. But both he and the Queen considered their daughter far too young for marriage, and warned the eager Lord Louis Mountbatten not to hurry things on too much. Princess Elizabeth did not share her parents' reservations. According to the King's official biographer (whose manuscript was read and approved by Queen Elizabeth II before publication), she had been in love with Prince Philip 'from their first meeting'.[31] In her private sitting room at Windsor, which she had been granted, along with her own lady-in-waiting, on turning eighteen, the Princess proudly displayed photographs of him. Queen Mary claimed that her eldest granddaughter was the kind of girl who, having fallen in love, would not change her mind. She would always remain 'very steadfast and determined' in her emotions.[32]

The second man now beginning to figure prominently in the princesses' lives was very different from the hearty Prince Philip. Early in 1944 King George VI, in an effort to associate himself more closely with the armed forces, decided to appoint young men with distinguished fighting records as temporary equerries. Since the Royal Air Force was the one service not yet represented at Court, the King approached Air Chief Marshal Sir Charles Portal, the Chief of the Air Staff, and asked him to choose a suitable candidate. Portal selected the much-decorated Battle of Britain pilot, Group Captain Peter Townsend.

Twenty-nine years old, married, and exceptionally handsome, Peter Townsend was, in royal terms, an outsider: a member of the middle classes (his father had been a colonial administrator in Burma) which had up till now played almost no part in Court life. Townsend, however, adjusted himself to his new environment so adroitly that in very little time he had become almost indistinguishable from those other polished figures surrounding the monarch. His appointment, intended to last for three months, was to last ten years.

Three years earlier, in 1941, Peter Townsend had married a brigadier's daughter, Rosemary Pawle. Theirs had been what he was to call a typically wartime wedding: the couple had hardly known one another. Townsend was something of a dreamer, imbued with a spirit of adventure; Rosemary was more conventional, more socially ambitious. 'We're made!' she exclaimed on being told of her husband's appointment as Temporary Equerry to the King. But they were not made; on the contrary, Townsend's appointment was to prove the unmaking of the marriage. In spite of the fact that the couple had two sons, and were given a grace-and-favour house, Adelaide Cottage, in Windsor Great Park, they gradually drifted apart. Instead of basking, as she had expected, in royal sunshine, Rosemary Townsend found herself living in dreary isolation while her husband's duties took him away for longer and longer periods. As Peter Townsend moved between Windsor, Buckingham Palace, Sandringham and Balmoral, his wife remained at Adelaide Cottage with their two little boys.

Although Townsend rightly dismissed a later claim that he became George VI's confidant and adviser, his relationship with the King was not unlike that between son and father. In many ways, the two men resembled one another. Both were slender, physically active men, shy, sensitive and most at ease in a small circle of people. The equerry could sympathize with the King's hesitancy of speech as he, too, knew 'the agonies of a stammerer'.[33] Like the King, Townsend was a religious man, with a fondness for biblical allusions and quotations, and for the rituals of the Church of England. He quickly learned how to cope with the King in his more fractious moments which, in this trying time of war, were not infrequent. Whenever the King was 'irked or rattled', says Townsend, his blue-eyed gaze would change into 'an alarming glare.... Then he would rant, noisily.'[34]

The Queen conquered Townsend as completely as she conquered anyone she met. Yet it did not take him long to appreciate that 'beneath her graciousness, her gaiety and her unfailing thoughtfulness for others, she possessed a steely will.' Only rarely, he wrote, did she show anger, 'and then it was in her eyes, which blazed, bluer than ever'.[35]

Townsend's first glimpse of the two princesses came immediately after his initial audience with the King. As Sir Piers Legh, the Master of the Household, was escorting him from the Regency Room in Buckingham Palace, two 'adorable-looking' girls, up from Windsor for a few days, came walking along the corridor. Townsend felt sure this meeting was no coincidence; the King, knowing that his daughters would be anxious to see a much-decorated war hero, had probably alerted them by internal telephone. The fighter pilot's record of his first impression of Princess Elizabeth and Princess Margaret is interesting. Both had inherited their parents' flawless complexions, small stature and blue eyes. The older girl, he found, was 'shy, occasionally to the point of gaucheness, and this tended to hide her charm'. Princess Margaret, at fourteen, was too young to make any strong impression on the newcomer. He described her as 'unremarkable' except for her dark blue eyes, 'like those of a tropical sea', and for her ability to come out with 'some shattering wisecrack'; then, 'to her unconcealed delight, all eyes were upon her'.[36]

Before many years had passed, Peter Townsend would decide that he found Princess Margaret to be a very remarkable person indeed.

'Events are moving very fast now,' wrote the King in his diary on 30 April 1945, the day on which Adolf Hitler committed suicide in the Führerbunker in Berlin.[37] Every day was bringing the end of the war closer. Hitler's 'revenge weapons' – the frightening V1 flying bombs or 'doodlebugs' and V2 rockets first launched the year before – had failed to hold up the steady progress towards victory. Although Princess Margaret and her fellow Girl Guides had once had to fling themselves to the ground as a V1 roared overhead, and although, by the end of the war, over three hundred high-explosive bombs had fallen in Windsor Great Park, the castle itself had escaped any serious damage. The Princess, on her journeys to or through London, was always surprised at how much of the capital had *not* been flattened. 'We heard so much about the bombing,' she says, 'that I expected everything to have been destroyed. There was really quite a lot still standing.'[38]

On the evening of Sunday, 6 May 1945 the royal family drove up from Windsor to London, expecting the formal announcement of the end of the war in Europe to be made the following day. For various reasons, the announcement was delayed until Tuesday, 8 May, which was officially declared 'VE Day'. Again and again that day, and on into the evening, the four royal figures – the King in naval uniform, the Queen in powder blue, Princess Elizabeth in the uniform of the ATS in which she had served briefly earlier that year, and Princess Margaret in a simple dress – appeared on the hastily draped central balcony of Buckingham Palace to greet the mass of cheering, singing, flag-waving people below.

For the last appearance on the balcony that night, the two princesses were not with their parents. Giving in to his daughters' entreaties, the King had allowed them to go out and mingle with the crowds. In the charge of their uncle, the Queen's youngest brother, David Bowes-Lyon ('It was really his idea; he organized it all,' says Princess Margaret [39]) and accompanied by a party of young officers, the two princesses slipped out of a side door and joined the surging, roaring, arm-linking revellers. After roaming the streets (it was presumably in order to save his daughters the sight of any unseemly sexual behaviour that the King forbade them to set foot in Piccadilly Circus), they forced their way into the great press of people outside the Palace gates. Here the two princesses stood yelling with the others, 'We want the King! We want the Queen!'

Half a century later, on the fiftieth anniversary of VE Day, mother and daughters were to re-enact the scene on the balcony to the hardly less enthusiastic crowds massed below.

CHAPTER 8

'Enfant Terrible'

Princess Margaret was now, wrote Marion Crawford of the autumn of 1945, 'at a girl's most awkward age, neither quite a child nor quite grown up'. The Princess had turned fifteen that August, but was 'mentally ahead of her age' and no longer prepared to devote herself to hours of schoolwork. The sisters appeared to be more of an age these days, Princess Elizabeth seeming younger than her years and Princess Margaret older.

The two princesses had always had different personalities, but now their interests began to diverge. At Balmoral for their first holiday after the war, Princess Elizabeth was introduced to the art of deerstalking by her father. She took to it with immense enthusiasm, even to the point of wearing a pair of the King's plus-fours as they tramped the hills. But Princess Margaret hated the sport. Nor did she share her mother's love of fishing. 'She did not care for sporting women and thought shooting unwomanly,' claims Crawfie,[1] while to her father's equerry, Peter Townsend, the Princess admitted that she 'detested stalking'. 'Oddly enough,' writes Townsend, 'I found this rather endearing. As time went on and I became something of an expert, she helped me not to take myself too seriously.'[2]

Princess Margaret's enthusiasms tended to be indoor ones. Although ready enough to join the family picnics in the heather or to gallop her horse across the hillsides ('Elizabeth, on a horse, was competent and classic,' wrote one member of the household, but 'Margaret was pretty and dashing'[3]), she was far happier in the drawing room. Like her mother, she adored parlour games and charades, and she was an avid canasta player, 'but with so little respect for the seriousness of the game that each coup was accompanied either by loud groans or gales of laughter'.⁴ The younger princess also read more than her sister, but most of all she enjoyed playing the piano and singing. One day, after the princesses had returned to live permanently in Buckingham Palace and were rummaging through the half-dismantled rooms piled with crates, Princess Margaret discovered an old piano. Dragging up a packing case, she sat down and began to play Chopin. As she touched the notes, great clouds of dust flew out. In the evenings, after dinner, she would entertain the company with her singing. Her musical tastes were catholic, her repertoire varied. She would belt out hits from American musicals, like 'Buttons and Bows' and 'I'm as corny as Kansas in August', or guy songs like 'I'm looking over a four-leafed clover', and she could imitate the raucous Ethel Merman to perfection. She could, too, be almost heartbreakingly moving as she sang, very softly, the old ballad, 'I gave my love a cherry, it had no stone'.

But not quite everyone was appreciative of her talents. Queen Mary's Lady-in-Waiting, Lady Airlie, invited to join the old Queen at Sandringham for the first post-war Christmas, had one or two sharp comments to make. Sandringham House, that riotously gabled, turreted, many-windowed mansion, looking like some vast station hotel set down among the flat marshlands of Norfolk, was King George VI's favourite home. It had been his father's favourite as well. Lady Airlie, who had known the house in King George V's day, found the atmosphere distinctly altered for the worse. The princesses were surrounded by young Guards officers; the radio 'blared incessantly'. 'During my visit to Sandringham I saw more of Princess Elizabeth than I had done for several years. In that family setting she seemed to me one of the most unselfish girls I had ever met, always the first to give way in any of the small issues that arise in every home.' No two sisters, continued Lady Airlie pointedly, 'could have been less alike than the princesses, the elder with her quiet simplicity, the younger with her puckish expression and irrepressible high spirits – often liberated in mimicry.' She considered Queen Mary's use of the word *espiègle* for her granddaughter to be exactly right, and felt that the King spoiled Princess Margaret, indulging her as an *enfant terrible*.⁵ Queen Mary judged Princess Margaret's character to be more complicated than her sister's, and could only hope that her outlook and attitude might improve.

By contrast, Princess Margaret's comments on her grandmother at this time are interesting. She was coming to appreciate the fact that, in spite of her forbidding appearance and manner, the old Queen was not quite the ogre of her childhood imaginings. 'Queen Mary was one of those women,' said the Princess in later life,

who prefer male company. Although my mother always said that she was a wonderful mother-in-law, Queen Mary didn't really like other women. She would put herself out tremendously for men, and could be utterly charming. After the war, when some of my men friends were obliged to sit next to Queen Mary at dinner, they would be terrified at the prospect. But they would come away enchanted. 'She was so interesting,' they would say, 'and she was so interested in what we had to say.'[6]

The King could find no fault with either of his daughters. One of his main worries, as far as they were concerned, was that 'they have never had any fun yet'.[7] Confinement at Windsor Castle and the austerities of post-war Britain hardly allowed them to indulge in the sort of fun enjoyed before the war by debutantes. Yet their lives were by no means dreary or uneventful. There were dances, and visits to the theatre – and in March 1946 Princess Margaret carried out her first solo public engagement, opening a new play-centre in North London for the Save the Children Fund. With the rationing of clothing by coupon still in force, there had to be a certain amount of making-do with dresses and hats, but, of course, money was not really a problem. A good deal of the royal family's much-vaunted wartime economizing had been an exercise in public relations, in example-setting by a family that was well able to afford anything it wanted. Besides, during the war, Mrs Ronald Greville – that relentless social climber in whose home, Polesden Lacey, the Duke and Duchess of York had spent part of their honeymoon – had died and bequeathed all her valuable jewellery to the Queen and £20,000 to Princess Margaret. (By today's standards, that sum would be equivalent to almost half a million pounds.)

King George VI was determined to enjoy the sort of family relationship which the war years had denied him. To him, his wife was simply 'the most marvellous person in the world', and his daughters hardly less marvellous. 'Our family, us four, the "Royal Family" must remain together,' he maintained;[8] and everything, wrote one member of the household, 'was subordinated to that warm, heartfelt sentiment'.[9] The four of them were very close; their talk among themselves was full of family catch phrases and private jokes. Their favourite standing joke took the form of a question which the princesses would ask their parents whenever they were in gala dress: 'Is this a special occasion?' The joke had its origins in a moment during the 1939 royal tour of Canada, when the King noticed that a local mayor was not wearing a chain of office. The King, thinking that he might present him with one, asked him whether or not he had a chain. 'Oh yes, sir,' answered the mayor, 'I have.' 'But I notice you're not wearing it,' said the King. 'Oh,' explained the mayor, 'but I only wear it on special occasions.'[10]

There was, confirmed Princess Alice, Countess of Athlone, 'something unique about the King's home life. Just a small, absolutely united circle of the King, the Queen and the princesses. They shared the same jokes and they shared each other's troubles.' For the gregarious Princess Alice, this self-containment smacked of insularity; 'they didn't seem to need anyone else,' she added, a touch reprovingly.[11]

The chief threat to King George VI's conception of cosy family solidarity was Prince Philip of Greece. By 1946 Princess Elizabeth was quite obviously in love with him and, just as obviously, determined to marry him. For a variety of reasons, not least because he could not bear the thought of parting from her, the King discouraged any talk of an engagement. But the Princess, normally so dutiful, stood firm. When Prince Philip proposed in the autumn of 1946, she accepted. But still the King insisted on keeping his daughter by his side for as long as possible.

A way out of the impasse presented itself in the form of the invitation from Field Marshal Jan Smuts, the Prime Minister of South Africa, for the royal family to tour his country during the early months of the following year, 1947. The King was adamant that all four members of what he called 'The Firm' should go, and that any announcement of Princess Elizabeth's engagement should be delayed until after the tour. In this he was supported by the Queen. The claim, sometimes made, that Princess Margaret championed her sister is apparently untrue – 'I knew nothing about the engagement,' she says.[12]

In the face of her father's determination, Princess Elizabeth gave way. The engagement remained secret, and on 1 February 1947 the royal family, with a suite of almost fifty, set sail for South Africa on board the battleship HMS *Vanguard*.

'I remember every minute of it,' claims Princess Margaret of this South African tour.[13] The vividness of her memories is understandable, for this three-month-long state visit was not only her first journey abroad, but also the first time that she was to be subjected to so continuous and relentless a public gaze. Except for a four-day break in the Drakensberg mountains, the family were on daily display for weeks on end. For a sixteen-year-old girl, much of whose youth had been spent out of the spotlight, it was a formidable baptism of fire.

Although the Princess would hardly have been aware of it, the object of the tour was chiefly political. Presented as a much-needed post-war holiday for the royal family and as a way of thanking South Africa for its contribution to the winning of the war, the state visit was the means whereby Smuts hoped to counter the growing threat of Afrikaner republicanism in South Africa. A one-time republican himself, Smuts was now an ardent, indeed sycophantic, monarchist. A South African election was due in 1948. Surely, in the face of this charming family, some of the opposition to the concept of monarchy would melt? Surely a successful royal tour would ensure that Smuts's party – the generally pro-British, anti-republican United Party – would be returned to power? About the infinitely more important question – that of black/white relations within South Africa – Smuts tended to be somewhat vague. The problem was not likely to be settled in his lifetime, he would muse.

HMS *Vanguard* docked in Table Bay on 17 February 1947, and for the following ten weeks the royal family was obliged to fulfil an extraordinary round of public engagements. At times, the pace was gruelling; day after day, often in murderous heat, the visitors were on show. Even the resilient Queen admitted that the tour was 'very strenuous'; the King lost over a stone in weight.[14]

The so-called White Train carried the family for thousands upon thousands of miles; to teeming cities, placid country towns and remote railway sidings. At these sun-baked wayside stations they would always alight to speak to the knot of people gathered there. 'These informal meetings were the most valuable of the tour,' the Queen said afterwards. 'One felt that one was really getting to meet ordinary people.'[15] And these ordinary people, expecting to be faced with a formal, unapproachably regal family, were delighted to find four such friendly, good-natured personalities, ready to talk about crops or cattle or the weather. Although the Queen was always unmistakable in her sumptuous hats and hydrangea colours, black children often had difficulty in identifying the other members of the family. A police officer was once heard explaining to a group of black children: 'That is Mr King and next to him Mrs King; then just behind, Princess Elizabeth King and Princess Margaret King.'[16] As to the 'problem' about which Smuts was so vague, Princess Margaret claims to have been especially struck, in those pre-apartheid days, by the neat and apparently unforced separation of the racial groups on these little railway stations.

Peter Townsend, who was the King's equerry on the tour, wrote that the younger princess's role was 'a relatively thankless one for, beside her sister, heir to the throne, she cut a less prominent figure'.[17] But, from the very outset, Princess Margaret made an impression. Beside her more stolid sister, who could look stiff and unsmiling, she was judged to be livelier, prettier, more sexually charged. With the sort of peaches-and-cream complexion seldom seen in hot climates and a vividly lipsticked mouth, she was already showing signs of a remarkable beauty. Unlike their mother, the princesses wore simple clothes; indeed, the chic of Cape Town's Mayoress, Miriam Bloomberg, caused Princess Margaret to complain that 'Next to Mrs Bloomberg, we look like housemaids.' Mrs Bloomberg's reply, on having the comment repeated to her, was wonderfully complacent. 'Nonsense,' she said serenely, 'they *also* had some lovely things.'[18]

Before long, stories of Princess Margaret's impishness and gaucheries were being widely circulated. She was seen to giggle at grossly fat, deeply curtsying officials' wives. Her eyes rolled heavenwards when an African chief, having lost his place in an interminable speech, started again from the beginning. 'Don't push!' she would snap, in full sight and sound of onlookers, if ever her sister accidently brushed against her. When Sir Ernest Oppenheimer, Chairman of the famous De Beers Mining Company, presented each of the princesses with a magnificent diamond, Princess Margaret asked innocently, 'And what about Mummy's?' Gallantly, Sir Ernest presented the Queen with a diamond from his own collection.[19] When the family attended a service in a Dutch Reformed church and the Princess rose to her feet at some point during the proceedings, she was tugged back into her seat by her more knowing Scots mother.

Southern Africa, claims the Princess, afforded her two of the most magnificent natural sights she has ever seen: the Drakensberg mountains, and Victoria Falls. It was during this tour, too, that she first flew in an aeroplane. One of her keenest pleasures were the early morning rides, invariably in the company of Peter Townsend, which the princesses were often able to enjoy: sometimes along the country's golden, deserted beaches, at others across the no less deserted veld. 'These were some of the most wonderful moments of the day,' she remembers.[20]

If, on this tour, Princess Margaret ever needed an example of royal dedication to duty, she had to look no further than her mother. Although the King was often fretful, short-tempered and ill-at-ease, the Queen's behaviour was impeccable. Her charm, stamina and sheer professionalism were extraordinary: she never put a foot wrong. One example, among many, must suffice. Late one night the White Train made an unscheduled stop. Because a little party of people had gathered in the pouring rain in the hopes of seeing the King, the local stationmaster had pulled down the signals and halted the train. Since the train was running late and the royal family had already retired to their compartments, the guard was all for giving the signal to restart immediately. Piet van der Byl, the South African cabinet minister in attendance on the royal family, was in a dilemma. Anywhere else, the disappointment of a handful of people gathered on the platform would not have mattered so much, but the train had just entered the Orange Free State, the most rampantly anti-monarchist province in the country. The non-appearance of the King could be very damaging.

And it seemed as though he was not going to appear. The distraught van der Byl, placating the disappointed local mayor on the one hand and the impatient train guard on the other, begged an equerry to coax the King to come out. Only after a nerve-racking delay did His Majesty appear. He was in a bad temper, and certainly in no mood to go down to greet a few people so late on a rainy night. 'Why wasn't I warned?' he asked angrily. As van der Byl was stammering out an answer, the Queen appeared in the doorway. 'I heaved a sigh of relief,' he said.

He had every reason to. Of course, said the Queen cajolingly to her husband, they must go down. Delaying just long enough to put her jewellery back on and to ensure that her daughters replaced theirs (the family were in evening dress), she led the party to the door. There she stood back to allow the King to alight first, and then down on to the muddy platform they all went. The Queen, appreciating the situation, 'walked more slowly, stopped more frequently and talked longer than usual. Sometimes the King would be ten yards ahead and had to wait . . .' writes van der Byl. 'Her Majesty, although very tired after a long day, did it wholeheartedly. I had never been so grateful to anyone in my life.'[21]

A frequently repeated claim that Princess Margaret and Peter Townsend fell in love with each other in the course of this South African tour is unsustainable. For the sixteen-year-old Princess the handsome Townsend would have been nothing more than a reassuring presence in a strange environment, while Townsend was so enamoured, not of the Princess, but of South Africa that he seriously considered settling there. He was going through a difficult period. A deeply sensitive, somewhat unresolved personality, Townsend was looking for what he called 'a feeling of permanence'. Seduced by the landscape of South Africa and by what he saw as the possibilities of leading a constructive life in this new country, he imagined that he might discover that elusive feeling of permanence there. His 'tortured thoughts', when relayed back to his wife Rosemary, were given short shrift; he was to put such hopelessly romantic ideas out of his head, she instructed firmly. She set his feet, he wrote, back 'on the straight, monotonous and narrow road, which leads on through a settled, conventional existence.'[22] Or so the two of them thought.

One of the highlights of the South African tour was the coming of age of Princess Elizabeth, who turned twenty-one in Cape Town on 21 April 1947. The occasion was marked by her famous wireless broadcast, in which she made what she called her 'solemn act of dedication' – a promise to devote her life to the service of the Commonwealth. The day ended with a spectacular display of fireworks and a ball at Government House, at which both princesses, in white tulle dresses sparkling with diamante and sequins, danced until the early hours. In the course of that day, Princess Elizabeth was presented with jewels whose combined value was well over £200,000.

Princess Margaret left South Africa with, among other gifts of diamonds, a bracelet made up of thirty-five of the stones.

The princesses made a positive, if inconsequential, contribution towards the political situation when, just before leaving South Africa, the King and Queen, on their own initiative, arranged a private meeting with the Leader of the (Nationalist) Opposition, Dr D.F. Malan and his wife. After a while, the two princesses were called into the room. 'As was only right,' said Malan afterwards of this royal charm offensive, 'nothing was discussed that had any political meaning. Our conversation was quite informal and friendly.'[23]

All in all, the political success of the tour was difficult to estimate. 'If, and I firmly believe it has,' wrote the King to Smuts on the voyage home,'our visit has altered the conception of monarchy to some South Africans . . . then our tour has been worth while.'[24] It was a vain hope. Just over a year later, South Africa went to the polls. Although Smuts's United Party won more votes, Malan's National Party won more seats. From that time on the National Party became ever more firmly entrenched until, in 1961, South Africa became a republic and ceased to be a member of the Commonwealth.

What effect had the tour had on Princess Margaret? She afterwards described the country as 'fascinating'; 'one could hardly have wished one's first journey abroad to have been to a more interesting country', she says.[25] It also gave her a taste for travel, for sunlit, exotic places. The Princess, wrote one member of the entourage afterwards, had matured during the journey. She had 'come on a lot. She was much more agreeable, less the Palace brat, and she was very good company. There must have been moments in the tour that seemed intolerable to both [princesses] but they behaved admirably.'[26]

On 10 July 1947, two months after the royal family had returned from South Africa, the engagement between Princess Elizabeth and Prince Philip was officially announced. By then the young man had changed his nationality, his name and his title. On becoming a naturalized British subject he had ceased to be Prince Philip of Greece, with the resounding surname of Schleswig-Holstein-Sonderburg-Glucksburg, and had adopted the anglicized version of his mother's name, Mountbatten. He became, quite simply, Lieutenant Philip Mountbatten. Not until his wedding morning was he created Duke of Edinburgh, and not until ten years later was he accorded the style and title of Prince of the United Kingdom by his wife.

The openly acknowledged romance did 'something wonderful for the Palace', says Marion Crawford mawkishly. She describes Princess Elizabeth as radiant, and Princess Margaret as 'sweet, happy in her sister's happiness as if it had been her own'.[27] At the time, Princess Margaret's opinion of the self-confident young man who was about to become her brother-in-law was not known; not until some years later was the prickliness of their relationship to become general knowledge. The young man's opinion of her was more apparent. 'He stood no nonsense,' says Crawfie. 'She was then at adolescence's most tiresome age, apt at times to be comically regal and over-gracious, and Philip wasn't having any.'[28] One day when a friend said jokingly to Prince Philip, 'You've chosen the wrong girl. Margaret is much better-looking!' his quick temper flared. 'You wouldn't say that if you knew them,' he protested. 'Elizabeth is sweet and kind, just like her mother. . . .' The implication was clear: that Princess Margaret was not sweet and kind.[29]

Although Peter Townsend maintained that he found Prince Philip a 'genial, intelligent and hard-hitting extrovert', other members of the royal entourage sensed a degree of hostility between the two men. Prince Philip, born royal, seems to have resented the other man's easy intimacy with the royal family. And Townsend, a shade defensively, says of Prince Philip that 'I never got to know him well.'[30]

With Princess Elizabeth busy making arrangements for her wedding, which was to take place that November, Princess Margaret undertook an important solo engagement. Accompanied by her recently appointed Lady-in-Waiting, Jennifer Bevan, and a detective, and with Peter Townsend acting as equerry, she flew to Belfast to launch the Union-Castle liner, *Edinburgh Castle*. At the Harland and Wolff shipyard she delighted the crowd by pulling a rose out of the bouquet just presented to her by the youngest shipbuilder and daringly inserting it in the blushing young man's buttonhole. It was the sort of spontaneous gesture which her more reserved sister would never have made. On spotting her recent hosts, the Mayor and Mayoress of Cape Town, among the dignitaries (the *Edinburgh Castle* was destined for the South African run) she assured them that instead of the customary champagne, she had smashed a bottle of South African wine against the ship's hull.

Princess Elizabeth's wedding, on 20 November 1947, was designed to be the first great royal occasion to recapture something of the splendour of pre-war years. The King, who, for all his modesty as a man, knew his responsibilities as a monarch, had ordered that the Sovereign's Escort of the Household Cavalry appear in full and glittering ceremonial uniform for the occasion. As members of foreign royal families poured into London (notable by their absence were the Duke and Duchess of Windsor and the bridegroom's sisters married to Germans), Princess Margaret was able, for the first time, to appreciate something of the scale of the great international and interrelated family of sovereigns to which she belonged. The gathering would also have underlined the fact that she was second in line to the throne of the world's foremost and most firmly established dynasty: beside the House of Windsor, these Continental houses, for all their past grandeur, seemed paltry.

Among the almost three thousand wedding presents on display in St James's Palace, Princess Margaret's struck an eminently practical note: a set of twelve engraved champagne glasses and a fitted picnic basket. Queen Mary, eagerly inspecting the presents, was incensed to see that Mahatma Gandhi had sent a loincloth, made from cloth he had woven himself (of what possible use this was to be to the nuptial pair cannot be imagined). 'What a horrible thing,' exclaimed Queen Mary. 'I don't think it's horrible,' countered the always outspoken Prince Philip. 'Gandhi is a wonderful man; a very great man.' Lips pursed, Queen Mary passed on. But the next day, when the royal family was making yet another inspection, Princess Margaret darted ahead of her slowly progressing grandmother and deftly hid the offending garment.[31]

'I hope people were not too taken up with the bride that day to notice her younger sister,' wrote Crawfie of Princess Elizabeth's spectacular wedding in Westminster Abbey. 'The full-skirted net frock Margaret wore made her look taller. She moved with extraordinary dignity and grace, her head held high. More than once the King and Queen exchanged a smile and a reassuring glance.'[32] Walking alone, directly behind the bride and three paces ahead of the other seven bridesmaids to emphasize her rank, Princess Margaret had to do some quick thinking when one of the two pages – Prince

William of Gloucester and Prince Michael of Kent – tripped over some broadcasting equipment. She caught him deftly and unobtrusively.

At the wedding luncheon at Buckingham Palace after the ceremony Princess Margaret was at her sparkling best – 'How pretty Margaret looked!' remembered one family guest.[33] It was she who marshalled the wedding party for the photographs, and who led the guests as they raced across the sanded quadrangle behind the landau that was carrying the newly married couple away to begin their honeymoon. The Queen, hitching up her long gold lamé skirts, was not far behind; together they pelted the departing carriage with paper rose petals. 'For a long time,' writes Crawfie, 'we could hear the cheers rising and falling, as the carriage passed through the crowds that lined the route all the way to Victoria Station.'

That evening, before changing for the night's party for the bridesmaids and ushers, Princess Margaret came to her governess's room. 'I can't imagine life here without her,' she sighed.

'Never mind,' answered Crawfie; 'you will be next.'[34]

CHAPTER 9

The Glamour Princess

FOR A DOZEN OR SO YEARS – from the marriage of her sister in November 1947 until her own marriage in May 1960 – Princess Margaret was regarded as one of the most glamorous figures on the world stage. There were very few women, and certainly no princesses, to challenge her public pre-eminence. Her elder sister, both as Princess Elizabeth and then as Queen Elizabeth II, was never able to fire the imagination to the same extent. She was considered too staid, too lacking in charisma to excite the enthusiasm of the press and the public. There was a dearth of young princesses during the 1950s; even Grace Kelly, who married Prince Rainier of Monaco in 1956, was regarded as only quasi-royal – a film star who had married a minor princeling. Other female celebrities of the period, such as Eva Peron, Marilyn Monroe and Elizabeth Taylor, were more like shooting stars, never serious rivals for the secure and established position held by the daughter of the King of England. Throughout the 1950s, Princess Margaret was one of the most illustrious, most talked about and most eligible women in the world. Her photographs appeared in newspapers and magazines almost daily; her picture had only to be featured on a magazine cover for circulation to rise. 'She is Britain's No. One item for public scrutiny,' trumpeted one American headline. 'People are more interested in her than in the House of Commons or the dollar crisis.'[1]

In 1948, Princess Margaret turned eighteen. She was very small, just over 5 feet tall but, as one admirer put it, 'perfectly made', with a 23-inch waist and a 34-inch bust.[2] Her hair was dark brown, her eyes deep blue, her complexion exquisite, her mouth sensuous and her smile dazzling. These striking looks were brought to life by her vivacity. Without being anything less than dignified on public occasions, she had that certain actressy air. In short, Princess Margaret had star quality.

The Princess's emergence into public life coincided, very happily, with a dramatic change in women's fashions, and in the years immediately ahead she was to earn a reputation as one of the most stylishly dressed women of her generation. Both her parents were very interested in clothes. 'My father,' says the Princess today, 'was very elegant. He had such a good figure for clothes and wore them beautifully.'[3] Although the King's taste was conventional, it was excellent. He insisted on beautifully cut garments and would happily spend hours with his tailors, Benson and Clegg, choosing cloth, discussing styles and trying on suits. The Queen, although by now distinctly plump, dressed with great panache. Her presentation of herself as a pretty-as-a-picture queen was deliberate. The lavish hats, fur trimmings, floating styles and, by night, glittering crinolines, were all designed to make her look both regal and romantic.

Inheriting this interest in clothes, Princess Margaret eagerly embraced the so-called 'New Look', launched by Christian Dior late in 1947. Dior had presented his collection at a show at the Savoy Hotel in London that autumn, and on the next day, at a secret showing at the French Embassy, the clothes were displayed privately to the Queen, Princess Margaret and the Duchess of Kent. Secrecy was necessary because it was thought that the conditions prevailing in post-war 'austerity' Britain could have turned this presentation of a French designer's extravagant collection into a 'politico-patriotic issue'.

Princess Margaret was completely won over. Blithely disregarding government disapproval (the formidable Labour MP, Bessie Braddock, had pronounced against such profligate fashions), the Princess lowered her hemlines. At the 1948 Easter race meeting at Kempton Park it was noticed that a fourth velvet band had been added to the three bands decorating a coat she had worn previously; and by 26 April, at the celebration of the King and Queen's Silver Wedding in St Paul's Cathedral, she had fully adopted the tightly waisted, bouffant-skirted, ankle-length New Look, with which she wore – and would always thereafter wear – very high heels and platform soles. Her example was immediately followed, it is claimed, by 'ten million British women'.[4]

An even wider stage was provided for the Princess's fashionable and newly sophisticated persona when she travelled to Amsterdam in September 1948 to represent King George VI at the Installation of Princess Juliana as Queen of the Netherlands, on the abdication of Queen Wilhelmina. Also in Amsterdam for the occasion was Princess Alice, Countess of Athlone, who was Queen Juliana's second cousin. She professed herself 'astonished' at the stir created by Princess Margaret. 'She really was the centre of attention,' she claims. 'The crowds went wild about her, shouting "Margriet! Margriet!" whenever she appeared.'[5] Arriving at the Installation in the magnificent Nieuwe Kerk, Princess Margaret, in a floor-length pink dress and small pink ostrich-feather hat, trailed a fox-fur cape (borrowed from her sister) along the floor behind her with all the aplomb of a fashion model.

By the Princess's side throughout four days of sightseeing and ceremonial – a canal trip, a tulip bulb auction, a tour of the Rijksmuseum, luncheons and banquets – was her father's equerry, Peter Townsend. At a ball held at the International Culture Centre, wearing a diamond tiara (borrowed, this time, from Queen Mary) she danced almost every dance with Townsend, and did not leave until after three in the morning. 'Without realizing it,' Townsend afterwards wrote, 'I was being carried a little further from home, a little nearer the Princess.'[6]

Back in Britain, Princess Margaret continued to carry out the less newsworthy duties that are the lot of every member of a royal family. By now she had her own suite at Buckingham Palace – her bedroom was painted salmon pink, and the old nursery had been converted into a sitting room – and the day would begin with the mail. Her Lady-in-Waiting, Jennifer Bevan, would screen the daily requests to endorse charities or make official appearances, and those invitations most likely to be accepted would be discussed with the Queen's Private Secretary, Major Tom Harvey. There were not, in these immediate post-war years, many family members available to undertake royal duties. The King was often unwell; Princess Elizabeth was twice incapacitated by pregnancies; while the King's younger brother and his wife, the Duke and Duchess of Gloucester, and his sister Mary, the Princess Royal, frankly lacked the sort of crowd-pleasing qualities needed on these occasions. This left only the Queen, Princess Margaret, the Duke of Edinburgh, and the widowed Duchess of Kent (the Duke had been killed in a flying accident during the war) to shoulder the responsibility. So Princess Margaret, by far the most glamorous member of the family, gamely presented freedoms of cities, launched ships, attended gala performances, inspected guards of honour, visited charitable institutions, toured hospitals and factories and newspaper offices.

How much, one wonders, did the Princess appreciate the atmosphere of unreality surrounding much of what she saw, or was shown? Was she taken in by all those deferentially bowing mayors, all those vociferously cheering schoolchildren, all that uproarious laughter at even the weakest royal joke? One national serviceman remembers that, in the frenzied whitewashing which took place in the camp at which he was stationed before one of the Princess's visits, even a heap of coal was painted white lest it offend the royal gaze. Another, as the member of the naval guard of honour at Gosport, claims that tailors were still busily pinning and tucking the newly unpacked uniforms just seconds before the Princess's arrival. The singer Peggy Lee, performing at the Pigalle, tells of the freshly ironed sheets that had to be laid over the kitchen floor of the club because Princess Margaret would be arriving by a back entrance.

Her views were treated seriously by even the most unlikely people. Once, at a Buckingham Palace reception, she spent twenty minutes arguing with the notoriously hard-line Russian communist, Andrei Vyshinski. He emerged from the conversation to announce that he had been deeply impressed by the then seventeen-year-old Princess's political acumen. 'If she had not been a princess, she would assuredly have made a most formidable advocate,' he said (a lawyer by training, Vyshinski had been a notoriously vindictive public prosecutor).[7] One can only assume that Vyshinski was as susceptible as the next man to a title and a pretty face.

The unreality of her existence also extended to those she met socially. 'I felt so sorry for her,' said one guest at a party for the Princess. 'She hasn't the faintest idea of what anyone is like. When she came into the room we all changed.' His listener, Lady Donaldson, knew exactly what he meant. 'Some years after this I had to destroy a photograph of myself talking to Her Royal Highness at some function and grimacing horribly in an over-extended effort to please,' she writes.[8] Such efforts to please could go very far indeed. Late one night, just as a newly fashionable Chelsea restaurant was about to close, a telephone booking was made for a party which included Princess Margaret. The manager, aghast at the dreariness of his by now completely empty restaurant, frantically summoned whatever friends lived nearby and ordered his more presentable-looking waiters to change into their street clothes. By the time the royal party arrived, the place was filled with apparently animated diners. 'And there we sat,' remembers one long-suffering waiter, 'nursing cup after cup of coffee, until almost three in the morning, when the Princess and her bloody chums finally decided to get up and go.'[9]

For the truth was that, by now, along with her reputation for beauty and vivacity, Princess Margaret was making a somewhat less admirable name for herself. She was emerging as the royal family's most ardent partygoer. Not – significantly – since the days when her Uncle David, as Prince of Wales, was the leading royal playboy, had a member of the family spent so much time in restaurants, night-clubs and at private parties.

The arrival of the new American Ambassador to the Court of St James's, Lewis W. Douglas, in the late 1940s, greatly enhanced the Princess's social life, for his daughter, Sharman, known as 'Sass' in her circle, became one of her closest friends. Two years older than Princess Margaret, with the wholesome blonde good looks and uninhibited charm of an American 'homecoming queen', Vassar-educated Sharman Douglas soon became the centre of a lively group of young people. The Princess was quickly drawn into this set, and although she later protested that the group was really made up of Sass's friends, it quickly became known as 'the Margaret Set'. To Sass Douglas, her royal friend was 'Magget'; only later would the Princess insist on being addressed as 'Ma'am'. The American girl is said to have spent 'hysterical' evenings at the palace, 'racing up and down the halls . . . creating chaos', and 'the better part of the next day in the Princess's bedroom, gossiping'.[10]

Princess Margaret's other women friends at this time – among them Lady Caroline Montagu-Douglas-Scott, Lady Rosemary Spencer-Churchill and Judy Montagu – tended to come from more conventional backgrounds than Sass Douglas. The American

Embassy was merely one of the settings for the many private parties and dances attended by this animated group. They knew all the popular songs, their conversation was full of the current catch phrases, they were *au fait* with the latest society gossip. 'She wanted to know everything, hear everything, see everything,' wrote one of her escorts.[11]

The men in the set were also members of the country's illustrious families: Princess Margaret's taste for unorthodox men in the arts had not yet been awakened. Chief among them were the Earl of Dalkeith and the Marquess of Blandford. Johnny Dalkeith, seven years older than the Princess, was heir to two Scottish dukedoms and three huge estates. Sunny Blandford, as the heir of the Duke of Marlborough, stood to inherit his father's title, and with it Blenheim Palace and its immense acreage. Others in the set were Lord Porchester, heir to the Earl of Carnarvon; the Hon. Peter Ward, younger son of the multi-millionaire Earl of Dudley; Lord Ogilvy, heir to the Earl of Airlie; the Hon. Dominic Elliot, the younger son of the Earl of Minto; and the immensely wealthy Billy Wallace. Of all these men, the Earl of Dalkeith was thought to be the most likely husband for Princess Margaret. As the future Duke of Buccleuch and Queensberry, and the heir to three stately homes and some quarter of a million acres of Scotland and England, Johnny Dalkeith seemed the obvious choice. But he was not the Princess's choice; nor she his. His interests were rural – hunting, shooting and fishing; hers were metropolitan. In any case, he was probably a little too staid for the effervescent Princess.

In no time, the names of all these escorts were being bandied about in the press. The Princess would be spotted in nightclubs and restaurants, at the theatre and at private parties. The 400 Club was one favourite haunt, the Milroy Club another; and she was often to be seen at that most famous nightspot of the period, the Café de Paris. Noël Coward, seeing her while he was performing there, wrote in his diary of 'the glittering audience headed by Princess Margaret . . . all very glamorous'.[12] At the age of nineteen, the Princess was first seen smoking in public. After dinner in a West End restaurant she lit a cigarette, which she smoked through a long ivory cigarette holder. In an age when women – or upper-class women, anyway – were supposed only to smoke in private, the incident both caused a stir and started a trend.

Almost daily the press carried stories about her partygoing. When she joined a group of friends in performing a spirited can-can at an American Embassy party, the next day's headlines read 'Princess Margaret High-Kicks It!' 'Look into my eyes,' she once instructed a dancing partner. 'Do you realize that you are looking into the most beautiful eyes in the world?' She then laughingly assured the abashed young man that she was quoting a recent press article about herself.[13] The American magazine *Newsweek* claimed that when, at about this time, she was asked to entertain a stiff-backed Presbyterian minister at the piano, she obliged with a raucous rendition of 'I'm jist a girl who cain't say no' from *Oklahoma!*[14] Perhaps more typical of the sort of incident reported in the press in the first years after the war was the story of a 'secret dinner' held in a London flat to celebrate the Princess's 'engagement' to Peter Ward. Having dismissed her driver and detective, the Princess had been driven back to Buckingham Palace by Peter Ward in his red sports car – or so the story ran. When it was discovered that the party had in fact been held to celebrate the return of Billy Wallace from a visit to the United States, the press decided that it was to him that the Princess had become engaged, and that it was he who had driven her home in his own, identical, red sports car. A curt statement from the Palace declared that the Princess had returned in the royal car.

Even innocent friendships and enthusiasms would attract attention, bringing with it the inevitable misinterpretation. One of the strongest of Princess Margaret's early theatrical obsessions was with the American comedian Danny Kaye. Having seen his act at the London Palladium, her admiration for his talents was almost unbounded. She sang his songs, imitated his dance steps and mimicked his patter. To her, 'his zanyish antics were like something from another world',[15] and she even insisted that the King and Queen go and watch him, but from the stalls, not the remote royal box. The Princess and the entertainer became friends. She would greet him with a kiss on the cheek and they were often seen dancing together. She – who would answer anyone who dared to refer to 'your father' with a withering 'Do you mean His Majesty the King?' – was delighted to be addressed as 'Honey' by the ebullient Kaye. When the Lord Chamberlain's office insisted on censoring the line 'Even Princess Margaret goes out with Danny Kaye' from the

London production of *Call Me Madam*, the public was only too ready to believe that there was rather more than just friendship between the Princess and the star.

Her late hours also frequently caused press comment. A typical headline, this time in the *Sunday Pictorial*, read 'Princess Margaret's Week of Late Nights'. Often she would not get back to Buckingham Palace until four in the morning, which hardly endeared her to the liveried footmen who were obliged to wait up for her. The photographer Cecil Beaton, commissioned to take her nineteenth birthday portrait, noted that she had been up until half-past five that morning and that towards the end of the session she began to wilt. No, she protested, 'she couldn't raise an elbow – it was an impossibility'.[16] Marion Crawford, finding her one-time charge becoming increasingly irresponsible, went to the Queen. 'I can do nothing with her,' complained Crawfie; 'she is tired out, and absolutely exhausted with all these late nights.' The Queen, as always, remained serene. 'We are only young once, Crawfie,' she answered. 'We want her to have a good time. With Lilibet gone, it is lonely for her here.'[17] Only when her wayward daughter appeared in public in an extremely *décolleté* evening dress did the Queen baulk, insisting that straps be added.

The marriage of Princess Elizabeth, and her move to the newly refurbished Clarence House, brought the Queen and her younger daughter even closer together. Both women had an unquenchable *joie de vivre*; both were interested in clothes, parties and witty conversation. Noël Coward described a 'gay, uninhibited evening' during the course of which both women had to leave to attend a staff ball at Buckingham Palace, after which they returned to listen to Coward singing 'till all hours'. He sang for them on another occasion at the American Embassy; the Queen 'really most obviously loved' his songs. 'Princess Margaret obliged with songs at the piano,' he goes on to say. 'Surprisingly good. She has an impeccable ear, her piano playing is simple but has perfect rhythm, and her method of singing is really very funny. The Queen was sweet on account of being so genuinely proud of her chick.'[18]

A less generous assessment of the Princess's gifts (the royal family could do no wrong in Coward's eyes) came from James Pope-Hennessy, the future biographer of Queen Mary. She was, he told a friend in 1949, 'high-spirited to the point of indiscretion. She mimics lord mayors welcoming her on platforms, and crooners on the wireless, in fact anyone you care to mention. She inadvertently attracts all the young eligibles to her feet, which doesn't endear her to the girls.'[19]

The publication of Marion Crawford's book *The Little Princesses* in 1950 – by which time Crawfie had married and left royal service – reinforced the public's perception of Princess Margaret as little more than a fun-loving maverick. Although the governess's picture of the Princess in childhood as spoilt, petulant and mischievous was bad enough, her contemporary description of her was worse. From out of the sentimental gush of Crawfie's prose there emerges an exacting, ill-organized and inconsiderate young woman. Princess Margaret, complained Crawfie, turned everything into a joke. When the governess berated her for lying late in bed when other young women had to get up and make their own breakfasts before going to work, the Princess answered that she could not possibly make her own breakfast as she had nothing to cook on. The fact that *The Little Princesses* became an international bestseller and was serialized in two women's magazines cannot have afforded the Princess much comfort.

But the book does not always show Princess Margaret in a negative light. One of her jokes, repeated by Crawfie, has become a classic quip. When, on 14 November 1948, Princess Elizabeth gave birth to a son, who was to be christened Charles Philip Arthur George, Princess Margaret imagined that from now on she would be known as 'Charley's Aunt'.

In the spring of 1949 Princess Margaret made official visits to Italy and France, and there had her first experience of the Continental paparazzi. Whereas in Britain and in the other countries she had visited – South Africa and the Netherlands – cameramen still behaved with restraint, the Italian and French press photographers showed no such consideration. Ostensibly, the journey to Italy was to allow her to visit British war graves, but the frantic photographers turned her stay into a nightmare of shouting, shoving and intrusion. A chambermaid, bribed by a journalist to reveal the secrets of the Princess's hotel room, came up with nothing more startling than that she used 'Tweed' perfume, 'Peggy Sage' nail varnish, and was reading *Busman's Honeymoon* by Dorothy L. Sayers. On Capri, a telephoto lens caught her swimming in a bathing suit so pale that it was rumoured that she had been bathing nude, and the photograph appeared in a number of Continental newspapers and magazines.

The crowds were equally inquisitive. Wherever she went – the exhaustive itinerary included Naples, Capri, Sorrento, Amalfi, Pompeii, Salerno, Rome, Florence, Siena, Bologna, Venice and Stresa – 'la bella Margherita' was mobbed; the sweating carabinieri were obliged to force a passage for her through the swarms of onlookers. She had to cope with more than crowds and photographers, however, for her visit to Pope Pius XII caused some controversy. Was it right for a Protestant princess to be granted an audience by the Pontiff? In fact, the audience was a great success. Dressed in black and with a black lace mantilla over her head ('I was so nervous I couldn't stop shaking', she remembers[20]), the Princess was given a small crucifix by the Pope. The crucifix stands on her desk in Kensington Palace to this day.

This Italian journey was to have an interesting sequel a few years later, in the shape of the film *Roman Holiday*. Released at the time of Princess Margaret's affair with Peter Townsend, it tells the story of a brief relationship between a princess touring Italy and a reporter. The leading roles were played by Audrey Hepburn, who looked extraordinarily like Princess Margaret, and Gregory Peck, who not only looked like Peter Townsend, but was said to be Princess Margaret's favourite film star at the time. At the end of the film, the Princess returns, reluctantly, to the royal treadmill. The parallel was 'milked for all it was worth', said Audrey Hepburn.[21]

From Italy, Princess Margaret went to Lausanne, in Switzerland, to visit the widowed ex-Queen Victoria-Eugénie (Ena) of Spain. Queen Ena, another of Queen Victoria's many granddaughters, was, in spite of her stately appearance and grand manner, a vivacious and warm-hearted woman. 'She was a great giggler,' says Princess Alice, Countess of Athlone.[22] 'Margaret darling, how are you?' Queen Ena would exclaim on meeting the Princess. 'Wonderfully well, Your Majesty,' the Princess would answer, 'wonderfully well.'[23] Queen Ena was greatly impressed by her attractive young visitor. 'She has blossomed out deliciously,' she exclaimed. 'What a success she will be in Paris!'[24]

And so she was, if the frenzy of the Parisian photographers was anything to go by. The fact that her apparently nude photograph had been reproduced in *France-Dimanche* merely heightened press interest. As the royal guest was hustled from one famous sight to the next, so was she jostled by a mob of cameramen. On hearing the band play 'Mean to Me' when she paid a midnight visit to a *boîte*, she said wryly, 'That tune is dedicated to some photographers.'[25] But the French were enchanted by this little figure, and by her almost Parisian elegance. 'Our visitor is all that we have dreamed in our childhood of a fairy princess,' enthused *Le Figaro*. 'All France is now nostalgic for a princess.'[26] Among the highlights of her stay in the French capital were her attendances at the fashion shows of Jean Dessès and Christian Dior. 'When I met Mr Dior in Paris,' said the Princess many years later, 'I thanked him so much for creating the New Look.'[27] 'Without consulting anyone,' claims one member of the household, 'she ordered a billowing ball-gown of white tulle with a strapless top.'[28] Significantly, another Parisian purchase, apparently, was a silk headscarf, decorated, for all to see, with the bold message, 'Toujours l'amour'.

Not long after the Princess's return from the Continent, that society gossip, Chips Channon, attended a ball at Windsor Castle. Here he found himself musing on the possible future of this small, soignée figure in her new Dior ball dress. 'Already she is a public character,' he wrote, 'and I wonder what will happen to her? There is already a Marie Antoinette aroma about her. . . .'[29]

It is not clear whether he meant that she was frivolous; or ill-fated; or both.

Throughout these apparently carefree years, Princess Margaret had had to contend with her father's declining health. Ever since returning from South Africa in 1947, King George VI had been unwell. He suffered painful cramps in his legs and one day, in the summer of 1948, as he was climbing Arthur's Seat, the hill that overlooks the Palace of Holyroodhouse in Edinburgh, he turned to Peter Townsend and exclaimed, 'What's the matter with my blasted legs? They won't work properly!'[30] That October he consulted his doctor, Sir Morton Smart and, after further consultations, he was diagnosed as suffering from arteriosclerosis. There was a fear that his right leg might have to be amputated. The news – as always with royal illnesses – was kept from the public and, after a period of rest in bed, the threat of amputation disappeared.

But because the King was still unwell, a planned state visit to Australia and New Zealand he was to have made with the Queen and Princess Margaret the following February had to be cancelled. Instead, on the morning of 2 March 1949, after he had suffered a thrombosis, George VI underwent an operation. It was performed at Buckingham Palace, since he had refused to go to a hospital; he had never heard of a king going to hospital, he declared. A right lumbar sympathectomy – the removal of a clot in his right loin – was successfully performed.

The King's recovery was slow, and during the following two years many of his duties were taken over by the Queen and Princess Margaret. (Princess Elizabeth spent several months in Malta, where her naval officer husband was stationed, and on 15 August 1950 she gave birth to their second child, who was christened Anne Elizabeth Alice Louise.) The King managed to open the Festival of Britain in May 1951, but by that summer he was again looking very ill. By then the doctors had discovered a 'shadow' on his left lung which they told him was pneumonitis. To avoid spreading alarm, he took to wearing heavy 'pancake' make-up for his public appearances. This merely added to the aura of unreality already surrounding the royal family. 'I remember seeing the three of them [the King, the Queen and Princess Margaret] at some ceremony in Westminster Abbey that year,' says one observer.

They had the sort of perfection that wax models have. The King was in naval uniform and his face was painted a deep bronze colour. Even his cheeks were rouged. The Queen was magnificent in velvet and furs and feathers and Princess Margaret looked ravishing. But all three looked more like actors on a stage than real people. They seemed almost artificial, as though they were in technicolor.[31]

On 21 August 1951, Princess Margaret celebrated her twenty-first birthday. In the Civil List Act of 1937, the payment of an annuity to Princess Margaret on attaining her majority had not, for some reason, been authorized in the correct statutory form. A bill was introduced to rectify this and an annual allowance of £6,000 (about £120,000 today) was agreed upon; Princess Elizabeth's allowance was £40,000, and the Duke of Edinburgh's £10,000. Princess Margaret's financial affairs would from now on be administered by Sir Arthur Penn, the Queen's Treasurer, and her official life managed by the Queen's new Private Secretary, Captain Oliver Dawnay. The Princess would still need the permission of her father – the Sovereign – to marry.

Her coming of age was celebrated at Balmoral, to which a group of her friends, including Johnny Dalkeith and Billy Wallace, were invited to join the celebrations. Both men, noted Peter Townsend drily, were tipped as possible husbands for the Princess. At dinner on the night of her birthday she wore a new Dior dress of white organza; 'a dream of a dress,' she exclaimed.[32] After dinner, her friends and the equerries formed a long line leading from the main door of the castle to the top of a nearby hill. In dramatic succession, the torches they were each carrying were lit, until the last member in this glittering chain set his torch to the specially prepared bonfire. The flames roared up into the night sky, exactly as, twenty-one years before, a bonfire at Glamis Castle had heralded the Princess's birth.

Whatever his joy in the celebrations of his younger daughter's majority, all was not well with the King. One evening, wrote Townsend, the King sent for him. In the monarch's eyes was that 'glaring, distressed look' which always indicated that he was feeling overwhelmed by his troubles. The room was reverberating with the sound of dance music from the drawing room below. 'Won't those bloody people ever go to bed?' shouted the King.[33] In truth, George VI was feverish throughout his stay at Balmoral, and on returning to London was examined again by his doctors, who this time discovered a malignant tumour. The whole left lung would have to be removed. On the morning of Sunday, 23 September 1951, the King was operated on, and although the surgery had to be more extensive than originally planned, the operation seemed to have been successful. Plans were made for him, accompanied by the Queen and Princess Margaret, to pay a convalescent visit to South Africa early the following year.

In mid-January 1952, Peter Townsend flew out to South Africa to inspect Botha House, the residence in the subtropical province of Natal which the South African government had offered the royal family as a holiday home. The *jeunesse dorée* – such as it was – of nearby Durban prepared itself for Princess Margaret's arrival. At Johannesburg airport Townsend was asked if he could confirm the report that Princess Margaret was going to marry Lord Dalkeith. 'I told him I could not,' wrote the equerry.[34]

It would be a mistake to dismiss Princess Margaret as having been, during these years, nothing more than a frivolous royal rebel. Hers was a complex character. For one thing, she had strong religious convictions. Like all her family, she attended church regularly, and never travelled without the small Bible, bound in white leather and blocked in gold, which had been presented to her on her confirmation at the age of sixteen. Her religious beliefs went beyond mere convention; she was interested in theology, and kept in close touch with one member of her set, Simon Phipps, formerly a major in the Coldstream Guards, who had since leaving the army been ordained, becoming a chaplain at Trinity College, Cambridge, before going on to minister to working-class congregations in Coventry and Huddersfield. During the frequent emotional crises in her life, Princess Margaret would always turn to the Church for solace. While researching his life of Queen Mary, James Pope-Hennessy once asked Dr Geoffrey Fisher, Archbishop of Canterbury from 1944 to 1961, about the old Queen's religious beliefs. Neither Queen Mary nor the Queen Mother were very concerned with religious doctrine, said His Grace. 'But take Princess Margaret, now,' he added, 'she understands doctrine – knows what it's all about. In fact, Princess Margaret is a thoroughly good churchwoman.'[35]

The Princess's glittery style of life tended to eclipse her more mundane activities, that dogged round of often unspectacular royal duties. Her much publicized attendance at late-night parties frequently followed an afternoon's trail round a hospital or a housing estate. Although such work might not have been especially onerous, it was not without its stresses and longueurs, while the fact that it was not newsworthy meant that the general public tended to remain unaware of it. In her capacity as Patron of this or President of that or Honorary Colonel-in-Chief of the other, she was obliged to make speeches, confer honours and present certificates.

Unlike her sister, Princess Margaret read widely, and by the early 1950s was gradually developing an interest in a number of cultural activities. She was also more loyal, generous and affectionate than many people imagined. And, in spite of her sophisticated manner, she suffered from a certain vulnerability. 'Behind the dazzling façade, the apparent self-assurance,' wrote Peter Townsend, who knew her in all her moods, 'you would find, if you looked for it, a rare softness and sincerity. She could make you bend double with laughing; she could also touch you deeply.' Townsend, of course, was hardly an impartial witness, for by now he was falling in love with her. She was, he writes lyrically,

a girl of unusual, intense beauty, confined as it was in her short, slender figure and centred about large purple-blue eyes, generous, sensitive lips and a complexion as smooth as a peach. She was capable, in her face and her whole being, of an astonishing power of expression. It could change in an instant from saintly, almost melancholic, composure to hilarious, uncontrollable joy. She was, by nature, generous, volatile. . . .[36]

His own marriage had fallen apart. In August 1950, he had been appointed Master of the Household, a permanent position in the King's service which meant that he had even less time to spend with his wife Rosemary, still living in Adelaide Cottage at Windsor. 'It was a difficult and sometimes heart-rending time,' he writes, 'with the growing conviction on us that a break-up was inevitable.'[37] It could hardly have been with much surprise that he heard that his wife was having an affair.

Equally heart-rending for Townsend must have been all the speculation about Princess Margaret's various suitors. One day at Balmoral, during the autumn of 1951, Sir Alan Lascelles, the King's Private Secretary, was delighted to be able to report to Townsend that Johnny Dalkeith (a relation of Lascelles) and Princess Margaret had been 'making sheep's eyes at each other last night'.[38]

By then, however, Peter Townsend knew that Princess Margaret was as much in love with him as he was with her. There can be no other explanation for the little episode which he recounts in his memoirs. One day, after a picnic lunch, Townsend stretched out on the heather for a nap. After a while, he was suddenly aware that someone was covering him with a coat. He opened his eyes to find Princess Margaret, her face very close to his, looking at him. Just beyond, he spotted the King, leaning on his stick, studying the two of them with an amused expression. 'You know your father is watching us?' whispered Townsend. The Princess laughed, straightened up and went to the King. 'Then she took his arm and walked him away,' wrote Townsend, 'leaving me to my dreams.'[39]

If King George VI did suspect that his daughter was attracted to his equerry, he would probably have dismissed the matter as no more than a schoolgirlish crush. Not for a moment would he have envisaged, or countenanced, a marriage between them. 'If the King had lived,' said her friend Colin Tennant many years later, 'he would have made Princess Margaret marry Johnny Dalkeith.'[40] The King would have seen his daughter's interest in Townsend as a passing phase, as just another aspect of her youthful unconventionality. He was always amazed and amused by what he considered her daringly emancipated way of life. But how, he once demanded, on being told that she was going to an after-theatre party in a flat in raffish Chelsea, would her chauffeur ever find the place? 'It's over a sweetshop near a bus stop,' she answered blithely.[41]

Princess Margaret was devoted to her father, a devotion that had deepened with the departure of Princess Elizabeth from the close family circle. It is, too, a curious and significant fact that all the men with whom Princess Margaret was to fall in love in some way resembled King George VI. She was never attracted to hearty extroverts; all her lovers were fine-boned, sensitive, somewhat vulnerable men. In a way, the King had provided his daughter with a template.

The Princess accompanied her parents to Sandringham for the Christmas of 1951. On the last day of January 1952, the three of them went to Heathrow airport to take leave of Princess Elizabeth and the Duke of Edinburgh, who were setting off on a Commonwealth tour. In spite of a bitter wind, the King stood hatless on the tarmac to wave goodbye. The family returned to Sandringham the following day. Five days later, while the King was out shooting, Princess Margaret went with her mother to visit the painter Edward Seago, who lived at nearby Ludham. After a cruise on the Norfolk Broads, they brought back some of Seago's paintings to show the King. After dinner that night, the Princess played the piano for her father while he did a crossword puzzle. At half-past ten he went up to bed.

King George VI died in his sleep during the early hours of 6 February 1952. He was found dead by his valet, James MacDonald, at half-past seven that morning. It was the Queen, herself heartbroken but composed, who broke the news to Princess Margaret.

PART THREE

The Queen's Sister

CHAPTER 10

Peter Townsend

THE DEATH OF KING GEORGE VI brought significant changes in the life of Princess Margaret. The royal centre of gravity, which had previously encompassed the King, the Queen and Princess Margaret, now shifted to the new monarch, Queen Elizabeth II, the Duke of Edinburgh and their two children. The royal residences – Windsor Castle, Buckingham Palace, Balmoral and Sandringham – passed into the charge of the new queen. King George VI's widow, now styled Queen Elizabeth the Queen Mother, and her younger daughter became, in a way, guests in the new sovereign's homes. Queen Elizabeth II was loath to leave Clarence House, and even toyed with the idea of using Buckingham Palace for constitutional and ceremonial purposes only, but she was talked out of this by the Prime Minister, Winston Churchill. A queen, he said, must live in a palace. So the two royal households exchanged homes. Queen Elizabeth II and her family moved into Buckingham Palace, and the Queen Mother and Princess Margaret moved into Clarence House.

Clarence House was to be Princess Margaret's home for almost eight years. This four-square, white-painted adjunct to St James's Palace, standing in its own garden, had been built by John Nash for the Duke of Clarence before his accession as King William IV in 1830. Long neglected, it had been renovated and enlarged, at a cost of £55,000, for the newly married Princess Elizabeth. It now underwent further refurbishment and alteration. Princess Margaret was given her own self-contained suite. But although Clarence House was an imposing mansion, with a large entrance hall and some good rooms, it was not a palace. Before long, however, the Queen Mother, with her sure eye and strong artistic tastes, had imbued the house with her own aura of majesty: for the next forty years, and more, Clarence House was to be one of London's important royal centres.

Until Clarence House was ready, Princess Margaret drifted between Buckingham Palace, Windsor Castle, Royal Lodge and Sandringham. This lack of a real home intensified her feelings of rootlessness. She had been deeply saddened by the death of her father. 'The King's death,' claimed a friend, 'was a terrible blow for Princess Margaret, she worshipped him and it was also the first time that anything really ghastly had happened to her.'[1]

'You know what a truly wonderful person he was,' she wrote in answer to Lady Astor's letter of condolence, 'the very heart and centre of our family and no one could have had a more loving and thoughtful father.

'We were such a happy family and we will have such lovely memories of him to remember when the grief of his loss has lessened. He was so kind and brave all his life.'[2]

In her grief, the Princess sought both spiritual and secular comfort. She joined the congregation at St Paul's Church, Knightsbridge, for a course of eleven half-hour Lenten lectures by the Bishop of Kensington, and attended post-confirmation classes at the vicarage. Her attendance at these lectures was unannounced: she was simply 'a black-clothed, sad little figure, inconspicuous in her pew'.[3] Inevitably, all this churchgoing gave rise to groundless rumours that she was about to embrace the Roman Catholic faith.

For comfort of a more earthly variety, Princess Margaret turned increasingly to Peter Townsend. The death of the King and the period of Court mourning meant that those people whose lives had once revolved about the monarch's were thrown into each other's company to an even greater extent. The Queen Mother, who was fond of Townsend and anxious to retain his comforting and competent presence, had him appointed to the important post of Comptroller of her Household. Quite oblivious to the romance burgeoning under her very nose, she felt that he would be a stabilizing influence on her often wayward daughter. During these months after the King's death, according to Townsend, he and Princess Margaret found 'increasing solace in one another's company . . . the King's death had left a greater void than ever in Princess Margaret's life, while my own was clouded by the failure of my marriage.'[4]

On the surface, though, the relationship between Peter and Rosemary Townsend seemed secure enough. Indeed, one day, in the summer of 1952, the Queen, the Duke of Edinburgh and Princess Margaret had tea with the Townsends in Adelaide Cottage. The Queen would have known nothing about Rosemary Townsend's extramarital affair; nor, of course, did she know anything about her sister's feelings for Peter Townsend. How much, one wonders, had the equerry's unavoidable neglect of his wife led her to look for affection elsewhere? And to what extent did he make use of this infidelity to justify his own relationship with Princess Margaret? It has been suggested that he 'needed his wife's guilt to salve his own conscience'.[5] Peter Townsend is always presented as a perfect gentleman, a blameless chevalier, but there must have been a certain amount of calculation in his behaviour. He could hardly have been blind to the opportunity opening up before him: a love-affair with – possibly even marriage to – a young, rich and beautiful princess, the most eligible girl in the world.

But if Townsend's motives were mixed, Princess Margaret's were not. By now she was passionately in love with this charming, serious-minded, still very attractive man, sixteen years her senior.

On 20 December 1952, Group Captain Peter Townsend was granted a divorce on the grounds of his wife's 'misconduct' with John de Laszlo, son of the celebrated society portrait painter, Philip de Laszlo. Townsend, the innocent party in the dissolution, was given custody of their two sons. Two months later, the former Mrs Townsend married her lover.

Early the following year, in what he described as his 'newly found state of bachelorhood', the thirty-eight-year-old Peter Townsend took up a spell of duty at Sandringham. Here, or so he claimed with deliberate vagueness, he and the twenty-two-year-old Princess Margaret 'rediscovered one another, and in a new frame of mind'. But he insisted that it was not until a few weeks later that they actually admitted to each other their love. Alone one afternoon in the Red Drawing Room at Windsor Castle when everyone else had gone up to London for some ceremony, Townsend told the Princess that he was in love with her. 'That is exactly how I feel, too,' she answered. It was, he wrote, 'an immensely gladdening disclosure'.[6]

This touching scenario may be a shade contrived. One can only assume that Townsend, in his memoirs, was anxious to spare

Princess Margaret any embarrassment and himself any charge of infidelity. By placing their declaration of love several months after his divorce, he hoped to clear them both of any hint of duplicity. But that afternoon at Windsor could hardly have been the first time that they each became aware of the other's feelings. Courts are notorious whispering galleries, and even before the King's death, there had been talk of 'an understanding' between them.[7] Townsend himself describes the two of them at Balmoral in previous years, walking 'a discreet but adequate distance from the rest of the party, so that we could talk *en tête-à-tête*'.[8] There was even a hilltop at Balmoral on which the two of them are said to have built a cairn, with the first one to reach the summit on subsequent visits having to add a stone. The resulting cairn was said to be almost three feet high. This is the behaviour of lovers, not just friends.

What was apparently settled in the course of that afternoon's talk in the Red Drawing Room at Windsor was an agreement to make an open acknowledgment of their love. The two of them wanted, says Townsend, to remain together, 'God alone knew how – and never be parted'.[9] He was right in imagining that only God knew how this life-long togetherness was to be achieved; no one else did. For the prospect of a marriage between the sovereign's sister and a divorced man was to raise – such were the conventions of the period – apparently insurmountable ecclesiastical and constitutional problems.

The first thing to be done was to tell the Queen. This Princess Margaret did alone. Elizabeth II, who was fond of her sister, was sympathetic. The Queen Mother proved equally understanding, although Townsend imagined that her reaction must have been 'this simply cannot be'.[10] It certainly was. In spite of her apparent composure in the face of the situation, the Queen Mother was deeply upset. When she discussed the news with one member of the royal household, she burst into tears for the first and only time in his long experience. Having been so intimately involved in the trauma of King Edward VIII's determination to marry the divorced Wallis Simpson, the Queen Mother could not bear the thought of going through the whole business again. The Duke of Edinburgh – in the course of an evening meeting between the Queen, Princess Margaret and Peter Townsend – treated the business in his customary bantering fashion.

There was no doubt that all three of these royal figures – the Queen, the Queen Mother and the Duke of Edinburgh – faced with this appalling conundrum, hoped that it would resolve itself: that, given time, the affair would run its course and that the feelings between the Princess and Townsend would cool. It was in this hope that the Queen asked the couple to wait a year before deciding on marriage.

Townsend himself broke the news to the man who was to play a significant part in the unfolding drama: the Queen's Private Secretary, Sir Alan Lascelles. With a lifetime of royal service behind him (he had been Assistant Private Secretary to the future King Edward VIII and to King George V, and Private Secretary to King George VI and now Queen Elizabeth II) Tommy Lascelles (as he was invariably known) was devoted to the monarchy. Although a stiff-backed courtier of the old school, he was something of a scholar, deeply interested in literature and always ready with an apt literary allusion. Almost alone at Court, Lascelles remained impervious to the Queen Mother's celebrated charm; indeed, he had always resented her influence over King George VI. She, for her part, found the Private Secretary's approach too drily academic. For Princess Margaret, Lascelles had even less regard: he considered her frivolous and irresponsible.

Lascelles's reaction, on hearing Townsend's news, was one of utter amazement. 'You must be either mad or bad,' he exclaimed.[11] In the Private Secretary's eyes, Townsend was simply a royal servant with ideas above his station, and one who should have known better than to encourage a silly young girl. In any case, his divorced status put paid to any hope of a marriage. Yet Lascelles did not actually tell Townsend that the thing was impossible. Nor did he speak directly about it to Princess Margaret. 'Had he said we couldn't get married,' complains the Princess, 'we wouldn't have thought any more about it. But nobody bothered to explain anything to us.'[12]

At its simplest, the explanation was this. Under the Royal Marriages Act of 1772 (instituted to prevent the dissolute sons of King George III from contracting undesirable marriages) Princess Margaret – until she reached the age of twenty-five – would have to obtain the Queen's consent to her marriage. It was highly unlikely that the Queen, whatever her private inclinations, would give this consent. Peter Townsend was a divorced man, and the Queen was the Supreme Governor of the Church of England, whose Canon 107 of the year 1603 expressly forbids divorce. Only if the Prime Minister were to advise the Queen in favour of the marriage would the royal assent be granted. This the Prime Minister was unlikely to do. After the Princess's twenty-fifth birthday, however, the sovereign's consent was no longer necessary; instead, the Princess would then need the consent of the British and Dominion parliaments. There was not much chance of her securing that, either. But whatever these complexities, it is difficult to take seriously Princess Margaret's protestations that she and Townsend did not understand the position in which they had placed themselves, or the dilemmas which their love-affair posed. Both were intelligent people, deeply interested in religious doctrine. 'He was very holy, always quoting the Bible,' claims one of the Princess's friends.[13]

The Queen certainly understood the position, particularly after it had been explained to her by the worried Lascelles. His advice was for her to send Townsend away as quickly, and as far, as possible. This, however, she could not bring herself to do. While agreeing to Townsend's instant removal from her mother's household, she merely appointed him to her personal staff as an extra equerry.

And so, for a while, matters rested. Nobody wanted to face the upheaval of a royal scandal just before the Coronation, set for that summer of 1953. Princess Margaret, having agreed to her sister's request that she wait a year, was apparently left with the impression that somehow or other things would work out; or that, at the very worst, she would have to wait until she turned twenty-five, in just over two years' time, before she could marry Peter Townsend. In the meantime, the affair was to be kept strictly secret.

The one royal figure who would have disapproved most strongly of what she would have considered a *mésalliance* – Queen Mary – departed from the scene at this critical juncture, for on 24 March 1953 she died at the age of eighty-five. During the last years of her life, she had established herself as an apparently indestructible part of national life: she had become, as one observer put it, 'like St Paul's Cathedral'.[14] Indeed, there was about Queen Mary's way of life something of the grandeur, precision and wealth of detail of a Baroque cathedral. 'She had such an image!' Princess Margaret exclaimed many years later.[15]

The death of the old Queen meant the cancellation of Princess Margaret's scheduled visit to Luxembourg for the wedding of Princess Josephine Charlotte of Belgium to Prince Jean of Luxembourg. But by May 1953, by which time Court mourning was over, she was able to fly to Oslo to represent Queen Elizabeth II at the marriage of her second cousin, Princess Ragnhild of Norway. The Norwegian wedding held a special significance for Princess Margaret, for Princess Ragnhild was marrying a commoner, Erling Lorentzen. The Norwegian princess's happiness, and the approval of her family, were very apparent.

The bulk of Queen Mary's wealth, which included her fabulous collection of jewellery, was left to Queen Elizabeth II. To Princess Margaret she bequeathed one of her favourite necklaces, a chain set alternately with large pearls and diamonds. To the very end, the overriding concern of the magnificent old Queen had been for what she had always regarded as the most sacrosanct of institutions, the monarchy. Although she had dearly wished that she might have lived long enough to see her granddaughter crowned, Queen Mary's final instructions had been that on no account was the Coronation to be postponed because of the mourning for her death. Royal obligation must take precedence above all else.

If Queen Elizabeth II was the most important royal figure at the Coronation on 2 June 1953, and the Queen Mother the most assured, then Princess Margaret was the most attractive. Her dress had been designed, as had those of the Queen and the Queen Mother, by Norman Hartnell; it was a creation of white satin, shimmering with pearls, crystal and silver thread. Over her shoulders she wore a robe of purple velvet trimmed with ermine. As the Princess, surrounded by the medieval figures of six heralds in their multi-coloured tabards, processed slowly up the nave of Westminster Abbey, 'a shaft of sunlight,' notes the proudly watching Hartnell, 'suddenly pierces the lofty stained-glass windows and splashes a pool of light on the carpets of blue and gold. . . . Her gaze steadily fixed upon the High Altar, she moves in white beauty like a snow-drop adrift from its stem.'[16]

The Princess was placed beside her dazzlingly dressed mother ('glittering from top to toe, diamonds everywhere, a two-foot hem of solid gold . . .', enthused one reporter[17]) in the front row of the royal gallery. Between the two women slipped the four-year-old Prince Charles in a white satin suit. Again and again, throughout the long and glittering pageant, Princess Margaret had to lean down to answer yet another question from the little boy. (Today, Prince Charles has no recollection of the Coronation whatsoever; 'I can only remember the gunge they plastered on my hair to keep it down,' he says.[18] At the climax of the ceremony – the actual crowning of the Queen – one member of the congregation noted that the Queen Mother 'raised her hand for one brief moment to her forehead', while Princess Margaret 'seemed tense with emotion'.[19] This solemn moment was followed by a fanfare of trumpets, a roll of drums and the distant sound of the guns thudding in salute in Hyde Park and at the Tower. 'I could have watched forever,' wrote Chips Channon in his diary, 'the red, the gold, the sparkle, the solemnity. . . .'[20]

Her train supported by her new Lady-in-Waiting, Iris Peake, Princess Margaret followed her mother's procession out of the Abbey. As she reached the specially built annex and stood waiting for her carriage, she saw Peter Townsend, slim and distinguished in his blue-grey, medal-bedecked RAF uniform. Looking, he said, 'superb, sparkling, ravishing', the Princess came up to him and, in a gesture of extreme tenderness and intimacy, brushed a bit of fluff off his tunic.[21] A hundred cameras flashed. By the following morning, the secret was out.

The secret was indeed out, although not yet in Britain. Just as it had at the time of Edward VIII's affair with Wallis Simpson, the British press remained silent on the issue. But not for long. With the Continental and American papers full of speculation about the Princess's romance, and with Fleet Street having been buzzing with rumours even before the Coronation, the British press could hardly be expected to ignore the story for ever. On Sunday, 14 June, twelve days after the Coronation, the *People*, employing the usual journalistic tactic of reporting an item while pretending to deny it, broke the news. In mock outrage, the newspaper claimed that there was no truth whatsoever in the 'scandalous rumours' that Princess Margaret was in love with a divorced man and wished to marry him. 'It is quite unthinkable that a Royal Princess, third in line of succession to the throne, should even contemplate a marriage with a man who has been through the divorce courts.'[22]

This breaking of the story, soon to be repeated throughout the national press, confirmed the Palace authorities in their opinion that Peter Townsend must be sent away. Already the matter had been thoroughly discussed with the Prime Minister. Hardly had Townsend told Tommy Lascelles that he and the Princess were in love than Lascelles had sent for John (Jock) Colville, Churchill's Principal Private Secretary. Lascelles had briefed Colville fully on the inadvisability, indeed impossibility, of the proposed match. Colville, in turn, had hurried down to Chequers, the country residence of Prime Ministers when in office, to explain the position to Churchill. To his Private Secretary's astonishment, the romantic old warrior had thrilled to the news. 'What a delightful match!' he exclaimed. 'A lovely young royal lady married to a gallant young airman, safe from the perils and horrors of war!' 'But Winston,' spluttered Colville, 'that isn't at all what Tommy was trying to say. . . .' At this point Churchill's wife, Clementine, had butted in. 'Winston,' she warned, 'if you are going to begin the Abdication all over again, I'm going to leave. I shall take a flat and go and live in Brighton.'[23] His wife's intervention had helped bring Churchill back to earth, and although he continued to feel some sympathy for the Princess's plight, he agreed that a scandal must be avoided at all costs. He asked Sir Lionel Heald, the Attorney-General, to prepare a report on the constitutional position and to canvass the views of the Commonwealth Prime Ministers. He himself held informal discussions on the matter with members of his Cabinet, almost all of whom advised against the marriage. The Prime Minister had duly reported all this to the Queen.

The disclosure in the *People* brought matters to a head. On the following morning, 15 June, Tommy Lascelles and the Queen's Press Secretary, Commander Richard Colville (Jock Colville's cousin), warned her that there was now no possibility of the rest of the press remaining silent. She must send Townsend away at once. Still the Queen demurred. The two men then visited the Prime Minister, and at an audience with Her Majesty the following day Churchill backed up their arguments. He again informed her that both the British Cabinet and the Commonwealth Prime Ministers were opposed to the marriage, and that there was very little likelihood of their approving it even after the Princess had turned twenty-five. He, too, urged her to send Townsend away. Reluctantly, the Queen agreed. Townsend would be sent abroad for two years, but to soften the blow, she asked for his departure to be held over until after 17 July, by which time Princess Margaret, who was due to accompany the Queen Mother on a sixteen-day tour of Rhodesia (now Zimbabwe), would have returned home. Townsend, unaware of all these machinations, was stunned to be summoned to Lascelles's office and told that he was to be posted abroad, as an air attaché, for two years. He was given a choice of postings: Brussels, Johannesburg or Singapore. He chose Brussels; at least that would ensure that he was relatively close, not only to Princess Margaret, but also to his two young sons, then boarders at a preparatory school in Kent.

The Queen Mother and Princess Margaret were due to leave for Rhodesia on 30 June. On the morning of the day before they left, Townsend went to Clarence House to say goodbye. With what he calls 'exquisite tact', the Queen Mother left the lovers alone. The Princess, he says, was 'very calm'.[24] Both felt confident, not only of their love for one another, but also that this would not be their last meeting before his posting abroad, for they would be seeing each other again on her return. At worst, their eventual marriage might have to be postponed for a couple of years.

Mother and daughter flew into Salisbury, Rhodesia, on 1 July 1953. The most important of the planned fifty-four engagements was the official opening of the Rhodes Centenary Exhibition in Bulawayo. Things got off to a bad start because the poorly advised visitors had arrived unprepared for the bitterness of the Rhodesian winter: their summery voiles and organdies proved quite unsuitable for the cold, if deceptively sunny, climate. But the Queen Mother was at her trouping best, smiling serenely through a specially composed anthem in praise of 'all descendants of Queen Victoria', and waving graciously as she drove under a triumphal arch proclaiming 'Greeting Great White Queen and Great White Princess'. The Great White Princess delighted all with her dazzling smile and fashionable, if flimsy, clothes.

The crowded schedule of events allowed only one, twenty-four-hour, rest period, which was spent at Leopard Rock Hotel, set among spectacular mountain scenery near Umtali, in the east of the country. And it was here that the Queen Mother broke the news to her daughter that Peter Townsend would not, as had been promised, be there to greet her on her return to London. His posting to Brussels had been deliberately brought forward to 15 July, the day before the Princess's return.

For the following four days, Princess Margaret vanished from public view. There are conflicting theories about this sudden disappearance. The official version is that because the Princess had succumbed to a sudden bout of 'Bulawayo flu', she had to be flown from Umtali to Salisbury, where she remained at Government House while the Queen Mother continued the tour. Not until 12 July did the Princess feel well enough to resume her duties. The other version – that she staged a scene, lapsed into a sulk and had to be flown to Salisbury – seems, on balance, more likely. Perhaps both versions are true, although the testimony of Lady Hambleden, the Queen Mother's Lady-in-Waiting, lends weight to the second. 'I was there when Princess Margaret was told about the Peter Townsend business,' she said many years later. 'It was *not* very pleasant.'[25]

If Sir Alan Lascelles imagined that the banishment of Peter Townsend would put an end to public speculation about the royal romance, he was soon proved wrong. Almost every newspaper in the land had something to say on the subject, even if only to voice a pretended disapproval of this 'ill-considered publicity about Princess Margaret's private affairs' and of the 'bandying about of her name in public gossip'.[26] It was left to Michael Foot, a future leader of the Labour Party, writing in *Tribune*, to strike a more honest note. He castigated the Cabinet for not allowing the Princess to marry Townsend, writing that 'This intolerable piece of interference with a girl's private life is all part of the absurd myth about the Royal Family which has been so sedulously built up by interested parties in recent years. . . .' The affair was not made any more savoury, Foot argued, by the fact that three members of the Cabinet – Anthony Eden, Sir Walter Monckton and Peter Thorneycroft – had themselves been involved in divorce cases. 'The laws of England say that a man, whether he has divorced his wife or been divorced himself, is fully entitled to marry again. In some respects, those divorce laws are still too harsh. But no self-appointed busybody has the right to make them still harsher. If these laws are good, they are good enough for the Royal Family.'[27]

In a poll conducted by the *Daily Mirror*, in which readers were asked whether the Princess should be allowed to marry Peter Townsend, over ninety-five percent voted in favour of the marriage.

While this storm was still raging, another blew up, when a proposed amendment to the Regency Act of 1937 brought Princess

Margaret's name back into the headlines. By the existing terms of this Act, in the event of the death or incapacity of the Queen, her sister would act as Regent until Prince Charles turned eighteen. It was now proposed that the Act be amended to allow the Duke of Edinburgh to replace Princess Margaret as Regent-Designate. Immediately, the antennae of the press began quivering. Either the way was being cleared for Princess Margaret's marriage, it was held, or she was being demoted. Introducing the amendment, the Chancellor of the Exchequer, 'Rab' Butler (acting as Prime Minister because Churchill had suffered a stroke) assured the House of Commons that it was not intended as a first step towards the Princess's marriage; it was simply an expression of the Queen's very natural wish that her husband should act as Regent for their son. Those who regarded the proposed change as some sort of slighting of the Princess were less easily reassured. 'May we assume that the contents of the proposed bill would be agreeable to all members of the royal family?' asked Clement Attlee, Leader of the Opposition. Butler's answer was a splendid example, says one observer, of 'triple tautology': 'Yes. I can give a definite answer to that in the affirmative,' he said.

But not even such public reassurances could lull public disquiet. During the autumn of 1953 press and politicians debated the matter. It was argued that as the Regency Act of 1937 had been expressly designed to settle the question, there was no reason to amend it. And why should the foreign-born husband of the Queen take precedence over the younger daughter of King George VI? Waxing more xenophobic still, some pointed out that not only was the Duke of Edinburgh foreign-born, but his grandfather had anglicized his German name of Battenberg to Mountbatten. 'Did Princess Margaret herself ask for this change [to the Regency Act], or was she asked to make the change?' demanded one Labour Member of Parliament. 'The matter was very clearly put to Princess Margaret, and she had every chance to consider it . . .' was the evasive reply made by the Home Secretary, Sir David Maxwell-Fyfe.[28]

In the end, the bill was pushed through the Commons and the Lords, and on 19 November 1953 it became law. Whatever its intentions or merits, the amendment edged Princess Margaret a little further from the throne, and a little nearer to a possible marriage to Peter Townsend.

CHAPTER II

The End of the Affair

WITH PETER TOWNSEND EXILED TO BRUSSELS, Princess Margaret resigned herself to getting on with her life until she turned twenty-five. This life remained what it had always been: one of extreme privilege, for which she paid with public duties which often meant little more than looking attractive, shaking a few hands and showing a polite interest. Her role, the Princess always maintains, is 'to help the Queen'.[1] This loose definition is open to a variety of interpretations. Whereas some sort of shape can be given to the lives of even the most amorphous of princes by putting them into the armed services, a princess, particularly an unmarried princess, needs to have an especially strong sense of direction if she is not to lose her way. Free of the disciplines and responsibilities of high office, Princess Margaret was able to do as much or as little as she pleased.

Her situation was a curious one. In the more egalitarian world of post-war Britain, she was in danger of developing into a relic from an earlier period: the world of the London Season, of Fridays-to-Mondays in great country houses, of debutante balls and presentation parties and society weddings. Whereas the royal generation that came after her would actively involve themselves in charitable causes, and the generation after that would actually earn their livings, Princess Margaret was not expected to do much more than display herself, as decoratively and as gracefully as possible, to the public.

Even her attempts at charity fund-raising tended to be imbued with a dated, patronizing flavour. In the summer of 1954 she was involved in an amateur production of Ian Hay's adaptation of the

Edgar Wallace novel *The Frog*, which was staged at the Scala Theatre in aid of the Invalid Children's Aid Association. By now the
Princess's interest in theatre was well known, although in this case
her involvement was primarily social. (She had recently defied the
strictures of an American cardinal by going to see the comedy *The
Moon is Blue*; His Grace had pronounced the piece to be immoral
because the word 'virgin' appeared in it.) The driving force behind
the production of *The Frog* was the Princess's friend Judy Montagu,
daughter of a former Secretary of State for India and granddaughter
of Lord Swaythling. The credentials of the rest of the company
were equally blue-blooded; in fact, it was almost 'the Margaret Set'
on stage. Colin Tennant played the Frog, Lord Porchester a police
sergeant, Billy Wallace a detective, the Duke of Devonshire a prison
governor, and various smaller roles were taken by Lord Norwich,
the Earl of Carnarvon, Lord Brooke and Lord Plunkett. The hero-
ine was played by the daughter of the romantic novelist Barbara
Cartland, the ineffable Raine Legge, afterwards Countess Spencer
and stepmother to the future Princess of Wales. The cast was round-
ed off by those two relentless social climbers, Elsa Maxwell and
Douglas Fairbanks, Junior. Princess Margaret, having obtained the
Queen's permission to involve herself in the business, did not actually play a part. Her role was that of associate director. Even so, her
most innocuous suggestions – such as 'I should take that a little
more slowly' – were hailed as irrefutable proof of her 'understanding of production techniques'.[2]

This aristocratic exercise, which played for a week, was roundly
slated by the critics. Few people were more scathing than Noël
Coward, who attended the first night with Vivien Leigh. His opinion, confided to his diary, is worth quoting at length.

The whole evening was one of the most fascinating exhibitions of incompetence, conceit and bloody impertinence that I have ever seen in my life.
With the exception of young Porchester, who at least tried to sustain a character, the entire cast displayed no talent whatsoever. Billy Wallace, the leading man, ambled on and off the stage with his chin stampeding into his
neck; nobody made the faintest effort to project their voices; Elsa Maxwell
appeared in a cabaret scene and made a cracking ass of herself. Douglas
Fairbanks played a small part in order, I presume, to prove that he was more
one of 'them' than one of 'us'. As a matter of fact, by now, he almost is. . . .

Those high-born characters . . . were unequivocally delighted with themselves from the first scene to the last which, I may add, was a very long time indeed. In the dressing-room afterwards, where we went civilly to congratulate Porchy, we found Princess Margaret eating foie gras sandwiches, sipping champagne and complaining that the audience laughed in the wrong places. We commiserated politely and left.[3]

Nevertheless, by the end of the run the Princess was able to announce that the sum of £10,000 had been raised for the charity. 'It's been my lucky week,' she said, for she had just won three guineas' worth of books for solving a *Country Life* crossword puzzle.[4]

More gratifying still was her appearance, in eighth position, on the New York Dress Institute's 1954 list of the world's best-dressed women. This was the last decade of formal, well-groomed, slavishly followed fashion, and Princess Margaret's clothes met all three criteria. Unlike her mother, who remained faithful to her own sumptuous style, or her sister, whose taste was unadventurous, Princess Margaret continuously changed her hairstyle, clothes and accessories to follow the latest trends. In this she was encouraged by the only other fashion-conscious member of the royal family, Princess Marina, Duchess of Kent. The latter had accompanied Princess Margaret on her second visit to Paris, late in 1951, where the two women had visited various couture houses. The older woman taught the younger a great deal about the art of royal dressing, even to the strategic pinning of a brooch in the small of the back so as to keep the sash of an order properly taut.

A source of additional gratification at Clarence House must have been the fact that the Duchess of Windsor, who for fifteen years had held the title of the world's best-dressed woman, had inexplicably slipped to a lowly tenth place that year. She bounced back, however. Two years later the Duchess tied with Princess Margaret for second place, the first going to that year's star personality, Grace Kelly.

The hopes of the rest of the royal family and of what was coming to be called 'the Establishment', that Peter Townsend's banishment would lead to a cooling-off of Princess Margaret's passions, proved fruitless. The couple frequently telephoned one another and wrote, says Townsend, 'almost every day'. Press speculation – that Townsend had 'faded from the limelight' and was 'lapsing into slow oblivion' – was wide of the mark.⁵ According to those who knew them well, the couple were real soul-mates and companions, deeply in love. There were certainly no grounds for the rumours that the Princess was about to become engaged to a member of the cast of *The Frog*: the handsome twenty-eight-year-old Colin Tennant, heir to Lord Glenconner, with whom she had become very friendly. 'Tennant To Marry Margaret' shouted the headlines when the Princess, accompanied by another of her ladies-in-waiting, Lady Elizabeth Cavendish, spent a few days at Glen, the house and 9,000-acre estate in Peeblesshire which Tennant was to inherit from his father.

In July 1954, Princess Margaret and Townsend organized a secret meeting, an almost ludicrously cloak-and-dagger operation. Under the assumed name of Carter, Townsend flew from Brussels to London. From the airport he was whisked off by car to Knightsbridge where, in the book department at Harrods, he was met by Brigadier Norman Gwatkin of the Lord Chamberlain's Office. Gwatkin drove him straight to Clarence House, where the Princess was waiting for him. 'Our joy at being together again was indescribable,' he wrote.⁶ For two hours they talked as though they had never been parted; clearly, their intense feelings for one another had not changed. All they needed to do, they imagined, was to wait another year until the Princess turned twenty-five, when she would be free of the Queen's official power of veto over her marriage.

After a short visit to his sons, Townsend flew back to Brussels. For once, the press had been caught unawares.

In her capacity as a representative of the Crown, Princess Margaret made two official tours during the following months. The first was a four-day visit to Germany in July 1954 to inspect British military units. As her stay included a formal luncheon in Bonn with President Heuss and Chancellor Adenauer, the visit was hailed as the first by a member of the British royal family to a German head of state since the days of Kaiser Wilhelm II. 'I was met by enormous crowds,' she said many years later, 'which surprised me so soon after the war.'⁷ She was being disingenuous. The reason why she was being so vociferously greeted with shouts of 'Heil Margaret Rose!' was because she was a young, beautiful princess involved in what was being called 'one of the greatest romances in history'.

Her second tour was more comprehensive, for she spent the month of February 1955 on an official visit to the Caribbean. Having flown out from London, she boarded the Royal Yacht *Britannia* to sail between Trinidad, Grenada, St Vincent, Barbados, Antigua, St Kitts, Jamaica and the Bahamas. The tour was an incomparable West Indian blend, as the Princess herself put it in her farewell speech, 'of great fields of sugar cane, of golden beaches and towering palms, and of an azure sea forever studded with the sails of your graceful ships'.[8] Enthusiastic crowds greeted her wherever she went; plumed-hatted governors bent over her hand; black guards of honour in white uniforms lined up for inspection; calypsos of varying merit were belted out – 'She ent married, she ent tall, like to dance, like to sing, like to try out anything.'[9] Her singing, in fact, caused an awkward moment in the Government House of one island when His Excellency shouted 'Turn that radio off!', only to be told that it was his royal guest singing in her bath.[10] Noël Coward, in Jamaica for the winter, pronounced the visit 'a very great success and everybody says she has done it exceedingly well . . . she was sweet and gay and looked radiant.'[11]

But the tour did not attract plaudits from all quarters. In Britain there was grumbling about the cost of it all: her thirteen-strong entourage, her 'fabulous wardrobe' designed by Norman Hartnell and Victor Stiebel, the £30,000-a-week expense of her 'floating palace', *Britannia*.[12] Matters were hardly helped by the statement issued by the Queen's Press Secretary to the effect that 'Her Royal Highness will, of course, shake hands with all of the considerable number of persons who are introduced to her' – as though that far from exacting exercise was all she was expected, or prepared, to do.[13]

Sir Hugh Foot, the enlightened Governor of Jamaica, was instructed that on no account was the Princess to be allowed to dance with any 'coloured person'. Noël Coward judged this to be 'a foolish edict'. 'Jamaica,' he wrote in his diary, 'is a coloured island and if members of our Royal Family visit it they should be told to overcome prejudice. I should think that any presentable young Jamaican would be a good deal more interesting to dance with than the shambling Billy Wallace.'[14] Foot was no stranger to royal race prejudice, however. He once expounded his arguments in favour of universal adult suffrage for Jamaica to the visiting Princess Alice, Countess of Athlone. Having heard him out, Her Royal Highness answered with a resounding, 'Foot! I have never heard such balder-dash in my life!'[15]

On Princess Margaret, this Caribbean tour made an indelible impression. The closing lines of her farewell speech – 'I hope one day I may come back' – were more than just conventional words of parting,[16] and in the years ahead she was to have a home in the West Indies. While the more orthodox members of the royal family would be shivering at Balmoral or Sandringham, she would be sunning herself in the Caribbean. This close, and enviable, association with such a captivating part of the world helped fix her image in the public mind as that of someone exotic, hedonistic, sybaritic.

On 21 August 1955, Princess Margaret turned twenty-five. She was, in accordance with the unvarying royal routine of the day, at Balmoral for the occasion. Her hopes of some sort of decision on her future marriage plans were obviously shared by the press, for hundreds of newsmen, British and foreign, were encamped around the castle. But no statement was forthcoming. The Queen seems to have distanced herself from the approaching storm; she was apparently ready to leave it to others to bear the responsibility for a resolution of her sister's future. Although Sir Alan Lascelles had retired from his post as Elizabeth II's Private Secretary in October 1953 and his place taken by Sir Michael Adeane, his unyielding views on the Townsend affair still influenced Palace thinking.

They were certainly reflected in the Cabinet; crucially, for it was now up to Parliament to decide whether or not permission was to be granted for the Princess's marriage. By this time the ailing Churchill had resigned from office and had been succeeded as Prime Minister by Sir Anthony Eden. A man who had divorced and remarried himself, the debonair-looking Eden had the unenviable task of bringing his Cabinet to some sort of a decision on the matter. Most vehemently opposed was the Conservative Leader of the House of Lords, the Marquess of Salisbury. A High Anglican and a man of considerable influence, Lord Salisbury – known as 'Bobbety' – threatened to resign from the Government if a bill were passed allowing the marriage. Although apparently quite prepared to serve under a divorced Prime Minister, Salisbury could not stomach the idea of being ruled by a sovereign whose sister had married a divorced man. Eden was forced to take Salisbury's threat of resignation seriously: his was the sort of gesture which brings down governments.

Lord Salisbury had influence in other quarters as well. He was highly thought of by the Queen Mother, his views often reflecting hers. In fact, by his insisting to her that the dignity and stability of the monarchy would be seriously endangered by this echo of the Abdication crisis, Salisbury was merely pushing at an already open door. The Queen Mother's attitude had hardened from one of sympathy for her daughter's feelings to one of strong disapproval of the affair. When the Princess asked for her advice at Balmoral that summer, the Queen Mother claimed that she was too upset to discuss the matter.

A few weeks after Princess Margaret's birthday, Sir Anthony Eden, accompanied by his second wife, Clarissa, arrived at Balmoral for the customary prime ministerial visit to the Sovereign's Scottish home. No doubt the Queen discussed the question of her sister's marriage with Eden, but at no stage was Princess Margaret involved in any talks. Throughout the Princess's stay at Balmoral the Queen was, she says, 'very nice but refused to discuss "it" at all'.[17] On the day that she was due to leave Balmoral for London in order to be reunited with Peter Townsend, the Queen purposely took the dogs out for a walk in order to avoid any discussion of the subject. Here was one of the earliest examples of the Queen's reluctance to involve herself in her family's intimate affairs: a reluctance that was to prove disastrous when applied to her own children.

Bewildered by her family's silence, but with her hopes still high, an excited Princess Margaret travelled south to meet Townsend.

The lovers met at Clarence House on the evening of 13 October 1955 – and for the following nineteen days were obliged to endure a nightmare of publicity. Their every move was followed by a horde of stampeding, shouting and gesticulating photographers and reporters. The restraint which had until now characterized the British press in its coverage of royal persons disappeared for ever. The final crisis of 'the world's greatest royal romance' was played out in the most merciless of spotlights.

It had started when Peter Townsend, imagining that he had foiled the press by flying into the tiny airfield at Lydd in Kent, was met by dozens of flashing cameras. Newsmen pursued him all the way as he drove to 19 Lowndes Square in London, where the Marquess of Abergavenny, a close friend of the royal family, had lent him his flat. The press remained encamped outside the flat for the rest of his stay. Braving them the following morning, Townsend set out for his meeting with the Princess. In her sitting room at Clarence House, the two of them re-entered their 'own exclusive world', realizing at once 'that nothing had changed'.[18] Their love for each other was as strong as ever. The couple arranged to meet the following day – a Friday – in order to spend the weekend together at Allanbay Park, the Berkshire estate of Major and Mrs John Lycett Wills: Jean Wills was the Princess's first cousin, the daughter of the Queen Mother's sister, Lady Elphinstone.

A plea to the newsmen from the Queen's Press Secretary that the privacy of Princess Margaret be respected proved futile. For the three days that the couple were at Allanbay Park the house was under siege; it was even watched from the air as aeroplanes chartered by the press circled overhead. When an attempt to bribe the Willses' butler with £1,000 failed, newsmen tried bribing their seven-year-old daughter – no more successfully – with chocolate. Provided they stayed out of sight, however, the lovers were at least able to spend time alone together. Perhaps inevitably, this weekend merely confirmed them in their determination to marry. Back in London, they met frequently during the following week, usually for dinner in the houses of various friends, and sometimes at Clarence House, on one occasion joining the Queen Mother for tea. The meeting gave rise to one inimitable American headline: 'Meg Sips Tea With Peter. Mom Makes It a Crowd.'[19]

And all the while the clergy, the press and the politicians were arguing the case. Canon Kirkland, an honorary canon at Canterbury Cathedral, declared that 'Princess Margaret contemplates doing something which is an affront to religion. Any person who marries a divorced person is unmarried in the eyes of the Church.' He was backed up by Dr Leslie Weatherhead, Chairman of the Methodist Conference, who argued that even if the Princess were to renounce her income and rights to the throne, for many people 'her example does not make it easier to uphold the ideal of Christian marriage'.[20] The Church was roundly attacked by certain sections of the press for such 'outdated and hypocritical' attitudes, for by now almost every newspaper carried photographs and reports of the couple's activities, and every leader-writer had an opinion. There were few households in the land in which the matter was not discussed. As in the case of Edward VIII and Mrs Simpson, the issue had developed into a simple one of love versus duty.

A particularly poignant reminder of the imperatives of royal duty came in the middle of the furore when, on Friday, 22 October, the Queen unveiled a statue of her late father, King George VI, in Carlton Gardens. Under an awning to shelter them from the driving rain, the royal family, including Princess Margaret, listened as the Queen paid tribute to the man who, in many ways, had laid down his life for the monarchy. 'Much was asked of my father in personal sacrifice and endeavour . . .' she said. 'He shirked no task, however difficult, and to the end he never faltered in his duty to his people.'[21] For Princess Margaret, the implication must have been only too apparent.

By this time, the matter had been fully thrashed out in Cabinet. In the course of a couple of specially convened meetings, the Government's resolve to oppose the marriage remained unshaken. If the Princess insisted on marrying Townsend, then a Bill of Renunciation would be placed before Parliament: a bill that would strip her of all her rights, privileges and income. She would have to be married abroad in a civil ceremony and be obliged to live out of the country for several years. What Princess Margaret was faced with, in short, was the prospect of being plain Mrs Peter Townsend, married outside the Church and living on whatever her husband could earn. All this was spelt out to Princess Margaret when she went to Windsor on Saturday, 23 October to spend the weekend with the Queen and the Duke of Edinburgh. The Duke, always outspoken, was by now extremely concerned about the ramifications of the affair.

This frank family conference seems to have proved a turning point; or, at least, to have dealt a final blow to the Princess's already fading hopes. On Sunday night she telephoned Townsend in great distress. Although she did not tell him 'what had passed between herself and her sister and brother-in-law . . . the stern truth was dawning on her.'[22]

It was dawning on him as well. In the course of the past week he had seen the Princess's earlier confidence evaporate and her normal gaiety disappear. 'We were both exhausted, mentally, emotionally, physically. We felt mute and numbed at the centre of this maelstrom.'[23] He also felt that he could not expect the Princess to make the expected sacrifices; they were in what he called a 'no deal' situation. Without consulting her, he scribbled out a rough renunciation on her behalf. When they next met, on the evening of Monday, 24 October, he realized that she, too, had come to the conclusion that marriage was impossible. 'We had reached the end of the road. Our feelings for one another were unchanged, but they had incurred for us a burden so great that we decided, together, to lay it down.'[24] So it was that, together, they worked on and finalized his suggested statement.

Yet, although the couple were willing to have the Princess's statement of renunciation issued immediately, the Palace authorities – in the form of Michael Adeane and Richard Colville – were not. They would apparently have preferred to have no statement issued at all; and they particularly objected to a phrase mentioning Townsend's 'devotion'. But the Princess held firm, and although she was obliged to wait a week before the statement was finally issued, it appeared very much as she and Townsend had written it.

This delay allowed *The Times* to publish, on Wednesday, 26 October, a ponderous editorial on the question. Not lending too much weight to the Queen's position as Supreme Governor of the Church, it stressed her standing as

the symbol of every side of life of society, its universal representative in whom her people see their better selves ideally reflected; and since part of their ideal is of family life, the Queen's family has its own part in the reflection. If the marriage which is now being discussed comes to pass, it is inevitable that this reflection becomes distorted. The Princess will be entering into a union which vast numbers of her sister's people, all sincerely anxious for her lifelong happiness, cannot in conscience regard as a marriage. . . .

The sharpest thrust came at the end. Whatever the Princess's decision, 'her fellow subjects will wish her every possible happiness – not forgetting that happiness in the full sense is a spiritual state and that its most precious element may be the sense of duty done.'[25]

In his biography of Peter Townsend, Norman Barrymaine dated *The Times* editorial two days earlier – to Monday, 24 October. Townsend repeated the error in his autobiography, with the result that the incorrect date appears in many subsequent books featuring the affair. One consequence is that this editorial is presented as a highly significant turning point in the drama; as an authoritative voice which finally forced the lovers to abandon all thoughts of marriage. But, of course, the decision had been reached, and the statement of renunciation drawn up and agreed, two days before the leader had appeared.

Her decision made, Princess Margaret went to Lambeth Palace on the evening of Thursday, 27 October to see Dr Geoffrey Fisher, the Archbishop of Canterbury. This visit, too, has given rise to another of the myths surrounding the affair. Writing in the *Spectator* almost three years later, Winston Churchill's son, Randolph, claimed that Dr Fisher, assuming that the Princess had come to consult him, had surrounded himself with various books of reference on the Church's attitude towards divorce and remarriage. 'When Princess Margaret entered,' wrote Randolph Churchill, 'she said – and the words are worthy of Queen Elizabeth I – "Archbishop, you may put your books away: I have made up my mind already."'[26] This romanticized account surprised Dr Fisher. 'I had no books of any sort spread around,' he told his biographer, William Purcell. 'The Princess came and I received her, as I would anyone else, in the quarters of my own study. She never said "Put away those books" because there were not any books to put away.'[27] Princess Margaret's own account is undoubtedly the correct one. Having greeted her, the Archbishop went over to a bookcase to take out a reference book. 'Put it back,' said the Princess crisply. 'I have come to give you information, not to ask for it.' She then told him of her decision not to marry Peter Townsend. 'What a wonderful person the Holy Spirit is!' said a beaming Dr Fisher.[28]

That night, Princess Margaret, resplendent in a pink and white satin dress and a tiara, sat with the Queen, the Duke of Edinburgh, the visiting President of Portugal, and Prime Minister Eden in the royal box at Covent Garden for a gala performance of Smetana's *The Bartered Bride*. It was noticed that although they were sitting side by side, not a single word was exchanged between the Princess and the Duke of Edinburgh.

All that now remained was for the lovers to take leave of one another. They spent a last weekend together at Uckfield House, the Sussex estate of Peter Townsend's friend, Lord Rupert Neville. As the Princess's statement of renunciation had not yet been published, the press and the public continued to pursue the couple with their usual relentlessness, and all sorts of subterfuges were necessary to get in and out of Uckfield. The couple said their final goodbye at Clarence House on the evening of Monday, 31 October. 'Without dishonour,' wrote Townsend, 'we had played out our destiny.'[29] As he drove back in the moonlight to Uckfield, and so eventually back to Brussels, the Princess's communiqué was being broadcast to the world.

I would like it to be known that I have decided not to marry Group Captain Townsend. I have been aware that, subject to my renouncing my rights of succession, it might have been possible for me to contract a civil marriage. But mindful of the Church's teachings that Christian marriage is indissoluble, and conscious of my duty to the Commonwealth, I have resolved to put these considerations before others. I have reached this decision entirely alone and in doing so I have been strengthened by the unfailing support and devotion of Group Captain Townsend. I am deeply grateful for the concern of all those who have constantly prayed for my happiness.[30]

From pulpits and editors' offices throughout the world, the Princess's statement was greeted either as a noble act of self-sacrifice for the sake of Church, Crown and country, or else as a decision imposed upon her by the forces of reaction. Cutting briskly through these thickets of sanctimoniousness and sentimentality was Noël Coward's remark that 'I hope that they had the sense to hop into bed a couple of times at least, but this I doubt.'[31]

What, exactly, was the nature of Princess Margaret's celebrated sacrifice? She had rendered, it has been fulsomely claimed, 'sovereign service to the monarchy, to the Church and to the divine institution of marriage'.[32] Mindful, as she herself put it, of the Church's teachings on the indissolubility of marriage and of her duty to Crown and Commonwealth, she had sacrificed her personal happiness. It was not quite as simple as that.

For what if the Government had agreed to the marriage? If she had been allowed to keep her royal status and income, would Princess Margaret have married Peter Townsend in spite of the Church's position on divorce? After all, she had been prepared to wait two years for the permission of Parliament, knowing full well that the reason why the Queen could not give her permission was because she was Supreme Governor of the Church of England.

Given her interest in religious doctrine, the Princess must have known exactly where the Church stood on the question of divorce. Perhaps the couple were hoping for some way round the impasse; may, indeed, have been encouraged by the fact that even the Duke of Windsor had managed to unearth a clergyman prepared to marry him to the twice-divorced Wallis Simpson.

In his autobiography, Peter Townsend points out that 'some of the Church's most devout and erudite prelates had contested the validity of the laws on divorce and remarriage', and that the Church of England had frequently remarried the 'innocent' or 'wronged' party of a divorce. He quotes the Archbishop of Canterbury himself as stating that 'I do not feel able to forbid good people who come to me for advice to embark on a second marriage.'[33] Perhaps the couple were hoping for some sort of dispensation. But if this had not been forthcoming, would the Princess's love for Townsend have proved stronger than her desire for a marriage sanctioned by the Church?

Looked at today, all this agonizing seems curiously irrelevant. Within a generation, divorce and remarriage had become common-place in the royal family. Princess Margaret herself is a divorcée, the Queen's daughter, Princess Anne, has been divorced and has remar-ried, and two of her sons are divorced. A marriage between Princess Margaret and Peter Townsend would have caused hardly a ripple today.

In the years ahead, reports of Princess Margaret's all-too-fre-quent emotional upheavals would be met with the stock answer: 'They should have let her marry Townsend.' But how successful – presuming that the Princess had been allowed to retain her royal position and privileges – would the marriage have been? In many ways, Peter Townsend would have made the perfect royal consort. He understood the formalities and restrictions, indeed, even the boredom, of Court life. He would have been tactful, discreet and dignified, quite prepared to walk the obligatory few paces behind his royal wife. By birth he was certainly as well-qualified as those royal consorts who came after him – Antony Armstrong-Jones, Mark Phillips, Timothy Laurence.

Success on the personal level is more difficult to gauge. 'She can't know, poor girl, being young and in love,' wrote a world-weary Noël Coward, 'that love dies soon and that a future with two strap-ping stepsons and a man [sixteen] years older than herself would not really be very rosy. . . .'[34] They were very different types. Peter Townsend was a serious-minded man who developed into something of a blimp, while Princess Margaret was a vivacious, mercurial young woman, anxious to sample life in all its variety. With the passing years the duality of her nature has become more pronounced: she is at once both more imperious and more of a maverick. She may well have proved too much for Townsend to handle. Would his character have been strong enough to match hers? Princess Margaret has never been an easy woman.

So what, then, if she had given up everything to marry him? They would have had to have gone abroad to be married in a civil ceremony, and although the Queen might well have granted her sister an allowance, life as Mrs Peter Townsend in an apartment on the Côte d'Azur would soon have palled. He simply did not have the weight, said Townsend many years later, to counterbalance what she would have lost. He could not, in other words, have afforded her. Marriage to Townsend would not only have deprived the Princess of her £6,000 a year, but also of the £15,000 (well over £200,000 today) which she would have been granted on contracting a more acceptable marriage. Princess Margaret took for granted, and greatly enjoyed, the privileges of her position: the luxurious homes, the liveried servants, the chauffeured cars, the couture clothes, the respectful entourage, the impeccable arrangements, the instantly obeyed orders. 'I cannot imagine anything more wonderful than being who I am,' she had once declared.[35] It seems likely, therefore, that, in the end, it was not so much that the Princess sacrificed her love for the sake of Church and Commonwealth, as that she was not prepared to sacrifice her style of life.

In addition, she was very conscious of being royal, of being a king's daughter. Here again, the Edward VIII/Wallis Simpson affair threw its long shadow: unconventional in some ways, Princess Margaret was not unconventional enough to risk losing the kudos of being a member of the world's most illustrious royal family. In short, she was not prepared to exchange that existence for the sort of trivial, tarnished, café-society life that the Duke and Duchess of Windsor led. 'She has always despised them as completely beyond the pale,' said a friend.[36]

It is also difficult to avoid the conclusion, that, in the end, Townsend lost his nerve. Imagining that he was about to hitch his

wagon to a star, he must have taken fright, not only at the prospect
of having to support this indulged and wilful young woman, but also
at the thought of having been responsible for depriving her of her
royal status. 'He was rather a weak man,' says someone who had
dealings with Townsend later, 'and wasn't to be trusted. He'd promise something and never deliver.'[37]

None of this is to imply that Princess Margaret was not in love
with Peter Townsend, nor is it to minimize the difficulties faced by
a girl then still in her twenties. Her dilemma was a real one. Some
measure of her love for Townsend can be gleaned from the fact that
it was not until she heard, many years later, that he was about to
remarry, that Princess Margaret herself decided to marry. First love
is often the strongest of all loves, and the cruel thwarting of the
Princess's love for Townsend may well have been the cause of the
subsequent turmoil of her emotional life. She certainly bore a
grudge against Sir Alan Lascelles, the man whom she considered
responsible for the mismanagement of the whole affair. Although
Lascelles lived, until he died at the age of ninety-four, in a grace-
and-favour house near the Princess's own home in Kensington
Palace, she never spoke to him again. One day – by then with one
failed marriage and many unhappy love-affairs behind her – she saw
Lascelles shuffling by. Turning to her companion, she said, 'There
goes the man who ruined my life.'[38]

CHAPTER 12

The Modern Princess

THE ENDING OF THE TOWNSEND AFFAIR – with all its romance, drama and heartbreak – trained an even brighter spotlight on Princess Margaret. She stood revealed as a more controversial figure than ever. While Townsend coped with the traumas of the affair in his way, by planning and then making, alone, a 60,000-mile journey around the world, the Princess coped with them in hers, by leading an ever more active social life. Those who imagined that she would shut herself away in Clarence House were soon proved wrong. Within a fortnight of the issuing of her famous renunciation, Princess Margaret 'plunged back into the social whirl with an extra zest'.[1]

She attended a ball at Winfield House, where she was seen smoking through a long cigarette holder and joking with an old friend, Mark Bonham Carter. A week later she accompanied another old friend, Sharman Douglas, to a performance of the musical *The Pyjama Game*, before going on to a party where she remained until three in the morning. She saw *Kismet* five times, and *Cinerama* four. In fact, more and more during the second half of the 1950s did Princess Margaret seem to be deserting the old aristocratic 'Margaret Set' for the infinitely brighter world of show business. Even on an official visit to the BBC's Lime Grove Studios, she astonished her hosts by knowing, and singing, all the words of 'You can't chop your Momma up in Massachusetts!' from the revue *New Faces*.

She went to hear performers like Lena Horne and Louis 'Satchmo' Armstrong. The famous trumpeter pronounced her to be, in the jargon of the day, 'one hip chick'.[2] 'This is a special for a fan of mine in the house tonight,' announced Satchmo on one occasion, before launching – to the Princess's obvious delight – into 'Mahogany Hall Stomp'.[3] One evening she arrived unexpectedly at a Count Basie concert at the Royal Festival Hall, stayed for two hours, and then came back at nine o'clock for the second two-hour-long concert. During these performances she frequently led the applause, particularly for Sonny Payne's show-stopping drum solo. 'From time to time,' said Count Basie, 'she used to catch the band in places outside London and she also came to a recording session.'[4]

The Princess also built up a sizeable collection of records, to which she constantly and enthusiastically added. Among her favourite performers were Ella Fitzgerald, Frank Sinatra and the guitarist Josh White; in time, she added Cleo Laine to this select group. With her Lady-in-Waiting and close friend, Lady Elizabeth Cavendish (who was associated with the show), the Princess attended rehearsals of *Cranks*, an innovative revue by the talented South African-born choreographer, John Cranko. 'I was rockin' and rollin' with Princess Margaret last night' was the exaggerated claim of one American journalist, when all he had done was to sit near her at *The Girl Can't Help It*, a 'rock-and-roll film' starring Jayne Mansfield.[5]

And, all the while, the royal engagements and appointments continued: the laying of foundation stones, the cutting of ribbons, the tours of inspection, the accepting of honorary colonel-in-chief-ships of this or that regiment. She had her portrait painted, in fifteen sittings, by Pietro Annigoni (she asked only for a bow on her dress to be removed and a strand of hair painted out), and her head sculpted by Jacob Epstein. In June 1956 she accompanied her Uncle Henry, the bovine Duke of Gloucester, Vice-Patron of the British Olympic Association, to Sweden to witness the equestrian events in the Olympic Games. There they were joined by the Queen and the Duke of Edinburgh, who had just completed a state visit to King Gustaf VI Adolf.

In September 1956 she undertook a more ambitious engagement, setting off on the sort of royal visit which seemed to reflect best her colourful image. This was the so-called 'Blue Lagoon' tour of Britain's East African and Indian Ocean possessions. The islands of Mauritius and Zanzibar and the coasts of Kenya and Tanganyika (which today, with Zanzibar, forms Tanzania) were highly exotic places, peopled by Arabs, Indians and Africans; even the Kenyan hinterland was imbued with an undeniable romance. Who better to mirror the langourous atmosphere and seductive setting than this beautiful young princess?

Yet for all Princess Margaret's much-vaunted modernity, her East African tour was an old-fashioned imperial gesture in a fast-changing world. The Mau-Mau rebellion in Kenya had only just been crushed, and her visit was designed to reassure public opinion. In fact the Mau-Mau uprising was to prove to be only a prelude to the wave of independence soon to sweep over these colonial possessions. Already, to the north in Egypt, President Nasser had nationalized the Suez Canal, until then under joint British and French control: a coup which was to spell the beginning of the end of Britain's role as a great imperial power.

Once again, as during her Caribbean tour, the Princess flew out from London, and then lived aboard *Britannia* for some of the time and in specially refurbished suites in Government Houses for the rest. And again, she delighted everyone with her radiant smile, fashionable clothes and apparent enthusiasm. Day after day she moved through a kaleidoscopic blur of beflagged streets, cheering crowds, tribal dances, garden parties, firework displays and game reserves. One or two things struck a more *outré* note. In the labyrinthine Arab quarter of Mombasa she sat drinking cups of coffee behind the delicate lattice screens with women in purdah. They presented her with a miniature Arab sword as a symbol, ran the somewhat disgruntled explanation, 'of the duties of men which in this age must be shouldered by women'.[6] On the sugar island of Mauritius she stayed in the Governor's residence, Le Réduit, where the ghost of a British admiral can be placated only by the nightly leaving of a glass of rum: the rum always disappears. On the spice island of Zanzibar she not only visited the world's longest-reigning sovereign, the seventy-eight-year-old Sultan of Zanzibar, in his white marble palace, but also met two African women, the one almost a hundred, the other over eighty-five, who had once been slaves.

In Arusha, Tanganyika, there was a meeting of a more poignant sort. There Princess Margaret was introduced to a tall, tanned, robust-looking District Commissioner. This was Peter Townsend's younger brother, Francis. With impeccable royal control, Princess Margaret flashed a smile, greeted him politely, and briskly turned her attention to the next person in the line.

But for all the enthusiasm with which she was greeted, and her obvious delight in so much that she saw, the Princess, noted someone travelling with her party, seemed 'a lonely little figure'. Already she was 'brandishing that conflicting blend of regal impatience and chummy amiability that made it hard to react to her approaches'.⁷

As a footnote to these royal occasions, two apparently off-the-cuff remarks made during the tour proved memorable. For a *baraza*, or tribal gathering, in Tanganyika, it was hoped to use the 'throne' upon which the Princess's Uncle David, as Prince of Wales, had sat over thirty years before. However, this venerable seat had been stored in a thatched hut for so long that it had all but crumbled away. 'Which decisively proves,' said the Governor, Sir Edward Twining, 'that people in grass houses shouldn't stow thrones.'⁸

The second story (although it is nowadays dismissed by the Princess) concerns another colonial administrator, Sir Evelyn Baring, the Governor of Kenya. Taking leave of him, the Princess, in a catch phrase of the period, said, 'See you later, alligator.' To the bemused Governor, a young aide explained that the correct answer to Her Royal Highness's remark should have been, 'In a while, crocodile.'⁹

In this same year, 1956, Princess Margaret was involved in a curious episode. With Peter Townsend out of the running, speculation about a possible future husband for the twenty-six-year-old Princess increased. There was no shortage of suggested candidates. Among the royal names which had been bandied about for years were King Baudouin of the Belgians, Prince George of Denmark, Prince Nicholas of Yugoslavia, Prince Bertil of Sweden, and Prince Christian of Hanover. In fact, the rumours of an engagement between the Princess and the tall, athletic, thirty-five-year-old Prince Christian of Hanover – brother of the controversial Queen Frederika of Greece – were so persistent that the Palace had to issue a formal denial. This was backed up by a denial from the Prince himself.

Nor was there any shortage of aristocratic names linked with hers, for the press was forever pairing her off with this or that scion of a noble house. To the consternation of the massed reporters, the Princess once arrived at the Red, White and Blue Ball at the Dorchester Hotel with no less than seven blue-blooded escorts. On another occasion, being discovered dining in a restaurant with the brothers James and Robin McEwen, she laughingly asked if she was expected to marry them both. By now, however, the ranks of the 'Margaret Set' were beginning to thin. One by one her previous escorts were married off: among them Sunny Blandford, Johnny Dalkeith, Mark Bonham Carter, Colin Tennant, Jocelyn Stevens, Henry Porchester and Peter Ward. By 1956 almost the only long-standing member of the group who was neither married nor involved in a serious relationship was Billy Wallace. And he was only too ready to marry the Princess.

Three years older than Princess Margaret, Billy Wallace was a tall, dark-haired, gangling young man, the most chinless-looking of the 'chinless wonders' surrounding her. But he was immensely rich. His father, Captain Euan Wallace, had been a Scottish landowner and a former Conservative cabinet minister; his mother, born Barbara Lutyens, was the daughter of the celebrated architect, Sir Edwin Lutyens. On her husband's death in 1941, Barbara Wallace had married another very rich man, an American named Herbert Agar. Of the five sons of Captain Euan Wallace (the two eldest by a previous marriage) only Billy, the youngest, had survived the Second World War. He was thus the sole heir to the family fortune, which included his mother and stepfather's country home, Beech-wood, near Petworth in Sussex.

From Eton, Billy Wallace had gone to Millfield in Somerset and then on to University College, Oxford. Great wealth and poor health (he suffered from kidney problems) are hardly incentives for the active pursuit of a career; Wallace's forays into the Stock Exchange and merchant banking led nowhere. He was far happier devoting his energies to social life, being 'endlessly socially ambitious', according to Colin Tennant.[10] Billy Wallace was to be seen at all the smartest places: playing polo at Cowdray Park, attending fashionable race meetings, gambling at Le Touquet, lunching and dining in London clubs, dancing at hunt balls, sitting up until all hours in nightclubs.

But for all that, he was not just another upper-class oaf. He was kind, with a good sense of humour and an informed interest in art, and he shared Princess Margaret's love of the theatre. An accomplished conversationalist, he is said to have been a great favourite with the Queen Mother, who found him more interesting than most of her daughter's many escorts. Throughout their long friendship (the Princess had attended his twenty-first birthday party at the Ritz in 1948) Billy Wallace had periodically proposed marriage to the Princess. Gently, because she was very fond of him, she had refused his offers. Now, however, in the bleak aftermath of the Townsend affair, with so many of the men in her life getting married and with the prospect of spinsterhood opening up before her, Princess Margaret accepted Billy Wallace's latest proposal. Her feelings for him were, at best, lukewarm, but he was, as she herself rather lamely put it, 'somebody one at least liked'.[11] He was also somebody who could afford to keep her in a style to which she was accustomed. Provided the Queen approved, the Princess told Wallace, she would marry him. Until such time, their engagement was to remain unofficial.

Delighted, Billy Wallace went off on a holiday in the Bahamas, where he joined a party of other wealthy bachelors at an exclusive leisure development near Nassau. While he was there, he enjoyed a brief holiday romance. On getting back to London, he took the extraordinary step of telling Princess Margaret about his fling. It is perhaps some measure of the tepidness of their relationship that he felt he could tell her something like this. But he had misjudged her. She was furious. Either that, or she used his indiscretion as an excuse to get out of a situation about which she was having second thoughts. She immediately broke off their unofficial engagement and refused to have anything more to do with him. Wallace professed himself 'rather surprised' by her attitude.

For several years Princess Margaret would not see Billy Wallace; she was, says Jocelyn Stevens, 'very bitter about Billy'.[12] Not until after her marriage to Antony Armstrong-Jones did she allow him back into her circle and when, in 1965, Wallace married Elizabeth Hoyer-Millar, the Princess attended their wedding. Twelve years later, in 1977, Billy Wallace died of cancer at the age of fifty. Princess Margaret, her own marriage in ruins by then, attended his funeral.

Except when engaged on such densely packed assignments as her East African tour, Princess Margaret led an enviably relaxed and luxurious life. Her days at Clarence House were cushioned and organized by a small army of attendants: ladies-in-waiting, equerries, secretaries, detectives, chauffeurs, maids and footmen. Her personal needs were met by her maid, Ruby – the same Ruby MacDonald who had been at 145 Piccadilly and who, having married a royal footman, was now Mrs Gordon. Like her sister, Bobo

MacDonald, who was the Queen's maid and confidante, Ruby was extremely possessive of her mistress. She alone was allowed to call the Princess 'Margaret', and she deeply resented what she considered interference on the part of the ladies-in-waiting. 'She was the bane of my life,' said one of the latter. 'She was in a very powerful position and was awful to the rest of the staff, and on tour to ADCs and practically governors. . . .'[13] On tour, Ruby always insisted that a tray of drinks be sent up to her room.

It was Ruby who brought in Princess Margaret's breakfast tray. Many years later when, in an effort to economize and simplify the running of the household, it was decreed that no more breakfast trays would be carried up to the bedrooms at Sandringham, the idea was quickly abandoned on the grounds that Princess Margaret would never stand for it.

When the Princess was ready to get up, Ruby would run her bath, lay out her clothes and help her dress. The Princess's wardrobes were full of beautiful couture dresses; her tiny shoes were handmade of leather as soft as silk. It was during these years that, in terms of style, Princess Margaret was 'taken in hand', as she later put it, not only by Princess Marina, but also by the Queen Mother's Lady-in-Waiting, Lady Jean Rankin, who introduced her to René, the hairdresser, and to Simone Mirman, the milliner. Although still faithful to Hartnell ('always so good at getting the balance right,' she says[14]) and Victor Stiebel, the Princess went to Dior and Jean Dessès for some of her clothes. Even if she were to spend the day at home, Princess Margaret never looked anything less than immaculate.

Living in the same house as her mother presented no problem for Princess Margaret. The two women led almost separate lives. By now the Queen Mother had overcome her undeniable, if understandable, resentment of the fact that she had been so suddenly robbed of the role of Queen Consort which she had enjoyed so much. As popular as ever, she led an extremely busy official and social life. In any case, she never interfered in her daughter's affairs. She never allowed herself to become upset by Princess Margaret's often capricious behaviour. 'You will see that this tiresome incident will have no effect on [the Queen Mother] at all,' a lady-in-waiting once assured a hostess whose plans had been upset by the Princess's sudden change of mind. 'She will enjoy her day as much as though it has never happened. Nothing will disturb her happiness.'[15]

If mother and daughter were both at home, they would lunch with the members of the household. The meal itself usually consisted of four courses, with the Princess smoking a cigarette while the rest of the company ate dessert. As both the Queen Mother and Princess Margaret were, and are, lively conversationalists, the atmosphere was always animated; the Queen Mother, says one of her ladies-in-waiting, 'was the greatest fun to be with'.[16]

In the household, Queen Elizabeth II was referred to as 'The Queen' and the Queen Mother as 'Queen Elizabeth'. Princess Margaret would expect her guests to speak of the Queen Mother as 'Queen Elizabeth', while she would refer to her as 'my mother' and address her as 'Mummy'. (A guest was once amused to hear the Queen Mother, then in her sixties, point to some table ornaments which she had inherited from her mother and say, 'Those belonged to Mummy'.[17])

Already a lover of hot climates, Princess Margaret enjoyed few things more than sunbathing in the secluded garden of Clarence House. This was something the Queen Mother would never dream of doing. She belonged to a generation of women that kept the sun off their skins. On one occasion Princess Margaret sent a gardener to tell her mother that a certain rose had come into bloom. Only after an interminable wait did the Queen Mother appear – in hat, gloves, summer coat and holding a parasol – in order 'to spend a few seconds inspecting a rose'.[18]

There were few evenings on which the Princess did not go out – to a party, show or restaurant. She would seldom arrive back before midnight; sometimes a bleary-eyed security man in the police lodge would log her in with the morning newspapers. Often, after the theatre, she would bring back a party of friends for supper, starting at eleven and continuing until almost dawn. She usually entertained her guests with songs at her grand piano. She was always loath to end a party and go to bed, particularly if she had been drinking too much. It was a rule that no one left a party until the Princess was ready for it to break up, and she was seldom ready for that.

During the second half of the 1950s, anecdotes about Princess Margaret's awkwardness and high-handedness began to circulate ever more widely. Servants at Clarence House are said to have complained about her unpredictable moods, her late hours, her unreasonable demands, her insistence on such little things as a plate being repositioned so that the coat of arms on the border was in precisely the correct place in front of her. A hole burned in a tablecloth by a cigarette would be lightly dismissed as she fixed another into her long holder. Even in other people's homes she would insist that her whisky be accompanied by what was then a relatively rare commodity – bottled, not tap, water. Lord Mountbatten's Private Secretary claimed that whereas Princess Margaret had inherited her mother's 'sardonic and really quite bitchy' nature, she had not inherited her 'common touch, her genuine interest in and enjoyment of people'.[19] Indeed, her reputation for causing scandal was such that, in the aftermath of the Suez Crisis in late 1956, with Britain having been forced to beat an ignoble retreat in the full glare of international publicity, a German magazine published a cartoon of the worried Queen Elizabeth II begging her sister: 'Say, Margaret, couldn't you do something to distract the horrid world press from our Suez débâcle?'[20]

In fact, the Princess came very close to causing just such a distraction on the occasion of the Queen's tenth wedding anniversary, which fell on 20 November 1957. The event was being celebrated by an intimate dinner at Buckingham Palace, to which only members of the family and a few very close friends were invited. Not only did Princess Margaret not attend the dinner, but she went instead with a party of friends to the Coliseum to see the musical *Bells are Ringing*. From there they went on to the Savoy for dinner where, because a table had not been reserved, the high-spirited party had to wait until one had been specially prepared. Towards midnight, the Princess was driven to the Palace, where she joined the dancing at her sister's party for less than an hour.

Her defiant behaviour was, in the words of one normally obsequious chronicler, 'inexplicable'.[21]

In the spring of 1958, Peter Townsend came back into Princess Margaret's life. Since their dramatic parting at the end of October 1955, the couple had had only one, secret, meeting. That was in September 1956, just before he had set out on a round-the-world tour. During the following eighteen months he had undertaken his 60,000-mile journey, travelling through Europe, the Middle East, India, Burma, Malaya, Australia, New Zealand, China, Japan, Canada, the United

States, South America and all the way up Africa from Cape Town to Algiers. But if he had imagined that this mammoth journey would help him forget Princess Margaret, he was wrong. No sooner had he arrived back in Brussels on 23 March 1958 than he felt compelled to telephone her. The Princess, apparently, was just as anxious to see him. They arranged to meet in London three days later.

Looking fit, bronzed and considerably younger than his forty-three years, Peter Townsend called at Clarence House on the afternoon of 26 March. Immediately the press was on the alert – 'They're Together Again!' trumpeted the headlines the following day. Much was made of the fact that the meeting had taken place while the Queen was away on a state visit to the Netherlands. In addition, Princess Margaret was accused of being headstrong, perverse, determined to steal her sister's thunder; while Townsend was said to be forcing the Princess to reconsider the question of their marriage. The press speculation was such that Townsend was obliged to issue a statement to the effect that 'there are no grounds whatsoever for supposing that my seeing Princess Margaret in any way alters the situation declared specifically in the Princess's statement in the autumn of 1955.'[22] Nevertheless, the couple decided that it would be wiser to postpone a second meeting, planned for that day; instead, Townsend sent the Princess four dozen red roses.

On the next day – 27 March – Princess Margaret flew off on an official two-day visit to Germany, while Townsend went down to Somerset to see his mother. He needed to deploy considerable ingenuity in order to evade the hounding press. Immediately on her return, the Princess telephoned Townsend; she told him that she had been 'persuaded' not to see him again during his present visit to England but they arranged to meet again after her forthcoming tour of the Caribbean. They felt 'confident that the present excitement would blow over'.[23]

It did not blow over. Three further meetings in the course of one week in May, on the Princess's return from the Caribbean, simply led to even more feverish press speculation. A report, by the London correspondent of the *Tribune de Genève*, that an engagement between Princess Margaret and Peter Townsend was soon to be announced was widely reported in the British press. Normally, the Palace did not deny such reports, but after the Queen had driven to Clarence House to see her sister, an official statement was issued:

The Press Secretary to the Queen is authorised to say that the report in the *Tribune de Genève* concerning a possible engagement between Princess Margaret and Group Captain Peter Townsend is entirely untrue. Her Royal Highness's statement of 1955 remains unaltered.[24]

But why did the couple keep meeting? If love has grown cold, it is quite possible for previous lovers, after a time, to meet as friends; if they have been forced to part, as these two had been, then love invariably becomes even stronger. Three meetings in one week between ex-lovers indicates more than just friendship. Were they still so attracted to one another that they simply could not bear to be apart? Were they still, in spite of everything, hoping to marry, or at least to establish some sort of permanent relationship?

Quite clearly, they could not. The situation was an impossible one. The harrowing scenario of two years before could hardly be played out a second time. Neither constitutionally nor ecclesiastically had anything changed. Hounded by the press and harassed, one may be sure, by the Palace, the couple had no option but to part once and for all. On 20 May they had their final meeting at Clarence House. 'Public curiosity killed our long and faithful attachment,' writes Townsend. 'That evening, Princess Margaret and I, warmly, affectionately, said adieu.'[25] The parting is reported to have been particularly poignant. For it was now, and not, as is generally believed, in 1955, that Princess Margaret's love-affair with Peter Townsend ended.

The couple did not see each other again for more than thirty years. Then, as an old man, Peter Townsend came to lunch with Princess Margaret at Kensington Palace.

By the late 1950s, Queen Elizabeth II's reign was going through the first of its troughs. Once all that heady talk about 'New Elizabethans' had died down, and the hopes of a new dawn had been proved to be unfounded, a sense of disillusionment set in. The Suez débâcle of late 1956 underlined the continuing loss of national prestige. The Queen herself was criticized for the manner in which she selected a new Conservative Prime Minister to replace Sir Anthony Eden, whose health had been broken by the strain of Suez. Her choice of Harold Macmillan, on the advice of two elder statesmen, Lord Salisbury and Sir Winston Churchill, laid her open to the

RIGHT: Princess Margaret in June 1931, aged ten months
(*Marcus Adams, Camera Press*)

BELOW: 'Golden Age': the Duke and Duchess of York with their daughters, Princess Elizabeth and Princess Margaret, 1931
(*Marcus Adams, Camera Press*)

RIGHT: Already a beauty:
Princess Margaret as a toddler
(Marcus Adams, Camera Press)

BELOW: The York family and
their dogs photographed
outside 'The Little House' at
Royal Lodge, Windsor, 1936
(Camera Press)

The King's daughters: Princess Elizabeth and Princess Margaret
(Marcus Adams, Camera Press)

ABOVE: The Queen watching the eleven-year-old Princess Margaret and the fifteen-year-old Princess Elizabeth at a dress rehearsal for the 1941 Christmas pantomime, *Cinderella*, at Windsor
(Camera Press)

LEFT: Princess Margaret in her Girl Guide uniform in Windsor Great Park, 1942
(Camera Press)

ABOVE: 'The Firm': the royal family in the gardens of Government House, Cape Town, 1947
(Author's Collection)

LEFT: The princesses in the locomotive of the White Train in South Africa
(Author's Collection)

FAR LEFT: The elegant, twenty-one-year-old Princess Margaret attending a fashion show in London
(Fox Photos, London)

ABOVE: Princess Margaret and Peter Townsend photographed leaving Windsor Castle two months before the news of their secret romance leaked out
(Popperfoto)

LEFT: Peter Townsend soon after his banishment to Brussels, 1953
(Camera Press)

A few hours after meeting Peter Townsend, for the first time in over two years,
Princess Margaret attended the premiere of the Hemingway film, *A Farewell to Arms*.
She was said to be looking far happier and more radiant than for a long time past

(Camera Press)

An official portrait by Cecil Beaton, to mark the Princess's visit to the West Indies, 1958
(Cecil Beaton, Camera Press)

The lovers: Princess Margaret and Antony Armstrong-Jones
(Camera Press)

ABOVE: Family gathering: Princess Margaret, Prince Charles, Prince Philip and Lord Snowdon, 1961
(Judy Appelbee, Alpha)

LEFT: Lord Snowdon with Princess Margaret holding their daughter in her arms. Lady Sarah Armstrong-Jones was born on 1 May 1964 at Kensington Palace
(Alpha)

ABOVE: 'A surprisingly successful mother': Princess Margaret with her children
Sarah and David, 1975 *(Alpha)*

BELOW: Three generations: Lady Sarah Armstrong-Jones, Princess Margaret and
the Queen Mother, at Badminton, 1976 *(Jayne Fincher, Photographers International)*

LEFT: In the gardens of
Les Jolies-Eaux, Mustique
(Alpha)

BELOW: The Princess by her
swimming pool on Mustique.
After visiting Mustique
during their honeymoon,
Lord Snowdon did not set
foot on the island again
(Alpha)

ABOVE: Royal triumvirate: the Queen Mother, Princess Margaret and the Queen, 1973
(Alpha)

BELOW: With the Queen Mother on the way to Prince Andrew's wedding
at Westminster Abbey, 1986
(Terry Fincher, Photographers International)

RIGHT: Looking splendid in green, Princess Margaret attends Royal Ascot, 1990
(Jayne Fincher, Photographers International)

BELOW: Princess Margaret and Lord Snowdon with the bridesmaids at the wedding of Lady Sarah Armstrong-Jones to Daniel Chatto, 1994
(Chancellor, Alpha)

Princess Margaret dancing
with Billy Wallace to whom
she was briefly, unofficially,
engaged
(Topperfoto)

LEFT: The Princess on
duty: opening a Church o
England school in Londo
(Camera Press)

RIGHT: Princess Margaret
setting off from Clarence
House for her wedding
on 6 May 1960
(Camera Press)

LEFT: The resplendent Princess, followed by Lord Snowdon, arrives at the Georgian Ball at the Mansion House *(Popperfoto)*

BELOW: Happy family: Princes Margaret, Lord Snowdon, Viscount Linley and Lady Sarah Armstrong-Jones pose in their latest car *(Tom Murray, Camera Press)*

RIGHT: The Snowdons with, among others, Paul Newman and Shirley MacLaine, at Universal Studios in Hollywood *(Walter Fischer, Camera Press)*

ABOVE: 'They were poets': Princess Margaret and The Beatles *(Popperfoto)*

LEFT: The ill-fated Robin Douglas-Home with whom Princess Margaret exchanged passionate love letters *(Rex Features)*

RIGHT: A photograph which seemed to bear out rumours of a rift between 'the highest paid performing dwarfs in Europe' *(Roger Garwood, Camera Press)*

The Princess in conversation with Peter Sellers, another of the men with whom
she was said to be romantically linked

(Popperfoto)

Roddy Llewellyn, the young man who revived the Princess's interest in life and provided the tabloids with headlines which considerably damaged her reputation

(Charles de la Court, Camera Press)

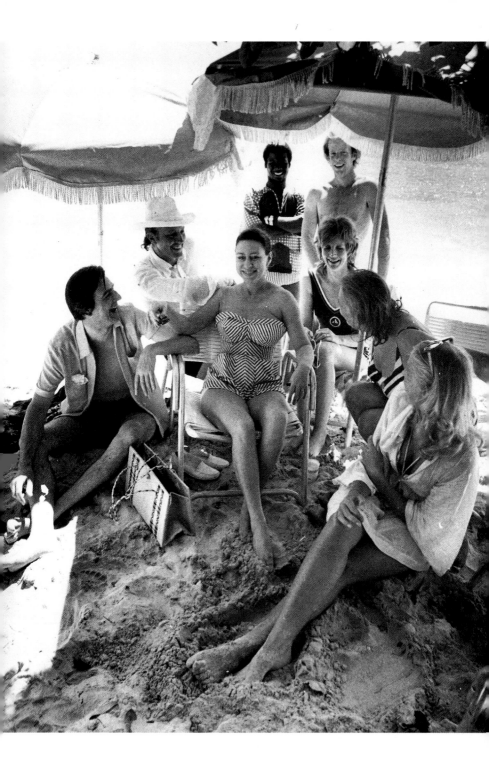

Princess Margaret holding court on Mustique with, from left to right, Dominic Elliot,
Colin Tennant, Princess Margaret, Basil Charles (of 'Basil's Bar'), Nicholas Courtney,
Anne Tennant, Judy Gendell and Bridget Sinclair

(Patrick Lichfield, Camera Press)

'The Sultan of Mustique': Colin Tennant, later Lord Glenconner
(Patrick Lichfield, Camera Press)

ABOVE: Not always eye-to-eye: the Queen and Princess Margaret at Windsor
(Srdja Dukanovic, Camera Press)

RIGHT: Masked but unmistakable, the Princess at a charity ball
with Norman Lonsdale
(Alan Davidson, Camera Press)

ABOVE: In spite of a lung cancer scare, Princess Margaret continues to smoke 'resolutely'
(Srdja Djukanovic, Camera Press)

LEFT: The Princess about to board the launch which will carry her back to *Britannia* during a Scottish holiday
(Glenn Harvey, Camera Press)

Often referred to as 'the Princess Diana of her day', Princess Margaret
with Diana, Princess of Wales

(Srdja Djukanovic, Camera Press)

accusation that she was too much under the influence of the old aristocratic order.

With Britain on the threshold of the 'Swinging Sixties', Elizabeth II did indeed seem to belong to an age that was passing. Her matronly clothes, her staid manner, her country interests, her colourless speeches, her schoolgirlish voice – all came in for censure. She was accused of having no intellectual or cultural tastes; of being entirely lacking in personal magnetism. She was surrounded, it was claimed, by a tweedy, conventional, hopelessly old-fashioned entourage. The Court, as Lord Altrincham put it in his celebrated tirade against the monarchy in the *National and English Review* of August 1957, 'has remained a tight little enclave of English ladies and gentlemen'.[26] Writing, he implied, more in sorrow than in anger, Altrincham regretted that the Queen was not taking advantage of her unique position to establish herself as a more assertive, articulate and enlightened personality. His views were widely echoed by several others, including the influential journalist and television commentator, Malcolm Muggeridge. Letters to the *Daily Mirror* showed that four correspondents agreed with Lord Altrincham to every one that did not; a poll for the same newspaper revealed a majority in favour of a less exclusive, less traditionally based Royal Household. It was even suggested that the Queen might be a bit too sedate for her more dashing husband. There were rumours of a rift between the couple, rumours which seemed confirmed when the Duke of Edinburgh set off on a four-month voyage in *Britannia* in the autumn of 1956. The Duke's answer to journalistic speculation about his married life was characteristic. 'Those bloody lies that you people print to make money,' he stormed.[27] (Princess Margaret's comment on frequent press reporting of 'royal rifts' – such as those between herself and the Queen – is equally characteristic. 'In our family we do not have "rifts",' she says. 'A very occasional row, but never a rift.'[28])

Out of this particular wave of public disillusionment, Princess Margaret emerged relatively unscathed. Whatever criticism she might have come in for, it was not for being old-fashioned; on the contrary, she was invariably described as 'the modern Princess'. The general public was unaware of her less admirable character traits; she remained, in the eyes of the majority of her sister's subjects, a beautiful princess who had sacrificed love for duty – a prime victim of the Palace's outdated attitudes.

Whereas, because of their conventional images, the Queen and her husband were now satirically referred to by the magazine *Private Eye* as 'Brenda' and 'Keith', Princess Margaret was given the nickname which seemed to capture best her brittle vivacity – 'Yvonne'. She could certainly be relied upon to bring a breath of fresh air into stuffy royal and official functions. The Queen, in an effort to meet some of the criticism of her exclusive way of life, initiated a few modest changes. She began to give small informal luncheon parties to which she invited the sort of people to whom she would not normally have a chance of speaking: newspaper editors, actors, clergymen, headmasters, businessmen, writers, industrialists. On these occasions, Princess Margaret proved invaluable. Unlike her reserved and conventional sister, she knew exactly what to say to people in the arts. She was sharp, witty, a good raconteuse.

Another break with the past came with the abolition of the long-established presentation parties at which hundreds of well-born or well-heeled debutantes would file past the Queen as part of their 'coming out' – the expression for a girl's being officially launched into society by way of the London 'Season'. By the late 1950s these socially divisive presentation parties had begun to strike an extremely false note in Britain's increasingly egalitarian society. To replace them, the number of royal garden parties was raised. At these less formal, and less class-based occasions, the Queen was again able to meet a much wider cross-section of people. With some eight thousand guests being invited to these three garden parties in the grounds of Buckingham Palace (and one at Holyroodhouse in Edinburgh) the Queen, trailing a selection of her relations – the men in morning dress, the women in flowered hats and chiffons – could exchange a few words with members of the public who had been invited because of their contribution to national life rather than because of their social status.

Here, too, Princess Margaret's presence proved a great boon. The brusqueness which was to characterize her public appearances in later life was not yet evident; admittedly, her air was often one of conscious *noblesse oblige* but, like her mother, she had an ease of manner which her less outgoing, and less articulate, sister so conspicuously lacked.

By now, there was talk of the Princess's social talents being put to better use; even some wild speculation that she might be given a governorship in the West Indies. In April 1958 she was again dispatched to the Caribbean: this time to represent the Queen at the inauguration of the Parliament of the newly created Federation of the West Indies. Although this somewhat shaky structure, designed to knit together various diverse and complex political strands, was destined to be short-lived, Princess Margaret approached the task conscientiously. She studied Foreign Office documents, acquainted herself with leading Caribbean political personalities, and listened to what the Under-Secretary of State for the Colonies, John Profumo, who was to accompany her, had to say.

Certainly she carried off the opening ceremony with great aplomb. In a gold-embroidered and lavishly beaded dress of white satin, and with a tiara glittering in her dark hair, she read the Queen's Speech from a throne set on a dais in the Legislative Chamber in Port of Spain, Trinidad. Everyone agreed that she did it beautifully. She even laid the ghost of a royal 'colour bar' by insisting on dancing – while in British Guiana (now Guyana), which she visited after Trinidad and British Honduras (now Belize) – with all the black officers of a volunteer regiment. And she kept on dancing until two in the morning.

Now hailed as 'Britain's Ambassadress', and apparently fulfilling the role as successfully as had her Uncle David, when Prince of Wales, in a previous generation, Princess Margaret was launched on a series of foreign visits. In July 1958 she attended the centenary celebrations of the founding of British Columbia, Canada, and then embarked on an extensive tour of that vast country. Two months later she was in Belgium for the Brussels Exposition. A visit to Rome allowed her to see her old friend Judy Montagu, now married to the American writer and art critic, Milton Gendel, and living in the Italian capital, and to sample, if not exactly *la dolce vita*, something of the warmth and vivacity of Italian life, to which she became increasingly attracted. On an official visit to Portugal she was wildly acclaimed; the tour producing a felicitous moment when a crowd of enthusiastic male students – latter-day Sir Walter Raleghs – flung their jackets to the ground to make a 'carpet of honour' for her to set her small, high-heeled shoes on.

If that was one side of the coin, another is shown by the writer Nancy Mitford, who attended a dinner in Princess Margaret's honour in Paris in April 1959. In a letter to her mother, Lady Redesdale, she had some characteristically acerbic comments to make about the Princess's appearance and behaviour. 'Dinner was at 8.30 and *at* 8.30 Princess Margaret's hairdresser arrived, so we waited for hours while he concocted a ghastly coiffure. She looked like a huge ball of fur on two well-developed legs. Shortest dress I ever saw – a Frenchman said it begins so low and ends so soon. In fact the whole appearance was excessively common.' The letter goes on to complain that the Princess looked 'cross', that she clearly 'didn't care about a rather pompous dinner party', and that she had already annoyed her previous hosts by 'suddenly chucking their luncheon'. 'Altogether she has not left a good impression and *France-Soir* mentioned the word *maussade* [sullen].'[29]

Nancy Mitford's opinion was echoed by the Princess's hostess, Lady Jebb, wife of the British Ambassador in Paris. The Ambassadress was appalled by what she described as her royal guest's flagrant behaviour. In her diary, Lady Jebb noted the Princess's rudeness, churlishness and inconsiderateness. She would ignore anyone whom she found boring, she made imperious demands, she was furious when the audience at a private theatrical performance did not rise when she entered. Faced with the prospect of what she had decided was to be a dreary lunch party, the Princess pretended to have a cold. This did not prevent her from having her hair done by Alexandre and a dress fitted by Dior. The trouble with the Princess, decided the Ambassadress, was that she insisted on being treated as a princess without being prepared to shoulder the responsibilities of being one.

It was Princess Margaret's unpredictability, grumbled one courtier's wife on another occasion, that made her so unpopular. She was 'nice one day and nasty the next. She was the only one who would come up to you at a party and really talk to you – but the next day she'd cut you. She antagonized her friends with her tricks, being horrid to their wives. She'd come up to a man and get him to dance with her, cutting out his wife. . . .'[30]

In August 1959 Princess Margaret turned twenty-nine. This, by the conventions of the period, was considered a particularly significant age for a woman. Thirty was especially late for a princess to be unmarried. Was Princess Margaret, in spite of her beauty, vivacity and eligibility, destined to remain a spinster? Perhaps there was some truth in the persistent rumour that she and Townsend had made solemn promises not to marry anyone else.

The answer came that October. While at Balmoral, Princess Margaret had a letter from Peter Townsend to tell her that he had fallen in love with a nineteen-year-old Belgian heiress called Marie-Luce Jamagne and that they planned to marry later that year. The unexpected news seems to have jolted the Princess into a decision. With her at Balmoral was the photographer Antony Armstrong-Jones, of whom she was very fond and who was only too ready to marry her. 'I received a letter from Peter in the morning and that evening I decided to marry Tony. It was no coincidence,' the Princess is alleged to have told Jonathan Aitken, the Conservative Member of Parliament, many years later.[31]

Perhaps her decision was not quite as unpremeditated as that. But two months later, in December 1959, the very month in which Peter Townsend married Marie-Luce Jamagne, Princess Margaret became privately engaged to Antony Armstrong-Jones.

CHAPTER THIRTEEN

Antony Armstrong-Jones

CONTRARY TO WHAT HAS OFTEN BEEN CLAIMED, Princess Margaret first met Antony Armstrong-Jones on 20 February 1958, only a month before Peter Townsend arrived back from his round-the-world journey. Nor was it until after the Princess and Townsend had parted for the last time, towards the end of May 1958, that the photographer began to feature in her life.

Antony Armstrong-Jones was presented to the Princess at a small dinner party given by Lady Elizabeth Cavendish in Cheyne Walk, Chelsea. Princess Margaret's ladies-in-waiting were always particularly intelligent women and Lady Elizabeth, with her strong artistic and intellectual interests, was more intelligent than most. Armstrong-Jones had taken the photographs for the revue *Cranks*, with which Lady Elizabeth had been associated. At the time of their first meeting, Tony Armstrong-Jones was twenty-seven, just five months older than Princess Margaret. Like her, he was small, only 5 feet 7 inches tall, and physically very attractive: slightly built, fair-haired, blue-eyed, with an engagingly toothy grin. His air was animated and energetic, and his manners charming. Astute beyond his years, he seems to have treated the Princess with just the right blend of deference and daring. She, who responded so eagerly to anything new, found him refreshingly different.

He belonged to a milieu that was part-aristocratic, part-bohemian. Born in London on 7 March 1930, he was the son of a barrister, Ronald Armstrong-Jones. His mother had been Anne Messel, daughter of Lieutenant-Colonel Leonard Messel, and sister of Oliver Messel, the celebrated theatrical designer. When the boy was four, his parents divorced. His beautiful mother then married Michael Parsons, Earl of Rosse, whose romantic good looks had earned him the title of 'the Adonis of the peerage'. As the Countess of Rosse, Anne now became the mistress of Castle Birr in County Offaly, Ireland, and of Womersley Park in South Yorkshire. His father's subsequent marriages were rather less illustrious. Ronald Armstrong-Jones first married a divorced Australian actress, Carol Coombe, and then an air hostess, Jenifer Unite. So, by a supreme irony, Princess Margaret, who had been forced to renounce the once-divorced Peter Townsend, was about to involve herself with a man whose parents and former stepmother could chalk up four divorces and seven marriages between them.

From Sandroyd preparatory school in Wiltshire, young Armstrong-Jones went to Eton. Neither academically nor on the sporting field did he show any promise. 'Maybe he's interested in some subject,' sighed one exasperated master, 'but it's not a subject we teach here.'[1] In any case, an attack of polio, which entailed a ninety-minute emergency dash from his father's home in North Wales to a hospital in Liverpool, and a year-long confinement to a wheelchair, severely interrupted the young man's education. The illness left him with one leg slightly shorter than the other.

Despite this setback, he managed to gain admittance to Jesus College, Cambridge, to read natural sciences. He apparently showed no great aptitude for this particular branch of study, either, and so switched to architecture. When this, in turn, proved fruitless, he decided to devote his energies to the one subject which did interest him – photography. Since boyhood, Armstrong-Jones had been an avid, if generally unappreciated, photographer and at Cambridge he was given his first opportunity when his shots began to appear in *Varsity*, an undergraduate newspaper. From here he progressed to taking photographs for various society magazines; and while pictures of the upper crust at hunt balls and point-to-points are hardly the stuff of great photography, they did bring him professional status.

Another field in which he proved himself while at Cambridge was rowing. Weighing only just over eight-and-a-half stone, he coxed the college rowing eight, and in 1950 he steered the Cambridge eight to a three-and-a-half length victory in that year's Oxford and Cambridge Boat Race. This particular race revealed a certain steeliness in his nature: when at one point the Oxford eight came too close to the Cambridge one, Armstrong-Jones astonished his rival cox by yelling, 'Why don't you fucking move over!'[2] The Oxford boat moved over.

The young man's language would have come as no surprise to those who had had dealings with him. 'He had,' remembers one of his contemporaries, 'a very bad reputation in the village [where his father lived] and was up to all sorts of oafish tricks. He was a terror at parties. He once tipped some jelly down the front of a young woman's beautiful new lilac evening dress. She was devastated but he found it highly amusing.'[3]

Although his mother, the Countess of Rosse, strongly disapproved of her son's proposed abandonment of architecture for photography ('Do not agree suggestion changing career,' she telegraphed in answer to his letter [4]), there was really no choice. Having failed the architectural examinations, he was in any case obliged to go down without a degree. He found his father more amenable. Appreciating that his son was determined to become a photographer, Ronald Armstrong-Jones stumped up the fee necessary for him to join the studio of Baron, one of the most fashionable society portrait photographers of the day. (Baron, much to the annoyance of his rival, Cecil Beaton, was highly thought of by the Duke of Edinburgh.) After six months, Tony Armstrong-Jones – again with financial help from his father – set up his own studio, first in Shaftesbury Avenue and then at 20 Pimlico Road. By taking advantage of his various aristocratic and university connections, and by the exercise of his own considerable talent, he soon established himself as one of London's most successful young photographers. He was especially interested in theatrical photography, but became equally well known for his atmospheric studies of such diverse subjects as Covent Garden porters, pub interiors, firemen at work, housewives queueing for food.

He was also ready to turn his hand to the more lucrative worlds of fashion and advertising. His small, stylishly dressed figure was to be seen in such smart West End advertising agencies as the J. Walter Thompson Company and in the offices of *Tatler*, *Vogue* and *Queen* – this last magazine having been bought, as a twenty-fifth birthday present to himself, by Armstrong-Jones's Eton and Cambridge friend, Jocelyn Stevens, the millionaire nephew of Sir Edward Hulton.

From here, Tony Armstrong-Jones progressed into the infinitely grander world of royal photography. In 1956 he photographed the young Duke of Kent and, the following year, was commissioned to take pictures of the Queen's children, Prince Charles and Princess Anne, and then of the Queen and the Duke of Edinburgh themselves. Once again, Cecil Beaton's jealousy was aroused. 'I don't think A. A. Jones's pictures are at all interesting,' he wrote of these royal portraits, 'but his publicity value is terrific. It pays to be new in the field.' It certainly did. Within a couple of years, Beaton was obliged to admit that Armstrong-Jones was enjoying

enormous success and indeed deserved it for his photographs were vital and he himself was a young man of great liveliness and a certain charm. The fact that he moved in the second-rate world of magazines and newspapers sullied him a great deal, but when I lunched with him in his studio basement I thought personally he survived with his freshness pretty well intact.[5]

This 'studio basement' was Tony Armstrong-Jones's Pimlico Road home. Wedged between the Sunlight Laundry and an antique shop, it consisted of a ground floor and a basement in a run-down block of Victorian flats. On the ground floor were his studio, his darkroom and his secretary's office (with a bed for guests shoved into a recess above the front door), and from here a spiral staircase, which he had designed himself, led down to his living quarters. His basement drawing room was decorated in an eclectic fashion: Aubusson carpets, Regency gilt furniture, a draped parachute and, against a wall, an antique bicycle. Most notable was the large looking-glass on which guests were asked to scratch their names, using a diamond.

Not unnaturally, his friends were an equally eclectic mixture, drawn as they were chiefly from the worlds of fashion, show business, the arts, advertising. Inevitably, many of his friends were gay: the columnist Nigel Dempster talks of the 'mainly male gatherings at No. 20', and quotes Princess Margaret as saying that the only reason she and Armstrong-Jones had been able to keep their love-affair secret for so long was 'because no one believed he was interested in women'. But 'whatever the stories', Dempster goes on to quote one of the photographer's friends as saying, 'there were always girls around Tony'.[6]

One of these girls, apparently, was a 'Eurasian beauty' whom Armstrong-Jones had photographed 'with a lighted candle in a strategic position'.[7] His secretary, Heather Crawford, is said to have been so shocked on accidentally developing these pictures that she resigned immediately. Another exotic-looking beauty with whom he was involved was Trinidad-born Jacqui Chan, the dancer who appeared in *Kismet*, *The Teahouse of the August Moon*, and *The World of Suzie Wong*. The relationship between the photographer and the dancer was close and attracted much comment, but any possibility of marriage was remote.

That possibility disappeared altogether once Antony Armstrong-Jones realized that his acquaintance with Princess Margaret could develop into something more serious. The young man, who has been described as an 'opportunist' with a 'calculating' charm, would have to have been exceptional not to have taken advantage of the dazzling opportunity which now presented itself.[8] In, one imagines, mounting excitement, he allowed himself to be cast into what Cecil Beaton – envious almost beyond speech – later described as 'this Cinderella-in-reverse' role.[9]

'He was such a nice person in those days,' said Princess Margaret in later life. 'He understood my job and pushed me to do things. In a way he introduced me to a new world.'[10]

Antony Armstrong-Jones's Pimlico Road studio was certainly a new world to Princess Margaret. Although always careful, in these early days, to address her as 'Ma'am' and to treat her with due respect, he gradually drew the Princess into his relatively unorthodox style of life. In his company, she felt, she says, 'daring'. After her long succession of blue-blooded escorts (and even Peter Townsend was a highly conventional man) she found Tony Armstrong-Jones delightfully nonconformist. She was intrigued by his casual clothes, his informal manners, his extrovert behaviour, his outspoken opinions, his irreverent attitudes. Here was a man who could discuss, quite naturally, the things in which she was interested: the ballet (she was President of the Royal Ballet Company), the theatre, stage design, interior decoration. As he was equally interested in clothes, he was quite unselfconscious about helping her design her dresses. In turn, he would ask for her advice about his work. In this he was not simply being diplomatic; he valued her opinion.

Evidence of Armstrong-Jones's high regard for the Princess's taste and intelligence comes from the writer, Kingsley Amis. At some time in 1958, the writer was to be featured in an article entitled 'Top Talkers' in *Queen* magazine. During a preliminary meeting to discuss the project, at which Armstrong-Jones, who was to take the photographs, was also present, the editor suggested that a colour picture of Princess Margaret, captioned 'Top Inspirer', be used to head the article. Both Amis and Armstrong-Jones, though for different reasons, objected to the idea. At that stage, of course, the still-burgeoning affair between the Princess and the photographer was a well-kept secret. Meeting Amis some time later, Armstrong-Jones asked him why he had objected to the Princess's photograph being used. 'Well,' answered Amis, 'just that the woman obviously has no mind at all. . . . I just thought that she didn't fit in very well with some of the people in the article in *Queen*. That's all.' To which the photographer replied: 'I can assure you you're quite wrong. She is in fact an extremely intelligent and well-informed woman.'[11]

Because Princess Margaret was determined that her developing relationship with Antony Armstrong-Jones be kept from the public, she could not risk too many visits to 20 Pimlico Road. Fortunately the press, assuming that he was involved with Jacqui Chan and that, as a mere photographer, he was hardly likely to be a candidate for the Princess's affections, paid them no attention. Moreover, whenever he visited Clarence House, it was usually as one of a party of friends. But there was one place where the two of them could meet unobserved – at 59 Rotherhithe Street, a small terraced house in Bermondsey, backing on to the Thames, where Armstrong-Jones had a room.

The house, set among the warehouses, council flats and pubs of this dockland area, was owned by a journalist, William Glenton, who had agreed to let the ground-floor room to Armstrong-Jones. The young man immediately set about making the large room habitable. He whitewashed the walls, scrubbed the beams and built simple pine cupboards, then furnished the place with pieces bought in local antique and junk shops and laid rush matting on the floor. (The lavatory, however, had to be shared with the landlord.) By March 1959, having broken permanently with Jacqui Chan, Armstrong-Jones felt confident enough of Princess Margaret to invite her to his Rotherhithe hideaway. Only after the news of their engagement had broken, almost a year later, did the press refer – with customary lack of originality – to his Bermondsey room as a 'love nest'.

To the Princess, it became 'the little white room' – a deliciously strange and romantic spot. 'It had the most marvellous view,' she remembers. 'One walked into the room and there was the river straight in front. At high tide swans looked in. And because it was on the bend of the river, you looked towards the Tower and Tower Bridge with the dome of St Paul's behind them, to the left, and the docks to the right.'[12]

Sometimes among friends, sometimes alone with Tony Armstrong-Jones, Princess Margaret could now play at *la vie simple*: eating shepherd's pie cooked by her lover, drinking cheap wine from the local off-licence, washing the dishes in the small sink. The couple addressed each other as 'pet' and 'love'. For months Armstrong-Jones's landlord remained unaware of the identity of his tenant's headscarfed and dark-spectacled visitor. Only the occasional presence of one of the Princess's ladies-in-waiting, arriving the next day to 'tidy up' (there were limits to the Princess's yearning for simplicity), and the fact that a superior brand of violet-tinted lavatory paper would suddenly come into use, aroused his suspicions.

Not everyone shared Princess Margaret's conception of the simple life, for what may have seemed like casual bohemian evenings to her were regarded as distinctly formal occasions by Armstrong-Jones's other friends. 'These evenings were rather stilted and stiff ...' wrote one of them. 'She wasn't at ease at the time, and nor was anyone else much. There were awkward questions of protocol – no one was supposed to leave before the Princess, which, as I was rehearsing early, was impossible for me. . . . I didn't enjoy them and soon stopped attending.'[13]

The couple's visits to Rotherhithe continued even after their marriage. The tie between the two of them seems to have been intensely physical. 'What he had foremost in common with Princess Margaret could be put in three words,' claims another of Tony Armstrong-Jones's friends, 'sex, sex, sex. Theirs was a terribly physical relationship, they couldn't keep their hands off each other, even with other people present. . . . He was very well made and obviously that had a lot to do with it.'[14]

* * *

But just as Princess Margaret was being drawn into Antony Armstrong-Jones's world, so, to an even greater extent, was he being drawn into hers. By the early summer of 1959, the Queen and the Queen Mother were aware of the Princess's deepening relationship with the photographer. Swallowing hard, they accepted the situation. Although it was not what they might have hoped for, after all the traumas of the Townsend affair they could hardly voice any objections. The Queen Mother, in fact, was rather taken with Armstrong-Jones; he was just the sort of lively, artistic, engagingly mannered young man that she liked.

One consequence of this growing royal approval was that he was invited to Royal Lodge to take a series of official photographs of Princess Margaret to mark her twenty-ninth birthday. 'I've been faithless to you,' she admitted to Cecil Beaton, on meeting him one day that summer, after she had sat for Armstrong-Jones. 'I knew at once that she meant that she had had her photograph taken by T.A.J.,' noted Beaton in his diary. 'This was a blow, but I thought it extremely honest and frank to tell me before the pictures appeared. I showed great tact by muttering, "I'm so glad. He's such a nice young man and deserves his success. If I have to have a rival, I'm glad it's him and not Baron."'[15]

But Cecil Beaton did not, at this stage, suspect that there was anything between sitter and photographer. And nor, when the pictures were published that August, did the press. Almost miraculously, the affair remained secret.

That autumn, the Queen invited Antony Armstrong-Jones to Balmoral. This annual Deeside sojourn was the supreme test for any prospective royal consort. If such a guest were a lover of the hearty outdoors life, then well and good; if not, his stay could be a form of torture. Try as he might, the photographer simply could not fit into the pattern. Being of Welsh descent, he was at least spared the kilt, but he tended to look even more out of place in his modish corduroy jackets and sharply brimmed caps. Only in the company of Princess Margaret did Armstrong-Jones seem completely at ease; cameras slung about their necks, the two of them would wander around taking innumerable photographs.

It was in October 1959, during the course of this Balmoral holiday, that Princess Margaret received the letter from Peter Townsend telling her that he was going to marry Marie-Luce

Jamagne. She regarded the news, she afterwards claimed, 'as a betrayal of an understanding that they had reached "concerning remarriage after divorce"'.[16] That same afternoon, while she and Armstrong-Jones were out walking, the Princess told him about Townsend's letter. Appreciating that her companion would now understand that she was free of any obligation to Townsend, and knowing that he wanted to marry her, the Princess none the less asked him not to propose. 'I didn't really want to marry at all,' she claimed many years later. 'Why did I? Because he asked me.'[17] Apparently Armstrong-Jones made his proposal in what she called 'a roundabout way'; 'It was very cleverly worded,' she added cryptically.[18]

Why, then, did Princess Margaret accept Antony Armstrong-Jones's proposal, having specifically asked him not to make one? Her motives were mixed. Although she later admitted that her acceptance, coming so soon after receiving the news of Townsend's impending marriage, was 'no coincidence', she also denied that she became engaged to the photographer 'on the rebound'. She was undoubtedly fond of him, she found him physically attractive, she was excited by his unconventional style of life, she shared many of his interests and enthusiasms. And, at the age of twenty-nine, with most of the other members of her circle married, she could not delay much longer.

There was another reason. 'Disobedience,' the Princess once told Jean Cocteau, 'is my joy!', and there was an element of this in her acceptance.[19] Antony Armstrong-Jones was a far cry from the sort of foreign princeling or landed aristocrat whom she would have been expected to marry. By choosing this somewhat unexpected candidate, she was thumbing her nose at tradition, underlining her reputation for being rebellious, emancipated, individual. Having kept the affair secret from the press was one triumph; having made so daring and unorthodox a choice was an even greater one.

The couple became privately engaged in December. The ring was a ruby surrounded by diamonds in the shape of a flower. Those who wondered how Armstrong-Jones could possibly have afforded so expensive a ring did not appreciate how successful he was in his photographic career; his work was to command even higher prices once his engagement to Princess Margaret became public. It was not until the following month – January 1960 – that he obtained the

Queen's formal consent. By then the royal family, with that clock-work regularity which ruled their lives, was at Sandringham. Even at this stage, an excuse had to be found to explain away, should the ever-curious press become interested, the young man's visit to Nor-folk. On the pretext of presenting to the Queen a new design for a pergola to house a statue of Buddha in the gardens of the house, Antony Armstrong-Jones – armed with a scale model – arrived at Sandringham one January morning. Having been kept waiting for a couple of hours, he was summoned, still clutching his model, into the Queen's presence. Here he asked for, and was granted, permis-sion to marry Princess Margaret. The Queen Mother, Prince Philip and the Princess herself then trooped in, ostensibly to view the model, but in fact to indulge in a flurry of congratulations. The model was never again mentioned.

As the thirty-three-year-old Queen Elizabeth II was then preg-nant for the third time, it was decided to postpone any announce-ment of the engagement until after the new royal baby had been born. The family returned to London at the end of January, and on 19 February 1960 the Queen gave birth to a boy, later christened Andrew Albert Christian Edward. Not until a week later, on 26 Feb-ruary 1960, was the engagement announced.

It is with the greatest pleasure that Queen Elizabeth the Queen Mother announces the betrothal of her beloved daughter The Princess Margaret to Mr Antony Charles Robert Armstrong-Jones, son of Mr R.O.L. Armstrong-Jones Q.C., and the Countess of Rosse, to which union the Queen has glad-ly given her consent.

The couple spent the weekend of the announcement at Royal Lodge, where the enthusiastic press and movie cameramen were allowed to record their comings and goings. Both very simply and neatly dressed, they might almost have been any young couple cel-ebrating their engagement. But as soon as this session was over, Armstrong-Jones, who had already slipped out of 20 Pimlico Road, was moved into Buckingham Palace. He remained there, firmly out of public reach, until his wedding day. From this point on, he was to be seen beside his fiancée in only the most socially acceptable of sit-uations: in white tie and tails in the royal box at the Royal Opera House, in trilby hat at the races at Newbury, in tweed suit at the Badminton Horse Trials. Hands clasped firmly behind his back, he had come to look like a carbon copy, in miniature, of Prince Philip, Duke of Edinburgh.

The news of Princess Margaret's engagement was received with astonished delight by the press and the general public. How gratifying that the bewitching Princess, cheated of her happiness with Peter Townsend, had found it at last with this man of the people. For, in its customary perverse way, the public both admired the bride-to-be for being royal, and her fiancé for being, not only a commoner, but a relatively humbly born commoner. There was, as *The Times* put it, 'no recent precedent for the marriage of one so near the Throne outside the ranks of international royalty and the British peerage'.[20] Even the left-wing *New Statesman* decided that the young man's qualification for becoming a member of the royal family had to be judged 'with a leniency which only a few years before would have been unthinkable'.[21] Not everyone displayed such 'leniency'. In aristocratic circles, the story was gleefully repeated of how, when Armstrong-Jones had come to take photographs at Wilton House, Lady Pembroke had made him eat his lunch in the servants' hall.

Suddenly, everyone was talking about, or claiming friendship with, Antony Armstrong-Jones. He was hailed as a photographic genius, a latter-day Michelangelo, a man of infinite talents. Acquaintances rushed into print with glowing tributes. 'Am I the only Fleet Street journalist,' demanded Sheila Logue in *Punch*, 'who isn't a personal friend of Antony Armstrong-Jones?'[22] One industrious genealogist even produced a family tree proving that the engaged couple were actually twelfth cousins twice removed, having a common ancestor in a certain Ievan of Bron y Foel.

But reaction to the match was not universally ecstatic. Armstrong-Jones's old friend, Jocelyn Stevens, one of the very few people to have been let into the secret of the couple's relationship ('there she was, grinning . . .' he said of his first astonished sight of the Princess in the Rotherhithe room), had all along considered the affair to be 'madness'. He appreciated that Princess Margaret was far too indulged and imperious, and Armstrong-Jones far too independent and assertive, for the thing to work. Now, in answer to his friend's telegram confirming the engagement, Stevens cabled back, 'Never has there been a more ill-fated assignment.'[23]

The prospective bridegroom's father, Ronald Armstrong-Jones, was equally apprehensive. Having just emphasized the chasm between the young couple's backgrounds by marrying, as his third wife, an air stewardess, Jenifer Unite, Ronald Armstrong-Jones was on honeymoon in Bermuda. 'I wish in heaven's name this hadn't happened,' he said. 'It will never work out. Tony's a far too independent sort of fellow to be subjected to discipline. He won't be prepared to play second fiddle to anyone. He will have to walk two steps behind his wife, and I fear for his future.'[24]

The envious Cecil Beaton pronounced Armstrong-Jones to be 'extremely nondescript, biscuit-complexioned, ratty and untidy'. The fact remained, he continued, that 'the young man is not worthy of this strange fluke [of] fortune, or misfortune, and because he is likeable and may become unhappy makes one all the sorrier.'[25]

Even within the royal family there was opposition. While the Queen and the Queen Mother resolutely closed their eyes to the possible future pitfalls, taking comfort in the fact that the young man seemed ready enough to adapt to their way of life, others were less tolerant. Noël Coward, visiting Princess Marina, Duchess of Kent, and her daughter, Princess Alexandra, noted what he called 'a distinct *froideur*' when he mentioned the engagement; 'They are not pleased.'[26] The Duchess of Kent, with her very Continental ideas about the exclusivity of royal families, considered it quite wrong for a king's daughter to be marrying a man who made his living by taking photographs.

From her Parisian exile, the Duchess of Windsor, so long spurned for not being good enough for the British royal family, wryly remarked that 'At least I'm keeping up with the Joneses.'[27]

Perhaps the doubters were right. Even at this early stage there were clashes between what were two very different styles of life. One Monday morning, as the couple were about to leave Royal Lodge to return to London, the Princess sat down on the drawing-room floor behind a high-backed sofa to sort through some records. Having made one pile, she rang for a footman to carry it out to the car. As the man crossed towards the door, Armstrong-Jones burst into the room. Not noticing the Princess behind the sofa, he said to the footman, 'I've been looking for you. Be a darling and . . .' At this, Princess Margaret leapt to her feet. 'Be a darling? What on earth do you mean, be a darling? Who are you talking to?' she demanded, in obvious fury. His explanation, that he was simply using an expression used widely in theatrical circles, seems not to have satisfied her. This was not the way one addressed a royal servant. 'You may go,' snapped the Princess to the embarrassed footman.[28]

Further evidence of these conflicting standards of behaviour came in March 1960. By then the wedding date had been set for Friday, 6 May. ('Marry in May and rue the day,' came a less than helpful piece of advice from one of the Princess's 'well-wishers'.[29]) Tony Armstrong-Jones had chosen as his best man – or 'groomsman' in royal circles – his friend Jeremy Fry, a member of the wealthy chocolate-manufacturing family. Soon after their engagement had been announced, the Princess and her fiancé had spent a Sunday with Fry and his wife in their beautiful William and Mary house, Widcombe Manor, in Bath. Also present for a large luncheon party was another of Fry's friends, Cecil Beaton. Beside the 'young men with long hair and jeans, young women with equally long hair and sweaters', Princess Margaret looked 'exquisitely pink and white and her hair was chic enough to differentiate her from the others,' noted Beaton.[30]

No sooner had it been announced that Jeremy Fry would be the best man than rumours began circulating about his conviction for a homosexual offence eight years before. By 6 April, one month before the wedding, he was obliged to announce that he was suffering from an attack of jaundice and would therefore be unable to act as best man. The fact that he had just returned from a skiing holiday, looking fit and tanned, did nothing to dispel public scepticism.

With Fry out of the running, it was hoped that another of Armstrong-Jones's friends, Jeremy Thorpe, might fill the vacancy. Thorpe, the future leader of the Liberal Party, had always joked that his greatest ambition was to marry Princess Margaret. Taking no chances this time, the Special Branch made discreet enquiries into Thorpe's sexual history. Conducted by the Chief Constable of Devon, Lieutenant-Colonel Ranulph Bacon (known, with heavy-handed police humour, as 'Streaky'), the investigation uncovered the same 'homosexual tendencies' which had rendered Fry unsuitable.[31] So Thorpe, too, was quickly dropped.

Eventually, from a shortlist of five, Armstrong-Jones chose Dr Roger Gilliatt, son of a former Surgeon-Gynaecologist to the Queen who, if not exactly an intimate friend of the prospective bride-groom, was at least an undeniably heterosexual one.

These homosexual flurries would not have bothered Princess Margaret unduly. As a worldly and uncensorious young woman, gay-ness was something with which she was quite at ease. Royal house-holds were always packed with gay servants; they tended to value the prestige of working for the royal family above the meagre wages. The theatrical and ballet circles in which the Princess moved were liberally peopled by gays. The Queen Mother had a penchant for cultured and amusing homosexual men; both she and Princess Margaret felt entirely comfortable in the company of people like Cecil Beaton, Norman Hartnell, Noël Coward, even Tony Armstrong-Jones's uncle, Oliver Messel. One of Princess Margaret's uncles, her mother's favourite brother, David Bowes-Lyon, was bisexual. So it would have been public reaction to the homosexuality of Fry and Thorpe, rather than the homosexual revelations themselves, that would have proved embarrassing to Princess Margaret.

Further embarrassments came when, one by one, invitations to the wedding were turned down by members of the various royal houses of Europe. It is difficult to believe that so many of them – Queen Juliana and Crown Princess Beatrix of the Netherlands, King Olav and Crown Prince Harald of Norway, King Gustaf VI Adolf of Sweden, King Baudouin of the Belgians, King Paul and Queen Frederika of the Hellenes, even the Spanish Pretender, Don Juan and his wife – were all too busy to attend the wedding of the sister of the Queen of England. Of them all, only Queen Ingrid of Denmark, whose mother had been a British princess, accepted the invitation. Some of the excuses were suspiciously lame. The truth was that, for all their populist, bicycling images, many of the royal families of Europe still regarded themselves – as did Princess Mari-na – as part of an exclusive clan: princesses married princes, not photographers.

The divergence of interests between bride and groom was high-lighted during their visit to Westminster Abbey to discuss details of the ceremony with the Dean, Dr Eric Abbott. So steeped in reli-gious doctrine and royal ceremonial, Princess Margaret was deeply concerned with such things as the form of service, the address, the prayers and the hymns. Tony Armstrong-Jones, on the other hand, 'could not have cared less whether the service, as Margaret wanted, was based on the Prayer Book of 1662 (with which he was barely familiar) rather than on the 1928 version; whether she should promise to obey him or not, or whether there was to be a special blessing for the wedding ring.'[32] He did, though, feign a polite interest. Only when the Princess suggested the installation of television monitors so that the High Altar would be visible to the entire congregation, did he appear genuinely interested.

Among other arrangements discussed with the Dean, the Princess decided that, instead of the customary address, the Beatitudes should be read. In view of the many calumnies being spread about, the Ninth Beatitude seemed especially appropriate: 'Blessed are ye, when men shall revile you, and persecute you, and shall say all manner of evil against you falsely, for my sake.'[33] She might almost have taken it as one of the leitmotifs of her life.

But nothing could spoil the splendour of Princess Margaret's wedding on Friday, 6 May 1960. It was both modern, in that it was the first royal wedding to be televised, and traditional, in its pageantry. It was the last occasion on which all the royal women wore fully formal, floor-length dresses. In superb spring weather and escorted by a dazzlingly uniformed detachment of the Household Cavalry, the Princess set out from Clarence House in the Glass Coach. Sitting beside her was Prince Philip, who was to give her away. Through dense, cheering crowds and along streets lined with white silk banners bearing the couple's entwined initials, she drove to Westminster Abbey.

Her dress was a complete break with royal tradition. Hartnell, summoned to Clarence House to discuss the design, had been horrified to be presented with Armstrong-Jones's sketch of a dress of almost nun-like severity. Overcoming his disapproval, the couturier adapted the design, producing a simple, V-necked, long-sleeved, tight-waisted, enormous-skirted creation of white silk organza. The veil was equally simple and generous. The bride's unadorned dress was not only a fashion statement, but also a statement of her individuality. The only glitter came from her headdress. Known as the Poltimore Tiara, it was a high, elegantly designed, all-diamond diadem, which had been privately bought at auction for the Princess, for a sum rumoured to be £5,000. By contrast, the bridegroom, as though to underline his non-royal status, wore morning dress instead of the customary uniform. Standing side by side at the altar, both bride and groom looked small, *soigné*, strikingly attractive.

The ceremony was conducted, as always on these occasions, with clockwork precision. The eight child bridesmaids (which ensured that no attendant towered over the couple), included the bride's niece, the plump, nine-year-old Princess Anne. They behaved impeccably. Such surprises as there were could be found among the guests, of which there were more than two thousand: William Glenton, the bridegroom's Rotherhithe landlord; Betty Peabody, his Pimlico Street charwoman; the postman from his father's Welsh village. There was particular press interest in the bridegroom's 'three mothers', although only his true mother, the Countess of Rosse, was allowed a place opposite the royal family by the High Altar. She was judged by women reporters as 'after the bride, the most beautiful single figure of the occasion'.[34] Other guests reflected the couple's cultural interests: among them the actresses Margaret Leighton and Joyce Grenfell, and the writers Jean Cocteau and John Betjeman.

Princess Margaret, whose performance throughout the ceremony was very assured, made only one mistake, when, during the exchange of vows, she gave her response ahead of the Archbishop of Canterbury. Instead of repeating a phrase, she spoke the next one: 'For better, for worse'. Nothing, as things turned out, could have been less appropriate.

The ceremony over, there followed the triumphant drive back to Buckingham Palace in the Glass Coach, the wedding breakfast, and the usual hilarious scramble as the guests, led by the Queen and the Queen Mother, flung rose petals at the departing couple as they drove away in an open-topped Rolls-Royce. With the Princess looking radiant in yellow shantung, they passed through the clamorous, tightly packed streets of the City of London on their way to Battle Bridge Pier to join *Britannia*, which was to take them on their Caribbean honeymoon. As they boarded the barge that would carry them out to the Royal Yacht, the roar of the crowds was augmented by a deafening chorus of ships' sirens, church bells, whistles and hooters.

Noël Coward, watching the departure of *Britannia* on television, admitted that 'it was moving and romantic and the weather still held, and when the Tower Bridge opened and the yacht passed through with those two tiny figures waving from just below the bridge, I discovered, unashamedly and without surprise, that my eyes were full of tears.'[35]

PART FOUR

The Snowdons

CHAPTER 14

The Performing Dwarfs

It was while on honeymoon in the Caribbean that Princess Margaret first saw the island of Mustique, a place with which, before many years had passed, she was to become indelibly associated. The newly married couple were by then halfway through their six-week-long cruise aboard *Britannia*. With official receptions being kept to the minimum, they were able to laze away their days on sunlit, isolated beaches and their evenings reading and listening to records on deck or in their luxurious stateroom. Their every need was catered for: the Princess even had, in addition to her own maid, a personal hairdresser, Sylvia Davies, a talented junior from René's hairdressing salon.

Britannia arrived off Mustique, one of the Windward Islands, on 26 May 1960. The unspoilt island had recently been bought by Princess Margaret's long-standing friend, Colin Tennant, who is said to have paid £45,000 for it. Only three miles long and one and a half wide, it had previously been owned by two spinster sisters. It had a small indigenous population, but was without roads, water or, of course, electricity. Tennant's plan was to create an exclusive colony of holiday homes by selling off parcels of land to rich buyers. When Princess Margaret's engagement had been announced, he had asked her whether she would prefer, as a wedding present, 'something wrapped in a box from Asprey or a plot of land on Mustique'.[1] The Princess chose the land, so Tennant promised her a ten-acre plot worth £15,000. He and his wife, Lady Anne (a daughter of the Earl of Leicester), were waiting to welcome the honeymooning couple to the island.

Princess Margaret's first view of Mustique enchanted her. She eventually chose a plot on a headland overlooking the sparkling blue waters of Gelliceaux Bay, and later built on it an elegant house to which she gave the name Les Jolies-Eaux – the original French spelling of the bastardized local version, Gelliceaux. In time, Mustique was to become an earthly paradise to her – and, to her critics, a symbol of what they regarded as her louche way of life.

Colin Tennant had equal reason to be pleased with his gift to the Princess. The cachet which her presence gave to the island ensured that there was no lack of buyers for the rest of his plots. The place soon became eagerly sought after by the rich and the famous; there are now about fifty holiday homes, as well as a hotel, on Mustique. In 1977 Colin Tennant sold the entire island for undisclosed millions; certainly enough to allow him to spend £3 million on a coconut plantation on the neighbouring island of St Lucia, which he then proceeded to convert into yet another holiday haven.

Princess Margaret's enthusiasm for Mustique was not shared by her husband. For one thing, Armstrong-Jones seems to have doubted the altruism of Tennant's gesture, allegedly suspecting that the Princess's friend was only too aware of the commercial advantages that her presence on the island would bring. For another, the bridegroom may well have been jealous of Tennant, not only of his longstanding friendship with the Princess, but also of the fact that this rich, landed aristocrat was in a position to give her a £15,000 wedding present. 'I think his dislike of Colin Tennant began when he was asked to take his wedding photographs,' says one member of the Princess's circle (Tennant had married Lady Anne Coke in 1956). 'They treated him in a very offhand manner.'[2] Indeed, Princess Margaret, who attended the Tennant wedding, was not even aware of the fact that her future husband had been present. 'Did Tony take the photographs?' she asked, many years later.[3]

But whatever the reasons for his disapproval of Colin Tennant, Antony Armstrong-Jones never set foot on Mustique again.

Always considered extravagant, Princess Margaret would from this time on be criticized, almost continuously, for what was regarded as her reckless expenditure. The carping had started with her wedding. On her marriage, the Princess's annual allowance from the Civil List was raised to £15,000. As if that were not enough for her critics, hardly had *Britannia* sailed away to the Caribbean than questions were raised in Parliament about the cost of all this royal junketing. The wedding had entailed an outlay of £25,000, of which £16,000 alone had been spent on decorations along the route. The six-week-long honeymoon on *Britannia*, with her crew of 20 officers and 237 ratings, added another £40,000 to the nation's bill.

On the couple's return – in mid-June 1960 – they were given a home in Kensington Palace. This charming, harmonious red-brick palace, designed by Sir Christopher Wren for the joint sovereigns King William III and Queen Mary II, was divided into a number of houses and apartments of differing sizes. It was irreverently referred to as 'the Aunt Heap' because it had housed, over the decades, so many royal widows. The newly married couple were given No. 10, Kensington Palace, the house in which Alexander, Marquess of Carisbrooke, Queen Victoria's last surviving grandson, had lived for many years. Known in the family as 'Drino', this dressy, gossipy, bejewelled old figure had died, very conveniently, three months before Princess Margaret's wedding.

Not until £6,000 had been spent on the house, however, did the Princess feel that she could possibly move into it. The alterations were supervised by Armstrong-Jones himself, with most of the rooms being painted white. But although No. 10 (now the London home of Prince and Princess Michael of Kent) boasted ten principal rooms and numerous other smaller rooms and offices, Princess Margaret described it as 'a doll's house'.[4] It was, she felt, not nearly grand enough for the sort of life which she intended to lead. Within months of having moved in, she began to agitate for a larger, more impressive home.

The couple employed a domestic staff of seven – butler, housekeeper, cook, footman, housemaid, chauffeur and the Princess's personal maid – as well as several part-time cleaners, which meant an annual wage bill of £6,000. The Princess also employed a private secretary, Major the Hon. Francis Legh, and made use of the services of an equerry and a lady-in-waiting. Unfortunately, within weeks of moving into No. 10, Kensington Palace, there was staff trouble when Thomas Cronin, the archetypal royal butler, found that he could not stomach Armstrong-Jones's informal yet interfering ways. He professed himself 'shocked' by what he regarded as his master's 'eccentric ideas': eating in his shirtsleeves with his jacket slung over the back of his chair, wearing a plum-coloured waistcoat to Buckingham Palace, appearing in the kitchen – 'a place I do not expect to see masters'. Cronin was especially affronted by Armstrong-Jones's tight trousers. 'The unusual circumstances of his life and his sudden elevation into the royal tradition,' the butler sniffed, 'may have had something to do with the lack of smoothness in our relations.' When Armstrong-Jones objected to Cronin's insistence on a third charwoman, the latter assured him that 'a royal residence is somewhat different from "digs"'. The butler deeply resented the fact that his master would check the accounts, and even refused his request for a hundred-pound float. They disagreed on the quality of the wine; even about the building of wine racks, which Armstrong-Jones felt they could quite easily do themselves. The final straw seems to have come when Armstrong-Jones once summoned Cronin by snapping his fingers.

Even with Princess Margaret, whom Cronin was careful not to criticize, things did not always go smoothly. Once, after a luncheon party, she reprimanded the butler. 'Cronin,' she said, 'unless Her Majesty the Queen is a guest in this house, you must always serve me first, regardless of the rank of my guests.' Not that the Queen ever needed to be served: Her Majesty visited the house only once, said the aggrieved servant pointedly. And, with the exception of the Queen Mother, no other member of the royal family ever called.

Whether Cronin resigned or was dismissed is a moot point, but on leaving No. 10, he 'did a Crawfie', making straight for the offices of the *People* in order to sell the newspaper his revelations. 'For the sake of the Royal Family, I must speak,' he proclaimed self-righteously. 'I was mortified by the strange standards imposed upon me.' Working for the royal family, declared the butler as a Parthian shot, was 'the highest possible honour for the lowest possible wage'.[5]

Cronin's departure was followed, within two years, by that of two further butlers and, worse still from the Princess's point of view, by that of her personal maid, Ruby Gordon. The always difficult Ruby had not endeared herself to the rest of the staff by her insistence on special treatment; among other things, she had refused to use the back door or to eat in the servants' hall with the others, demanding that her meals be served in her room. It was almost inevitable that the self-important and possessive Ruby should clash with Armstrong-Jones; she left, it is said, 'in a huff'.[6] Inevitably, news of all this staff trouble would have been relayed to the Queen by her own long-serving personal maid, Bobo MacDonald, Ruby's sister. Bobo kept in touch with whatever was happening in the various royal households 'by her private network of informers among the older servants'.[7]

Hardly had the £6,000 been spent on No. 10, Kensington Palace than a more grandiose home was agreed upon. This was the nearby Apartment 1A, Clock Court, which, despite its modest title, occupied one complete wing of Kensington Palace's quadrangle. A visitor who passed through the archway under the Clock Tower into the great paved courtyard would find that Princess Margaret's apartments made up the entire right-hand side. She lives there to this day.

On four storeys, the twenty-one-room apartment had been lived in by various members of the royal family down the centuries. The last occupant had been Queen Victoria's daughter, the 'artistic' Princess Louise, Duchess of Argyll, who lived there until her death, at the age of ninety-one, in 1939. Since then the apartment, which had anyway not been renovated since 1891, had stood empty. Not only was a complete redecoration called for but the actual fabric of the building – the walls, ceilings, floors and other woodwork – had to be comprehensively restored. One of the minor alterations waiting to be done was the opening up of a certain doorway leading into the garden: Princess Louise had had it bricked up to prevent her husband, the Duke of Argyll, from slipping out into Hyde Park in search of soliciting guardsmen.

The estimated cost of the work on Apartment 1A was £70,000. Of this £50,000 would be met by the Ministry of Works, with the remaining £20,000 coming from the Queen's 'personal funds'. This 'personal' contribution was not quite what it seemed: it would come from 'a grant-in-aid included in the Ministry of Work's estimates every year and placed at the Queen's disposal for the maintenance of royal palaces'.[8] In the event, the final bill was £85,000.

Not unnaturally, there were protests in Parliament. The Princess was blamed for this extravagant expenditure at a time of national economy. 'Is it not a deplorable priority,' asked that scourge of the monarchy, the Labour MP Willie Hamilton, 'that when there are thousands of homeless in London, this kind of money should be spent on this apartment?'[9] Warming to his task, Hamilton inveighed against 'a tiny, highly privileged, in the main useless minority', and described Princess Margaret as 'idle' and 'a kept woman'.[10] Alongside such vigorous attacks, the defence by the Minister of Works, Lord John Hope, that he was merely preserving a historic building, sounded very lame.

Once the furore had died down, the work been completed, and the bills paid, Princess Margaret was left in possession of a suitably impressive royal residence. A spacious hallway with a black-and-white tiled floor led to the main ground-floor rooms: the drawing room, dining room, garden room and Armstrong-Jones's study (for parties, the reception rooms could accommodate a hundred people). The couple had separate bedrooms, with a shared bathroom, on the first floor. There were other bedrooms on this and the second floor, with staff sleeping quarters on the third floor and in the basement. Also in the basement were, among other rooms, the secretary's office and Armstrong-Jones's darkroom.

The heart of the apartment was the large drawing room: its walls kingfisher blue, its curtains pale grey, its sofas and chairs echoing the muted shades of blue, grey, apricot and gold of the huge, specially made carpet. At one end of the room were a grand piano and a tall mahogany cabinet housing a collection of porcelain; at the other, the Princess's desk and two large, highly ornamental figures of blacks holding torches aloft. The whole effect was of a room both elegant and stylish, capturing something of the spirit of the eighteenth century. Perhaps above everything, however, the Princess's apartment gave off the atmosphere of a country home, an impression heightened by the fact that it had its own garden and, beyond that, the great stretch of Kensington Gardens. 'It's wonderfully quiet; it's hard to believe that one's in the middle of London,' she says. 'And the air is so fresh these days. When I first came here, before the "Clean Air Act", I used to have to wipe every single leaf of my camellias by hand.'[11] It is a diverting image.

From this decorative home, the young couple were launched on their active, controversial and highly publicized professional and social lives. They became, in the words of the satirical magazine *Private Eye*, 'the two highest-paid performing dwarfs in Europe'.[12]

Princess Margaret had not been married long before a spoof advertisement appeared in the 'Situations Wanted' columns of a London newspaper: 'Cambridge Blue, 29, well-connected, forced to give up lucrative professional career, seeks release from social round. Own car. Suggestions welcomed.'[13] For all its jokey tone, the advertisement contained more than a grain of truth. On his marriage, Antony Armstrong-Jones suddenly found himself without a job. There is, as his niece by marriage, Princess Anne, was later to say, 'a special difficulty' about the status of a princess's husband. 'After all, we normally still think of the husband as number one and the wife as number two, whereas in the case of a royal female who has public duties to perform, it's rather the other way round.'[14] When that royal female was someone as conscious of her status as Princess Margaret, the problem was compounded.

The truth is that the Princess would have been far better off married to someone like Prince Philip, a man totally dedicated to helping his wife in her royal calling, or to someone like Princess Alexandra of Kent's future husband, the Hon. Angus Ogilvy, who was content to leave his wife to get on with her public engagements while he concentrated on his own career. Even men like Peter Townsend or Princess Anne's second husband, Commander Timothy Laurence – discreetly supportive and publicly unassertive – would have suited Princess Margaret better. But Antony Armstrong-Jones fitted no such bill. He was an ambitious, aggressive and talented career man, accustomed to living his own life.

At first, he tried to adjust himself to his new situation, becoming, in a way, a scaled-down version of Prince Philip. Whenever he accompanied his wife on official engagements, he behaved with dignity and circumspection: he dressed more formally, he spoke more slowly, he even employed the royal 'one' in conversation. The couple were seen together at all the traditional royal occasions – the Royal Tournament at Earls Court, the Chelsea Flower Show, the Buckingham Palace garden parties, Ascot, Trooping the Colour, gala performances and charity balls – as well as carrying out the no less traditional round of royal duties ranging from the consecration of Guildford Cathedral to the inspection of a new council development in Dunbartonshire. They represented the Queen at the marriage of King Baudouin of the Belgians to the Spanish aristocrat, Dona Fabiola de Mora y Aragon, in Brussels in December 1960, and at the marriage of Princess Astrid of Norway to plain Herr Johan Ferner in Oslo in January 1961.

In August 1962 they again represented the Queen, this time at the granting of independence to Jamaica. At a midnight ceremony, of a type which was becoming increasingly familiar during these years as, one by one, former imperial possessions became independent, Princess Margaret watched the Union flag being hauled down and the new national flag being run up. On the following day, resplendent in white satin and glittering tiara and with her husband, in morning dress, standing sedately by her side, the Princess opened Jamaica's new Parliament.

From time to time, the couple even became pawns in the diplomatic game. Early in 1963 the French President, General Charles de Gaulle, vetoed Britain's entry into the European Economic Community. The British Government's response was to cancel the proposed visit of Princess Margaret and her husband to Paris. As an excuse for the cancellation, the British Ambassador in Paris explained that because the Queen was away on a Commonwealth tour, Princess Margaret's 'constitutional responsibilities' prevented her from leaving the country. 'The excuse might be transparent,' admitted the Ambassador, 'but that does not really matter. . . .'[15]

But for Armstrong-Jones, this sort of public gallivanting was not enough. The work he was doing on the restoration of Apartment 1A, Kensington Palace, and the occasional solo engagement, could not satisfy his urge to be involved in something more constructive. His creative energies needed an outlet. He also needed – for the sake of his pride, if for nothing else – to earn some money. If, in the eyes of Willie Hamilton, MP, Princess Margaret was 'a kept woman', then how much more so was her husband a kept man.

Yet when he did find some more intellectually rewarding, and eventually gainful, employment, there was an outcry. The first of these jobs came early in 1961 when he joined the Council for Industrial Design, which might have been thought blameless enough. He was to be there, it was explained, in an advisory capacity only and would receive no fee or salary. Playing the dutiful wife, Princess Margaret paid a highly publicized visit to her husband's new office off Haymarket. Her gesture was hardly likely to pacify the press, and there was considerable criticism of her husband's 'sinecure'. There was still more criticism when, later that year, it was announced that London Zoo had chosen a design by Armstrong-Jones, working with an architect and an engineer, for a new aviary.

Again there were accusations of favouritism., and he was mockingly hailed as one of Britain's leading birdcage designers, in 'a not over-crowded profession'.[16]

Such carpings were as nothing compared to the uproar that start-ed up when, in January 1962, it was announced that the Princess's husband had been appointed artistic adviser on the soon to be launched *Sunday Times* colour magazine. Although it was long believed that Armstrong-Jones's old Cambridge friend, Marc Boxer, the magazine's first editor, had offered him the job, the Princess her-self appears to have had a hand in his appointment. Aware of her husband's mounting frustrations, she had approached Jocelyn Stevens about the possibility of Denis Hamilton, editor of the *Sunday Times*, appointing him.[17] Not unnaturally, Hamilton was delight-ed: to get, at one stroke, a talented photographer and the Queen's brother-in-law to work on his projected colour magazine would be a considerable coup. Armstrong-Jones was no less delighted. A salary of £5,000 a year, with liberal expenses and opportunities for inter-national travel, in return for working on an innovative, trend-setting magazine, was exactly the sort of thing he was looking for. With the Queen's permission, he accepted the job.

The reaction to the news was immediate and infuriated. The Hon. David Astor, editor of the rival Sunday newspaper, the *Observer*, denounced the appointment on the grounds (or so he claimed) that it would harm the monarchy. The *Sunday Times*, thun-dered Astor, was simply making use of the Crown in order to line its own pockets. Left-wing papers resented the link between Princess Margaret's husband and the Tory press, and even *The Times* voiced its disapproval. The presence of more than fifty jostling photogra-phers waiting to greet the new artistic adviser on his arrival at the newspaper's office, coupled with the fact that he had to hurry away from his first editorial conference in order to attend a Buckingham Palace lunch in celebration of the tenth anniversary of the Queen's reign, hardly mollified his critics. It was left to William Connor, the incomparable 'Cassandra' of the *Daily Mirror*, to introduce a breath of common sense into the overheated atmosphere. His paper would happily sign up Princess Margaret as a women's features editor, he announced.

Disapproval over his job was only a part of what Antony Armstrong-Jones had to face, for yet another flutter was caused by the question of a title for him. Thus far, Princess Margaret had refused to add the suffix 'Mrs Antony Armstrong-Jones' to her name, and expressed a weary contempt for the heavy-handed humour of those who insisted on referring to her as 'Mrs Jones' or even 'Maggie Jones'. But by the spring of 1961 she realized that she was pregnant, and this reopened the matter of a title for her husband. Her children could hardly be expected to enter the royal line of succession as plain Mr or Miss Armstrong-Jones. It was widely rumoured that she would be satisfied with nothing less than a dukedom for her husband, but it was unlikely that the Queen would ever have considered transforming Antony Armstrong-Jones into a duke. The Princess denies that she ever demanded, or even expected, a dukedom: 'I know my place!' was her wry comment on the matter.[18]

In the end, Armstrong-Jones was granted an earldom, a title ranking two places below that of a duke. After much discussion, he decided on the title of Earl of Snowdon, Viscount Linley of Nymans (the latter also being the courtesy title that would be used by his heir). Snowdon is the highest mountain in Wales and thus an acknowledgment of his Welsh ancestry; Linley was chosen as a tribute to his maternal grandfather, Linley Sambourne, the illustrator and *Punch* cartoonist; and Nymans was the name of the Messel family home in Sussex. His choice of title was announced on 3 October 1961. From now on he would be known as Lord Snowdon, and his wife became officially HRH the Princess Margaret, Countess of Snowdon. Together, husband and wife were usually referred to as 'the Snowdons'.

The *Daily Mirror*, which had already dismissed the idea of a title for Armstrong-Jones as nonsensical, was now joined by the *Sunday People*, which bemoaned the fact that he had 'lost his most precious asset, his birthright'.[19] The *Guardian* recorded a 'tinge of disappointment that plain honest Mr Armstrong-Jones should have a title thrust upon him'.[20] But the sharpest comment on Snowdon's title came from some unnamed wit. 'They have made a mountain,' he said, 'out of a molehill.'[21]

On 3 November 1961, exactly one month after Lord Snowdon had been granted his title, Princess Margaret gave birth at Clarence House to a son, a healthy baby weighing 6 pounds 4 ounces. 'It's much less painful than you think,' she assured Nenne Glenton, the wife of Snowdon's Rotherhithe landlord. 'The worst part is waiting weeks beforehand. I used to get a little irritable.'[22] The Princess belonged to a generation of royal women who kept themselves out of public view when they were pregnant, which, in view of that self-confessed irritability, was probably just as well. As it was, press and public seemed genuinely delighted by the birth, and for a time the proud parents basked in something approaching approval.

Six weeks later, on 19 December, the baby, wrapped in the traditional Victorian lace robe, was baptized by the Archbishop of Canterbury in the Music Room at Buckingham Palace. The baby's godparents – 'sponsors' – were the Queen, Lady Elizabeth Cavendish, Lord Plunket, Lord Rupert Neville, and the Reverend Simon Phipps – no one, apparently, was prepared to risk asking one of the father's friends to be a godparent. Having automatically assumed his father's subsidiary title of Viscount Linley at birth, the baby was given the names of David Albert Charles. Although it was afterwards claimed that the name David had been chosen because of its Welsh connotations or in honour of the Queen Mother's favourite brother, David Bowes-Lyon, it was widely believed that the puckish Princess Margaret had named her son after her fellow royal maverick – her Uncle David, the disgraced Duke of Windsor.

Within weeks, the public glow of approval surrounding the royal mother disappeared. Leaving their eight-week-old baby in the care of a nanny, Verona Sumner, and a nurse, the Snowdons flew off to Princess Margaret's beloved Caribbean. While Britain shivered, the couple sunned themselves on the island of Antigua for three weeks. Understandably, the Princess was sharply criticized, privately and publicly, for being 'callous, selfish and perverse'.[23] Her mail brought innumerable poison-pen letters.

Matters were hardly improved when it was revealed that the whole of the first-class section of a Britannia aircraft (operated by BOAC), normally seating sixteen people, had been taken over by the Princess, Lord Snowdon, a maid and a detective. 'Considerably more than the cost of the fare is being paid to us,' announced a BOAC spokesman defensively. True or not, the royal couple's action was insupportable. If the Princess had indeed paid well over £3,000 for sixteen seats, then she was being extremely profligate; if she had not paid the full value, she was being granted an unfair privilege; she was also, of course, denying use of the first-class section to other passengers. 'This type of thing does great harm to the monarchy, which is traditionally chary of claiming privilege except as an inherent part of performing a duty,' claimed one normally sympathetic observer.[24]

This special treatment, coming on top of the grumbling about the cost of the Princess's Kensington Palace renovations and her husband's well-paid *Sunday Times* job, damaged the Princess's reputation considerably. She was labelled high-handed, self-indulgent, pleasure-loving, yet she herself would blithely complain that the press were 'just vultures waiting for an accident'. She used to get 'appallingly upset', she is reported to have said some years later, at having 'no way of hitting back. I was an absolute wreck after some of the publicity.'[25]

In spite of, or possibly because of, all this controversy, the Snowdons quickly established themselves as Britain's smartest young couple. Throughout the 1960s they were a focus of national and international attention. Everything they did made news, and they came to be regarded as the epitome of glamour and modernity. Still in their thirties, they were young enough, and certainly ready enough, to identify themselves with the innovative, classless and liberated mood of the era. With the monarchy still floundering about in its efforts to make itself more relevant to contemporary national life, this quasi-bohemian, quasi-intellectual couple seemed to provide the answer. The Snowdons became the monarchy's contribution to the 'Swinging Sixties'. Their style has been described as 'hip plush'.

They certainly looked daringly modern. Under her husband's guidance, Princess Margaret's clothes became simpler, more in tune with the skimpy fashions of the period. Although she never wore a miniskirt, she wore skirts shorter than those of any of the other royal women. Her hairstyle, seldom the same two days running, was transformed by the addition of hairpieces and padding into towering concoctions. She wore fashionably pale lipstick, heavy eye make-up, dangling earrings. At night, her evening clothes revealed a *décolletage* that was provocatively low. Snowdon's clothes were equally modish. He affected velvet jackets, outsize caps, drainpipe trousers, voile shirts. Even at Buckingham Palace gatherings, he would wear a white silk polo-necked shirt with his dinner jacket. 'We hated black tie,' says Princess Margaret. Instead, their male guests would arrive for dinner in 'the most beautiful shirts'.[26] At a Clarence House reception Lady Jebb was struck, not only by what she called Snowdon's sun-lamp complexion but by his brightly tinted hair. Sacheverell Sitwell described the colour as peach but she considered it to be more apricot.

Snowdon initiated the Princess into an entirely new way of life. In headscarf and dark glasses she would sit on the pillion of his motorcycle as he went roaring through the traffic. Together they visited street markets, where Snowdon bargained for valuable finds amidst the junk. They were once even spotted on the London Underground. They bought themselves one of those quintessentially Sixties cars, a Mini. (A fellow lunch guest was once flabbergasted to hear that the Queen Mother had just arrived 'in a mini', until he realized that it was the car and not the skirt.) The couple went to jazz clubs, avant-garde films, intimate theatres. They mingled with many of the people thrown up during these years of dissolving class barriers, of new talents, of uninhibited behaviour. Their circle included the designer Mary Quant, the hairdresser Vidal Sassoon, the writer Edna O'Brien, the actors Peter Sellers with his wife Britt Ekland, and Bryan Forbes with his wife Nanette Newman. The dancer Rudolf Nureyev would arrive at Kensington Palace dressed from head to toe in skintight black leather, or wrapped in an ankle-length fur coat. Another friend from that world was Dame Margot Fonteyn, for Princess Margaret loved the ballet. 'I had shivers down my back watching. My hands are quite worn out from clapping,' she once admitted to Dame Ninette de Valois after attending a performance at Covent Garden.[27]

Such an unconventional *mélange* of guests could bring its problems. After a party at Kensington Palace for Marlene Dietrich, the Princess was furious to find that four bottles of very rare vodka, which had been given to her, had disappeared. With that streak of royal parsimony that goes hand in hand with her extravagance, she spent the whole of the following morning ringing round until she had tracked down the culprit. The bottles were returned.

Inevitably, the Snowdons befriended those icons of the period, the Beatles – to John Lennon, the couple were 'Priceless Margarine' and 'Bony Armstrove'.[28] 'I adored them,' says the Princess, 'because they were poets as well as musicians.'[29] This friendship was not without its risks. Once, at a Chelsea party given by the artist Rory

McEwen, the Beatle George Harrison, having just been arrested, charged and bailed for possessing drugs, came dashing up to the Princess. 'Guess what?' he exclaimed, 'we've been busted! [The police] planted a big block of hash in my bedroom closet.' 'How terrible,' murmured the Princess diplomatically. But Harrison was after more than her sympathy. 'Do you think you might get the charges dropped?' he asked. 'I don't really think so. It could become a little sticky. Sorry, George.' The situation became more awkward still when Patti Harrison's sister, Paula, casually strolled up and offered the Princess 'a drag on a joint that was being passed around the room'. Hurriedly, the Snowdons left.[30]

Their friendship with Peter Sellers and Britt Ekland led to the couple starring in a home movie. One scene had Sellers announcing that he was going to give his 'celebrated impression of Her Royal Highness Princess Margaret'. He stepped back and disappeared behind a screen, apparently flung off several items of clothing and then the real Princess Margaret emerged from behind the screen. Waggling her hips like a conjuror's assistant, she blew a kiss to the camera and disappeared. Another scene had Sellers and Snowdon, as a couple of American gangsters, discussing ways of killing another mobster. 'If it's not the light switch, and it's not the East River, how are you goin' kill him?' asked Sellers. After a long pause, Snowdon dropped his wrist in a camp gesture and lisped, 'That's *entirely* my concern.' The film ended with the Princess, Snowdon and Sellers giving a high-kicking chorus-line rendition of the *Gang Show* signature tune 'Riding along on the crest of a wave'.

When Sellers screened the film to a party of friends, including the Snowdons, the Princess, who had insisted upon sitting on a footstool and not a chair, afterwards exclaimed in her 'clear high voice' to actor Graham Stark, who was sitting behind her, 'Oh, I do feel such a fool. Me, an amateur, being watched by all you professionals.' The next day Sellers telephoned Stark to tell him that he had made a 'great hit' with the Princess. 'Evidently you called her darling all evening and she loved it.'[31]

The Princess's interest in show business also brought her into contact with the celebrated drag artist, Danny La Rue, although her first visit to his club caused him some embarrassment. Just as he was about to start his act, he noticed a party making its way through the darkness to a table. Danny La Rue hated latecomers. 'Good evening,' he shouted to the woman leading the group, adding, 'Sorry, darling, I didn't recognize you with your clothes on.' The audience laughed and applauded to an extent which the corny old crack hardly seemed to merit – only afterwards was La Rue told that the woman had been Princess Margaret.

After that, the Princess often came to his club. Once, when the drag artist was changing, someone hammered on his dressing-room door, shouting, 'Danny, it's Princess Margaret. Quick!' 'Piss off!' shouted the star, opening the door. But it was indeed the Princess, and La Rue, who was stark naked at the time, found that he did not know 'whether to bow, curtsy or cover myself up'.[32]

Danny La Rue's name features in one more royal story, worth repeating since Princess Margaret was present. At a show staged at the Talk of the Town in London in aid of the World Wildlife Fund, the royal family, including the Queen and and her sister, attended in force. That celebrated theatrical figure, Lord (Bernard) Delfont, was sitting beside the Queen when the romantic novelist Barbara Cartland (whose presentation of herself has been described as 'a cross between the Queen Mother and Mae West'[33]) swept past the royal table in a flurry of chiffon and ostrich feathers. The Queen, whose sense of humour is often underrated, revealed it on this occasion. 'Who is that?' she asked Bernard Delfont. 'Danny La Rue?'[34]

Danny La Rue, who describes Princess Margaret as 'witty and highly intelligent', claims that 'you always knew you were in the presence of a princess'.[35] Meant as a compliment, it pinpointed the awkwardness of her situation. For no matter how hard she tried to immerse herself in *la vie bohème*, she remained, in looks and attitude, indubitably royal. The cut-glass accent, the carefully coiffured head, the couture clothes, the expectation of some show of deference – all this set her apart from the sort of people by whom she wanted to be accepted. Nothing could disguise her natural hauteur. She had a way of ignoring any remark that displeased her, and of cutting short any unwelcome conversation. Her glare of disapproval was, and is, legendary. If ever she felt that she was being treated with too much familiarity by her fellow guests, she would simply walk out.

'No one seemed to behave naturally when she was there,' says one observer. 'She tried her best but it always came across as condescension. She had that royal way of moving on, of not wanting to be left too long with anyone. She never really seemed to belong to that arty world.'[36] This distance between her two worlds was vividly illustrated when the actor Jack Warner once warned his tarty girlfriend, 'Don't say "shit" in front of the Princess.'[37]

'Although we got along well enough,' wrote William Glenton, the journalist who had let the Rotherhithe *pied-à-terre* to Armstrong-Jones, and who came to know her very well,

I do not think Margaret really ever understood me. I think perhaps the main reason was that I did not really fit in with her set ideas about people. She appears to have a much more Victorian concept of people than the average person today, dividing them distinctly into upper, middle and lower classes, without recognizing the many social nuances that now exist. From a strictly personal point of view, too, she sees them as being either pro- or anti-royalist. As I did not fit into any of these categories very obviously she sometimes seemed puzzled, but I did nothing to ease her curiosity, feeling this could easily lead to argument. In explaining myself I would also be attacking her own position, and Margaret can be very emphatic when on the defensive.[38]

In fact, her forays into the world of arts and letters often brought her up against people who were either unimpressed by, or actually hostile to, her royal status. Once, at an evening of avant-garde films, Princess Margaret was introduced to the playwright Harold Pinter and his first wife, the actress Vivien Merchant. Automatically, Her Royal Highness put out her hand. But either because she wanted to show her disapproval, or because she spurned such conventional gestures, the actress ignored the Princess's outstretched hand. 'I put out my hand which was refused,' remembers the Princess. 'So I sort of drew it up as if it were meant for another direction.'[39] By contrast, the critic Kenneth Tynan, who was almost invariably described as a 'champagne socialist', found that he was always having to defend his friendship with Princess Margaret. He liked her, he said, because of her 'appetite for the theatre, her wit and her loyalty to her friends'.[40]

Indeed, Princess Margaret's loyalty to her friends is often cited as one of her more endearing characteristics. In this, apparently, she differed from her husband. 'When we were married,' she says, 'I pressed him to keep up with his old chums, but the funny thing about Tony is that he is a friend-dropper. After the marriage nearly all his old friends vanished and I never saw them again. I'm not like that, I don't discard people. My friends are old friends.'[41]

Another point of divergence between husband and wife was the Princess's continuing refusal to go to bed at a reasonable hour. Towards midnight, Snowdon would begin to indicate that it was time for guests to leave, but the Princess would insist that they stay on, sometimes until three in the morning. And no one – not even, during these early years of marriage, her husband – could leave the party until Her Royal Highness had given the signal.

But these were minor marital differences. In these first years husband and wife were very close; 'They were times,' as Princess Margaret's authorized biographer has put it, 'of tactile gestures, private asides, shared laughter and shared confidences.'[42] It was apparent to all their friends that there was a strong sexual chemistry between them. As another of the Princess's biographers has quoted, somewhat less elegantly, 'theirs was a very passionate and physical marriage and she certainly didn't go short in that direction'.[43]

On 1 May 1964, at Kensington Palace, Princess Margaret gave birth to a daughter. Seven weeks earlier, on 10 March, the Queen's fourth and last child, Prince Edward Antony Richard Louis, had been born. Princess Margaret's baby was baptized by the Dean of Westminster in the private chapel at Buckingham Palace, and given the names Sarah Frances Elizabeth (with the style of Lady Sarah Armstrong-Jones). Her five godparents were Jocelyn Stevens's wife, Jane, and his stepsister Prudence Penn, Marigold Bridgeman, the Earl of Westmorland, and a friend of Lord Snowdon's from his Cambridge days, Anthony Barton.

At the champagne reception afterwards, Snowdon's father, Ronald Armstrong-Jones, asked Princess Margaret about the 'little white room' – the dockland 'love nest' in which she and Snowdon had spent so many happy hours. On one memorable night, after their marriage, they had taken the Queen Mother to see it. On the way, they had stopped the car and let Her Majesty out, so that the unmistakable figure of the Queen Mother was to be seen enjoying a casual stroll along Waterloo Road, where she showed especial interest in the window of a well-known tattooist. 'I haven't enjoyed myself so much since I was a girl of twenty,' she exclaimed afterwards.[44]

Among Snowdon's later improvements to the room had been the installation of a lavatory in a cupboard which, since the tiny cubicle had no window, had to be done without planning permission. In a mock opening ceremony, Princess Margaret cut a blue ribbon stretched across the door. Having declared the lavatory open, she instructed her husband to flush it. She then proposed a toast to 'the great and glorious future of our loo'.[45]

By 1964, however, the local authority, deciding that the row of artisans' homes was of no interest or value, had condemned the houses as slums and bulldozed them. 'They are simply brutes,' complained the Princess.[46] Although Snowdon kept some of the furniture, the double divan which he had bought for a pound had to be jettisoned. Together, he and Princess Margaret launched it out of the window and into the Thames where, 'moving sluggishly, it drifted upriver on the tide – and out of their lives'.[47]

Some time later, Cecil Beaton was commissioned to photograph the Snowdon family. Posed in Clock Court, Kensington Palace, with little Lord Linley perched on his father's shoulders, Lady Sarah Armstrong-Jones cradled in her mother's arms, and the parents gazing lovingly into each other's eyes, anyone would have taken them for an ideal and blissfully happy little family group.

CHAPTER FIFTEEN

$\mathcal{D}$ivisions

NOTHER EXAMPLE OF PRINCESS MARGARET'S breaking with royal tradition came with her choice of holidays. Ever since the accession of her grandfather, King George V, in 1910, British monarchs have spent their holidays in Britain. The royal roster had become sacrosanct: Christmas, New Year, January and much of February at Sandringham (although for several years, as her family expanded, Elizabeth II spent Christmas at Windsor), and most of August and September at Balmoral. Significantly, the only monarch to break this rule was King Edward VIII, when he took Wallis Simpson on his highly publicized cruise along the Dalmatian coast in 1936. So although the sovereigns went abroad on official visits, they almost always remained at home when it came to private vacations.

Once married, Princess Margaret lost very little time in stepping out of this pattern. Having spent their first Christmas together as a married couple at Sandringham, husband and wife took off for Ireland in order to see the New Year in at Castle Birr, the Irish home of the Princess's mother-in-law, Lady Rosse. Birr, a nineteenth-century Gothic Revival pile set in a large wooded estate, was the scene of a sizeable house party that season. The Princess had invited her old beau, Billy Wallace, to show him that now, safely married herself, she had forgiven him for his philandering; her husband had invited Jeremy and Camilla Fry, to prove that Fry's replacement as best man had not weakened their friendship. They were joined by Lord Rupert Neville and his wife and by the bridegroom's sister, Susan, Viscountess de Vesci.

The visit seems not to have been a great success. The Princess found the Irish too hearty, too devoted to the sporting life, for her taste; 'I really don't like sports at all,' she maintains.¹ Nor, apparently, did she much like her mother-in-law. She is reported to have made cutting remarks about Lady Rosse's insistence on elaborate dressing for dinner, and she demanded the deference she felt to be her due. 'She was really wicked,' claims one witness, 'because she never told Tony's mother to call her anything familiar, although Anne was allowed to kiss her on both cheeks – after curtsying.' In the end, poor Anne Rosse compromised by calling her daughter-in-law 'Darling'.²

Another, later visit to Ireland, early in 1965, was marked by national, as opposed to domestic, friction. Princess Margaret and Lord Snowdon were spending a private holiday with his sister Susan and her husband John, the sixth Viscount de Vesci, and their three young children at their home, Abbeyleix in Laois. On this occasion the Princess had to pay the price of what she represented: the British Crown. Although 'the Troubles' had not attained the terrifying scale they were to reach in the years after 1969, the IRA were in full cry at the thought of this representative of an oppressive foreign power being in the country they wished to see united as a republic. She was subjected to the whole range of IRA protests: abusive posters, seditious pamphlets, road blocks, explosions, power failures. The Princess kept her nerve, however, insisting, among other things, on being taken on a pub crawl which ended up at the celebrated Paddy Burke's in Clarinridge, County Galway.

The visit ended in a typically Irish muddle. The Garda, desperately worried about IRA bombs, assured the Princess that if her driver kept behind a car marked 'Follow Me', she would be led directly to her aircraft waiting on the runway at Dublin airport, thereby avoiding the potentially dangerous VIP lounge. But the leading vehicle, mistaking the royal car, led a quite different vehicle, containing two bewildered American tourists, to the Princess's plane. This left the Princess's car stranded in the middle of what was, thankfully, a very good-natured crowd. They cheered, they thumped on the roof, they broke into hearty choruses of 'For She's a Jolly Good Fellow!' Eventually the Snowdons had to get out and make their own way on foot to the very VIP lounge that they had been instructed to avoid. Their progress was followed by a stream of cheerful badinage about the Queen Mother's well-known love of racing. 'Next time bring your mother,' shouted one member of the crowd. 'And tell her to bring the horse,' yelled another. 'What if it doesn't win?' quipped back the Princess. 'It will,' came the reply, 'we'll carry it round.'[3] One can hardly blame Princess Margaret for complaining, in her dry fashion, that she found the Irish boisterous.

Other foreign holidays accorded better with the Princess's more sophisticated tastes. In September 1963 the Snowdons accepted an invitation from the rich Greek shipowner, Stavros Niarchos, to spend a few weeks on his private Aegean island, Spetsapoula. With them was one of the Princess's old escorts, Sunny, Marquess of Blandford, who had divorced his wife to marry Tina Livanos, who was herself the ex-wife of another rich Greek shipowner, Aristotle Onassis. In this moneyed, smart, international society, of which the women were often the products of an English education and Swiss finishing schools, the Princess felt eminently at ease. Niarchos proved the perfect host. The island was stocked with especially imported game birds to provide sport for shooting parties, and the luxurious Niarchos yacht took the party on expeditions to Delphi and Corinth. Wandering around in her cotton dresses and sandals in the clear Greek light, the Princess must have felt a million miles from the bracing winds of Balmoral.

An even more exotic holiday location was provided by the young, handsome, British-born Aga Khan, Prince Karim, always known to his friends as 'K', and who was regarded by the Ismailian sect of Muslims as their hereditary Imam or spiritual leader. The young man's latest, more secular, interest was the establishment of a holiday resort on the Costa Smeralda, on the Italian island of Sardinia, on which he and his associates were lavishing £80 million: a collection of dazzlingly white, gracefully arcaded buildings set against the blue waters of the Mediterranean. With one eye on the publicity value of the visit, he invited the Snowdons to be his guests for a few weeks in August 1964. They were delighted to accept. The Aga Khan brought them to the island in his private plane, put them up at the Hotel Pitrizza, as his own extensive villa was considered too modest, and placed his well-appointed yacht, *Amaloun*, at their disposal. The couple were able to swim, sail, sunbathe and water-ski in relative privacy. After that first visit they returned to Sardinia on several occasions throughout the 1960s, the Aga Khan's generosity allowing them to keep within the holiday allowance limits imposed at that time by the British Treasury. Nor did their two small children present any problem: they were always left, in the care of Nanny Sumner, with the Queen at Balmoral.

Each Sardinian visit provided its incidents. One one occasion *Amaloun* hit a rock off the little island of Sofia, sprang a leak and appeared to be sinking. While Snowdon dived into the sea, the Princess and the rest of the party clambered into a dinghy, from which they were rescued by a passing yacht. To offset the inevitable exaggerated press reports of the incident, the Princess cabled the Queen to assure her that all was well.

On another occasion the Snowdons accepted an invitation to visit the yacht of Arndt von Bohlen, an extremely rich scion of the German arms-manufacturing Krupp family. The Princess knew Bohlen by reputation only: he was celebrated for what was described as his 'flamboyant lifestyle and eccentricity'. As the couple strolled towards the spot where the Krupp yacht was moored, the Princess saw their host waiting on deck to greet her. Only on coming closer did she notice that his cheeks were rouged, his eyelashes mascaraed, and his lips painted bright red. With that inborn royal instinct for self-preservation, she stopped short. Shouting out to Bohlen that she had suddenly remembered something, she made her apologies and briskly led her husband away. Although Princess Margaret would not, herself, have minded about her host's particular 'eccentricity', she appreciated what the press would make of the encounter.[4]

In the Sardinian *beau monde*, the Snowdons were always regarded as the most socially desirable visitors to the island. The celebrated hostess Ann Fleming reported that her house guest, the writer and critic Cyril Connolly, was made 'fearfully restless by the vicinity of the Snowdons, saying that not to meet them was like being in the Garden of Eden without seeing God'. She eventually wangled for him an invitation to a dinner party being given for 'Margaret and Tony' by a 'local tycoon', which she describes as having been 'wholly successful.' 'But social scene grows tense on Highness's departure,' continues Ann Fleming in her staccato style, 'she tells tycoon she has no plans for the morrow, he is filled with despair, for the poor brute is lunching with me. I ask all to lunch. Cyril beams....'[5]

On two occasions the Snowdons flew to mainland Italy after their Sardinian holiday. In 1964 they joined Jocelyn and Jane Stevens at the Palladian villa, La Malcontenta, near Venice. The days were spent in relentless sightseeing, with Princess Margaret approaching the whole business with a Queen Mary-like thoroughness. She planned the excursions, took a highly intelligent interest in everything she was shown and, on returning home each day, would write up notes in her diary. Tirelessly, she would question the rest of the party about what they had seen. 'Now,' she would say briskly, pen poised, 'what did we see in the Giotto chapel?'[6] The evenings were spent in a more relaxed fashion with the four of them dining in Venice, either with friends in their palazzos or in places like Harry's Bar.

The foursome were in Italy again the following summer, and again the Princess enjoyed herself in a singularly un-Windsor-like fashion: staying with a count in a thirteenth-century castle near Brindisi; racing along in Snowdon's newly delivered Aston Martin to Rome; visiting her old friend Judy Montagu and her art critic husband; being received in private audience by the Pope at his summer residence, Castelgandolfo; and going on to stay with yet another count in a superb Palladian house in the foothills of the Dolomites near Treviso. With each visit to Italy, her delight in the country intensified.

But things were not quite as idyllic as they seemed. That 1965 Italian holiday, said the Princess many years later, 'was the last really happy holiday Tony and I spent together'.[7]

For the truth was that, by now, Princess Margaret's marriage was beginning to fall apart. It is almost always impossible to pinpoint a time at which, or to give a single reason as to why, a relationship begins to go sour. Nor, of course, can the blame always be put on one partner. In the case of the Snowdons' marriage, things apparently began to go wrong early in 1964, less than four years after their wedding and just before their second child was born.

Quite clearly, Lord Snowdon was beginning to have second thoughts about the marriage. What had once seemed like the glamour and prestige of being a member of the royal family had gradually worn off. While still not quite impervious to the status and advantages of his position as a royal consort, he was beginning to find these increasingly irksome. So energetic, so ambitious, so attuned to the variety and creativity of the period, he was simply not content to follow dutifully in his wife's footsteps. His work on the *Sunday Times* was taking him all over the world; he was involved with the sort of people whose lives were infinitely distanced from the traditionalism of the House of Windsor. He was feeling increasingly trapped. 'I am not a member of the royal family,' he would snap, 'I am married to a member of the royal family.'[8] The distinction was too fine for most people. If, for instance, he were out on some photographic assignment, he would invariably find himself the target of other photographers. This dichotomy, allied to the frustrations of his situation, made him moody, irritable, even vindictive.

Had Antony Armstrong-Jones married a different sort of woman, even a different sort of princess, things might still have worked out. But the couple were too alike. Both husband and wife were volatile, self-centred, arrogant, accustomed to getting their own way. Raised in the unreal atmosphere of the Court, Princess Margaret had very little experience of genuine human relationships. She had never really known people with whom she could be totally relaxed; even within the family, contact tended to be formal, superficial, cushioned by circumstances. She had never had to adjust her way of life to someone else's; on the contrary, she always expected others to adjust to her. Orderly and punctual in a particularly royal way, she found her husband's behaviour irritatingly erratic. She was also extremely possessive. There was, says one witness, 'a neurotic, obsessive quality' about Princess Margaret's love.[9] For all these reasons, Lord Snowdon's striving for independence took the Princess by surprise. She felt bewildered both by his occasional withdrawal from her, and by his sudden bursts of temper. She began to feel, she complained, as though she were married to a stranger. Her initial distress at this rejection was so serious that her doctor was worried about its effect on her second pregnancy.

In these early days, the clashes between husband and wife were intermittent; they were, however, still real enough. Once, during their second holiday on the Italian mainland, Snowdon lapsed into a sulk lasting for a couple of days, and was discovered by Jocelyn Stevens 'sitting cross-legged on a flat-topped chimney' on the roof.[10] At Kensington Palace, he took to spending more and more time in his work rooms, where his secretary-assistant, Dorothy Everard, organized his various professional commitments. Among these was the preparation for publication of his latest photographic book,

Private View. One day, while he was discussing some technical point with a colleague, Princess Margaret suddenly came into the room. 'Never come in here without knocking!' barked Snowdon. The Princess, says the embarrassed colleague, 'went as white as a sheet'.[11]

Needless to say, Princess Margaret could give as good as she got. Once, while Snowdon was in his dressing room having his hair cut, she came in to ask him if he would be in for lunch, as guests were coming. He did not answer, simply went on reading his newspaper. 'Darling, I'm talking to you,' said the Princess sharply. 'Darling, I'm listening,' drawled Snowdon, still reading. 'Well, will you be home for lunch?' 'No.' Shouting that she would not entertain his friends by herself, the Princess stormed out of the room, slamming the door so hard that she shattered the mirror fixed to the back of it. Oblivious to the hairdresser's discomfort, Snowdon calmly carried on reading his newspaper.[12]

Among the many positions held by Princess Margaret was the presidency of the Dockland Settlement and she never missed the association's annual ball. One evening, while choosing a partner (she always chose a different partner for each dance), she noticed that Snowdon was keeping resolutely to the same attractive girl. Between dances the Princess walked over to the young woman. 'Are you enjoying yourself?' she asked. 'Very much so, Ma'am,' came the reply. 'That's enough, then, for one evening,' said the Princess icily. 'Run along home.' The poor girl blushed deeply and hurried away. Snowdon refused to dance again that evening.[13]

A more serious rift was caused by the choice of a country retreat. Both husband and wife were anxious to have a weekend place outside London. Princess Margaret favoured the building of a home at Sunninghill, near Windsor. In the days after the birth of their daughter, the Snowdons had often water-skied on Sunninghill lake and picnicked on its banks, and she had her heart set on a country retreat beside the lake. Such a home would be well within the orbit of Windsor Castle and Royal Lodge.

Snowdon had other ideas. Now that he was earning good money from his *Sunday Times* job and his books, he was anxious to establish his independence by creating a country place of his own; he wanted, in short, to be free of any obligation towards the royal family. He planned to renovate Old House, a semi-derelict cottage set in woodland at Nymans, the Messel family estate at Handcross in Sussex. He was especially anxious that their children should be raised more naturally than other royal children. He wanted them to enjoy the informality of Old House, released from the stultifying, nanny-supervised atmosphere of the sort of royal residence that his wife had in mind. But Princess Margaret disapproved strongly of the idea, arguing that Old House would be inaccessible, inconvenient, not at all the sort of place in which she wanted to spend her weekends. In any case, she claimed, it was haunted.

At loggerheads, the couple asked their business manager to act as arbiter. Not unnaturally, he sided with the Princess: Sunninghill would be the better proposition. According to Princess Margaret, Snowdon, having deferred to the arbiter's decision, then simply ignored it and, 'behind his wife's back', went ahead with the renovation of Old House. The Princess expressed herself 'crushed' by his blithe disregard of the agreement.[14] Whatever the truth, Snowdon flung himself with customary energy and expertise into the restoration of Old House, 'cannily employing enthusiastic but cheap student labour during the holidays'.[15] When the work was complete, he invited the Queen Mother to cut a ribbon in a mock-ceremonial opening. Nothing more was heard of the Sunninghill project.

Princess Margaret hated Old House, and seldom stayed there. For all her professed bohemianism, she much preferred to spend her weekends amid the elegance of her mother's beautifully run weekend home, Royal Lodge, with its four-course meals, deferential footmen, frequent changes of clothes, and reassuringly regal ambience. 'The row over Old House was not so much the cause of the eventual break-up as a sign,' says Jocelyn Stevens. 'It wasn't so much a stupid squabble over who lived where but the seeds had been planted a long time before and now they were being reaped.'[16]

But, for the moment, at least, the show had to go on. Side by side, as though nothing were wrong, the couple carried out their various engagements: British Week in Denmark; the British Fair in the Netherlands; an official visit to Uganda in the spring of 1965, where they received a warm welcome from Mutesa II, Kabaka of Buganda. Known in the Western press as 'King Freddie', the Kabaka had spent some years in exile in London where he had been much fêted by the *beau monde*. Restored in 1955, his period of power hardly outlasted this royal visit for, in 1966, poor King Freddie was deposed by his Prime Minister, Milton Obote. He died, penniless, in London three years later. Obote, in turn, was ousted by Idi Amin.

In November 1965 the Snowdons set out for the United States, undoubtedly their most important tour to date. An invitation from the Princess's old friend, Sharman Douglas, to visit the family ranch near Tucson in Arizona was transformed into an official, flag-showing royal tour with engagements in San Francisco, Los Angeles, Washington and New York. 'I enjoyed it all enormously,' says the Princess, 'and I have kept an abiding love for the United States ever since.'[17] Lord Snowdon had equal reason to be pleased: the visit coincided with the American publication of his book *Private View*. He must also have been gratified by the fact that, after the tour, he was voted the man with whom most American women would like to be marooned on a desert island.

Princess Margaret was especially intrigued by her encounters with various film stars while in Hollywood. The stars were no less intrigued by this real princess. To them, she seemed astonishingly regal. These encounters brought the inevitable crop of film-star anecdotes; many of them apocryphal, and some belonging to quite different periods of the Princess's life. When, for instance, Richard Burton gave his wife Elizabeth Taylor a ring in which sparkled the famous Krupp diamond – a 33.19 carat jewel then worth over $300,000 – Princess Margaret pronounced it to be 'the most vulgar thing she had ever seen'. Inevitably, the remark was repeated to the actress. Some time later, on meeting the Princess at a party, Elizabeth Taylor asked her if she would like to try on the famous ring. Princess Margaret slipped it on to her finger. 'Doesn't look so vulgar now, does it?' asked the actress, smiling her cat-like smile.[18] Another of the Princess's abrasive remarks was directed at that actress-turned-princess, Grace Kelly, by then Princess Grace of Monaco. 'Well, you don't *look* like a movie star,' said the Princess on their first meeting. 'Well,' the other replied, 'I wasn't born a movie star.' The normally composed former actress was said to 'flush red with anger' whenever she repeated this story.[19]

The British Princess was, however, put firmly in her place, in the course of this Hollywood visit, by the legendary Judy Garland, whom she had often met before. At a party at the Beverly Hills Hotel, Her Royal Highness sent a message across the room to say that she would like to hear Miss Garland sing. The singer was appalled, both by this trivializing of her talent and by the Princess's lordly tone. 'Go and tell that nasty, rude little princess that we've known each other for long enough and gabbed in enough ladies' rooms that she should skip the ho-hum royal routine and just pop over here and ask me herself,' said Garland. 'Tell her I'll sing if she christens a ship first.'[20]

The highlight of the Snowdons' American tour came with a White House reception given by President Lyndon B. Johnson. In a shimmering evening dress and jacket of pink and silver, Princess Margaret looked suitably radiant; more than once, Lady Bird Johnson was caught gazing in admiration at this assured and vivacious little figure. The Princess's charm, when she chose to exercise it, could be prodigious, and there can be no doubt that on occasions during this visit to the United States, she revealed her slightly 'actressy' quality to the full. 'I'll tell you what it is,' decided one observer, on seeing her at a ball at the Waldorf-Astoria Hotel in New York. 'It's a put-on; campy; tongue-in-cheek camp. She's doing an impersonation of herself.'[21]

As was only to be expected, back in Britain the irrepressible Willie Hamilton, MP, launched a tirade against the Princess's American tour. Determined, he said, to enjoy what he called the 'pop culture' of the United States, she had agreed to undertake a handful of public engagements only on the understanding that the Foreign Office would foot the bill, which came to more than £30,000. Hamilton's accusations were taken up by certain sections of the press, which published emotive headlines about 'Jet-Set Parties', 'Luxury Tour', 'Own Hairdresser' and 'Who Pays?' Princess Margaret was attacked for being a 'very expensive young lady'.[22] The *New Statesman* described the Snowdons as acting like 'Barbie and Ken, the real-life dolls for children who can afford to buy miniature clothes costing hundreds of dollars'.[23] But even the briefest glance at her itinerary shows that the tour consisted, very largely, of the sort of exhibition-opening, museum-visiting, fund-raising, speech-making activities that are the lot of all royal visitors. 'Three weeks for £30,000?' decided one commentator. 'The British Foreign Office considered it a bargain.'[24]

No one, seeing the Snowdons in the course of this American tour, looking 'as engaging as a little bride and groom on top of a wedding cake', would have taken them for anything other than an ideally suited, happily married couple.[25] By now, however, even if they had not yet admitted it to themselves, the gulf between them was becoming unbridgeable.

As her marriage deteriorated so, slowly at first, and then more and more surely, was Princess Margaret drawn down into a desperate emotional and sexual spiral. A young, highly sexed woman with, according to someone who knew her well, 'positively Hanoverian' appetites, she felt increasingly insecure, increasingly in need of attention and reassurance.[26] Before her marriage, she had been accustomed to a considerable amount of male attention; now, suddenly, she found herself without it. With her husband so often away from home on foreign photographic assignments, and her children cared for by a nanny, she frequently felt lonely and, more important, unloved.

The Princess's first recorded extramarital affair was with Anthony Barton, the Cambridge friend of her husband's who had stood as godfather to her daughter Sarah. In fact, there is a theory that Lord Snowdon purposely threw the two of them together. 'I've no doubt that Barton was originally encouraged by Tony,' said Jocelyn Stevens. 'If you yourself are playing around, then your conscience is eased if your partner does the same.'[27] Tall, dark-haired and very good-looking, Barton belonged to a family whose business was the production and shipping of wine. The firm of Barton et Guestier had been established in Bordeaux for well over a century and a half, and Barton, with his Danish-born wife and their two children, had been living there for some years. The Bartons and the Snowdons were good friends.

Early in 1966, while Lord Snowdon was on a *Sunday Times* assignment in India, Anthony Barton – allegedly on Snowdon's suggestion – called on the Princess at Kensington Palace. There apparently followed a short-lived, highly charged affair, which would have remained a secret had the Princess not, as is claimed, telephoned Barton's wife, Eva, to confess all and to say how sorry she was. Why did she do this? A Barton family friend is quoted as saying that Princess Margaret 'obviously enjoyed the role of *femme fatale*'. She is, continued the friend, 'a typical Leo – devious, destructive and jealous'.[28]

Although Eva Barton never really forgave the Princess, Snowdon seems to have lost no time in exonerating Barton, and the two men soon returned to their previous close friendship. Quite clearly, if the Princess had imagined that the confession of her affair with Anthony Barton would arouse Snowdon's jealousy and bring him to heel, she was mistaken. He continued to go his own way. It was noticed that husband and wife would attend the same function in different cars. When Snowdon was away from home he neither wrote nor telephoned; people he worked with expressed surprise at the fact that he never even mentioned his wife.

By the end of 1966 Princess Margaret was in a highly emotional state – smoking almost continuously, drinking her favourite Famous Grouse whisky in alarming quantities, telephoning her friends at dead of night to bemoan her unloved state. Early in 1967 she was admitted to the King Edward VII Hospital for Officers, ostensibly for a 'check-up'. The fact that her husband was away in Japan simply fuelled rumours that something was wrong between them. It was even reported that the Princess had deliberately overdosed on alcohol and pills; that her admittance to hospital was in the nature of a *cri de coeur*.

In this low and feverish state, Princess Margaret embarked on an ill-starred love-affair with a man named Robin Douglas-Home.

CHAPTER 16

Affairs of the Heart

ROBIN DOUGLAS-HOME WAS THIRTY-FIVE at the time of his affair with Princess Margaret. He was exactly the sort of sensitive, unorthodox man to whom she was invariably attracted, though his background was conventional enough. His father had been a major in the army and a noted ornithologist. His mother had been born Margaret Spencer, daughter of the sixth Earl Spencer, of Althorp in Northamptonshire – the house in which the future Diana, Princess of Wales was to grow up. More significantly, his uncle was Sir Alec Douglas-Home, formerly the fourteenth Earl of Home until he renounced his title in order to succeed Harold Macmillan as Conservative Prime Minister in 1963, an office he held for just a year. Both at Eton and later in the Coldstream Guards, young Robin Douglas-Home had rebelled against authority: at Eton by writing an article criticizing the rituals of beating, and, as a captain in the army, by filing a report attacking the War Office. Not unnaturally, he left the service soon afterwards.

Well-connected and good-looking in a fair, somewhat effete fashion, Robin Douglas-Home could boast only one real accomplishment: he was a talented pianist, although one whose repertoire was almost entirely restricted to popular songs of the period. On leaving the army he had played the piano in various nightclubs, and it had been in one of them that, during the 1950s, he had first met Princess Margaret. He became a fringe member of her set and gradually established a reputation as a ladies' man. Few women, it seemed, could resist his quiet charm, seductive manner, and way of bestowing all his attention on whoever he happened to be with. By 1956, when he was twenty-four, his family had managed to find him a proper job: as a trainee account executive with that smartest of advertising agencies, the J. Walter Thompson Company in Berkeley Square. ('He was a nice enough chap,' remembers one colleague, 'but a lazy bastard.'¹) At night, however, he still played the piano in the cocktail lounge of the Berkeley Hotel in Piccadilly.

Socially ambitious, Douglas-Home had always gravitated towards the more important members of society and by late 1956 he had landed a very big fish indeed: Princess Margaretha, the twenty-two-year-old granddaughter of King Gustaf VI Adolf of Sweden. They had met at a party in London and in no time the Princess had become besotted with the romantic piano player. He, who was given to falling in love very easily, was equally enamoured of her. Although he appreciated that he was in no financial, or even social, position to meet the expected royal standards, he nevertheless began thinking in terms of marriage. Princess Margaretha's mother, the widowed Princess Sibylla, was appalled at the prospect – her daughter was ordered home to Sweden immediately.

Nothing daunted, Robin Douglas-Home wrote a formal letter to Princess Sibylla asking for her daughter's hand in marriage. It was firmly refused. The Master of the Swedish Royal Household issued a statement to the effect that the business was being regarded as 'an innocent affair in London as so often happens between young people', and that the Swedish Court considered the matter closed.² In fact, it was not closed until the following year when, on a visit to Sweden, Douglas-Home was assured by King Gustaf VI Adolf himself that there was not the slightest chance of a marriage. Six years later, Princess Margaretha married a London businessman named John Ambler.

Hardly had Douglas-Home's relationship with Princess Margaretha ended than he married the beautiful Sandra Paul, a top fashion and photographic model, then just eighteen years old. The couple had one child, a son whom they christened Sholto, but almost from the start the marriage ran into trouble. Douglas-Home was simply too unreliable, too irresponsible, too obsessed with seducing as many women as possible, for the relationship to succeed. They separated and, in 1965, were divorced. (Sandra Paul went on to marry, as her fourth husband, Michael Howard, afterwards Home Secretary in the Conservative Government.)

By now, Robin Douglas-Home had become a somewhat tarnished figure. His hair was thinning, his waist thickening, he was drinking and gambling too much. He lived well beyond his means. The advertising job had not lasted long and his attempts at alternative careers – as a photographer and as a writer – never really took off; furthermore, in his two unsuccessful novels and in his newspaper column (dealing with the activities of international high society) he revealed himself as a betrayer of confidences. He capitalized on his friendship with Frank Sinatra to dash out a skimpy biography of the singer, and he used his still considerable personal charm to worm his way into the confidence of the world's most famous widow, Jacqueline Kennedy, whose trust he repaid by publishing details of their private conversations in the tabloid press. Even as a pianist his undoubted talent was proving unsuccessful: in the era of rock and roll and the Mersey beat, Douglas-Home's relaxed, sophisticated style sounded distinctly dated.

But he remained a dedicated and surprisingly successful womanizer. Although his tastes were catholic – affairs with society beauties gave him as much satisfaction as sex with girls in the backs of taxis – his speciality seems to have been the seduction of neglected wives. And, late in 1966, Robin Douglas-Home found himself once more in the orbit of that season's most celebrated neglected wife, Princess Margaret. Although the two of them had met intermittently during the previous decade, and the Princess had actually lunched with him before attending Billy Wallace's wedding in 1965, they had not really been close. But meeting her again in late 1966, Douglas-Home immediately recognized in her the signs which, throughout his long career as a Lothario, had invariably led to sexual conquest.

A mutual love of music, and particularly songs from the shows – the music of George Gershwin, Jerome Kern, Cole Porter, Sammy Cahn – was a strong bond between them. (It was a taste which Snowdon, who was tone deaf, never shared.) Douglas-Home would play, while Princess Margaret sang. From here it did not take long for the Princess – by now thoroughly unhappy, insecure, lonely – to be emotionally drawn towards this attentive and understanding man. When Snowdon went off to Japan early in 1967 on a lengthy photographic project (from where he apparently never bothered to contact his wife), she responded even more eagerly to Douglas-Home's flattering attentions. The couple would meet either in

Kensington Palace or at Douglas-Home's small Cromwell Road house; they apparently even spent a weekend together in his country cottage, Meadowbrook, in West Chittington, Sussex.

Robin Douglas-Home, who may well have embarked on the affair with a degree of opportunism, found himself increasingly infatuated by Princess Margaret. After all, she was still an attractive, voluptuous and interesting woman. He took to writing her long poetic letters (some in a sort of musical code) in which he made his feelings for her abundantly clear. Her replies, although affectionate, were more guarded.

Their intense, month-long relationship was brought to a dramatic halt by the press. After completing his assignment in Japan, Lord Snowdon had moved on to New York and it was here that he heard about his wife's association with Douglas-Home. So, too, had the newspapers. Seizing on Snowdon's prolonged absence, the Princess's sudden admittance to the King Edward VII Hospital for Officers, and a spate of rumours about her affair with Douglas-Home, the press reported a break-up of the marriage. Snowdon, on being tackled by American reporters, professed himself amazed at the speculation about a rift between the Princess and himself. He blandly assured the newsmen that whenever he was away on an assignment, he kept in constant touch with his wife. 'He never wrote or rang when he was abroad,' snaps Princess Margaret.[3]

On 27 February 1967 news of the rumoured rift – or, rather, of Snowdon's emphatic public denial of a rift – was carried by almost every newspaper in Britain. Yet despite that smoothly delivered denial, privately Snowdon deeply resented his wife's relationship with Douglas-Home. Or, at least, he seemed to. It may be that he was just pretending to resent it, for, as one observer has put it, 'the incident had its advantages for him – it served to allow him greater freedom in the future in his own actions.'[4]

The flurry of press speculation did have the effect of making both husband and wife think again, though. Divorce, then, was out of the question. Nor was either of them prepared for a public separation. For the sake of their two children, not to mention the image of the monarchy, it would be best for them to remain together. That being so, some sort of public gesture of reconciliation was necessary. It was agreed that Princess Margaret would fly to New York, collect her husband at Kennedy airport, and the two of them would fly on to the Bahamas, where the faithful Jocelyn Stevens had offered them the use of his Lyford Cay house, near Nassau.

On 10 March the manoeuvre was duly put in train. The couple were seen chatting happily together at Kennedy airport, and throughout their stay in the Bahamas they behaved with something of their old affection towards each other. They were joined by Princess Margaret's first cousin, once removed, Patrick, Earl of Lichfield, another of those aristocratic bohemians, already well on his way towards establishing himself as a successful photographer. Together, the three of them enjoyed the sort of pranks which had characterized the early days of the Snowdons' marriage. In Britain, public opinion was reassured by press photographs of the couple strolling arm-in-arm in the Caribbean sunshine.

On her return, Princess Margaret decided that she must break off her affair. Even if her marriage was to be the sort of open arrangement into which it seemed rapidly to be developing, she must, she knew, do all she could to preserve at least its outward aspects. On 25 March 1967 she sat down at her desk in Kensington Palace to compose a farewell letter to Robin Douglas-Home. In due course some of these letters turned up at auction in New York (was this yet another betrayal, another desperate money-making bid on Douglas-Home's part?), and although their history is chequered, they have since been published in a book by the journalist Noel Botham.[5] There seems to be no reason to doubt their authenticity.

Among this correspondence was the Princess's final letter to Douglas-Home. In intimate, romantic, kindly worded terms, she sets out to explain why their association must end. Addressing him as 'Darling', she thanks him for the heart-lifting beauty and poetry of his last letter to her. She tells him about Snowdon's extreme anger about the affair and assures him that, in a curious fashion, his love was helping her in her determination to make her marriage work. 'Trust me as I trust you and love me as I love you,' she writes. 'Our love has the passionate scent of new-mown grass and lilies about it. Not many people are lucky enough to have known any love like this. I feel so happy that it has happened to me.' She would try, she said, to come back to him one day.[6]

Robin Douglas-Home is said to have been 'shattered' by this break with Princess Margaret.[7] He began to talk of suicide. Desperate for money, he was given a job by John Aspinall, the zoo-owner, who wanted someone to play the piano at his gaming club, the Clermont in Berkeley Square. As usual, Douglas-Home repaid this act of kindness with a betrayal: he sold a photograph of Aspinall in his swimming pool with a tiger cub, which he had taken at a private session, to the gossip columnist on the *Daily Express*. Aspinall sacked him immediately.

By now cripplingly short of money, and having lost his lover as well as a good many friends, his last romance was his most bizarre. He fell in love with a photograph of the twenty-two-year-old Miss United Kingdom, Kathleen Winstanley, and decided that he must marry her. He invited the girl down to his country place in West Chittington on the pretext of taking photographs of her but, on launching into his practised routine, found that the old charm simply did not work on her. Firmly but kindly, Kathleen Winstanley explained that she already had a boyfriend.

On 15 October 1968, eighteen months after the end of his affair with Princess Margaret, the thirty-six-year-old Robin Douglas-Home committed suicide in his cottage by taking an overdose of pills. The Princess did not attend his funeral.[8]

An indication that the Snowdons were resolved to lead separate lives came with the building of Princess Margaret's house on the island of Mustique. While the couple were staging their show of reconciliation in the Bahamas in March of 1967, the Princess had telephoned Colin Tennant to ask if she could finally take him up on his generous offer of a plot of land on Mustique. He confirmed the gift, and later came to Kensington Palace with a map of the island so that the Princess could choose her plot. She decided on that headland above Gelliceaux Bay where she had picnicked during her first visit to the island while on honeymoon, seven years before. Any hopes she may still have had that her husband might interest himself in the project, let alone design a house, were vain. Snowdon wanted nothing to do with a holiday home on Mustique.

Early in 1968, while recovering from an operation to remove her tonsils, Princess Margaret flew out to Barbados to spend a holiday with Snowdon's uncle, the stage designer Oliver Messel, who, because of his declining health, now lived permanently in the Caribbean. From his elegant colonial mansion, the Princess visited Mustique. With Colin Tennant only just beginning his programme of development, the island was still very primitive and the Princess's party had to hack their way through dense growth until they reached the chosen spot above Gelliceaux Bay. The views across the sea towards the neighbouring islands were magnificent, and the Princess pronounced herself delighted with her present. 'What about the house?' she then asked Tennant. Having a labour force and all the materials on the island, he assumed that he would be able to build one quite cheaply. But with Snowdon showing no interest in designing a house, the Princess turned to Oliver Messel. Messel duly visited the island, landing in a light plane on the bumpy earth airstrip, and drew up his plans. What with Messel's design and 'other little refinements', Colin Tennant's wedding gift turned out to be 'decidedly more costly' than he had at first imagined.[9]

The result was charming. Les Jolies-Eaux is a relatively modest – it can sleep ten – single-storey stone villa built in a U-shape around a paved courtyard. It is shaded by two giant cedars, and its roofs are pitched in such a way as to collect precious rainwater. The glass-panelled sitting-room doors can be folded back to frame an unbroken panorama of the glittering sea. The bamboo furniture and the tiled floor complement exactly the airy, informal, sun-steeped atmosphere of the house. From a roofed dining terrace, steps lead down to a lawn set in a garden bright with oleanders, bougainvillea, hibiscus and calla lilies. Beside a swimming pool stands a small thatched summer house. Pine-scented paths wind down the head-land to the sands of Gelliceaux Bay and Deep Bay.

If the building of Les Jolies-Eaux proved 'costly', it did at least provide, if unintentionally, a second dwelling. With the house com-plete, the Princess's furniture had arrived from London in a vast wooden container, which it took all day to unload. By that same evening the empty container had been converted into a home by an impoverished island family. Windows had been cut into the sides and a verandah, roofed in palm fronds, added. On the sides of this 'house' their remained stencilled, in bold black letters, the words 'HRH Princess Margaret'.

Once Les Jolies-Eaux had been completed, Princess Margaret visited it twice a year; in February and again in the late autumn. These tropical holidays, in the course of which the Princess would be photographed in various hedonistic situations, invariably aroused critical comment. More than any other place, Mustique came to symbolize, in the public mind, Princess Margaret's sensual and sybaritic nature. Indeed, the island was to be the setting of one of the climactic episodes of her life.

Meanwhile her life as a member of the royal family continued. During the second half of the 1960s Princess Margaret paid official visits to Hong Kong, France, Belgium, and another to the United States. At home, in addition to the usual round of engagements, she played her part in all the great state occasions. But even here, among the overwhelming traditionalism of the Court, the Princess could strike a discordant note. Barbara Castle, who served in various Cabinet posts in Harold Wilson's Labour Government during the second half of the 1960s, encountered her at a state banquet at Buckingham Palace. The setting, wrote the politician, was 'pure Ruritania: gold plate, knee-breeched gentlemen advancing in an organized phalanx to serve the courses, roses everywhere, minstrels in the gallery, and the dining room dominated by a huge canopied throne'. After the meal, as the Minister stood talking to the Queen, Princess Margaret strolled over to join them. In her *décolleté* dress and towering coiffure she looked, remembered Castle, 'very *outré*'.

'You've got to go back and vote or something,' she said to the Minister, and on being told that the vote was on the question of the reintroduction of the death penalty, commented cryptically, 'Ooh, you musn't miss that. I care very much about that.' Barbara Castle knew better than to ask a member of the royal family for her views on such a controversial subject.

The Queen, who was 'very relaxed', spoke about Prince Charles's forthcoming examinations, at one point turning to her sister and remarking, 'You and I would never have got into university.' Barbara Castle, a *soignée* woman herself, then complimented the Queen on her 'ravishing, gossamery' evening dress. Her Majesty's 'obvious pleasure' at this was immediately nullified by the Princess, who pointed a finger at the order pinned on the Queen's right breast. 'That's rather prominent, darling,' she said. 'Well, it does rather stick out.' Having delivered this deflating comment she wandered off, saying, 'I suppose we ought to permeate.' Her manner throughout, thought Barbara Castle, was 'positively brash'.[10]

'She has a way of putting you down,' says another observer, 'of making you feel either stupid or over-effusive.'[11] On one occasion an elderly retired woman journalist, thrilled at being invited to a reception for Princess Margaret, was even more thrilled on being presented to her. The journalist immediately launched into a recital of the occasions, dating back to King George VI's Coronation, on which she had reported the Princess's activities. The latter cut her short, asking icily, 'Are you one of those terrible reporters who tell lies about us all the time?' The poor woman could only stand, open-mouthed and blushing deeply, as the Princess moved away.[12]

One of the major royal occasions of this period was the Investiture, on 1 July 1969, of Prince Charles, as Prince of Wales. The ceremony took place at Caernarvon Castle, and although the overall responsibility for this great event lay with the Earl Marshal, the Duke of Norfolk, the Queen asked Lord Snowdon – whom she had already created Constable of Caernarvon Castle in 1963 – to design the pageant. He did it beautifully, with simplicity the keynote. Firmly rejecting the usual ornate royal style, he kept decoration to a minimum. A transparent perspex canopy covered a plain circular dais on which stood three stool-like thrones made of slabs of Welsh slate – for the Queen, Prince Philip and Prince Charles. The canopy was topped by a nine-foot high representation of the three feathers of the Prince of Wales's badge, carved in moulded polystyrene. For himself, Snowdon designed a dark green uniform with narrow trousers and a zip-fastened roll-collared jacket, although this had the slightly unfortunate effect of making him look not unlike a cross between a space traveller and the pantomime character 'Buttons'. Only the royal women, including Princess Margaret, struck a more traditional note in their pastel colours and elaborate hats.

The Investiture at Caernarvon greatly enhanced Snowdon's professional standing; indeed, as Princess Margaret's reputation plummeted, so did his soar. Already, as a member of the Committee for the National Fund for Research into Crippling Diseases, he was involved in work for the disabled, his boyhood experience of polio giving him an insight into the problems of the wheelchair-bound. Among his many contributions in this field, Snowdon designed a 'motive power pack' which allowed greater mobility than a conventional wheelchair. The disabled journalist Quentin Crewe, to whom one of the power packs was presented, claimed it to be the result of one of those 'great leaps in imagination'.[13]

Snowdon was branching out in other ways as well. He was commissioned by the Columbia Broadcasting System to make a documentary film about old age. The resulting film, *Don't Count the Candles*, made in collaboration with the television journalist, Derek Hart, won international acclaim and many awards. They followed this with further documentaries, including *Happy Being Happy*, about the achievement of personal happiness, and *Born To Be Small*, which dealt with the problems of midgets or, more tactfully, 'people of restricted growth'. When the actor Gordon Jackson, who had been invited to one of the Queen's special luncheon parties, congratulated Princess Margaret on her husband's *Born To Be Small*, her reply was dismissive. 'Not my cup of tea at all,' she shrugged. 'Bit too near home, I'm afraid.' Jackson suddenly realized, he said, that all the royal women were 'TINY'.[14]

Not that Snowdon himself was much taller. There is a story about a row between him and one of his journalistic colleagues. In the course of a telephone conversation between the two men, tempers became increasingly frayed. 'Everyone knows,' yelled Snowdon, 'that you're the biggest shit in London.' 'Well,' the journalist shouted back, 'everyone knows that you're the smallest shit in London.'[15]

Lord Snowdon's successes underlined, to a marked degree, the fact that whereas he was winning public respect by his personal achievements, Princess Margaret's claim to recognition rested solely on an accident of birth. And she was coming to be regarded as being unworthy even of that. Somewhat unfairly, she was seen as lacking in any sense of royal dedication. Her dogged fulfilling of her engagements went largely unappreciated; she was better known for her less admirable activities. Lacking her sister's iron sense of duty and her mother's charm and showmanship, the Princess gave the impression of being a royal freeloader. In retrospect, she would have done better, and certainly have improved the public view of her, to have taken up – as her niece Princess Anne was to take up – some praiseworthy and newsworthy charitable cause, and to have dedicated her undoubted talents to that. Such enthusiasms as she did have – for various branches of the arts – were not especially profound, and her self-conscious forays into the world of rock stars or fashion models were hardly calculated to win her wide public approval. Gradually she came to be spoken of as a woman without a cause, as a princess without any real sense of purpose.

None the less, in September 1969 the Snowdons set out on one of those gruelling, densely packed, three-week-long tours which, since they are scantily reported, earn very little recognition at home. This one took them to Japan, Hong Kong, Cambodia, Thailand and Iran. The climax of their nine-day stay in Japan was the opening, by the Princess, of yet another British Week, this time in Tokyo. While they were there, the Princess met her cousin, Prince William of Gloucester, eldest son of her Uncle Henry, the bluff-mannered Duke of Gloucester. The dashing, twenty-seven-year-old Prince was serving as Commercial Attaché at the British Embassy in Tokyo, but during the Snowdons' visit acted as a liaison officer between them and their Japanese hosts. Like Princess Margaret, Prince William was something of a free spirit. Refusing to live in one of the mock-Queen Anne houses in the Embassy compound, he had found himself a traditional Japanese house, and it was here that he entertained the Snowdons. 'Thank you for your lovely party. We so enjoyed it,' wrote the Princess to him afterwards. 'It was such fun with such nice people and heavenly food and I adored your house – also one can't imagine anything more blissful, after tramping through all those excellent department stores, to be asked to take one's shoes off.'[16]

Like his cousin, Prince William too found himself 'torn between the yoke of his birth and his longing for freedom'.[17] And, like her, he tended to fall in love with unsuitable people. In Tokyo he became involved with an older woman – a Hungarian-born, twice-divorced *femme du monde* named Zsuzui Starkloff. The Prince was set on marrying her but, knowing only too well what his family's reaction would be, he discussed his problem with Princess Margaret. She advised him to 'wait a bit and then come home and see how everything looks'.[18] Better than anyone, she would have realized exactly how everything would look to the young man's parents. Nor did it take Zsuzui Starkloff long to appreciate the situation. Brought to England to meet the Duke and Duchess of Gloucester, she saw that marriage was out of the question. 'William's devotion to his parents, and his sense of responsibility towards what he is,' were too strong, she admitted. 'He's too much of a man to be happy in the Prince's role and he's too much of a Prince to be happy in an ordinary man's role', was her summing up of Prince William's dilemma.[19] Her conclusions might have applied equally to Princess Margaret.

Under the pressure of this Far Eastern journey – this kaleido-scopic jumble of flights, train journeys, exhibitions, receptions, ban-quets, luncheons, tours of inspection and visits to assorted mosques and temples – the relationship between the Snowdons deteriorated still further. By the time they reached Iran they were hardly on speaking terms. A guest at a reception at the British Embassy in Tehran gives a vivid picture of the two of them: 'She came in with a face like thunder and immediately asked for a drink. Then she put a cigarette into a long holder and began puffing away. She made no effort whatsoever. He made conversation here and there but she obviously couldn't be bothered to mingle with the guests. They didn't say a word to each other. I'm sure that they'd just had a flaming row. It was very embarrassing.'[20]

Lord Snowdon had always been very attractive to women. In the course of his work he was, not unnaturally, associated with many fashionable beauties, and was often to be seen lunching or dining with good-looking models or career girls. 'He has the talent,' said a friend, 'for soft-soaping them quite skilfully.'[21] There is no reason to believe that these encounters were anything other than innocent, but in the late 1960s Snowdon's name became linked, more seri-ously, with that of the young Lady Jacqueline Rufus Isaacs.

Lady Jackie, as she was usually called, was the only daughter among the four children of the third Marquess of Reading. The Readings' country home, Staplefield Grange, was less than half a mile from Snowdon's restored weekend retreat, Old House. Inevitably, he became friendly with his neighbours, and would often stroll over from Old House to have tea or drinks or even din-ner with the Readings. Lady Jackie, who turned twenty-three in November 1969, was an extremely attractive young woman who earned her living, in a desultory, ex-debutante sort of way, as a model in a fashionable dress shop and as an organizer of society par-ties. Before long, she had apparently fallen for Lord Snowdon's cel-ebrated charms. The unsuspecting Princess Margaret liked Lady Jackie and her older brother, Lord Anthony Rufus Isaacs – who ran a company which made television films – and added them to her Kensington Palace invitation list.

It was not until towards the end of 1969 that members of the Princess's circle first began to suspect that there was something going on between Lord Snowdon and Lady Jacqueline Rufus Isaacs. On 11 December Princess Margaret attended the charity première of the new Peter Sellers film *The Magic Christian* (which also starred the Beatles' drummer, Ringo Starr) at the Odeon cinema in Kensington. The film was followed by a party at one of the Princess's old haunts, the nightclub Les Ambassadeurs, to which such contemporary luminaries as David Frost and Ringo Starr himself were invited. It was immediately noticed that whereas Princess Margaret sat at one table, between Patrick Lichfield and Jocelyn Stevens, Snowdon – who had arrived alone – sat at another table, beside Lady Jackie. When some of the party moved on to that other fashionable nightspot, Annabel's, Lady Jackie accompanied them. Photographs of Snowdon, in velvet jacket and loosely knotted scarf, sitting at a table with his lovely companion, seemed to tell the whole story.

Throughout the following year, 1970, Lord Snowdon and Lady Jackie allegedly saw each other regularly. He continued his visits to Staplefield Grange, where the unsuspecting Readings welcomed him as before, but his more private meetings with their daughter are said to have taken place in her London flat in Cundy Street, not far from his old Pimlico Road studio. It is impossible for an outsider to know the true nature of their relationship, but, quite clearly, Lady Jackie was very taken with Snowdon. When he entered the London Clinic for an operation for haemorrhoids in December 1970, it was noticed that she visited him more often than did Princess Margaret – the two women sometimes missing each other only by seconds. ('Tony tried to ban me from visiting him,' claims the Princess.[22]) Snowdon's stay in hospital proved a blessing in one way: it allowed him to miss the awkwardness of the Royal Family's Christmas gathering.

The business came to a head in January 1971, when Lady Jackie, with her eldest brother Simon, Viscount Erleigh, set off to spend a holiday, in accordance with upper-class ritual, in the Swiss ski resort of Gsteig. Hardly had they arrived before the *New York Daily News*, the largest-selling newspaper in the United States, broke the story of the 'romance' between Princess Margaret's husband and Lady Jacqueline Rufus Isaacs. By midday press placards throughout London were proclaiming the rumour, and by that evening the news was being broadcast on all television and radio stations. For the following three days Lady Jackie was besieged in her chalet by the paparazzi. The Marquess of Reading, appalled by the news, hotly denied it, meanwhile advising his daughter to say nothing to the press. His advice was backed up by Snowdon. He, too, was determined to say nothing, not least because he realized that any official denial would simply give credence to the rumour. Lord Reading is said to have banned Snowdon from his house and the 'affair' died a quick death.[23]

The real casualty in the Lady Jackie affair was Princess Margaret. She was furious; not only about the rumoured romance, but also because of the damage that the news of it would inevitably do to her reputation. Involvement in this sort of scandalous episode was exactly what the public had come to expect of her. That she was the innocent party in the affair made no difference: it seemed merely to emphasize her scandal-racked way of life. She never forgave Lady Jackie for this indiscretion. When, a couple of years later, the Princess was placed near the young woman at a luncheon party, she studiously ignored her, except to raise her voice whenever the unfortunate Lady Jackie opened her mouth to speak.

Although the Snowdons tried to make good the damage in what was becoming the usual way, by flying off to the West Indies and having themselves photographed in happy poses on the beach, the public remained sceptical. Perhaps the Princess would have won a little more public sympathy if her reconciliations with her husband had not always taken place in the Caribbean sunshine while Britain shivered. But whatever public face they chose to put upon their relationship, in many ways the Lady Jackie affair marked the beginning of the end of the Snowdons' marriage.

CHAPTER SEVENTEEN

Goon Show

'PRINCESS MARGARET,' announced one of her friends at about the time of Snowdon's association with Lady Jackie, 'needs a man.'¹ That she did not have one was not because of any lack of masculine attention. Throughout the deterioration of her marriage, her name continued to be linked, with or without foundation, to men of varying suitability. During the early 1970s, a figure from the 1950s, the Hon. Dominic Elliot, a son of the Earl of Minto, re-entered the Princess's life. Divorced from his wife, Countess Mari-anne Esterházy, he was ready to renew their old relationship. After an official tour of the Virgin Islands in March 1972, Princess Margaret went on to Mustique. There she was joined by Elliot who, before flying off to the West Indies, had assured clamouring reporters at Heathrow that he and the Princess were merely 'old friends'.² Once on the island – he was there as a guest of the Ten-nants – he had proved the perfect companion; the two of them swam, picnicked, dined either alone or with friends, and invariably ended the evening dancing to the gramophone in the Beach Bar.

A more exotic association was with that dazzling star of the peri-od, the rock singer Mick Jagger. The darling of society, the leader of the Rolling Stones was attending the sixteenth birthday party of the Hon. Victoria Ormsby-Gore when he found himself being beckoned over by Princess Margaret – 'wearing a low-cut gown that revealed ample cleavage'. Renowned, among other things, for his animal magnetism, Jagger could also be a charming and entertaining con-versationalist, and the Princess spent more than half an hour chat-ting to him on that occasion. After this initial meeting, says one close associate, 'they spoke on the phone constantly and Margaret invited him to social events. Like many other women, she found him sexy and exciting. If you saw them laughing together, dancing, the way she'd put her hand on his knee and giggle at his stories like a schoolgirl – you'd have thought there was something going on.'³ The Princess suggested that the singer should visit Mustique, which he duly did; indeed, in time he built himself a holiday home there.

A better authenticated, though hardly less bizarre relationship was that between Princess Margaret and the actor Peter Sellers. Although Sellers and his second wife, the Swedish-born actress Britt Ekland, had been friendly with the Snowdons for several years, it was not until the end of the 1960s that Peter Sellers declared himself in love with the Princess.

Born in 1925, Sellers had risen from his modest Jewish background by virtue of his extraordinary talent – mainly for his astonishingly diverse personality disguises. Having gained enormous popularity on the BBC's long-running radio comedy, *The Goon Show*, he had developed into an international film star, with his career reaching its peak in the mid-1960s with such films as *Dr Strangelove* and *The Pink Panther*. The Snowdons' eager embracing of bohemia had soon brought them into contact with this offbeat comedian and his wife, Britt, whom he had married in 1963. To the delight of Peter Sellers – who, in his characteristically thin-skinned way, was both impressed by, and determined to prove himself the equal of, the Snowdons – the two couples became great friends. The actors would entertain the royal pair in their house in Elstead, near Farnham in Surrey, and would in turn, be entertained at Kensington Palace. And not only Kensington Palace, but, more significantly, at Royal Lodge and Windsor Castle. The Queen Mother, with her penchant for unorthodox characters, was very taken with Sellers. This fondness may well have dated from the occasion when, on being presented to the actor in one of the usual line-ups after a film première, she had asked him the usual question 'What are you doing now?' – to which she had received the unusual answer, 'Why, standing here talking to you.'⁴ Peter Sellers and his wife were often invited to Royal Lodge and Clarence House.

The actor was made equally welcome at Windsor Castle. Having a taste for buffoonery, the Queen and Prince Philip greatly admired Sellers. In fact, the celebrated home movie in which both Princess

Margaret and Lord Snowdon had featured, had been made by Sellers (at a personal cost of £6,000) as a birthday present for the Queen's thirty-ninth birthday in 1965; the film is still regularly shown at family gatherings. Sellers's greatest fan, however, was Prince Charles. Besotted by *The Goon Show* (he admits that the 'Ying-Tong Song' is the only song he knows by heart) the Prince once stoutly declared that 'no matter how much "fashion" in humour changes, there will always be thousands of people whose minds are attuned to the kind of mental slapstick and imaginary cartoonery that typifies Goonery.'[5] He would on occasion happily spend hours with Sellers, playing Eccles to the other's Bluebottle.

The ex-Goon himself was apparently quite happy to be cast in the role of Court Jester, joining with relish in the charades and other parlour games which provided the entertainment at Windsor Castle. Britt Ekland writes that she would 'squirm with embarrassment at the demeaning lengths [Sellers] would stoop to in order to ingratiate himself with the royal family. It was contemptible.'[6] In his eagerness to identify himself with his illustrious hosts, Sellers even took up shooting. Once, while water-skiing on the lake in Windsor Great Park, he caused much hilarity by falling off his skis. Not realizing that his ducking was an illustration of his incompetence rather than of his clowning, the assembled royals burst into a Goonish catch phrase, 'He's fallen in da wahtar!'[7]

To his wife's increasing irritation, Sellers loaded the Snowdons with gifts. Lord Snowdon had only to admire some new lens (Sellers had taken up photography) for it to be handed over to him. The actor also gave him cameras, hi-fi equipment and a CIA bugging device, and sold him an Aston Martin for a fraction of its cost. Sellers's little daughter, Victoria, was heartbroken when he gave her palomino pony, Buttercup, as a present to Princess Margaret's children. Even more irritating was his habit of retrieving gifts already presented to others and of sending them on to Princess Margaret instead. He once gave the pianist Alan Clare an electric piano, a so-called 'mellotron' ('all tubes, flues, flashing lights and gears'), only to take it back in order to have it sent to Kensington Palace. The Princess, apparently, loved it and, pretending to be 'coming up through the floor in an Odeon', would sit perched on the stool 'playing arpeggios'. As much as she loved it, though, Snowdon hated it; for him, the mellotron became, it is said, 'a symbol of the couple's dissent'.[8]

In the summer of 1967, with his own marriage, like the Snowdons', now falling apart, Sellers bought a £150,000, 50-foot yacht. Having christened the vessel *The Bobo* (the title of his latest film), he suggested that both couples make use of it while holidaying in Sardinia. There they were joined by Princess Margaret's cousin, Princess Alexandra of Kent and her husband, the Hon. Angus Ogilvy. In Sardinia the entire group was able to celebrate Princess Margaret's thirty-seventh birthday at a party given by the Aga Khan. But not even this illustrious gathering could satisfy Sellers's soaring social ambitions: he now wished that, like Snowdon, he could be a famous photographer, rewarded with an earldom.

Peter Sellers's divorce from Britt Ekland in 1968, and his awareness of the imminent collapse of Princess Margaret's marriage, caused him to imagine that his ambitions might yet be realized. Although dazzled by the Princess's status, the actor was alive to her vulnerability; to the fact that, for all her apparent and often sharp-tongued self-assurance, she felt isolated and unhappy. This meant not only that he declared himself to be in love with her, but that he genuinely imagined that she might agree to marry him. To the famous clairvoyant, Maurice Woodruff, whom he found indispensable to his life, Sellers claimed to be having an affair with the Princess, and to the *Daily Mirror* he jokingly protested that they were 'just good friends', knowing full well the implications of that phrase. He wrote her romantic letters, took her out to meals *à deux*, and entertained her in his lavishly decorated Clarges Street apartment. To him, she was 'Ma'am darling'. He even confided to the actor Laurence Harvey that the Princess had breasts of the same size as the subject of one of his earlier obsessions, Sophia Loren: 'the same cup size exactly'.[9] And as his obsession grew, so did his actions occasionally verge on the bizarre. On one occasion, in order to convince the Princess's detective that she was attending a large party and not dining alone with him in his apartment, Sellers answered the door disguised as an old manservant while, in the background, a tape played sounds of lively talk and laughter. Fooled by this apparent evidence of a substantial gathering of people, the detective retreated to wait downstairs.

Sellers adopted a proprietary attitude towards Princess Margaret, deeply resenting her friendship – even her acquaintance – with other men. Once, on the set of *Casino Royale*, he proudly announced that the Princess was due to come and see him work that morning, and promised Orson Welles that he would present him to Her Royal Highness. She duly arrived, walked straight past Sellers and made for Welles. 'Hello, Orson,' she exclaimed, 'I haven't seen you for *days*.' Sellers, said Welles, 'went as white as a sheet.'[10]

For all his buffoonery, and the occasional oddity of his behaviour, Peter Sellers could be an astute observer. He has an interesting comment to make on the strange dichotomy of Princess Margaret's position. 'I've never known her especially enjoy protocol . . .' he said, 'yet I have taken her out to lunch without a detective or chauffeured car and she simply doesn't enjoy that.'[11] In other words, without actually wanting the royal trappings, she was uneasy about functioning without them. She remained, in her bones, a princess first and a maverick second.

What were the Princess's feelings towards Peter Sellers? He was, she once admitted, 'the most difficult man I know', but she was clearly attracted to him.[12] Sometimes, though, he could go too far, as when he telephoned her and, pretending to be Lord Snowdon, embarked on a raunchy description of his alleged nights with Lady Jacqueline Rufus Isaacs. This time, Her Royal Highness was not amused. Sellers was a great womanizer, and many women found him irresistible, but however close the relationship, at no stage did the Princess envisage marrying him. This realization seems to have cooled his ardour. 'It's amazing,' he said naïvely. 'Princess Margaret has made it quite clear she won't marry again. Having been through it once and, God knows, marriage breakdowns happen all the time, she won't do it again. She is a very resolute woman.'[13] His acceptance of this state of affairs, combined with the fact that, in 1973, the Princess became involved with an infinitely more desirable man, marked the end of Peter Sellers's dreams of ennoblement and a royal marriage. Gradually, his association with Ma'am darling died a death.

The last, inevitable, question is whether their relationship had been actively sexual. When Sellers's biographer, Roger Lewis, caused enquiries to be made on this delicate subject, he received a characteristically tart answer from one of her staff. 'Well, if she did,' came the reply, 'she had her eyes closed and she forgot about it immediately afterwards.'[14]

* * *

By now, Princess Margaret and Lord Snowdon were barely on speaking terms. On the rare occasions when he was home during the day, he would lock himself in his study or his studio. At night he would go out alone, never saying where he was going and often not returning until the following morning. If the couple did bump into each other at home, the Princess's greeting would be rewarded with a grunt; if Snowdon did want to communicate with her, it was invariably by a tersely worded note left on her desk. To a close woman friend, she confided that Snowdon had even left a note on her dressing table headed '20 reasons why I hate you'.[15] Once, when she was entertaining some of her friends at a formal party in Kensington Palace, Snowdon arrived with a group of leather-jacketed companions, nodded briefly to his wife's guests, and marched his party through to another room. On another occasion, when Princess Margaret passed through a room, Snowdon dropped a mock curtsy behind her retreating back.

Matters became even worse, however, when they were obliged to spend time in each other's company. 'There was an atmosphere you couldn't kick your way through,' said Jocelyn Stevens, and Lord Lichfield described them as 'trading insults like gunfire'.[16] Peter Sellers's secretary, Hattie Stevenson, was shocked by the bitterness between the couple. 'PM used to be very nasty to her husband,' she says. 'They used to say the most awful things to each other. I can remember dinner parties and they'd argue right across the table.'[17] 'She could be incredibly sharp,' said another observer, 'and would cause him to lose his temper.'[18] In this, though, he was more than a match for her. 'Oh, God, you bore me!' he would say in public, and he once exclaimed, 'You look like a Jewish manicurist and I hate you.'[19]

This permanent marital tension began to affect the Princess's looks. While her husband remained slender and stylish, she became fat and frumpish. Unhappiness always caused her to put on weight and whereas the Queen Mother cleverly converted her plumpness into an added dignity, Princess Margaret looked merely unfashionably dumpy. In 1970 the satirical magazine *Private Eye*, quick to reflect current rumour, featured a cover photograph of the Snowdons, both grinning broadly as their car is being driven through the crowds. 'What's all this about us rowing in public?' asks the Princess in the caption. 'Shut up you fat bitch and keep smiling,' answers Snowdon.[20]

Such holidays as the couple still took together soon deteriorated into open warfare. On one annual Sardinian visit Snowdon is said to have purposely remained on the Aga Khan's yacht, maliciously leaving the Princess to force her way alone through a crowd of shoving, shouting, camera-clicking tourists as she made for the safety of the waiting car. In 1973, on their last Sardinian holiday together, the couple were accompanied by their two children. David, Lord Linley, was now eleven and at boarding school, and Lady Sarah Armstrong-Jones was nine. They were both attractive, affectionate, well-mannered children, with David resembling his father in appearance and temperament and Sarah looking more like her mother; both were to develop strong artistic interests. ('My children,' Princess Margaret would always explain, 'are not royal. They just happen to have the Queen for an aunt.'[21]) Whatever their other failings, Princess Margaret and Lord Snowdon were devoted parents, always very interested in their children's progress. In Sardinia that year, however, any hope that the presence of the children might improve the holiday atmosphere between the parents proved to be vain. 'Tony was bolshie from the start, late for meals or not turning up at all, that sort of thing,' complained the Princess. 'And more than anything, he was rude to me in front of the children.'[22] 'Papa, Mummy is talking to you,' one of the children would say, only to be answered with a curt, 'I know.'[23] Within a week, Snowdon had returned to London, leaving his wife and children behind.

On an earlier holiday, this time in the Caribbean, there had been a scene at a charity ball. Princess Margaret had agreed to attend the local Red Cross Ball on Barbados, knowing that her presence would stimulate ticket sales. Although suffering from one of her recurrent migraines, she insisted on attending so as not to disappoint the guests, both black and white, so demonstrating once again her often underestimated and unappreciated sense of royal obligation. The Princess endured the evening bravely but, towards midnight, decided that it was time to go home. Lord Snowdon, however, was nowhere to be seen. When the Princess's detective was unable – or diplomatically claimed to be unable – to find him, the exasperated Princess asked Jonathan Aitken, who was her host's cousin, to see if he could unearth her husband; it would not do for husband and wife to be seen leaving the ball separately. Primed by the detective, Aitken discovered Snowdon under a table with a girl who worked in a local boutique, and explained that the Princess was desperate to leave. 'Fuck off, arselicker,' came the answer. Together, Aitken and the detective heaved Snowdon to his feet and marched him off to the waiting Princess.[24]

Lord Snowdon seems to have been equally difficult at the Badminton Horse Trials in the spring of 1972. To the Duke of Beaufort's relief, he had refused to accompany Princess Margaret to the horse trials because, he said, they bored him. But two days before the start of the event he changed his mind, deciding to attend after all, which entailed much reorganizing of the accommodation. Hardly had Snowdon arrived before he infuriated the Duke by pronouncing hunting to be cruel. The Duke – the Master of the Beaufort Hunt – hotly denied this, but his guest then annoyed him further by saying that 'the competitors in the horse trials must be terrified.' 'Equestrians are never terrified,' barked the Duke. 'Only cissies are terrified.' In his fury, he attacked the fire with a poker. Princess Margaret, anxious to calm her raging host, said, 'Tony doesn't mean terrified really, he means nervous.' 'No, I don't,' insisted Snowdon, 'I mean terrified.' The by now apoplectic Beaufort banged the poker so violently that he bent it. 'Damn this fire, I tell you. Damn it, damn it!' he thundered. That same afternoon, Lord Snowdon left Badminton, without saying goodbye.[25]

Another telling, and rather different, picture of the Snowdons together is given by the writer James Lees-Milne. He was invited to a small dinner party given in a private room at Rules restaurant in London, to honour the poet John Betjeman. Other guests included Prince Charles, Princess Margaret and Lord Snowdon. Lees-Milne described the Prince of Wales as charming and polite and Snowdon as 'full of vitality and cheer'. His comments on the Princess are rather more critical. 'You know Jim?' Snowdon asked the Princess as they came face to face with Lees-Milne. 'Yes,' she answered curtly, and immediately moved away. 'Princess Margaret,' writes Lees-Milne, 'is far from charming, is cross, exacting, too sophisticated, and sharp. She is physically attractive in a bun-like way, with trussed-up bosom, and hair like two cottage loaves, one balancing on the other. She wore a beautiful sapphire and diamond brooch. She smoked continuously from a long holder. . . .'

After the dinner, when the hostess, who had slipped out of her shoes, walked downstairs barefoot to see Prince Charles off,

Princess Margaret picked up her shoes and put them on her plate. This annoyed Snowdon. 'It is unlucky, and I don't like it,' he snapped. The Princess transferred the shoes from the plate to the seat of her chair and strode huffily to the window. Then, having announced that she wanted to leave, she finally induced Snowdon to take her home. Somewhat to the discomfiture of the other guests, he insisted that they all come back to Kensington Palace. In her own home, says Lees-Milne, the Princess was rather more gracious to him, but he still 'did not find conversation very easy or agreeable'.[26]

The writer Richard Hughes experienced a similar conversational awkwardness when seated at dinner next to Princess Margaret who, without Snowdon, was visiting Lord and Lady Harlech on their Welsh estate. Among other novels, Hughes was the author of *The Fox in the Attic*, which is, in part, a chilling account of the rise of Nazi Germany. 'I haven't read *The Fox in the Attic*,' was the Princess's opening and intimidating remark. 'Tell me what it's about.' Having stumbled his way through that, Hughes, frantically searching about for something further to say in the face of Princess Margaret's unnerving silence, blurted out what he instantly realized was the wrong question. 'Have you seen Snowdon?' he asked. 'Do you mean the man,' she answered icily, 'or the mountain?'[27]

Most other couples, given such insurmountable marital incompatibility, would have settled for a divorce. But although Snowdon apparently told friends that he would have no difficulty in getting a divorce, Princess Margaret was not prepared, at this stage, to consider it. And nor, of course, were the Queen and the Queen Mother. For the second time in her life, the long shadow of the Duke of Windsor's marriage to a twice-divorced woman was falling across Princess Margaret's path. To the Queen Mother, the whole idea remained anathema, and even the Queen, who took a rather more tolerant view, appreciated that a divorce would do incalculable harm to the image of the monarchy. The situation was further complicated by the fact that both women remained very fond of Lord Snowdon. Not unnaturally, they always saw him at his best, and both were quite ready to believe that much of the fault lay with the always wayward Princess Margaret.

The first divorce of one of King George V's direct descendants had taken place as recently as 1967. This was after Queen Elizabeth

II's cousin, the Earl of Harewood, had been sued for adultery by his first wife. Nothing could have illustrated better the royal family's attitude to divorce than the complications surrounding Harewood's attempts to end his first marriage and remarry. His mother, Princess Mary the Princess Royal, only sister of the late King George VI, had been appalled at the idea. Yet the members of the royal family were so inarticulate, so determined never to discuss unwelcome subjects, that Harewood only once mentioned his marital problems to his mother. She listened to what he had to say in complete silence, making no comment and showing no understanding. Not until he mentioned the word divorce did she speak up. 'What will people say?' she exclaimed.[28]

She was, however, to be spared this, to her, dreadful scandal, for she died soon afterwards. Just over two years later, by which time Lord Harewood was already living with the woman who was to become his second wife, he was granted a divorce from his first. This should have left him free to remarry, but in practice it did not. By the conditions of the Royal Marriages Act, the Sovereign's consent was needed for his remarriage. This the Queen would have been willing to grant – albeit reluctantly – were it not for the fact that giving that consent would look as though she, as Supreme Governor of the Church, were condoning divorce. What was she to do? A way out of the impasse was provided by the then Prime Minister, Harold Wilson. He put the matter to the Cabinet, which advised the Queen to grant permission; and she, as a constitutional monarch, was obliged to take their advice. The divorced Lord Harewood married for a second time, and a royal precedent was set.

But the Queen's permission had not meant the Queen's approval. For many years after his divorce, Lord Harewood was cold-shouldered by the rest of the royal family, the Queen Mother remaining especially strong in her condemnation. It is hardly surprising that in such a climate of disapproval, and conscious of the Church's teachings, Princess Margaret should have put aside all thoughts of divorce. In any case, as her authorized biographer has put it, the Princess 'neither wanted nor approved of divorce'.[29]

In the early 1970s, with her life in this unsettled state, Princess Margaret became involved in yet more controversy, this time concerning her allowance from the Civil List.

Under the operating rules of the Civil List, the Sovereign and several other leading members of the royal family receive annuities from the Treasury. These annuities are not salaries: they are designed to reimburse members of the family for the expenses incurred in the carrying out of their public duties. Nevertheless, the misconception that the Civil List provides family members with personal spending money, rather than with the means of meeting their official expenses, dies very hard. By 1972, this question of the royal finances had become the subject of a particularly heated public debate.

Long gone were the days when a Civil List could be fixed at the start of a reign in the certainty that its provisions would be adequate at the end of it. (It is an illuminating fact that, on her accession to the throne in 1952, Queen Elizabeth II needed to be granted only £5,000 more than her great-grandfather, King Edward VII, had been apportioned on his accession in 1901.) By the year 1970, with inflation rampant, the monarchy was, as Prince Philip bluntly put it, 'in the red'. The annual £475,000 established by the Civil List Act of 1952 was proving hopelessly inadequate; the deficit for the year 1970 alone was £270,000. The same was also true of the provisions made for other leading members of the family, including Princess Margaret, although the amounts involved were smaller.

To meet the Queen's request for an increase in the Civil List, the Prime Minister of the day, Harold Wilson, set up a Select Committee to examine the subject. On the fall of the Labour Government in June 1970, the new Conservative Prime Minister, Edward Heath, set up yet another committee. But not until 1972 was the whole complicated and controversial question of the royal family's finances thrashed out in Parliament. In the end, the Queen's allowance was more than doubled to £980,000 a year, and increased annuities were paid to other members of the family.

It was this question of increased payments to other members of the family that had caused most controversy during committee sessions – and it was Princess Margaret who had come in for the roughest treatment. Her annual annuity, granted on her marriage in 1960, was £15,000, and it had been proposed, by the Palace, that her allowance now be raised to £35,000. The committee, however, was having none of it. Having noted that £80,000 had already been spent on the restoration of her Kensington Palace apartment, the members of the committee went on to argue that she was not really earning her allowance. During 1970, they maintained, the Princess had spent only thirty-one days outside London on official engagements. 'Since the Princess has a working husband and since her public engagements appear to be extremely limited in number, scope and importance, your Committee do not feel it right to ask the taxpayer to continue the annuity; free housing should be adequate recompense for services rendered.'[30] In short, the committee was suggesting the complete abolition of Princess Margaret's annuity.

The Princess was incensed. She could point out that in 1970 she had undertaken 117 official engagements, including 7 to units of the armed forces. Between 1970 and 1972, she had paid official visits to Yugoslavia (as the first member of the British royal family to visit a communist country), France, Canada, the British Virgin Islands, Italy, West Germany, the Seychelles, Western Australia and Singapore. It was not, she protested, as though her allowance went on drink, cigarettes, holidays and private entertaining: it was used to cover the costs of carrying out her royal duties. These included secretarial and staff salaries; the rates, heating and lighting of her Kensington Palace home; the running and maintenance of her official car; the costs of such things as telephone calls, office equipment, stationery and postage. During recent years, as her original £15,000 annuity had become increasingly – and, finally, hopelessly – inadequate, she had had to supplement her expenses from her own funds. She might also have claimed that having – by her renunciation of Peter Townsend in 1955 – opted to continue a life of public service, she was fully entitled to a Civil List allowance.

The House of Commons debate on the matter was extremely heated. When, in the course of it, Willie Hamilton referred to Princess Margaret as 'this expensive kept woman', the Conservative MP Norman St John Stevas became almost apoplectic with rage. He rose to quote against Hamilton 'the parliamentary bible of Erskine May [the authoritative work on parliamentray procedure]. "Disrespectful use of Her Majesty's name would normally give offence outside of Parliament; and it is only consistent with decency that a member of the legislature should not be permitted openly to use such language in Parliament".' Should not that rule, demanded St John Stevas, apply equally to disrespect shown to the Queen's sister?[31] In the end, however, the Select Committee's recommendation that Princess Margaret's annuity be abolished altogether was defeated; in fact, the Conservative majority in the House of Commons ensured that not one of the committee's radical recommendations was adopted. In spite of the blistering denunciations of Hamilton and other Labour members, all the original proposals for a general increase in the Civil List were carried. As had been proposed, Princess Margaret's allowance was raised from £15,000 to £35,000.

Within five years this seemingly generous increase had, in turn, been swallowed up by inflation, and the Queen was once again obliged to ask Parliament for increases in the Civil List. And once again the indefatigable Willie Hamilton was on his feet to denounce what was generally, if inaccurately, referred to as a 'royal pay rise'. But once again the increases were granted, Princess Margaret's allowance rising from £35,000 to £55,000. This time, though, the machinery for granting such increases was altered: instead of a new Act of Parliament to sanction each increase, the matter of the royal finances would in future be subject to the same procedure as any other government expenditure. Even this could not spare the Princess the embarrassment of such recurring tabloid headlines as 'Is She Worth It?' and 'Does She Earn It?' – headlines which were invariably accompanied by inaccurately low estimates of the number of her public engagements and all too accurate proofs of her low ratings in popularity polls.

Not all the comment was hostile. 'I do wish they would leave poor Princess Margaret alone,' wrote Princess Alice, Countess of Athlone, to a friend at this time.[32] Princess Alice, who was by then Queen Victoria's last surviving granddaughter, lived in Clock House, Kensington Palace, which lay across the courtyard from the Snowdons' apartment, and was thus a close neighbour. Widowed since 1957, she turned ninety in 1973, and had lived exactly the sort of active, dedicated, meaningful life that Princess Margaret ought to have been living. Her late husband, the Earl of Athlone, had been Governor-General of, first, South Africa and then Canada, and she had, until very recently, been Chancellor of the University of the West Indies. Like Princess Margaret, Princess Alice adored the Caribbean, and each year would travel out by banana boat to spend the worst of the British winter in the sunshine.

Princess Alice was very fond of Princess Margaret, whom she thought 'so pretty, and so lively and intelligent. She's full of spirit. And she gets about.'[33] Being herself very interested in clothes, she would often stand at a window to watch Princess Margaret leaving her apartment opposite, just to see what she was wearing. The younger princess was equally fond of 'Aunt Alice'; 'If ever I could get past that dragon, Miss Goldie [Princess Alice's secretary],' she would say, 'I would go and see her.' Since Princess Alice was by then very deaf, visiting her was not the easiest of duties but Princess Margaret would sit in Aunt Alice's elegant drawing room, gamely bellowing away at the little bird-like figure.

In old age, Princess Alice would proudly tell of how, as a child, she had met a woman who had attended the Duchess of Richmond's ball in Brussels on the eve of the Battle of Waterloo in 1815. Princess Margaret, whose sense of history is highly developed, delighted in that snippet of information. 'I used to tell my children to remember, in their old age,' she says, 'that when they were young they had known someone who had known someone who had danced at a ball just before the Battle of Waterloo.' (It is this same sense of the importance of the past which makes the Princess bemoan the fact that the Queen Mother has never kept a diary. 'We've begged her to write down her memories or even tape them, but she won't,' she sighs.[34])

Other complimentary comments on Princess Margaret come from someone who often met her at parties during the early 1970s. 'She was very warm and witty and could be the greatest fun,' he says. 'She had a way, if there was a harsh overhead light, of shielding her eyes with her hand and peering about in mock despair that was really very funny. And some of her take-offs were hilarious. One heard all sorts of stories about her rudeness but she was always charming to me.'[35]

The singer Cleo Laine was equally appreciative of the Princess's many good qualities. When she and her husband, the musician John Dankworth, launched a centre for music in the village of Wavendon in Buckinghamshire – the Wavendon Allmusic Plan – Princess Margaret gave them unstinting support, attending concerts, raising funds, presenting awards, and opening a new extension to the building. Cleo Laine and John Dankworth were always invited to the Princess's Christmas carol party at Kensington Palace, at which the

Queen was often present. 'I remember one occasion John and I arrived late to find everyone waiting to begin the carolling. We were hurriedly introduced by the Princess to those present: "Lord so and so, Lady do-da, the Hon. what's it, you know my sister . . .".'[36]

Indeed, it was among show business people that the Princess often exhibited her own film-star quality. On once visiting Brinsworth House, the actors' retirement home in Twickenham, she was mistaken for an actress by an elderly resident. 'Hello dearie,' exclaimed the old lady. 'It *has* been a long time. What are you in nowadays?'[37]

CHAPTER 18

Joy Boy

O N 21 AUGUST 1973, Princess Margaret turned forty-three. Just over a fortnight later, she met the young man who was to revive her interest, her energies, her exuberance and enthusiasm, and, eventually, to land her in the most serious emotional, marital and public upheaval of her life. His name was Roderic Llewellyn, and he was twenty-five at the time of their meeting.

The couple met at the Café Royal in Edinburgh on 5 September 1973. Princess Margaret, with her two children, was on her way from Balmoral to Glen, Colin Tennant's house near Innerleithen in Peeblesshire, where she was to join the house party. Lacking a man to balance the numbers (the Princess had been late in accepting the invitation), the desperate Colin Tennant had telephoned his great-aunt by marriage, the redoubtable London hostess, Violet Wyndham, for help. She immediately suggested Roddy Llewellyn. Several telephone calls were necessary to track down the elusive young man who, once found, and although he had never met the Tennants, accepted their invitation. They apparently assured him that they would pay his fare up to Scotland. He was to join the lunch party, which would include the Princess and her children, in Edinburgh, and they would then all drive on to Glen.

In Roddy Llewellyn the Tennants – or rather Mrs Wyndham – had made an excellent choice. Although not invited specifically because he might pair off with Princess Margaret, he turned out to be exactly her type. Looking not unlike the young Antony Armstrong-Jones – small, slender and handsome in a way that was both sensitive and sensuous – he had the same slightly vulnerable air, although, in

Snowdon's case, that had turned out to be deceptive. His fair hair was long and shaggily cut; he was well-mannered, well-spoken and amusing; above all, he was very sweet-natured. The Princess responded to him immediately. Throughout lunch the two of them chatted easily and happily together. When she heard that he had not brought any bathing things (Glen had a heated outdoor swimming pool) she took him shopping after lunch. Together, they chose a pair of swimming trunks decorated with the Union Jack.

For Princess Margaret, that house party at Glen turned out to be magical. In spite of the eighteen years' difference in their ages, she and Llewellyn established an extraordinary rapport. They talked, they swam, they went walking in the superb weather, they sang songs round the piano, they held hands. The Princess, who had gone through so much emotional upheaval during the past few years, was delighted with this fresh-faced young man, while Llewellyn, whose experience of women was limited, was clearly fascinated by this seductive and vivacious *femme du monde*. By the time the house party broke up, it was generally assumed that Princess Margaret and Roddy Llewellyn were in love. Colin Tennant could congratulate himself on having done the Princess another favour.

There might have been a formidable hurdle to this new liaison, but in the event Princess Margaret's children – the twelve-year-old David and the nine-year-old Sarah – seem to have accepted the situation quite happily. They were accustomed to their mother's various men friends and, sophisticated beyond their years, understood that this was all part of the pattern of their parents' marriage.

At first sight, Roddy Llewellyn's social credentials seemed eminently appropriate. Born on 9 October 1947, he was the second son of Lieutenant-Colonel Sir Henry (Harry) Llewellyn, Bart, and his wife 'Teeny', formerly the Hon. Christine Saumarez. The family home was Llanvair Grange, an impressive estate near Abergavenny in South Wales. And although by the time Roddy and his elder brother, Dai, were growing up, the Llewellyn and Saumarez fortunes had been considerably reduced, the family was still quite well off.

Whatever the comforts of his home, however, even as a child, Roddy Llewellyn had been something of a misfit. He never really took to the hearty, sporting life so eagerly embraced by his domineering father (who had captained the winning British show-jumping team at the Olympics in Helsinki in 1952) and more extrovert brother. In temperament, he was more like his mother, to whom he was devoted. At his preparatory school, Hawtreys, he had shown that his interests lay in music, poetry and gardening, rather than in games. Deeply disappointed at not being able to follow his brother to Eton, he had had to make do with five years of schooling at Shrewsbury, which he hated. He described his school as uncivilized, and apparently took refuge from what he regarded as its philistine atmosphere by an avid reading of *Burke's Peerage*. 'It is fair to say that he is slightly snobbish,' wrote his brother Dai some time later. 'He was always attracted by bluebloods. . . . He loves the great houses. The old families.'[1]

On leaving school at the age of eighteen in 1966, the younger Llewellyn embarked on a somewhat aimless, nomadic existence, having no strong interests, no ambitions, no qualifications. An unproductive spell at university in Aix-en-Provence was followed by a visit to South Africa, where his maternal grandfather, Lord de Saumarez, was living. Unable to find much work as a male model, he drifted up Africa, working for a while at a mine near Bulawayo in what was then Southern Rhodesia, and then touring East Africa. On returning to Britain he became an apprentice brewer at Tennants in Sheffield, a subsidiary of Whitbread of which his father was a director. Roddy loathed provincial Sheffield, but a move to the Whitbread Brewery in London, in 1969, pleased him no better, and he quit the job after three months. On inheriting £3,000 from Lord de Saumarez, who died in 1969, Roddy became co-partner with a cousin in a mobile discothèque, which they called 'Elevation Entertainment'. When this venture, in turn, proved unsuccessful, he took a job as a researcher tracing genealogies at the College of Arms. He augmented his meagre salary by working as a part-time sales assistant in a branch of the Piero de Monzi fashion business, of which Lord Snowdon's one-time friend, Lady Jacqueline Rufus Isaacs, was a director.

By now, Roddy Llewellyn was very much a part of that particular London world in which the divisions between classes, social circles, professions, and even sexes, were blurred. Still in his early twenties, he was an impecunious upper-class drifter, apparently unresolved sexually, and given to bouts of almost suicidal depression. In 1972 he took up with a homosexual, Eton-educated interior designer named Nicky Haslam. Their nine-month-long relationship included a stay in the United States where, in Los Angeles, Roddy aped

Haslam in wearing a single earring and going to parties in skintight black leather and chains. But their association was always stormy and in 1973, after yet another quarrel, he left Haslam's studio apartment and moved in with his brother Dai. But his relationship with Nicky Haslam did bring one positive result. When Colin Tennant asked Violet Wyndham to suggest a suitable man for his house party, she remembered Haslam's presentable and attractive young friend. She then immediately set in train the series of telephone calls which tracked Roddy down and which, eventually, brought him to that lunch table in the Café Royal, Edinburgh. 'In our tiny way, darling,' Mrs Wyndham remarked afterwards to Nicky Haslam, 'I do believe we might have changed the course of history!'[2]

They had certainly changed, for a time, at least, the course of Princess Margaret's history. To her, Roddy now became 'my darling Angel' and, deaf to any criticism of the footloose young man – or, indeed, to any warnings about the unsuitability of the match – she flung herself wholeheartedly into this new relationship. She slimmed down, she regained her *joie de vivre*, she tackled all aspects of her life with a new zest. The Princess had never known anyone quite like Roddy. Listening to his accounts of what, to her, must have seemed like an extraordinarily chequered career, she saw in him one of life's victims, someone who needed nurturing and protecting. By now wholly taken up with him, she telephoned him constantly, arranged for him to be invited to private dinner parties, and saw him as often as possible.

Since, in his new role of royal favourite, Roddy could hardly go on living in his brother's flat (Dai Llewellyn, an accomplished womanizer and popular socialite, always the envy of his immature younger brother, was flabbergasted by the turn of events), he set about finding a place of his own. He chose a basement flat in Walham Grove, a leafy avenue in Fulham. It was paid for by his equally flabbergasted parents. Princess Margaret, transported back to her days with Tony Armstrong-Jones in the white room in Rotherhithe, offered not always practical advice and help and, together with her Lady-in-Waiting, Annabel Whitehead, was to be spotted in shops like Peter Jones, ordering things for the flat.

Early in 1974, five months after their first meeting, Princess Margaret invited Roddy Llewellyn to spend a holiday with her on Mustique; he was assured that he need pay for nothing other than tips for the staff at Les Jolies-Eaux. The couple travelled separately (the Princess's love was not quite so reckless as to risk exposure by the press) and, with Colin and Anne Tennant as fellow guests, spent a blissful three weeks on the island. Unlike the energetic Snowdon, Roddy was quite happy with the sort of lotus-eating life that the Princess lived on Mustique. Sporting his Union Jack swimming trunks and a silver stud in one ear, he would spend hours on the beach.

Yet while he was there he was able to put to use his one real talent – for gardening. With the aid of the Princess's gardener, Roddy reorganized and planted the grounds of Les Jolies-Eaux. In doing this, he discovered his *métier*: three years later, having graduated from an agricultural college, he became a professional and highly successful landscape gardener.

The holiday over, the Princess flew home – with Roddy discreetly following a day later. She was met at Heathrow by her husband. As part of the charade, Lord Snowdon had solicitously brought along a mink coat for her to wear over her summery dress. Side by side, smiling their bright public smiles, the couple were driven home to Kensington Palace.

Running almost parallel to Princess Margaret's affair with Roddy Llewellyn was her husband's with a young woman named Lucy Lindsay-Hogg. An attractive brunette in her early thirties, she was the daughter of a successful fabric designer and the ex-wife of a film director, Michael Lindsay-Hogg. The couple had had no children. After the divorce, Lucy had worked as a production assistant with a film company and had met Lord Snowdon through his close associate, Derek Hart. Before long, she became Snowdon's production assistant. She was very good at her job, ideal for him, said one of her colleagues.

She was ideal, in fact, in many ways. In due course the couple fell in love. As Lucy lived in a small flat in Kensington Square, a short walk from Kensington Palace, Snowdon could visit her quite easily. 'There he was, living in my house, thinking he could have a lovely affair,' fumed Princess Margaret at a later stage. 'I asked him for a separation but he laughed in my face. I would only know he was back at night when I heard him banging about in the bathroom – it was all hours. . . .'[3]

The one thing still uniting this estranged couple was their concern for their children. By 1973 David had been a boarder at Ashdown House for four years, by which time it had become apparent that his exam results would never be good enough to get him into Eton, as his parents had originally planned. His strengths were artistic rather than academic. At no stage, apparently, had the Snowdons thought of following the Queen's example of sending her sons – the Princes Charles, Andrew and Edward – to Gordonstoun; they would have disapproved of the aggressively spartan, self-consciously character-building ethos of Gordonstoun, so much admired by Prince Philip. Instead, it was agreed that David would go to Bedales, the progressive, coeducational school in Hampshire at which there was a strong emphasis on creativity. In time, he was to be followed by his equally artistic sister, Sarah, who was then a pupil at the Francis Holland Church of England School near Sloane Square.

Another aspect of the Snowdons' life in which they had, at least, to appear united, was in the carrying out of the Princess's official engagements. There were many which she carried out alone, but on the occasions when they were obliged to appear together, it was imperative that a façade of marital harmony be maintained. Together they attended the various state and dynastic occasions which marked the first half of the 1970s: the celebration, in St Paul's Cathedral in 1972, of the twenty-fifth anniversary of the Queen's marriage; the wedding of Princess Margaret's niece, Princess Anne, to Captain Mark Phillips in Westminster Abbey in 1973; the funerals, in St George's Chapel, Windsor, of her uncles the Duke of Windsor in 1972 and the Duke of Gloucester in 1974.

For the Princess, the funeral of her Uncle David was to have a curious sequel. In May 1974, the Snowdons paid an official visit to the United States and Canada. While they were in New York – where Princess Margaret, in her capacity as President of the Royal Ballet, had to attend a gala performance of the touring Royal Ballet company – they were suddenly brought face to face with a controversial figure from the Princess's past – the Duchess of Windsor.

The late Duke's seventy-six-year-old widow was making what, as it turned out, would prove to be her last visit to her native America, and was staying, as usual, in a suite at the Waldorf Towers. The Snowdons, arriving at the same hotel, astonished to hear that the Duchess was also there, felt that it would be churlish not to offer to go up and see her. A strictly private meeting followed, with no members of the Princess's entourage accompanying her. Only very rarely, and then always on formal occasions, had she met the woman whose marriage to her uncle had so dramatically affected her own life. (There is an apocryphal story that while attending the Duke of Windsor's burial at Frogmore at Windsor, the Duchess, drugged and disorientated, had slipped her arm through Princess Margaret's and asked, 'Having a good time, honey?'[4]) On Princess Margaret's suggestion, this private meeting in the Waldorf Towers was photographed. It is difficult to know why she had agreed to this. It may be that by now, with the Duke of Windsor safely dead, even the implacable Queen Mother had decided that a little show of family forgiveness would do the monarchy no harm.

In fact, Princess Margaret went further than this. 'I once saw the Duchess of Windsor in a hotel in New York,' she said many years later. 'She looked so gloomy that I sent her a signed photograph of myself, just to cheer her up.'[5] It is to be hoped that the Duchess was duly cheered.

However euphoric Princess Margaret might have been feeling about her new romance, Roddy Llewellyn seems not to have been anything like as happy with the situation. For one thing, he was not accustomed to life at so elevated a level: the Princess, for all her approachability and affection (at least where he was concerned), still lived and behaved like a member of the royal family. In every way – age, wealth, status, experience and sophistication – she was his superior. He was uneasy, too, about her husband: 'Tell your friend to keep out of my house,' a seething Snowdon had advised Nicky Haslam.[6] Although Roddy tried his best to befriend the Princess's children, he must have been conscious of the fact that he was nearer in age to David than he was to David's mother. And financially, of course, he was very much out of his depth. Earning £70 a month from his job at the College of Arms, he could not hope to match, let alone contribute to, Princess Margaret's style of life. This, too, undermined his self-confidence.

It was undermined still further when, appreciating that he simply had to earn more money, he accepted a job which had been arranged by the ever-sympathetic Colin Tennant. Appointed personal assistant to J. 'Algy' Cluff, a dynamic young man who was busily making himself a fortune by astute speculation in North Sea oil, the job could hardly have suited Roddy less. He had no head for business, and it was soon obvious to everyone at Cluff Oil that the boss's personal assistant had no idea what he, or anyone else, was supposed to be doing. 'I lasted just two months and it's a miracle it wasn't two days,' he afterwards admitted.[7]

But perhaps most stressful of all was the intimate side of the relationship with Princess Margaret. Roddy Llewellyn had apparently never before had a long-term affair with a woman, and adjustment to this mature, possessive, demanding personality, so accustomed to getting her own way, cannot have been easy. Before long, he began to feel claustrophobic. When the couple, having celebrated their first 'anniversary' at Glen, moved on to spend a weekend at Llanvair, the Welsh home of the Llewellyns, Dai noticed that his brother seemed under tremendous pressure. Not only was Roddy finding his new job depressing but, according to Nigel Dempster, Dai realized that 'the physical side of the relationship was proving too difficult to sustain'.[8]

In such circumstances, something was bound to give. Hardly had the couple returned to London than Roddy cracked. If he had remained in London for one minute more, he afterwards claimed, he would have shattered into a million pieces. One day, while at lunch in a restaurant, he suddenly leapt up from the table, dashed home to pack a suitcase, withdrew some money from the bank, telephoned both his mother and Princess Margaret to tell them that he was going away indefinitely, and headed for Heathrow airport. He took the first available plane, which happened to be going to Guernsey. Within a couple of days he was back at Heathrow. This time, looking distrait and unshaven, he boarded a plane bound for Istanbul, flying off with a vague notion of making a long and leisurely tour of India.

But Roddy never reached India; instead, he spent several weeks travelling round Turkey by bus. To someone he met on his travels, he confided that he 'had been having an affair with a married woman and that it had all got too much for him and the sex had become a problem.'[9] He was fleeing abroad to escape the situation. After three weeks, however, he felt more composed and decided to return home, though it was not, for the moment, to Princess Margaret that he was returning. He planned, instead, to embark on a five-month-long tour of South America. Having arranged to let his Walham Grove flat, he set off, in early February 1975, for Barbados as a first step on his South American adventure. Here his behaviour became increasingly erratic – he was clearly heading for a mental breakdown. Worried friends contacted his father and it was arranged for Roddy to be flown back to London in the care of a psychiatrist. He spent three weeks in the Charing Cross Hospital and, on being released, went home to Wales.

Roddy Llewellyn's sudden flight to Turkey had a dramatic effect on Princess Margaret. His disappearance, combined with the strain of her highly charged relationship with her husband, caused her to suffer a nervous collapse. Desperately needing rest, she took rather too many sleeping pills with the result that a couple of her engagements had to be cancelled. On 15 November 1974, her office announced that she was suffering from a severe cold. But, inevitably, a rumour began to circulate to the effect that she had tried to commit suicide, had purposely overdosed on Mogadon tablets. The Princess afterwards dismissed the idea as ridiculous, and a friend was probably right in describing it as a *cri de coeur* rather than a serious attempt to take her life. Her long-standing friend Jocelyn Stevens agreed. 'It would be totally out of character . . .' he maintained. 'She loves life too much. She would never do it.'[10]

Stevens's contention was echoed, if in more cynical terms, by the Queen. One weekend, Princess Margaret telephoned a male friend who was hosting a house party to threaten that if he did not come over immediately, she would commit suicide by throwing herself out of the bedroom window. Desperately worried, the friend rang the Queen and explained his fears. 'Carry on with your house party,' answered Her Majesty calmly. 'Her bedroom is on the ground floor.'[11]

Life in the tranquillity of the Welsh countryside gradually restored Roddy Llewellyn's equilibrium. He was always at his best among growing things and, encouraged by his adored and adoring mother, he reorganized the gardens and greenhouses at Llanvair. Then, in June 1975, he was invited to join a commune at Surrendell Farm, near Malmesbury in Wiltshire, where a handful of friends were busy restoring the derelict property in an idealistic attempt to become self-sufficient by living off the land. As an extra source of income they planned to open a restaurant in Bath, and Roddy was to be responsible for providing the restaurant with fresh fruit and vegetables grown in Surrendell's kitchen garden. Nothing could have suit-

ed the young man better. It was the start, he said, of the most
rewarding year of his life. Toiling in the overgrown kitchen garden
and keeping company with a shifting population of aristocrats,
actors, artists, playwrights and pop singers, he was in his element.

His newly found composure also restored his faltering relationship with Princess Margaret. Once she had recovered from her own
nervous breakdown, she did what she could to see Roddy through
his more serious psychological troubles. As a woman of the world,
she appreciated that he needed his own breathing space. She kept
in touch by telephone, by sending him encouraging messages, and
by arranging to see him from time to time. Gradually, they resumed
what has been called their 'loving friendship'.[12] Delighted that he
was at last involved in something fulfilling and creative, the Princess
shared his enthusiasm for the commune. She visited it a couple of
times, once even spending the night in the very spartan conditions
of the renovated farmhouse. 'There she was in the evening in her
pearls,' remembers one member of the commune, 'muddling along
with a game of mah-jong which she said she hadn't played since she
was a child. She endeared herself to us all.'[13]

But what seemed like a harmless rural idyll to Princess Margaret
was viewed quite differently from Buckingham Palace. Although
the Queen and the Queen Mother were by now accustomed to the
Princess's whimsicality, and were not too disturbed by her association with what to them looked like a colony of drop-outs, they must
have disapproved strongly of her relationship with Roddy
Llewellyn. By now this unseemly affair between the Queen's sister
and an apparently rootless young man eighteen years her junior was
being widely talked about in royal and society circles. To the
Queen, Roddy epitomized what she called 'my sister's guttersnipe
life'.[14] Her Majesty's own marriage may have had its ups and downs,
but her private behaviour had always been beyond reproach. Normally tolerant of her sister's unconventionality, her patience seems
finally to have snapped during the Roddy Llewellyn affair, while
her husband's disapproval was, if anything, even stronger. Llewellyn's slap-happy way of life ran counter to everything that the
dynamic Prince Philip believed in and was constantly advocating.
Just able to tolerate Snowdon's bohemian behaviour, he was prepared to make no allowances whatsoever for the object of his sister-
in-law's latest infatuation.

Nevertheless, Roddy was invited – or rather taken – to Royal Lodge to meet the Queen Mother (he was certainly never invited to Windsor). She, apparently, made no comment to the Princess about the affair. The Queen Mother has the happy knack of not allowing herself to become too involved in other people's troubles, something which contributes to the celebrated optimism and serenity of her temperament. But she could hardly have approved of the relationship. Both she and the Queen remained deaf to any suggestion that Lord Snowdon's behaviour might have been in some measure responsible for the collapse of the marriage, and for Princess Margaret's subsequent romantic entanglements. 'Tony was so oily to my mother and sister,' she complained.[15] It was, in any case, not until mid-1975, after Snowdon and Lucy Lindsay-Hogg had spent several months filming in Australia, that Princess Margaret realized that her husband was in love with his assistant. Unlike her affair with Roddy Llewellyn, his was conducted with the utmost discretion, something which was to make it very easy for Snowdon to appear – when the news of his wife's affair finally hit the headlines – as the injured party.

That news broke, with dramatic suddenness, early in 1976. In February the Princess and Roddy, their love-affair back on course, had flown out to Mustique. Also on the island was a photographer, a New Zealander by the name of Ross Waby. He worked for the New York bureau of News International, a network of tabloid newspapers, including the *Sun* and the *News of the World*, owned by the Australian press baron, Rupert Murdoch. Waby had managed to evade Colin Tennant's ban on newsmen by posing as a tourist, complete with wife, who had come on a package holiday to stay at the Cotton House Hotel. The sole purpose of his visit, however, was to take a photograph of Princess Margaret with Roddy Llewellyn.

Usually, Princess Margaret kept well away from the guests at the hotel, spending most of her time at Les Jolies-Eaux or on the nearby private beach. Her only sortie into public view was when, very occasionally, she took a party of her house guests to the Beach Bar. It was here that Waby, his wife by his side, stationed himself for the better part of each day. In time, his patience was rewarded. He managed to take a somewhat blurred photograph of the Princess sitting at a wooden table beside Roddy, with Viscount Coke (Anne Tennant's brother) and his wife Valeria sitting opposite. All four were wearing swimming costumes. Within days the photograph appeared on the front page of the *News of the World*. Cannily, however, the picture had been cropped to cut out the Cokes, so that what the public saw was a photograph of the forty-five-year-old Princess Margaret sitting *à deux* in the Caribbean sunshine with her long-haired, bare-torsoed, deeply bronzed twenty-eight-year-old lover.

The publication of the photograph caused a sensation. The resulting scandal finally blew the Snowdon marriage apart. Lord Snowdon, able to claim that he had been publicly humiliated, promptly moved out of Kensington Palace. Showing what Princess Margaret called 'devilish cunning', and despite the fact that he had been seriously involved with Lucy Lindsay-Hogg for well over a year, he emerged from the drama as the wronged partner. The Princess came hurrying back from Mustique without Roddy and, after consultation with the Queen and her advisers, decided on an immediate separation. Under the terms of this, the children were to remain with their mother at Kensington Palace, and their father, on whom the Princess agreed to settle a six-figure sum, was to have free access to them. On 19 March 1976 a statement was issued from Kensington Palace:

HRH The Princess Margaret, the Countess of Snowdon, and the Earl of Snowdon have agreed mutually to live apart. The Princess will carry out her public duties and functions unaccompanied by Lord Snowdon. There are no plans for divorce proceedings.

On that very day, Snowdon flew off to Australia to organize an exhibition of his photographs in Sydney. Here he appeared on television and, looking harassed and disconsolate, issued a short statement. 'I am naturally desperately sad in every way that this had to come,' he said. 'I would just like to say three things: firstly to pray for the understanding of our two children; secondly to wish Princess Margaret every happiness for her future; thirdly to express with the utmost humility my love, admiration and respect I will always have for her sister, her mother and her entire family.'

Princess Margaret was able to watch this affecting performance on the BBC television news. 'I have never seen such good acting,' she commented wryly.[16]

By now the newshounds were in full cry after Roddy Llewellyn.

Pockets stuffed with bribe money, a pack of photographers and reporters laid siege to Surrendell Farm, setting up long-lensed cameras and begging for interviews. To heighten the contrast between the Princess and her young lover, Roddy was inaccurately described in the press as a 'hippie' living on the dole. Appreciating that all this media attention was unfair on his colleagues, he decided to escape from Surrendell. Trailed by a stream of press cars, he took refuge with a friend who lived nearby. Together, they agreed that the only way to stop this harassment would be for Roddy to issue a statement to the press. Having drawn one up, they decided to clear it with Princess Margaret's office before telephoning it through to the Press Association.

It was as well that they did. The Princess's Private Secretary, Lord Napier and Ettrick, had taken over the post three years earlier from the even more fulsomely named Lieutenant-Colonel Frederick Barnaby-Atkins. A sensible and worldly man, tough-minded enough to handle his capricious royal employer, Lord Napier was appalled by the statement. It was full of the sort of high-minded, commune-inspired jargon that would have proved a gift to the tabloid press. Under no circumstances, he ordered, was the statement to be issued in its present form. Instead, Roddy composed a more conventionally worded one which, having been passed by Kensington Palace, was issued on 24 March 1976. 'I am not prepared to comment on any of the events of last week,' it read. 'I much regret any embarrassment caused to Her Majesty the Queen and the Royal Family for whom I wish to express the greatest respect, admiration and loyalty. I thank my own family for their confidence and support. . . .' He went on to express his gratitude to his colleagues at Surrendell.

In fact, the drama marked the end, not only of Roddy's association with Surrendell, but also of the whole experiment. Parsenn Sally, the community's restaurant in Bath, collapsed under a mountain of debt and, within a few months, the farm itself was abandoned and the various members drifted away. Roddy retired, as often before, to the tranquillity of his parents' home in Wales.

The one thing that did survive the furore was the relationship between Princess Margaret and Roddy Llewellyn. But it would be as well, she advised him, for them not to be seen together until the present excitement had died down.

CHAPTER 19

Divorce

Those who imagined that Princess Margaret would lie low after the turbulence of her separation were soon proved wrong. Several things – a lust for life, a defiance of public opinion, even a royal sense of obligation – ensured that her life continued much as before. In the course of the following year her official engagements took her to North Africa (where the King of Morocco, Hassan II, assured her that 'if your husband is no good, you are quite right to get rid of him'), Cyprus, Italy and the United States.[1]

Her highly publicized association with the various worlds that made up the pop culture of the day continued unabated. 'The whole night was very odd,' remembers a writer of song lyrics who had been invited to one of the Princess's after-the-show parties. 'The thing that amazed me was that there didn't seem to be any kind of security at Kensington Palace, other than a policeman at the gate. You just rolled up, knocked at the door and were let in. The other thing I remember is that, getting out of the car, I split my trousers at the crotch . . . a lady-in-waiting sewed them up for me.' A further memory is of other guests 'getting plastered in a back room'.[2]

After attending Elton John's concert for the Invalid Aid Association, Princess Margaret had become an ardent admirer and, soon afterwards, asked her friends Bryan Forbes and his wife Nanette Newman to arrange for the singer to give a private command performance. 'She said she'd been telling the Queen Mother about Elton,' said Nanette Newman. 'The Queen Mother was terribly keen to see him as well.' The first of Elton John's many private royal command performances took place at Royal Lodge. The Queen

Mother proved as enthusiastic as her daughter; to their delight, Elton John, in singing 'Your Song', deftly changed the line 'I'd buy a big house' to 'I'd buy Windsor Castle'. The performance over, the Queen Mother announced that there would be dancing. She crossed to the record player, put on her own favourite, a piece called 'Slattery's Mounted Foot', and seizing the singer – still dressed in his cream canvas suit, embroidered with the chinoiserie artwork from the cover of his album *Goodbye Yellow Brick Road* – partnered him in a vigorous dance round the room.[3]

Although generally sceptical of the lavish praise of her own voice, Princess Margaret never needed much persuasion to do a little singing herself, even in public. Many years before, having listened to the famous contralto, Kathleen Ferrier, singing at a private party, the Princess – displaying what one fellow guest tactfully describes as 'enormous spirit' – got up and sang herself. 'Normally,' says the observer, 'no singer would care to follow Kathleen and risk comparison', but Miss Ferrier was 'the first to lead the applause', generously declaring that the Princess was so good that she could have earned her living as a performer.[4]

Not everyone showed the same appreciation. One night, at a ball given by the celebrated hostess, Lady Rothermere, the Princess 'grabbed the microphone from the startled leader of the band, whom she instructed to play songs by Cole Porter'. Obediently, all the guests stopped dancing and stood listening to the Princess's performance. As they 'shouted and roared for more' she became, says Lady Caroline Blackwood, who was watching, 'a little manic', with her swaying, full-skirted ball gown proving quite unsuitable for her 'slinky' gyrations. She had just launched into 'Let's Do It' when, from the back of the crowded ballroom, came loud sounds of booing and barracking. The rest of the place fell silent. Mortified by this unprecedented show of hostility, the Princess abandoned the microphone and hurried out of the room. The culprit was the painter Francis Bacon, blind drunk as usual. 'Her singing really was too awful,' he afterwards said. 'Someone had to stop her.' (Bacon's outrageous behaviour on that occasion seems to have left no lasting impression on his host. On being introduced to the famous painter again some years later, Lord Rothermere politely asked, 'And what do you do?' Once more, Bacon proved brutally frank. 'I'm an old poof,' he answered.[5])

Another of Princess Margaret's highly acclaimed talents was for mimicry or, rather, for assuming various accents and dialects. Fawning references were always being made to her skill in impersonating cockneys or Southern belles or obsequious town clerks. Her close association with Peter Sellers considerably broadened her repertoire, and she added impressions of the Goon characters Major Bloodnok, Eccles and Bluebottle, and of *The Pink Panther*'s Inspector Clouseau, to her list. There is a story that the biographer Michael Holroyd, invited to a lunch party by the Princess, dutifully screamed with laughter, and even banged the table in admiration, on hearing what he took to be his hostess's Bluebottle impersonation. Unfortunately, the Princess had been speaking in her normal voice.

If her liking for pop culture, and her readiness to perform in public herself, were viewed with suspicion by some, Princess Margaret's holidays on Mustique continued to provide her critics with what looked like evidence of a raffish way of life. By the late 1970s the place was firmly established as 'the most exclusive island in the Caribbean'; the 'glittering meeting place' as one visitor put it, of 'the talented, the artistic and the mega-rich from all over the world'.[6] Although still primitive in some ways – the single landing strip had to be illuminated by car headlights in emergencies, and the airport building was simply a small hut – it boasted dozens of million-dollar holiday homes. Some of them came to be owned by anonymous bankers and businessmen; others by stars such as Mick Jagger, David Bowie and Billy Joel. The hub of island life was Colin Tennant's hotel, the Cotton House, a converted eighteenth-century warehouse built of coral and stone, and decorated by Oliver Messel. Rooms in the twenty or so suites dotted about the hotel's palm-shaded grounds could cost more, per night, than the transatlantic flight. Life on Mustique, says someone closely associated with it, was 'like a very grand Scottish house party. It was all great fun.'[7]

Princess Margaret's days on the island were delightfully relaxed. She would rise late and, surrounded by a small court of house guests or local friends, would sunbathe in her boned and skirted swimsuit, lunch in the summer house or picnic on the beach, and go swimming in the warm water in her 'slow-motion style'. The evenings would be given over to cocktails, dinner parties, parlour games or the weekly 'jump-up' at the Beach Bar.

The Princess's late-autumn visit to Mustique in 1976 was made memorable by Colin Tennant's famous fiftieth birthday party. At his own expense, Tennant flew his guests in from all over the world, Princess Margaret heading the list of such contemporary celebrities as Mick and Bianca Jagger and Patrick Lichfield. The week-long celebrations culminated in the 'Gold Night' fancy-dress ball, for which guests were obliged to sport something gold. The Princess, her skin specially darkened, struck a highly exotic note in caftan and turban. Glitteringly bejewelled, she looked the very epitome of languorous glamour.

By now, however, this Caribbean paradise was beginning to act as a magnet for some of society's more disreputable elements, and Princess Margaret sometimes found herself indirectly involved in unsavoury scandals. One of these concerned John Bindon, an East Ender with a criminal record who visited the island on a couple of occasions. He briefly met the Princess, who was said to be amused by his cockney rhyming slang and his hilarious stories of his time in gaol. (Bindon was apparently very proud of his 'enormous penis', which he would display in the palm of his hand; talk on the island was that he had even once 'flashed it for Princess Margaret'.[8])

In 1978 he was involved in a fight in a seedy London drinking club, in the course of which he knifed to death an underworld figure named John Darke. While Bindon was on remand in Brixton gaol his girlfriend began negotiating with the *Daily Mirror* for the sale of his story, which included the claim that, while on Mustique, he had been a close friend of Princess Margaret. On his acquittal, on the grounds that he had killed Darke in self-defence, the *Daily Mirror* paid him £40,000 and serialized his memoirs, printing, as one of the illustrations, a blurred photograph of the Princess and Bindon among a group of people at a picnic on Mustique. Although the East Ender's boast of his close friendship with Princess Margaret was debatable, the publicity did her reputation no good.

Nor was it improved by another Mustique photograph. One day when the Princess was on the beach with Colin Tennant, Roddy Llewellyn and Nicholas Courtney, Tennant asked if he could take off his swimming trunks. The Princess not only agreed but, with the other two having taken off their trunks as well, she photographed the three of them. Somehow or other, the photograph of Princess Margaret's three men friends, unmistakably naked, found its way into the *News of the World*.

Yet however scandal-racked or sybaritic she might appear, it did not do to forget that she was a princess. Her unpredictability, her expectation of being treated as an equal at one moment and as royalty the next, never ceased to confound those who had dealings with her. The theatre director Peter Hall, having escorted her to the opening night of *Bow Down* at the Cottesloe Theatre in the summer of 1977, was astonished to discover that she had been 'very affronted' by the production.[9] She ought not, she protested, to have been invited to see it. It was not so much, apparently, that she was shocked by its powerful theme as that, as a representative of the monarchy, she should not have been seen attending a controversial play in her official capacity.

On another occasion, a student at Keele University, of which Princess Margaret was Chancellor for thirty years, was once put firmly in his place for being too familiar. In the course of dancing a lively cha-cha with the Princess at a university ball, he said, in an effort to match her informality, 'I am not sure what to call you.' He was rewarded with 'the Windsor glare'. 'Why not try Princess Margaret?' answered Her Royal Highness.[10]

Within weeks of the Snowdons' official separation, Princess Margaret and Roddy Llewellyn were seeing each other again. Sometimes, if the Queen were away, the Princess would take him and her children swimming in the pool at Buckingham Palace; at other times he would visit her at Kensington Palace. They would often spend the evenings alone together, watching television, singing at the grand piano or playing backgammon, at which the Princess is very adept. In the summer of 1976 she paid another visit to Llanvair, where the cachet of a royal visit doubtless compensated his parents for their continuing unease about the relationship.

Later that year Roddy, who since the collapse of the Surrendell commune was again without work, was accepted as a student by the Merrist Wood Agricultural College in Surrey. He threw himself with enthusiasm into the year-long course, even to the extent of turning down his invitation to Colin Tennant's fiftieth birthday party on Mustique that November. Princess Margaret, in turn, skipped her usual February visit to the island the following year because Roddy again felt that he should not interrupt his studies, and she did not want to be at Les Jolies-Eaux without him. She would telephone him at his lodgings, often twice a day and, very gradually, began to allow herself to be seen with him in public. Accompanied by her long-standing friend, the Conservative MP Norman St John Stevas, the Princess openly took Roddy to the theatre to see *Donkey's Years*. On another occasion, when flying back from a stay at Glen, the Princess was followed out of the plane by the broadly grinning Roddy Llewellyn, to the delight of the waiting reporters. To celebrate his thirtieth birthday, in October 1977, she gave a formal dinner followed by a large party at Kensington Palace. Quite clearly, Princess Margaret's intention was to have the young man accepted by the public as part of her life.

But not yet, apparently, as part of Queen Elizabeth II's life. When, in November 1977 the Queen interrupted a tour of the West Indies to visit her sister's home on Mustique, Roddy was obliged to wait on Barbados until the royal visit was over. The journalists' disappointment at being denied any indication of a royal blessing on the romance was compensated for when, later that same day, they were able to photograph the Queen boarding Concorde on Barbados, bound for Britain, at the very time that Roddy was boarding a small island-hopper plane, bound for Mustique.

Such subterfuges emphasized the awkwardness of his position. 'This is a very difficult and unique situation for me,' he complained to a reporter. 'I have been in a terrible dilemma. I had a choice of becoming a total nervous wreck or of trying to enjoy myself in this impossible situation. And I have decided to make damned sure that I enjoy myself. . . . I am tired of having to avoid being seen. I think the time has come to hold up my head and smile.' Asked about his love-affair with Princess Margaret, he declared it to be a 'taboo subject'.[11]

On leaving Merrist Wood in 1977 with his National Certificate of Horticulture, he registered himself as Roddy Llewellyn Landscape Limited, with a view to tackling any gardening job from window boxes to country estates. But not even the notoriety of his association with Princess Margaret brought him much work and, ever the optimist, he decided on yet another change of career. He now wanted to become a pop singer.

If Roddy Llewellyn's relationship with Princess Margaret had not initially benefited his gardening career, it was certainly exploited to the full by those who planned to launch his singing career. Through his brother Dai's many social and business connections, Roddy met

Claude Wolff, the husband and manager of the singer Petula Clark. In a blaze of publicity, it was announced that Roddy, who apparently had a pleasant enough voice, had been signed up by Wolff. Inflated estimates of his possible future earnings were bandied about; he was invited to appear on television; he was accepted as a client by a celebrated public-relations adviser; and a firm of West End estate agents were finally able to boost the sale of a penthouse on the strength of of its having a Roddy Llewellyn-designed roof garden. His career was launched with the singing of a duet with Petula Clark on French television. 'His voice is certainly good enough to get him a Number One,' announced a generous Petula Clark.[12]

Quite what Princess Margaret thought of all this is difficult to gauge. According to Roddy, she approved heartily of his new career move; after all, it was part of the world in which she moved. And it is probably true that, wanting only what he wanted, the Princess encouraged him in this, the latest of his many ventures. What is certain, however, is that she remained blind to the incalculable harm which her association with the young man was doing to her reputation. Already the flood of publicity about Roddy's career was focusing renewed attention on their relationship. A series of newspaper articles, although containing nothing new or startling, none the less underlined the apparent unseemliness of the affair between the Princess and the pop singer.

Things came to a head in March 1978. As so often before, the setting for the drama was the West Indies. Soon after Roddy had arrived on Mustique, direct from a recording session, he announced that he felt ill. The Princess sent for a local doctor, who insisted that the patient be flown for emergency treatment to Barbados, where he was diagnosed as suffering from an 'upper gastro-intestinal haemorrhage'. Two days later, the worried Princess flew to Barbados to be at his bedside, the friend with whom she was staying there assuring reporters that although she was 'obviously very upset', she was keeping calm.[13] Within days, pictures of the lovers – Roddy sitting up in his hospital bed and Princess Margaret enjoying herself in the sunshine – began to appear in British newspapers. They unleashed the worst storm of Princess Margaret's always stormy life.

For the following few months Princess Margaret was subjected to a tirade of abuse in the press. Her attendance at Roddy's sickbed on the tropical island of Barbados coincided with the Parliamentary Review of the financial provisions to be made to those members of the royal family on the Civil List, including Princess Margaret. This had proposed that her annual annuity be raised from £55,000 to £59,000, a proposal which enabled Willie Hamilton to launch his most virulent attack yet. Pointing out that the Elizabeth Garrett Anderson Hospital for Women in Euston was facing closure because lift repairs would cost between £20,000 and £30,000, he suggested that the necessary sum be taken from the annuity of 'the young lady now holidaying in the West Indies. If she thumbs her nose at tax-payers by flying off to Mustique to see this pop-singer chap, she shouldn't expect the workers of this country to pay for it.'[14]

Other Labour MPs joined in the attack. Douglas Hoyle suggested that the Princess's annuity be taken from her and distributed among other members of the royal family who were 'pulling their weight'; meanwhile, she should decide whether to carry on 'swanning around in the West Indies or get on with her job'. Dennis Canavan went further. Referring to her as a 'parasite', he boldly declared that it was 'intolerable that the public purse should subsidise the Princess's second honeymoon'.[15]

Matters were hardly helped when Roddy Llewellyn, arriving back in Britain one week after Princess Margaret, spoke out publicly on the issue. 'I would like to see Willie Hamilton or any of the others do all her jobs in the marvellous way that she does,' he said. 'People love the monarchy and appreciate with their whole hearts the job she does. I shall go on seeing Princess Margaret when and where I want. Let them all criticize – I don't mind. . . . I certainly don't believe that Princess Margaret has done anything to give the royal family a bad name, as suggested.' To this outburst, Willie Hamilton had a telling reply. Princess Margaret, he pointed out, had fulfilled exactly eight public engagements in the last three months, during which time she had drawn about £14,000. Not bad, he said, for eight performances. The royal family, he surmised, 'must be very disturbed by the defence coming from this quarter [from Llewellyn]. I think that is the last thing they should want.'[16]

It was the last thing they wanted, and things were made even worse by Roddy's tendency to get himself involved in escapades that kept his name in the newspapers. 'I wish,' said Dennis Canavan, 'that he would get himself a job so he can support his girlfriend instead of her living off the state. It's quite obvious that even people who have a great admiration for the royal family think she has let them down. If she would do us the favour of retiring from public life she would not be missed.'[17]

This theme of her possible retirement from public life was taken up by the tabloids. On 5 April 1978 the *Sun*, under the banner head-line 'Give Up Roddy or Quit', printed what it called an exclusive story in which the Princess was reported to be struggling with her conscience after having received an ultimatum from the Queen: she must either end her love-affair with Roddy or withdraw from public life. The *Daily Mirror* went further: Princess Margaret's future, it claimed, was now in the hands of Prince Philip. He had had enough of her irresponsibility and had told her that it was time to retire, a view with which the Queen, apparently, had agreed.

Needless to say, there was no truth in these reports whatsoever. But by now even the Church had joined in the discussion of the errant Princess's future. 'If you accept that you are a public person,' lectured the Right Reverend Graham Leonard, Bishop of Truro, 'you do accept limitations that don't apply to others. I would have thought that the thing that had to be resolved now was in fact how far she can go on being a public person. If you accept the public life, you must accept a severe restriction on your personal conduct.' Withdrawal from the public arena, he suggested, would be the only possible way of sorting out her affairs.[18]

But Princess Margaret had her defenders. Various newspapers could point to the fact that her controversial way of life tended to overshadow her less newsworthy activities, and that she fulfilled as many public engagements as did most other members of the royal family. 'While Princess Margaret plays hard,' declared the *People*, 'she works hard too.'[19] The *Daily Telegraph* asked if there was any evidence to suggest that she 'refuses or evades public engagements which she ought to fulfil'.[20] The theatre critic Milton Shulman, writ-ing in the *Evening Standard*, robustly declared that 'Princess Mar-garet still has a useful role to play and she should be allowed to perform it without being harassed by sanctimonious abuse and hyp-ocritical cant.'[21] The *Times*, changing its tune since the days of the Peter Townsend affair, decided that 'the high standing and efficient work of the monarchy does not require that every member of the extended royal family should be a paragon of virtue or a model of decorum, and that all who fail that test should be withdrawn out of range of royal duties and rewards.'[22]

One short-term solution to the Princess's problems would have been for Roddy Llewellyn to keep out of sight. He is said to have received instructions from 'on high' to leave the country for three months and to grant no interviews during that period. Obligingly, and because he was now earning some money from his various singing and gardening ventures, Roddy slipped off to North Africa. While in Tangier, he gallantly resisted a £150,000 offer from an American publication for his story.

The reason why Roddy Llewellyn had been told to get out of Britain became clear on 10 May 1978. On that day it was announced that Princess Margaret was finally suing for divorce.

Ever since the official separation two years before, Lord Snowdon had been moving from one London address to another. First he had stayed in his mother's house in Stafford Terrace, Kensington, and then he had moved into the basement flat of the Belgravia home of his old friend Jeremy Fry. Towards the end of 1977 he had finally moved into a home of his own, in Launceston Place, Kensington. Princess Margaret visited the house once only. On that occasion she had gathered that, in spite of her husband's continuing relationship with Lucy Lindsay-Hogg, he was not thinking in terms of divorce and remarriage.

One of the effects of the separation was that Lord Snowdon had become increasingly isolated from the rest of the royal family. This isolation was graphically illustrated during the celebrations marking the Silver Jubilee of Queen Elizabeth II's reign, which took place in the summer of 1977. The climax of these festivities was the Thanksgiving Service in St Paul's Cathedral on 7 June. While Princess Margaret and her two children were driving in procession through the vociferous crowds in an open landau, Snowdon sat waiting inside the cathedral with the rest of the congregation. He could only watch while his wife, his children and the other members of the royal family moved slowly up the nave between hedges of curtsying women and bowing men.

The Queen's Silver Jubilee proved that, in spite of the many political and domestic upheavals of her reign – and not least the caprices of her only sister – the Sovereign herself remained as popular as ever. By the second half of the 1970s it was becoming increasingly difficult for anyone in Britain to remember a time when this small, slight, perfectly groomed figure had not been head of state. In a fast-changing world, she stood as a familiar, constant, stable factor. And while it is unlikely that she was quite as astounded by the warmth of public reaction as her grandfather, King George V, had been on the occasion of his Silver Jubilee, there can be no doubt that the Queen was highly gratified at the fervent demonstration of national loyalty. She was not to know that, in many ways, the 1977 Silver Jubilee marked the climax of her reign. From this point on, the royal family was to become increasingly enmeshed in domestic strife and scandal.

Certainly, by the time the Snowdons were next due to be brought together for a dynastic event, the storm of criticism about Princess Margaret's affair with Roddy Llewellyn was at its height. The occasion was the confirmation, on 5 April 1978, of their daughter, Lady Sarah Armstrong-Jones (Lord Linley had been confirmed three years earlier). The ceremony took place in St George's Chapel, Windsor, where Dr Donald Coggan, the Archbishop of Canterbury, was able to confirm a whole clutch of royal children: the fourteen-year-old Lady Sarah was joined by the Queen's youngest son, Prince Edward, the Duke of Kent's daughter, Lady Helen Windsor, and Princess Alexandra's son, James Ogilvy. This time it was Princess Margaret who was excluded from the family gathering, but only because she was ill. She had developed flu and her doctors had expressly forbidden her to attend the confirmation service, though she was able to look in at the celebratory lunch that followed. Inevitably, however, there was public speculation about the real reason for the Princess's absence from so important an event in her daughter's life. It was suspected that, given the virulence of the calumny by then being heaped on her, which reached a climax that very week, she simply could not face the strain of a public appearance. But it is far more likely that her illness had been brought on by the hurricane of criticism: that, in her buffeted state, she had succumbed more easily to the virus.

But Princess Margaret was nothing if not resilient. Driven both by her sense of duty and by her determination to avoid any further accusations of slacking, she was back on the royal treadmill within three days, and fulfilled several engagements in the course of the following three weeks. It was, however, obvious that she was still not well, and on returning from a day's engagements in Manchester 'feeling like death', she sent for her doctor.[23] His suspicions of hepatitis were confirmed by a blood test. The Princess was rushed to the King Edward VII Hospital where, because the condition is contagious, she was kept in isolation. As part of the cure, she was obliged to abstain from drinking alcohol for a year.

By now, the Snowdons had decided on a divorce. On 10 May 1978, the day before the Princess was released from hospital, a statement was issued from Kensington Palace:

Her Royal Highness The Princess Margaret, Countess of Snowdon, and the Earl of Snowdon, after two years of separation have agreed that their marriage should formally be ended. Accordingly Her Royal Highness will start the necessary legal proceedings.

The Queen's solicitor added that it had been agreed that the Princess should institute the divorce proceedings. Since the necessary financial arrangements had been made at the time of the separation two years before, and since there was no dispute over custody of and access to the children, the divorce would be a straightforward affair. Neither party would need to appear in court.

On 11 May, eight days after she had been admitted, the Princess left hospital. Wearing a grey coat and a silk headscarf and accompanied only by a nurse, she was driven back to Kensington Palace. Her ill and doleful appearance, coupled with the announcement of the impending divorce, raised not only considerable public concern, but also public compassion. Suddenly, newspapers began to produce a flurry of sympathetic articles. The coals of the Townsend affair were duly raked over, and the recently maligned figure was now presented in a more tragic light; as 'the Princess whose fairy tale never came true'.

Princess Margaret's petition was heard on 24 May 1978 by Judge Roger Willis in Court No. 44 of the London Divorce Court. The Princess was represented by her solicitor, Mr Matthew Farrer, and Lord Snowdon by Mr John Humphries. Within minutes of the hearing, the decree nisi had been pronounced and rubber-stamped. Six weeks later, on 11 July 1978, Princess Margaret was granted a decree absolute.

PART FIVE

The Divorcée

CHAPTER 20

Tragic Princess

THE YEARS FOLLOWING THE BREAK-UP of Princess Margaret's marriage brought a spate of books and articles about her. Almost all of them presented her as a tragic figure, leading an unfulfilled, unproductive, directionless life. She was pictured as a woman whose frenetic search for personal happiness was proving fruitless; as a spoiled and wilful creature whose antics were doing the monarchy immense harm.

Increasingly bizarre theories were put forward to explain her behaviour. She was said to be an hysteric, a manic depressive, a woman of voracious sexual appetites. One writer even claimed that she suffered from the 'royal malady' – porphyria. This hereditary disease, which can manifest itself in violence and insanity, was thought to be responsible for the celebrated 'madness' of King George III. Although there is very little evidence that it ever surfaced again in the British royal family, James Brough, the author of *Margaret: The Tragic Princess*, argued that she suffered from porphyria. Brough claimed that a Fleet Street reporter, alerted to the fact that the Princess had inherited the condition, consulted an unnamed 'British specialist on the subject'. Having warned the reporter that he would deny the story if ever it appeared in print, the specialist confirmed his suspicions. Others 'familiar with porphyria' had put together their 'long-range observations' of the Princess and had arrived at the same 'provisional diagnosis'. Only a form of this inherited madness, implied Brough, could explain Princess Margaret's erratic behaviour.[1]

Nonsensical and exaggerated as many of these claims and theories were, they all helped to point up the contrast between Princess

Margaret and the rest of the royal family. By the end of the 1970s, Queen Elizabeth II had been largely successful in presenting the monarchy as a respectable and stable institution; the origins of the troubles that were to beset it in the years ahead were not yet apparent. The Queen herself was known to be virtuous and dutiful, a monarch in whom any lack of charisma was compensated for by an undeniable dignity. She had developed an air of exclusiveness, of reserve, of being one stage removed from ordinary life. As a princess, and as a young queen, she had been thought too matronly; now that she was a matron, she seemed to have come into her own. She was admirably supported by Prince Philip, for while the marriage might have had its difficulties, these had never been made public. The Prince was seen as dynamic, intelligent, straight-talking, and no less dedicated to serving the monarchy.

Although their two youngest sons, Prince Andrew and Prince Edward, had not yet had the opportunities to make their marks, the two older children, Prince Charles and Princess Anne, had both emerged as hard-working and conscientious figures. Prince Charles, with his wide-ranging interests and enthusiasms, and his well-meaning, if somewhat vaguely expressed, sympathies for the underprivileged, was busy instituting various projects and administering assorted trusts. His more aggressive sister, Princess Anne, having for years fought a running battle with the press, eventually established herself, largely through her tireless work for the Save the Children Fund, as one of the family's most industrious and, latterly, most admired members. And, as an example to them all, as proof that it was possible to be colourful without ever putting a foot wrong, there was the Queen Mother. At almost eighty, she continued to carry out her engagements, her apparent tirelessness matched only by her charm, enthusiasm and professionalism.

When set against the worthy behaviour of the other members of what King George VI used to call 'The Firm', Princess Margaret's way of life did seem scandalous and self-indulgent. True, she had only herself to blame for the fact that her contribution to the national life (other than as fodder for journalists) went largely unnoticed and unappreciated. Equally true, however, was the fact that her reputation for irresponsibility was often compounded by bad luck or bad health. In the autumn of 1978 she flew 6,000 miles to represent the Queen at the granting of independence to Tuvalu, a group of islands in the South Pacific which had formerly been part of the British colony of the Gilbert and Ellice Islands. A combination of humidity, tropical showers and dramatic changes of temperature proved too much for her constitution; she had still not fully recovered from hepatitis. After a first day crowded with engagements, she returned to sleep aboard the Royal New Zealand Navy frigate *Otago*, which was lying offshore. During the night, she began to feel desperately ill. Telephoning her soundly sleeping Private Secretary, Lord Napier, she was just able to whisper, 'Thank God you've answered. I'm in great pain . . . I can't breathe.' Within minutes the ship's doctor was at her bedside. The Princess had contracted viral pneumonia: she had a temperature of 105°, and was sinking into a state of delirium. 'I very nearly died,' she afterwards affirmed.[2]

While Lord Napier took her place at the independence ceremonies the following day, arrangements were made to fly the Princess to the nearest fully equipped hospital, which was in Sydney, Australia, over 2,500 miles away. A Hercules military transport was converted into an air ambulance, complete with bed and medical equipment and, once it was considered safe for the Princess to travel, she embarked on the nine-hour flight. Although weak and by now painfully thin, she refused to be carried off the plane on a stretcher. Smiling tremulously, she greeted the Governor of New South Wales and walked unsteadily to the waiting car.

'In our family,' Princess Alice, Countess of Athlone, used to say, 'we never make a fuss about illness.'[3] Within nine days of leaving Tuvalu, Princess Margaret had resumed her tour. She flew to Japan to bestow the honorary Cross of the Order of St Michael and St George on Princess Chichibu, sister of the Emperor Hirohito. From Tokyo she flew to the United States for a three-day private stay in Los Angeles, and then on to Mustique before paying an official visit to Dominica. She returned to Britain in November 1978.

Here Princess Margaret was met by the news that Lord Snowdon was to marry Lucy Lindsay-Hogg. The Princess and her former husband had one of their customary rows, this time about whether or not he had warned her of his plans, and she insisted that he be the one to break the news to their children. On 15 December 1978, just over five months after his divorce from Princess Margaret, Lord Snowdon married Lucy Lindsay-Hogg at the Kensington register office. In contrast to the glittering, widely televised ceremony in

Westminster Abbey eighteen years earlier, this one took place in semi-darkness. To foil any attempt by the photographers massed outside to take pictures through the windows, the bridegroom had insisted that the main lights in the office be turned off.

Since remarrying, Lord Snowdon has led an admirably fulfilled and useful life. His children took quite happily to his new wife without ever becoming alienated from their own mother; indeed, they developed into two remarkably well-adjusted young people. Both the Queen and the Queen Mother are devoted to them, and have remained on good terms with their father since the divorce. The Queen Mother even went so far as to suggest that Lord Snowdon continue to be invited to join the royal family for Christmas. 'Really, my mother!' exploded Princess Margaret.[4]

All in all, the year 1978 had proved disastrous for the Princess. It had seen the furore sparked off by her rush to Roddy Llewellyn's sickbed in Barbados; the vehement public debate in the press and in Parliament about her official role; her divorce; three serious illnesses; and, finally, the remarriage of her husband. It is little wonder that she afterwards described it as the worst year of her life.

Throughout all these vicissitudes, Princess Margaret was sustained by her affection for Roddy Llewellyn. The relationship might not have been as passionate as once it had been, but it remained a source of great comfort. The couple continued to meet at Kensington Palace or in the homes of friends; they would holiday together on Mustique or Spain's Costa del Sol; they would go to the theatre, sometimes with the Princess's children; they would attend balls and parties. The American dress designer, Halston, notorious for his wild entertainments, once invited them to a party at the Savoy, where they joined people like Liza Minnelli and Andy Warhol. One of the guests took a photograph of the Princess and Roddy together. Always wary of adverse publicity, she begged him to hand over the film, but although he refused, the pictures were never published.

She was less fortunate with some photographs taken at Glen, where she and Roddy were part of the Tennants' 1979 autumn house party. Princess Margaret, in fancy dress as Sophie Tucker, did a raunchy impersonation of the singer, and her 'act' was photographed by Anne Tennant. Once the pictures had been developed and printed, the negatives were put away in a drawer, where they were discovered by the Tennants' eldest son who, in need of cash, arranged for them to be sold to the *Daily Mail*. The country was duly faced, one morning, by a three-page spread of Queen Elizabeth II's sister impersonating the Last of the Red-Hot Mommas. It was hardly the image of the monarchy which Her Majesty was trying so hard to preserve.

However great the affection between them, Princess Margaret was forever being caught up, directly or indirectly, in the publicity engendered by Roddy Llewellyn's every move. In October 1978 his LP, titled simply *Roddy*, was launched. Neither his royal connections, however, nor the extensive media coverage of the launch could boost sales, which proved to be dismal. Within weeks, the record had disappeared, and Roddy never cut a second. This failure marked the end of his brief career as a pop singer.

Then, early in 1979, he was arrested for drink-driving. Taking a woman friend named Naima Kelly home from a party in his van, Roddy collided with a police car. Thoroughly alarmed, he careered away in the direction of Kensington Palace, pursued by the slightly damaged police vehicle, until his flight was ended when he crashed the van into a bollard. He failed a breathalyser test and, when the case came to court, he was fined and banned from driving for eighteen months. Since transport was essential for his gardening business, he was faced with the prospect of earning even less money than usual.

Roddy's friendship with Naima Kelly proved even more awkward for Princess Margaret when, later that year, the *News of the World* carried a story that Kelly's husband was planning to divorce her, citing Roddy as co-respondent. Although the report was subsequently found to be false, it caused the Princess acute embarrassment, for it had been cynically timed to coincide with her return from Mustique. Arriving at Heathrow, tired after a long flight, she was met by a horde of reporters and cameramen, only too ready to record her distress.

More distressing still was the same newspaper's publication, early in 1980, of Dai Llewellyn's 'story'. Roddy's elder brother had sold his revelations twice before, and on this occasion was being offered a rather greater sum of money on the understanding that he would produce new and yet more revealing information about the

Princess and Roddy. The story, which appeared in four instalments, duly upset most of Dai's family and friends. The *News of the World* journalist who interviewed him for the pieces had apparently pressed the older Llewellyn to discuss what he called Roddy's 'sensitive areas' – in other words, his alleged homosexuality – but this Dai says he refused to do.[5] He did, however, say that Nicky Haslam, the interior designer with whom Roddy had once lived, had described him as 'a lovely, sweet angelic boy'. He also repeated an apocryphal story concerning their father who, on being told about Roddy's affair with Princess Margaret, is said to have exclaimed, 'Well, at least it makes a change from Italian waiters!'[6] The Princess herself refused to read the articles, though doubtless she was perfectly well aware of their content. 'I've been misreported and misrepresented since the age of seventeen,' she said loftily, 'and I gave up long ago reading about myself.'[7]

Princess Margaret's feelings for Roddy Llewellyn were in no way affected by this barrage of adverse publicity. In spite of the disapproval of her family and of many of her friends, she refused to hear a word against him, let alone break with him. To those who accused him of using their relationship to further his career, she replied that he was simply being taken advantage of by unscrupulous people.

And, in a way, she was right. Roddy Llewellyn was far from being a mephistophelean figure, a mercenary toy boy preying on a vulnerable, middle-aged woman. No one, seeing the two of them together, could doubt that their feelings for each other were warm and sincere. They would hold hands, share private jokes, go out walking arm-in-arm. While he was always careful to address her as 'Ma'am' in public, she would call him 'darling' or 'my love'. Close friends like Colin Tennant always maintained that Roddy was 'an angel' with her: the only man ever to have treated her with care and kindness. One day, while they were playing gin rummy with a party of friends, the Princess asked Roddy for the score, and he passed her the pad. When she turned the page, she saw that he had written her a message. 'You are looking very beautiful today,' it read.[8]

Late in 1979, Princess Margaret became embroiled in a serious political controversy. This had its origins in the violent murder, on 27 August that year, of Earl Mountbatten of Burma, the uncle of Prince Philip, an important member of the royal circle, and a distinguished figure in the nation's life. While Lord Mountbatten and his family were on holiday in the Irish Republic, his yacht was blown up by a remote-controlled IRA bomb. Mountbatten, one of his grandsons and a young crewmate were killed instantly; his son-in-law's mother died from her injuries the following day. The Earl's daughter, Lady Brabourne, her husband and their son were severely injured. Not unnaturally, the royal family was deeply shocked and saddened by this brutal and callous slaughter.

Some six weeks later, in her capacity as President of the Royal Ballet, Princess Margaret set off on a two-week visit to the United States to help raise funds for the Royal Opera House. Over £7 million was needed for the redevelopment of the backstage facilities. By mid-October the Princess was in Chicago ('not, to my mind, an altogether straightforward piece of fund-raising, given that we are in the heart of the Middle West,' drily remarked the British Ambassador, Sir Nicholas Henderson[9]) where she attended a dinner given in her honour. There she was seated beside Mrs Jane Byrne, the Mayor of Chicago, who told her royal guest that she had attended the funeral of Lord Mountbatten as part of a ten-member delegation from the United States. According to Irv Kupcinet, a columnist on the *Chicago Sun-Times*, the Princess had replied, 'The Irish – they're pigs,' and had followed this with an immediate, 'Oh-oh, you're Irish.' The 'very, very Irish' Mrs Byrne, claimed Kupcinet, left the party 'as soon as possible'.

The allegations were denied by the Princess's Private Secretary, Lord Napier, who issued a statement to the effect that no such remark had been made, and that Mayor Byrne had not left the party early. In addition, Kupcinet's informant could not possibly have heard a conversation over the amplified music in a crowded, noisy room. But both Mayor Byrne and the Princess's hostess, Mrs Abra Anderson, confirmed that the royal guest had made 'an Irish slur'. The Mayor issued a statement in which she claimed that she understood the remark to have referred to the IRA terrorists and not the Irish people. 'The mayor felt "pigs" was an unfortunate choice of word, and one she would not have used, but she understood it was in context with terrorists and murderers.'[10]

Whatever the truth of the matter, Princess Margaret's alleged remark infuriated a certain section of the Irish-American population, and gave to the IRA's cause in North America a wonderful rallying cry. Militants threatened to disrupt her visit to San Francisco by releasing a thousand pigs through the streets by way of protest. (In the event, only one pig could be rustled up, and there were fewer than a hundred demonstrators.) By the time the Princess reached Los Angeles, however, a more serious IRA threat had been uncovered by the police. Captain Larry Kramer of the Los Angeles Police Department claimed to have discovered a plot to assassinate her; it was said that a high-ranking IRA man, on the run since the Mountbatten murder, and an American accomplice were involved in the conspiracy. As a result, Princess Margaret was protected by what was described as 'presidential-style' security: a bullet-proof car, an armed police motorcycle escort, plain-clothes State Department agents, and a helicopter fitted out as an air ambulance. Doctors at selected hospitals along her route were given details of her medical history, blood type and drug allergies. This tight security was explained away as official protection made necessary by the outcry caused by her alleged 'Irish pigs' remark.

The Los Angeles visit brought social problems as well. When the celebrated Hollywood producer, Ray Stark, held a cocktail party for the royal visitor, he ensured that such ageing stars as Cary Grant and Gregory Peck (once Princess Margaret's favourite) were all assembled by half-past six. But the guest of honour did not arrive until a quarter to eight, by which time most of the celebrities had given up and gone home.

A formal dinner given by one of Hollywood's leading theatrical agents proved even more disastrous. The Princess was seated at a table with such glitterati as Barbra Streisand, Jack Nicholson, Clint Eastwood, Michael Caine and, by her special request, Barry Manilow. Also at the table was the Governor of California, Jerry Brown, whose opening remark to the Princess broke all royal protocol. 'Good evening, Your Highness,' he said airily, 'I just dropped by to say hello. I have another appointment so I'm only staying for the first course.' To have left the word 'Royal' out of her title was bad enough, but to have casually announced that he was planning to leave a formal occasion before she did was, by her reckoning, unforgivable. Without saying a word, the Princess simply turned her back on Governor Brown and took no further notice of him, not even when he left. She afterwards described him as 'a dreadful man'.

But there was worse to come. The singer Linda Ronstadt, who was Jerry Brown's companion for the evening, was seated at another table. As the Princess's table was served first, Miss Ronstadt strolled over and, standing behind the Governor's chair, asked, 'What are we having to start?' She then leaned over with the intention of taking a piece of food off his plate in order to taste it. In doing so, she not only put one hand on the Governor's shoulder, but she also put the other on the Princess's shoulder. 'I have seen people shrug many times,' says Michael Caine, who was watching, 'but the Princess's shoulder shrugged like a punch from a boxer and with almost the same effect on Miss Ronstadt. She almost overbalanced and fell on the floor.'[11] At no point did Her Royal Highness even look up.

This trouble-fraught fund-raising trip is said to have raised a mere half-million dollars, and much of that had been pledged before Princess Margaret left Britain. It must, therefore, have been with considerable relief that she flew off to join Roddy Llewellyn on Mustique. Even he had suffered as a consequence of her widely reported 'Irish pigs' remark. Some of Fulham's Irish community had smashed the terracotta pots outside his flat, and emptied their contents into his basement area.

Nor was this tour the Princess's last taste of Irish-American opposition, for her projected visit to Washington the following year had to be cancelled because of the threat of pro-IRA demonstrations. Sir Nicholas Henderson, attending a party given by Douglas Fairbanks, Junior, for the incoming United States Ambassador to the Court of St James's, was standing talking to the Queen when, to his surprise, Princess Margaret strolled over and butted into their conversation. They discussed the cancellation of her Washington visit. She clearly thought that the loss was the American capital's, not hers. 'Serves 'em right,' she exclaimed, thus striking what Sir Nicholas gallantly describes as 'an admirably self-assured and undefensive note'.[12]

Due to turn fifty in August 1980, Princess Margaret decided to take herself in hand. In January that year she underwent plastic surgery to remove lesions or bumps from her jawline. Although the operation was not, as the press inevitably claimed, a full face-lift, she nevertheless emerged from hospital looking younger and prettier, and with no trace of what had fast been developing into a double chin.

She also lost almost two stone in weight, and even tried to cut down on her smoking. Able to wear more stylish clothes she looked, exclaimed one spectator at a fashion show, 'absolutely stunning'. On another occasion, a woman journalist wrote of watching the Princess arrive at the Cathedral Green in Ely, looking 'startlingly slender, glamorous even, in a primrose yellow suit, with softly waved hair, pink lipstick and a relaxed smile. . . .'[13] The official birthday photographs that year, taken by Norman Parkinson in the Princess's blue-walled drawing room at Kensington Palace, perfectly capture her svelte, sparkling, newly revived film-star quality.

For Princess Margaret, and in contrast to previous years, 1980 was packed with engagements. Perhaps she was spurred on by the fact that her annual Civil List allowance had been raised yet again, this time to £82,000. She visited British military bases in West Germany where, admittedly, the weather was so cold that she left one guard of honour uninspected and, instead, asked for a gin and tonic to revive her circulation. She undertook a sixteen-day tour of the Far East, to Singapore, Malaysia and the Philippines, where the ineffable Imelda Marcos all but overwhelmed her with hospitality in an effort, she explained, to 'compensate' her royal guest for years of adverse publicity. She paid an official visit to Canada, where her exhausting schedule included a prairie-style barbecue at which she looked superb in a pink *fin-de-siècle* costume. The trip was marred only by an editorial in the *Toronto Sun*. 'She is out West being given the top hat and curtsy treatment as if she were something special,' it grumbled, 'rather than a Royal Baggage who has, by her lifestyle, forfeited all right to respect and homage.'[14]

At home, her engagements were no less numerous: eight in one week alone in May. 'Princess Margaret,' noted one surprised reporter, 'seems to be returning to the respectable routine of royal duties.'[15] Then, on 15 July 1980, came one of those great royal occasions by which the monarchy captures the imagination of the people: the Service of Thanksgiving in St Paul's Cathedral to mark the Queen Mother's eightieth birthday. In full panoply – marching bands, open carriages, the Sovereign's Escort of the Household Cavalry – the royal family passed in procession through wildly cheering crowds, everyone anxious to pay tribute to the nation's most popular figure. On 4 August, the actual date of the anniversary of the Queen Mother's birth, a smaller but no less enthusiastic crowd gathered outside Clarence House, for it had by now become traditional for a faithful band of her admirers to pay this annual homage. Helping their mother receive gifts and flowers from scores of children were the Queen and Princess Margaret. Seen together like this, the three royal women – all beautifully groomed, their necks roped with pearls, their feet shod in high-heeled white sandals – looked as though nothing in the world could disturb the harmony of their family relationship.

But Roddy Llewellyn remained a source of dissension. Although the Queen Mother had entertained him at Royal Lodge (his boast was that he had once danced with her), the Queen resolutely refused to invite him to any of her homes. Roddy had, however, once met her, although in embarrassing circumstances, at Royal Lodge. Wearing only a shirt and underpants, he had gone in search of Nanny Sumner to have a button sewn on, and had suddenly come across her in conversation with the Queen. 'Please forgive me, Ma'am, I look so awful,' the young man spluttered. 'Don't worry, I don't look very good myself,' answered the Queen calmly, and left the room.[16] Not until the following morning were they formally introduced by Princess Margaret after morning service in St George's Chapel, Windsor.

The Queen's antipathy to her sister's lover came to a head during discussions about the party to mark Princess Margaret's fiftieth birthday. Although the actual date was celebrated, as usual, at Balmoral on 21 August 1980, the official party was to be held on 4 November, at the Ritz Hotel in London. The royal family would head a group of forty who would dine at four tables; at half-past ten more than a hundred other guests would arrive to dance. The Princess wanted Roddy to be among the favoured forty sitting down to dinner; the Queen did not want him to come at all, not even with the after-dinner guests. There were several rows. Princess Margaret's long-standing friend, Dominic Elliot, took the Queen's part, and eventually, after yet another blazing argument, refused to attend at all, whereupon he was told by the furious Princess that she never wanted to see him again.

In the end, a compromise was reached. The Princess's closest friends, the Tennants, who would normally have been invited to the dinner, were detailed to take Roddy out to eat elsewhere, and the Queen agreed that he could come to the dance with the lesser guests. Throughout the evening, he kept well clear of the royal family, only dancing with Princess Margaret after the Queen and Prince Philip had gone home.

By now, Princess Margaret and Roddy Llewellyn had been together for over seven years. In some ways they were not unlike a married couple; ill-assorted, admittedly, but accustomed to one another. For him there was the continuing excitement, glamour and social advantage of being associated with a princess; for her, there was the reassurance of a good-looking and good-natured young escort. She had built up his self-confidence; he had reawakened her interest in life. 'They need each other,' said Colin Tennant, who probably knew them as well as anyone did.

'If our relationship ended,' Roddy once said, 'life for me would rather lose its point. We sing, we dance, we're generally happy and I don't see why things should not continue as they are for ever.'[17] But at his thirty-third birthday party, on 9 October 1980, given by the night-club-owner Peter Stringfellow (from which the Princess was absent, feeling that it would be unwise to attend what was a commercially driven function), Roddy found himself in the company of an attractive dark-haired woman of his own age named Tatiana Soskin. Always known as Tania, she was the daughter of a Russian-born film producer, the late Paul Soskin, and had trained as a fashion designer in Paris. In fact, Roddy and Tania had known each other for several years, but it was not until that evening that he began to fall in love with her.

In the course of the following four months, as Roddy's feelings for Tania deepened, he realized that he would have to break off his close relationship with Princess Margaret. In February 1981, when the two of them were again on Mustique, things came to a climax. When the Princess tackled Roddy about what she had noticed was his uncharacteristically taciturn behaviour, he confessed that he was in love with Tania and wanted to marry her. One cannot know Princess Margaret's precise reaction to the news; some claim that she was devastated, others that she was relieved. As a woman of the world, she probably appreciated that the affair, already somewhat lukewarm, could not last indefinitely, though she would no doubt have preferred to have been the one to end it. All she could do was to give Roddy her blessing and to advise him to propose to Tania as soon as possible. 'I'm really very happy for him,' she afterwards said. 'Anyway, I couldn't have afforded him much longer!'[18]

Graciously, on her return to London she gave a small luncheon party at Kensington Palace for Roddy and Tania and, on the announcement of their engagement on 4 April 1981, assured them that she would be delighted to attend their wedding. A ceremony and reception in Wales were planned for 27 June 1981, but because this was going to prove inconvenient, the place and date were switched to Marlow in Buckinghamshire – where Tania Soskin's uncle had a home – for 11 July. This date, however, did not suit the Princess: she was due to visit Canada and the United States as part of the Royal Ballet's fiftieth anniversary celebrations. So, in the end, the wedding took place without her, which was, perhaps, just as well. The press would have relished nothing more than to picture the rejected but bravely smiling Princess Margaret, facing up – in journalistic jargon – to yet another broken dream, yet another fairy tale that had not come true.

Roddy Llewellyn's marriage to Tania Soskin proved to be very successful. The couple had children, and Roddy's career as a garden designer flourished. Although Princess Margaret might not have been as heartbroken by his defection as many imagined, it must have deepened her feelings of isolation, her sense of emotional failure. Behind her lay a trail of unfulfilled relationships: Peter Townsend, Antony Armstrong-Jones, Robin Douglas-Home, Roddy Llewellyn. And even if she were to find some suitable male companion, marriage for the Queen's divorced sister, in the climate of the early 1980s, was still unthinkable. 'I'm back to where I started with Peter,' she sighed, 'but this time *I'm* divorced. . . .'[19]

CHAPTER 21

Aunt Margot

THE GRANDIOSE WEDDING OF CHARLES, Prince of Wales to Lady Diana Spencer in St Paul's Cathedral on 29 July 1981 marked, in many ways, a turning point in Princess Margaret's life. The focus of public attention shifted to a younger generation. As the young Princess of Wales gained in confidence and chic, so did she begin to take the position which the young Princess Margaret had held in the 1950s. People began to talk of the older woman as having been 'the Princess Diana of her day'. The relentless media attention was now directed away from the Queen's sister; not only towards the Princess of Wales, but also towards the increasingly newsworthy lives of a whole new royal generation. Not yet, but in time, Princess Margaret's once scandalous-seeming antics would pale in comparison with those of the latest breed of family members.

Other weddings, this time of members of her household, increased Princess Margaret's awareness of changing times. Two of her ladies-in-waiting were married during this same year: the Hon. Davina Woodhouse married Earl Alexander of Tunis, and Elizabeth Paget married Dr Angus Blair. The Princess's ladies had always been friends rather than employees and, married or not, continued to be in attendance. (On once being asked how new ladies-in-waiting knew what to do, the Princess answered, in her languid fashion, 'They learn, they learn'.[1]) Anne Tennant who, on her husband's succession to his father's title, became Lady Glenconner, often acted as a lady-in-waiting. Although a close friend, she unquestioningly accepted the fact that Princess Margaret belonged to a royal generation whose members expected to have everything done for them.

Colin Glenconner once explained that his wife was quite happy to spend a morning packing the Princess's clothes. 'But it's something,' he added, 'my children simply can't understand.'[2] For Princess Margaret, it seems, the generation gap is not confined solely to the royal family.

The first of the new family members temporarily to eclipse Princess Margaret – in the eyes of the public, although certainly not in the latter's own – was Princess Michael of Kent. In the year of Princess Margaret's divorce, her thirty-five-year-old cousin, Prince Michael of Kent, contracted a highly controversial marriage. His bride, the Austrian-born Baroness Marie-Christine von Reibnitz, could hardly have been a less suitable choice – she was a Roman Catholic divorcée. Obstacles to the marriage had seemed insurmountable: the Vatican forbade the remarriage of divorced Catholics; the Act of Settlement of 1701 forbade the marriage of members of the British royal family to Catholics; and the Royal Marriages Act of 1772 forbade the marriage of a royal person without the Sovereign's permission.

These problems were overcome in various ways: initially, by the Pope annulling the first marriage; secondly, by Prince Michael, who was only sixteenth in line of succession, giving up his rights to the throne; thirdly, by the Queen granting her permission. A further rumpus was caused by the Pope refusing to allow a church ceremony on the grounds that if the couple had children, these were to be raised as Protestants. Disappointed, they were married in the Rathaus in Vienna in June 1978. This highly complicated process brought home to Princess Margaret the difficulties she would face if ever she contemplated marrying again. 'One couldn't get married in this country – look at Michael and Marie-Christine,' she sighed. 'Remarriage would be a devil of a trouble. . . .'[3]

Ushered into the royal family on a whirlwind of publicity, Princess Michael of Kent adroitly managed to keep herself in the public eye. Before long, she was being generally referred to as 'Princess Pushy'. Princess Margaret's aversion to her cousin's wife seems to have been almost immediate. Thirty-three at the time of her marriage, Princess Michael was tall, slender, *soignée*, with the sort of conscious charm that the rest of the royal family found distinctly grating. Princess Margaret is alleged to have regarded her as an unctuous, limelight-seeking adventuress, far too eager to force her way into the inner circle of the royal family; to the rest of them, she was 'the Valkyrie' or 'You-Know-Who'. When the newly married couple were given a home in Kensington Palace (in fact, the house occupied by the Snowdons at the start of their marriage), Princess Margaret's reaction was decidedly cool.

Her antipathy was once vividly, and very publicly, demonstrated during the traditional carriage procession at Ascot. The two princesses had been seated side by side, and while Princess Michael babbled on in an effort to be friendly, Princess Margaret rewarded her relentless flow with an occasional grunt. 'Why did you put me next to that woman?' she demanded of the Queen at the end of the drive. 'Because I knew that it would give you a chance to do what you like best,' answered her sister. 'Concentrate on the two attractive men sitting opposite.'⁴

The relationship between the two princesses was hardly improved when Princess Margaret's son, Lord Linley, once loudly announced that, as a Christmas gift to his worst enemy, he would give 'dinner for two with Princess Michael'. The quip was immediately reported back. Princess Michael's riposte, made in a public speech, was that Linley's insult had brought three sackloads of mail from men only too anxious to proclaim themselves to be Lord Linley's worst enemy, and thus become eligible for a dinner date with her.

A still more embarrassing situation developed when, at a private party attended by Princess Margaret, the Earl of Dudley revealed that he had written a satirical poem about Princess Michael. 'Let's hear it,' said a delighted Princess Margaret. As his recitation progressed and the verses became increasingly scurrilous, Lord Dudley wondered whether he should continue, but the Princess's appreciative 'Wow!' gave him all the encouragement he needed.⁵ Inevitably, reports of the poem, and of Princess Margaret's enthusiastic reaction, got back to Princess Michael.

John Barrat, who had been Lord Mountbatten's private secretary and who, after the earl's murder, went to work for Prince and Princess Michael of Kent, has some telling comments to make on the antipathy between the two princesses. Princess Margaret's staff could not wait, he says, 'to pass on the latest titbit about Marie-Christine's behaviour'. Princess Michael was very conscious of the fact that Princess Margaret 'hated' her, a hatred from which Barrat was to suffer. On Mountbatten's death, Princess Margaret had written the private secretary 'a lovely letter', but as soon as she heard that he had gone to work for Princess Michael, she 'cut him dead'.[6]

In time, Princess Michael's increasingly assertive behaviour, allied to newspaper rumours about her affair with a Texan millionaire, accusations of plagiarism in a book she had written, and the revelation that – unbeknown to her – her father had been a member of the Nazi SS, caused her to be cold-shouldered by the rest of the royal family. By the late 1980s her brief starburst of fame had burnt itself out.

Whatever her other failings or shortcomings, as a mother Princess Margaret was extremely successful. Her often rackety way of life seems to have had no adverse effect upon her two children. 'In her odd, detached way,' says Lady Elizabeth Cavendish, 'she's been a very good mother. Against all the odds.'[7] She and Lord Snowdon were sympathetic, interested, supportive parents, never forcing their children – as the Queen and Prince Philip had tended to force theirs – along paths that were alien to their natures. The tendency on the Princess's part to leave things in the hands of the nanny had been counteracted by Snowdon's insistence on educational toys, practical hobbies, instructive holidays. Both Lord Linley and Lady Sarah Armstrong-Jones had been boarders at Bedales in Hampshire and, like any other parent, Princess Margaret had sat uncomplainingly through sports days, prize-givings, pantomimes and nativity plays. During school holidays she had taken the children to exhibitions, galleries, concerts, theatres and cinemas.

She could be surprisingly strict. Once, in the course of an Italian holiday, the Princess and her two children were taken by Gore Vidal to visit a monastery above Naples. In the refectory, where there was a row of carved wooden seats for the high-ranking members of the order, Lord Linley immediately plonked himself in a seat several places below the abbot's chair and ordered his sister into the seat below his. 'Each knew his exact place in succession to the crown,' commented Vidal. But the Princess was not amused. '"Stop *that*," [she thundered] . . . in her best Lady Bracknell voice.' Interestingly, Vidal goes on to make an astute observation about Princess Margaret. 'She is far too bright for her station in life,' he writes, 'which she takes altogether too solemnly.'[8]

It is highly unlikely that either of David Linley's parents would have wanted him to follow the traditional royal route into the armed services; in any case, as a pacifist, he would have resisted any such notion. At Bedales he had shown a strong interest in carpentry (he had spent much of his free holiday time in the Buckingham Palace workshops, helping to repair and restore furniture) and, on leaving school, had enrolled in a two-year cabinet-making course at the John Makepeace School for Craftsmen in Wood at Parnham in Dorset. On leaving the John Makepeace School, at the age of twenty in 1982, he and a partner set up their own cabinet-making business in Dorking. Within three years he had proved successful enough to open a shop in the New King's Road, Fulham, trading as David Linley Furniture Limited.

Although there can be no doubt that being the son of Princess Margaret brought considerable advantages – including the advantage of being able to charge hefty prices – David Linley's workmanship was of a high enough standard to bear comparison with that of most of his competitors, his marquetry pieces being particularly impressive. His mother was extremely proud of his achievements. Glass in one hand and cigarette in the other, she was often to be seen admiring his work at launch parties or exhibition openings. 'This is David's,' she once exclaimed, on seeing a walnut table inlaid with ebony, priced at £7,500, at the Ideal Home Exhibition; 'Look how beautifully crafted it is!'[9]

In 1985, the year in which he opened up in Fulham, the twenty-three-year-old Linley bought his own flat and moved out of Kensington Palace. In the same way that she had always encouraged her son to follow his creative talents, so did Princess Margaret understand his need to have a home of his own. Although, physically, he resembled his father, he had inherited many of his mother's characteristics: he was volatile, nonconformist and, in spite of a determination to make his own way in the world, not beyond insisting on being treated with the deference due to his royal descent; the Kensington Palace staff had to address him as 'Sir'. From both parents, Linley had inherited a strong interest in clothes: his taste was stylish and adventurous. By the time he moved out of his mother's home, he had a regular girlfriend, Susannah Constantine.

He also had a passion for cars, which Princess Margaret indulged. He owned several and was often in trouble for motoring offences.

But in spite of the many tabloid stories to the contrary, Linley was never just another roistering young royal. Receiving nothing from the Civil List, he had to earn his own living. Ever the entrepreneur, and in spite of the success of his furniture business, he went into partnership with Patrick Lichfield to open a restaurant in Chelsea, which they called Deals. Astutely, Linley invited a group of taxi drivers to the opening so that, in future, they would be sure of the address. Within a few years, he had opened a second restaurant.

Like her brother, Lady Sarah Armstrong-Jones had inherited her parents' looks and artistic interests. Leaving Bedales with one A level in art, she went on to Camberwell School of Art where, with her broad grin, untamed hair and casual clothes, she was indistinguishable from her fellow art students. She even pedalled her way on a push-bike from Kensington Palace to the art school every morning. On completing her course, she spent a year doing odd jobs. Taking advantage of her various family connections, she joined her father in India, where he was shooting photographic stills for David Lean's film *A Passage to India*; she worked for the film producer, Lord Brabourne, the late Lord Mountbatten's son-in-law; she studied wood gilding with her father's cousin, Thomas Messel. Her year's sabbatical over, she enrolled for a two-year course in textile and fabric design at Middlesex Polytechnic, and in 1988 she entered the Royal Academy Art School. Not long after she turned twenty-one, on 1 May 1985, Lady Sarah, again like her brother, moved out of Kensington Palace into a home of her own. This has been described as a 'cottage-style' house in a leafy Kensington street, midway between the homes of her divorced parents. It was bought for her by her mother.

Princess Margaret has always made a point of explaining that her children are not members of the royal family. Although they were often to be seen at such family occasions as weddings and christenings (Sarah was a bridesmaid to the Princess of Wales), they carried out no official public engagements. There were the expected visits to Balmoral and Sandringham, the Queen being very fond of the Snowdon children, particularly of Sarah; 'They love the Queen and she loves them,' said one member of the household.[10] An exception to the rule of no public duties came when both children accompanied their mother on an official visit to China and Hong Kong in May 1987. The traditional formal portrait to mark this visit – of

Princess Margaret and her two children – was taken by none other than Lord Snowdon. It showed the three of them grouped around a symbol of their journey, a large globe.

Whatever their other differences, Princess Margaret and Lord Snowdon were united in their concern and affection for their children. Once officially free of one another, the couple were able to meet on more amicable terms, and Snowdon has been scrupulous about never speaking publicly – to authors or the press – about his stormy relationship with his first wife. He could, at one stage, have earned enormous sums for his revelations about their married life, and he still has the power to damage her reputation. The late Jackie Onassis, in her capacity as a consultant for an American publishing house, Doubleday, is reported to have once offered him about two and a half million dollars for his autobiography. But he has kept his admirable silence.

No one, seeing the four members of the Snowdon family entertaining the Queen Mother at a convivial lunch given for her eighty-ninth birthday at Linley's restaurant, Deals, would have imagined that they were anything other than a blissfully happy and united family. It is only in private that the Princess refers to her ex-husband as 'the Rat'.

Both intentionally and unintentionally, throughout the 1980s Princess Margaret still kept herself in the news. Indeed, in 1981 she allowed herself to be featured in the media in a way that would have been unthinkable for a member of the royal family a few years before, when she appeared on Roy Plomley's BBC Radio Four programme *Desert Island Discs*. Always unpredictable, the records she chose were not the expected Noël Coward or Frank Sinatra songs, but such stirring tunes as 'Rule, Britannia!', 'Scotland the Brave', a Sousa march and a Welsh hymn. Perhaps she was trying to play down her perceived public image. (The truth is, however, that the Princess's musical tastes are a good deal more serious than many people imagine. She may not like opera, but she greatly enjoys most classical music, and often listens to concerts on BBC Radio Three.) Her views, as they were expressed on the programme, were rather more predictable. She complained bitterly to Plomley about misrepresentation and misreporting in the press; she said that she loved the theatre, particularly ballet; she admitted that she enjoyed life far too much to be able to live alone on a desert island. The 'luxury item' she would have wanted on a desert island was a piano; her choice of book would have been *War and Peace*.

Princess Margaret was also the first member of the royal family to act, rather than just to appear, in a broadcast production when in 1984 she played herself – as President of the National Society for the Prevention of Cruelty to Children – in the long-running BBC radio soap opera *The Archers*.

In 1981, she again revealed herself to the public by being photographed in her drawing room at Kensington Palace for the *Observer* magazine series 'A Room of My Own'. It was her favourite room, she announced, because it was the largest room; she had been 'brought up in very large rooms' and 'always gravitated to the biggest rooms around'. But she insisted that the highly polished doors be kept shut at all times; she had an aversion to sitting in rooms with open doors. The article also revealed that, in spite of its splendour, the room had a reassuringly informal air; surfaces were cluttered, her desk was covered in what she called her 'own system of mess', paper carrier bags were propped up in one corner.[11]

In another feature, this time a 1986 *Sunday Times* magazine excerpt from the book *The Englishwoman's Wardrobe* by her friend Angela Huth, the Princess spoke about her clothes. 'I'm always conscious of what's in fashion,' she said, 'because without following it too strictly, one must get the line right.' Twice a year, the piece continued, she subjected herself to the planning and fitting of her summer and winter wardrobes. All her clothes were what she called 'working clothes', which in practice meant that they were like most women's 'best clothes'. There were certain unchanging rules for royal women: skirts could not be too tight because of climbing stairs and getting in and out of cars; sleeves had to be loose to allow for waving; fabrics had to be uncrushable; as much attention had to be paid to the back view as the front; clothes had to photograph well; dresses with matching coats were more practical for changing climates. Although she did not really like hats, they were obligatory for certain occasions. (In the early days of their marriage, Lord Snowdon had designed a special back for an aeroplane seat which enabled her to wear a hat in comfort.) Living, as she did, in the public eye, meant considerable yearly additions to her wardrobe. At least four new outfits were necessary for Ascot alone; a foreign tour usually meant a complete new wardrobe. She made use of several designers but, if touring abroad, felt obliged to wear only British-designed clothes. The Princess's personal preferences were more revealing. She never wore trousers; she preferred city to country clothes; she found brown depressing; she liked only smooth fabrics; what she enjoyed wearing most were grand evening dresses. She greatly regretted the passing of any sense of occasion: of bathing and changing into something special for the evening. Even when everyone else was wearing short dresses at night, she wore long, and she loved evening dresses in sumptuous materials – velvets, satins, taffetas. 'But not too much *décolletage* these days,' she added. 'I think when you're older exposing too much skin is hideous.' She was photographed for the feature in an ivory-coloured evening dress created by her friend, the theatrical designer Carl Toms. 'Carl has me absolutely right,' she said. 'He's used to small people because of designing for ballet dancers.'[12]

There were some aspects of her dressing which the Princess did not mention. Blithely ignoring current conservationist thinking, she continued to wear a full-length mink coat. Even the Queen Mother, who loved fox furs, had by now had hers put into cold storage. The Princess was also criticized for her choice of shoes: regardless of fashion, she stuck resolutely to the high-heeled, platform-soled, peep-toed styles that she had worn in the 1950s. But, even given such criticisms, there was no denying that, on occasions like a gala première or the State Opening of Parliament, Princess Margaret could look extremely striking: elegant, opulent, every inch a princess.

She continued to make news in less complimentary ways as well. Her off-the-cuff, characteristically sharp remarks were still avidly reported. In 1982 the Princess attended an award ceremony for the pop group Culture Club, whose song 'Do you really want to hurt me?' had become a No. 1 hit record in fifty-one countries. The group's lead singer was Boy George, as celebrated for his lavish make-up and androgynous clothes as he was for his voice. The Princess turned down Boy George's request that she be photographed with the group, with the alleged remark that she did not 'want to be photographed with that over-made-up tart. I'm too old for that sort of thing.' To this, the singer replied, 'I don't give a damn. I didn't want to talk to her anyway. She doesn't mean a thing to me . . . I bring more money into the country than she does.'[13] He then went on to demand an apology. None, of course, was forthcoming. It was claimed that the words 'over-made-up tart' had been a mishearing of the Princess's reference to the singer's make-up looking like a *commedia dell'arte* mask. The long-suffering Lord Napier was obliged to protest that Her Royal Highness would never have dreamed of making such a remark.

Above all, of course, it was for her love life that Princess Margaret remained a source of abiding public interest. Not long after her divorce, her name was coupled with that of a wealthy Italian merchant banker named Mario d'Urso. Seven years younger than the Princess, d'Urso was the London representative of an American banking house. In August 1978 she had spent a holiday in the d'Urso family villa in Amalfi, and when the two of them, accompanied only by a detective, flew off together, there had been considerable press speculation about d'Urso being, not only 'the new man' in Princess Margaret's life, but possibly her future husband.

Another such candidate was a wealthy property owner, Ned Ryan. Three years older than the Princess, Ryan was a self-made man. The son of a Tipperary farmer, he had had a varied career which had included jobs selling carpets, driving buses and manning a street stall. By his drive and business acumen he had become a millionaire, with a house in Knightsbridge and a circle of smart friends. He was exactly the kind of amusing, outspoken, unaffected man that appealed to the Princess; he had, too, the sort of cheek that would penetrate her hauteur. Once, at a Rolling Stones concert at Wembley, a naked man streaked across the arena. Ned Ryan immediately clapped his hands over his eyes. 'You're supposed to clap a hand over my eyes!' exclaimed the Princess. 'I did think about it,' answered Ryan, 'but I thought you'd be disappointed if I did.'[14]

But no more than Mario d'Urso was Ned Ryan ever a serious love of Princess Margaret's life. He was simply an occasional escort, a good companion, her 'Court Jester'.

The man whose name was most persistently linked with hers at this time was Norman Lonsdale. The two of them had known each other for many years but in 1981, with the death of Lonsdale's wife and the marriage of Roddy Llewellyn, they had drawn closer together. A rich, handsome, Eton-educated businessman, four years older than the Princess, Lonsdale made an eminently suitable companion. His career, like Ryan's had been varied: among other things he had been a banker, restaurateur, even a ranch hand in Montana. His frequent escorting of the Princess, their holidays together on Mustique, their dinners *à deux* in his Fulham home, led to the inevitable news reports that they were about to marry. Lonsdale's answer to this was that he had never proposed marriage to the Princess and was not likely to do so. The Princess's answer was more trenchant. 'Absolute rubbish!' she said.[15]

But the story died hard. In 1988, six years after the marriage rumours first surfaced, the *People* featured a double-page spread of the Princess and Norman Lonsdale in swimming costumes on the secluded terrace of a villa in Italy. The pictures were obviously taken with a camera equipped with a telephoto lens; the couple were obviously quite unaware of the fact that they were being photographed. 'For ten long, hot summer days and nights,' read the perfervid text of the accompanying article, 'the princess and her perfect gentleman kissed and caressed as they strolled near the remains of an ancient temple of love. . . .' It was as well, as one of Princess Margaret's biographers remarks, that she had long ago given up reading articles about herself.[16]

'My vices are cigarettes and drink,' Princess Margaret once announced. 'And I don't see myself giving those up.'[17] Certainly they are the two things with which she is invariably associated. 'Have been meditating a poem on Princess Margaret, having to knock off first the booze and now the fags,' wrote the poet Philip Larkin early in 1985, when the Princess went into hospital. 'Now that's the kind of royal poem I could write with feeling.'[18]

Her drinking, first of gin and later of whisky, was legendary. Guests at Kensington Palace were amazed at the number of drinks she could down during the course of a meal, let alone a party. 'I just couldn't believe how often her glass was refilled,' says one observer. 'Yet she never seemed to get drunk.'[19] Once, on Mustique, after a party which lasted until two in the morning and at which she sang 'Walk On By' to the guests, she appeared at half-past nine the following morning, beautifully groomed, to fly off to Barbados to fulfil an official engagement. But as the flight was delayed, she had to wait in the bar of the Cotton House Hotel until the plane took off. Fixing a cigarette into her holder, which she naturally expected someone else to light, she announced, 'I'll have a gin and tonic, please. A large one.' She had two more large ones before she finally took leave of the curtsying women and head-bowing men and – in perfect control, as ever – flew off.[20] (These days the Princess's lunchtime drinking is confined to lemon barley water. She makes a great ritual of slicing the lemon to go into the drink.)

Her smoking was equally unrestrained. 'She hardly touched her food,' says one Kensington Palace guest, 'just pushed it round her plate but she smoked almost non-stop. A silver cigarette box and an ashtray were beside her plate and she was forever discarding one filter from her long holder and replacing it with a new one.'[21]

The outspoken newspaperman, Derek Jameson, tells the story of an encounter with the Princess at the Boat Show at Earls Court. Before the opening ceremony, the two of them stood sipping champagne and drawing on cigarettes. The Princess was smoking untipped Players, which moved Jameson to say, 'That's a rough old fag you've got there, Ma'am.' 'What do you mean?' she asked. 'Well,' he explained, 'they're plain and very strong. You'll do yourself a mischief smoking those. Top of the coffin nail league.' The Princess, however, obviously knew her subject. 'No, they're not,' she snapped back. 'Capstan Full Strength are worse.'[22] The two of them went on to discuss the efficacy of filter tips and cigarette holders and the impossibility of ever giving up smoking.

A guest at one of her Kensington Palace show-business parties claimed that the Princess 'richly lived up to her reputation for earthy eccentricity'. As the pop artists lined up to greet her, 'they noticed the evidently essential accoutrements of gin and tonic and wreathing smoke.' At one point, mislaying her pack of American cigarettes, Her Royal Highness allegedly turned to a footman and demanded, 'Where are my fucking Winstons?'[23]

The one time that Princess Margaret might have felt compelled to give up smoking was early in 1985. She had seen the New Year in at Sandringham, where she was reported to have been 'in cracking form', but on 5 January she was admitted to the Brompton Hospital in London, which specializes in heart and respiratory problems. She had been suffering from chest pains and a persistent cough for some weeks and had gone in for an 'investigation'. Not unnaturally, it was feared that she might have lung cancer. (The four most recent British monarchs – Edward VII, George V, Edward VIII and the

Princess's own father, George VI – had all died of smoking-related illnesses. George VI had had to have his left lung removed because of a malignant growth, brought about by heavy cigarette smoking.) An X-ray showed a shadow on the Princess's left lung. But when a small area of the lung was removed during an operation, the growth was found to be non-malignant. Greatly relieved, the Princess spent nine days in her £165-a-day private room. As was the way with royal illnesses, this one was played down. The Queen and the Queen Mother remained firmly at Sandringham, and the Princess's children did not cut short a holiday they were taking in Venice. Not until after the Princess had returned to Kensington Palace was she visited by the Queen.

'Give Them Up, Ma'am!' trumpeted the *Daily Mirror* on her emergence from hospital. That, however, was too much to expect. At her first public appearance after the operation, when she went to Cambridge early in March to see her nephew, Prince Edward, take part in a revue, she was seen inserting a cigarette into a holder and lighting up. And by the following month, when she made the presentations at a radio and television awards ceremony in London, she was obviously quite prepared to be photographed smoking; only now it was filter tips through an even longer holder.

Five years later she was being more careful, not about smoking, but about being photographed smoking. 'The Princess smoked resolutely throughout,' reported Alan Clark, who was sitting near her at a window in Admiralty House, where they had gathered to watch a parade in honour of the Queen Mother's ninetieth birthday. At one point the Princess reprimanded Prince Charles 'who had moved *out* of her line of sight, thus exposing her to a telephoto lens'.[24]

Contrary to public perception at the time, the extended royal family, which included the Gloucesters and the Kents, was not a single, united entity. Its members saw each other very seldom, meeting only on state occasions such as weddings, funerals or thanksgiving services, or over Christmas. But by the mid-1980s even the latter annual family gathering had been slimmed down. With the Queen having decided that the Christmas jamboree at Windsor had become too unwieldy, the inner core of the royal family had reverted to spending Christmas at Sandringham. Although Princess Margaret was a part of this inner core, and was usually to be found at

Sandringham at the end of the year and at Balmoral for a week or two in the autumn, she was hardly a follower of the rigid royal routine. She did not even always spend her birthday with her family. Turkey, Italy (where she sometimes stayed with Sir Harold Acton in Tuscany) and, of course, Mustique, were her preferred holiday places.

Nor was Princess Margaret especially close to the other members of the royal family, apart from the Queen and the Queen Mother. There had never been much rapport between her and Prince Philip. Their relationship was friendly enough but they were hardly soul mates. She found him aggressive; he found her languid. The Queen's three sons, although different from each other, all shared a somewhat uneasy relationship with their 'Aunt Margo'. She was too blasé, too brittle, too piquant for their tastes. She, for her part, did not feel particularly drawn to any of her nephews. None of them had the sort of 'outsider' quality that she liked; they were all, in their different ways, conformist. Prince Charles took himself too seriously; Prince Andrew was too hearty; not even Prince Edward, who had theatrical ambitions, seemed to interest her.

But when Prince Charles married Lady Diana Spencer in 1981, the new bride found an ally in Princess Margaret, later admitting that the Princess had given her the most help in finding her feet in the rarefied royal atmosphere. As the Queen came to realize that Diana was not the sort of country-loving girl she had imagined her to be, but was more interested in clothes, shopping and pop music, so did the Princess of Wales come to rely on Princess Margaret. 'I've always adored Margot,' she later said. 'I love her to bits and she's been wonderful to me from day one.'[25]

Princess Margaret shared some of Diana's tastes and could sympathize with her complaints of being treated as nothing other than a royal fashion model. 'In an interview on television last year,' Princess Margaret once said, 'the Princess of Wales said all the things I was saying twenty-five years ago. Clothes aren't her prime concern. They weren't mine. But the fashion writers insist on treating her, as they did me, as if we were just unreal figures straight from *Dynasty*.'[26] It was with a mixture of wry amusement and relief, therefore, that Princess Margaret watched the frantic media concentration on the Princess of Wales as, over the years, she gradually transformed herself into a royal megastar.

For Sarah Ferguson, whom Prince Andrew married in 1986, Princess Margaret had very little time. The new Duchess of York was far too bouncy and boisterous, and the Princess would no doubt have agreed with the Queen's one-time Private Secretary, Lord Charteris, that 'Sarah Ferguson was not cut out to be a royal princess in this or any other age.'[27] As for 'Fergie' (as the media dubbed her), she, for all her brash self-confidence, must have found Aunt Margot intimidatingly cool.

Princess Margaret's somewhat detached attitude towards her nephews could not have been more vividly illustrated than by her absence from the christenings of their children. Impervious to family disapproval and press censure, she stayed away from the christenings of Prince Charles's sons, the Princes William and Harry, and from those of Prince Andrew's daughters, the Princesses Beatrice and Eugenie. 'I don't think it is essential to be at the christening of your nephew's children,' was the somewhat defensive statement from Kensington Palace.[28] Being Aunt Margot was bad enough; being Great-Aunt Margot was horrendous.

In her niece, however, Princess Margaret saw a kindred spirit. When Princess Anne first entered public life, it was her Aunt Margo who advised her on clothes, make-up and deportment. Different in so many ways – the one so metropolitan, the other so sporty – the two women did have certain things in common. Both were independent, sharp-tongued, disdainful of public opinion; both had married commoners; both had suffered intense media criticism and harassment; both had been cast as family black sheep. 'But Anne's much more positive than I was,' admits Princess Margaret. 'She's much tougher, too, she's been brought up in a different atmosphere.'[29] There was, though, another difference between aunt and niece: Princess Anne, having endured enormous unpopularity, had by the 1980s become one of the most admired members of the family. Without in any way softening her attitudes, she had won – mainly by her dedication and her work for the Save the Children Fund – the sort of public esteem which was always to be denied to Princess Margaret. It would be small comfort to the older princess to see that there was one more way in which her niece's life paralleled her own: by 1992, both would have had marriages which, after sixteen years, had ended in separation and eventually divorce.

Of all her family, Princess Margaret was probably closest to her mother. Even during her daughter's most reckless periods, the Queen Mother remained largely uncensorious. The two women were in constant touch, with Royal Lodge an ever-welcoming weekend home for the Princess (it is believed that she will one day inherit the use of the place). And although she did not share her mother's passion for racing and fishing, they had many tastes in common: the theatre, music, parties and travel (the Queen Mother would often slip off to France on private visits). Where Queen Elizabeth II was quite content to spend her evenings alone at home, eating supper off a tray in front of the television set, her mother and sister would be only too ready to change into their evening dresses, put on their jewellery, and entertain or be entertained. 'She's the greatest fun,' the Queen Mother would exclaim, while Princess Margaret might say, 'Isn't my mother looking wonderful?' – although any answering reference to 'your mother' – instead of to 'Queen Elizabeth' – would be met with an icy stare.[30]

The Princess never criticized her sister, the Queen. On one occasion, when Gore Vidal told the Princess that Jackie Kennedy had complained that she always found the Queen 'pretty heavy-going', the Princess had answered briskly, 'But that's what she's there for.'[31] Once Roddy Llewellyn had faded from the scene, the Queen and Princess Margaret resumed their easy relationship. 'The royal family is very inward-looking and finds it hard to welcome strangers,' noted Lord Mountbatten's private secretary, 'and the Queen, particularly, finds it very difficult to relax unless she is surrounded by those with whom she feels at home.'[32] With her sister, the Queen felt eminently at home, not least because there was a strong bond, born of shared experience, between them. To some observers it seemed as if they were almost telepathically linked, and this despite the fact that the Princess did not share her sister's horsey, county tastes. She seldom rode, and attended the races for social, or traditional, reasons only. She did not even own a dog. As a child, she had played with her parents' corgis, and later owned dogs of her own. (Her aunt, Princess Alice, Duchess of Gloucester, tells the story of how once, despite being bitten by one of the Gloucesters' Scotch terriers, the little Princess Margaret – knowing that the dog should not have been in the room – never said a word.) In the end, however, her active way of life did not allow for the keeping of dogs at Kensington Palace.

The longest time that the sisters would spend in each other's company would be at Balmoral in the autumn. Guests were often struck by the contrast between the stuffiness of the royal family ('You'd get this chilling po-face. Princess Margaret's very good at it. . . .'[33]) and the childishness of the things which amused them. One day, during a shooting lunch, a young footman serving coffee to Princess Margaret failed to realize that the small spirit burner which kept the silver coffee-pot warm had stuck to the bottom of the pot. As he was filling her cup, the burner fell, setting her napkin alight. The rest of the family 'fell about laughing, delighted, and the Queen called out, "Oh, look – they're trying to burn Margo!"'[34]

It was at night that Princess Margaret came into her own. The trick for guests who wanted to get to bed was to time their departure with that of the Queen, who usually retired at midnight, which gave others the chance to follow her upstairs. 'If they miss the cue,' reports one member of the household, 'they're up until two in the morning listening to Princess Margaret playing and singing at the piano. While she is holding court there is no escape.'[35]

CHAPTER 22

The Survivor

O N 21 AUGUST 1990, Princess Margaret turned sixty. She was still an attractive woman, with her sexual allure almost undimmed, but whereas, in youth, she had had her mother's prettiness, she now looked very much her father's daughter: hers was a feminine version of his lined, sensitive, wide-mouthed face. Unlike the Queen, who looked distinctly matronly, Princess Margaret was smart and slender, her hair expertly dyed, her air as actressy as ever. Although often chillingly regal, she could still cause surprise by the indiscretion of her conversation and the sharpness of her tongue. She would blithely refer to a black man, in company, as a 'rug head'.¹ Accustomed to being stared at all her life, she seemed oblivious to the impression she was creating: guests at her table have been astonished by the way in which she would unselfconsciously repair her bright red lipstick during the course of a meal.

By now her life followed a well-established pattern. Having gone to bed in the early hours of the morning, she would be late getting up. It was usually well after nine before her maid brought a tray of Lapsong Souchong tea to her large bed with its lemon-yellow silk canopy. She would read her personal mail and glance at the morning papers – *The Times*, the *Daily Telegraph* and the *Daily Mail*. She usually managed to finish *The Times* crossword during the course of the day. Her mind is described as agile rather than intellectual.

Whatever her plans for the day, she would dress formally and would always wear jewellery: necklace, earrings, brooch, rings. Her hair, done by Josef, of David and Josef in Berkeley Street, would be dressed high and well off her face; sometimes she would visit him in his salon; at other times he would come to Kensington Palace. (On important tours abroad, Josef would accompany her.) On ordinary days, her maid would do her hair. Once, when the Princess was inspecting a medical company's new factory, she put on the obligatory white coat but refused to wear the equally obligatory, but hideous, hair covering. 'I would not say it was vanity,' explained the discomfited managing director. 'She just ignored our request to wear it.'[2]

For breakfast the Princess would have fruit, occasionally toast, and always Brazilian coffee. Most mornings would be spent at her untidy desk in the corner of her drawing room. Here she would attend to her official and personal correspondence (perhaps surprisingly, she was an efficient two-finger typist) and fill in her diary, which she has kept faithfully since childhood, wearing the large, boldly framed spectacles she now had for reading. She would discuss various duties and commitments with Lord Napier, who had his offices across the courtyard, and would go through her official letters with her personal secretary, Muriel Murray Brown. Lord Napier, who had been through so much with her, claimed that the Princess was excellent at summing up a problem and coming to a quick decision.

The Princess employed a staff of ten, who were divided into household and domestic. The household staff consisted of her Private Secretary, her personal secretary, and their secretary. Making up her domestic staff were her butler, housekeeper, personal maid, chef, chauffeur, and two part-time domestics. Her ladies-in-waiting, all of whom were friends, accompanied her on official engagements whenever necessary. Almost every morning the Princess would telephone the Queen and the Queen Mother, speaking to them on her telephone with its specially extended cord trailing behind her as she moved about the room.

As she disliked eating alone, she often invited a friend to lunch. Sometimes an actor whose performance she had admired, or a writer whose books she had enjoyed, might find themselves at her table. She was always ready to share her memories with reputable biographers or historians. 'I can't think why she didn't come and see me about it,' she would say of some author, as though coming to see someone with so fearsome a reputation were the easiest thing in the world.[3] Like all the royal women, the Princess never moved without a handbag, which at mealtimes she would carry to and from the table. Determined to keep slim, she picked at her food, eating very little, and she never served potatoes, and never ate puddings. On one occasion, when she thumped a poppadom on her side plate, scattering pieces all over the floor, a startled guest leapt to his feet and started gathering them up. 'Don't do that,' she drawled and, nodding her head towards the butler, added, 'let him do it. That's what he's here for.'⁴ To another guest, daunted at having to help himself from a dish of tagliatelle which the butler was holding too far away from him, she said, 'Dear, just drag it orf. That's what I do.'⁵

If there was no afternoon engagement, she might spend the time pasting photographs into albums. Possessed of a strong sense of the past, she was very interested in keeping a record of her own life. Photographers were forever getting demands from Kensington Palace for a copy of this or that picture, or being asked if they had taken photographs of her at certain functions: 'Her Royal Highness would like to know if you have a picture of her at the Chelsea Flower Show' would come the request from her office. When the photographer Jayne Fincher came to take a set of pictures for a magazine, she found her subject – whom she had been apprehensive about meeting – astonishingly professional, interested and helpful. Sensing that the photographer thought her dress too dark but was afraid to say so, the Princess immediately offered to change into something lighter. When she posed in front of the famous Annigoni portrait of herself, she said, without explanation, 'Don't do a Cecil, dear.' Only later did the bemused Jayne Fincher learn that when Cecil Beaton had photographed the Princess in the same position, his lights had reflected off the Annigoni portrait. Typically, Her Royal Highness had expected her to know this.⁶

Photographing royalty brings its own special problems. The late Norman Parkinson, a great favourite with the royal family, once decided to photograph the Queen, the Queen Mother and Princess Margaret dressed in identical blue satin capes. The session brought unexpected problems. His instructions of 'Chin up a little, Ma'am' and 'Could you just turn to the right, Ma'am?' caused endless confusion. 'It's absolutely no use you Ma'aming us like this,' exclaimed Princess Margaret. 'We haven't the slightest idea who you are referring to. We are *all* Ma'am.'⁷ The resulting photograph of the three satin-swathed royal women looks not unlike a picture that might be used on a record sleeve, and has been dubbed 'The Latest Hits of the Windsor Sisters'.

Princess Margaret also collected cartoons, not only of herself, but also of other family members as well. When the cartoonist Trog (Wally Fawkes) did a strip depicting the bizarre penetration of Buckingham Palace security by the intruder Michael Fagan, who ended up chatting to the Queen in her bedroom, the Princess contacted the cartoonist to ask for the original. He was only too happy to oblige. The strip no doubt joined all those framed addresses of welcome and freedoms of cities which line the walls of her downstairs lavatory.

The Princess was also often obliged to sit for her portrait. The painter Richard Stone, commissioned by the Royal Anglian Regiment, of which Princess Margaret was Deputy Colonel-in-Chief, found her to be a highly entertaining and amusing sitter. He was given twelve sittings for preliminary sketches, one of which she rejected on the grounds that he had managed to capture exactly, she said, the fact that she had been suffering from flu at the time.

Regularly, the Princess and her domestic staff would set about cleaning her enormous collection of shells, which are displayed in large, specially built cabinets in the pink and green Garden Room at Kensington Palace. Collected in the course of her travels all over the world, the result has been described by London's Natural History Museum as the most comprehensive collection of shells in individual ownership. The Princess would wash each fragile shell herself, carefully replacing it in its labelled position.

Princess Margaret had very little to do with the other members of the family living in Kensington Palace. In the early 1990s the Palace was also home to the Prince and Princess of Wales, the Duke and Duchess of Gloucester, and Prince and Princess Michael of Kent. None of them would have dreamed of simply dropping in on one another; their very rare meetings were by invitation only. They might see each other on state occasions, in which case they would leave the Palace in strict order of precedence: first the Waleses, then Princess Margaret, then the Gloucesters, and finally the Kents. The Waleses were the only neighbours with whom Princess Margaret had much contact. The Gloucesters would have been too unsophisticated for her taste; and she and the Kents were barely on speaking terms.

But the Princess did have a circle of close friends. 'She is probably the loyalest friend you could have, once she's decided she likes
you,' said Lady Elizabeth Cavendish. But that was the difficulty:
the Princess was as strong in her dislikes as in her likes. 'All her
geese are geese and all her swans are swans,' said one of her oldest
and closest friends, Lord Glenconner.[8] He had reason to know. In
August 1988 the Princess was absent from the traditional birthday
lunch held for the Queen Mother because she was staying with the
Glenconners in Scotland. Those who dismissed this as a typically
capricious act on the part of the Princess did not know that she had
gone north to comfort her friends. Of the Glenconners' three sons,
the eldest had become a heroin addict; the second was very ill; and
the youngest had been involved in a motorcycle accident which had
left him paralysed. Faced with the choice between a royal family
celebration and supporting old friends, the Princess had not hesitated. (Unlike the Queen, who finds it difficult to express her feelings,
Princess Margaret always writes heartfelt letters of condolence or
commiseration.)

Another example of her loyalty, or partisanship, was her refusal to
accept any invitations from another old friend, Jocelyn Stevens,
after he was divorced, in case his ex-wife, Jane, be hurt. Jane
Stevens remained one of her closest friends.

In spite of her intimacy with various women, Princess Margaret
was much happier in the company of men. She had never really out-
grown her youthful flirtatiousness, her delight in being the centre of
masculine attention. Even directors of her charities would find her
taking their arms and speaking to them in a surprisingly conspirato-
rial, intimate manner. At parties she would ignore wives and monop-
olize husbands, provided they were attractive and entertaining.
Because Roddy Llewellyn still had the power to charm her, her
hosts would often ensure that he and his wife Tania were invited to
any occasion at which the Princess was expected. Entertaining her
was always a daunting business, however. She expected, as well as a
supply of interesting men, a certain level of splendour. (One hostess
was obliged to reopen a long-disused drawing room because the
Princess made her dislike of a small sitting room abundantly clear.)
If she was to fulfil some official engagement in a certain neighbour-
hood, she would never hesitate to invite herself to stay with friends
nearby. Quite when she would arrive was another matter. 'One of

the troubles is that she's always so late,' complained one member of her set. 'You ask her for lunch at one and it's often two-thirty before she turns up. By then the food is ruined.'⁹

Her intimate circle included the Glenconners, Lady Penn (Jocelyn Stevens's step-sister, Prudence), Jane Stevens, Ned Ryan and Norman Lonsdale. They kept her amused, organized her social life, travelled with her – often on charter flights – to Turkey and Italy and, in return, were entertained by her on Mustique. 'Well, I can provide a car,' she could be heard saying on the telephone to a friend who had proposed some entertainment, exactly as though she were being invited to join some adolescents' outing.¹⁰

Another of the Princess's old and trusted friends, whom she did not see very often, was one of Lord Linley's godparents, Simon Phipps, the former Guards officer who had entered the Church and who had now become the Bishop of Lincoln. Once, on an official visit to Coventry, the Princess delighted the vicar at Willenhall by agreeing to attend a service in his church. Willenhall was where, in her young days, she had used to visit Phipps, who was then a simple curate living in a council flat. Now, as Bishop of Lincoln, he preached the sermon during her visit. His address made no concessions whatsoever to the leading member of the congregation: it was about unemployment.

Throughout her life, Princess Margaret retained her interest in ecclesiastical matters, and was often to be seen in animated conversation with clergymen. She was especially friendly with the somewhat exotic Donald Harris, vicar at the fashionable St Paul's in Knightsbridge, whose flamboyant manner and particular brand of Anglo-Catholicism appealed to her. (She apparently never minded waiting at the west door of St Paul's while he stood grooming his hair in the vestry.) With the passing years, the Princess's religious feelings had intensified, her preferences inclining towards High Church services and the old Book of Common Prayer. 'You've never seen so much genuflecting,' said one member of her circle, irreverently.¹¹ St Paul's, Knightsbridge, the very antithesis of Low Church plainness in its services, suited her religious inclinations very well.

Perhaps as the result of a combination of influences – a fondness for her friends, a deeply felt conception of royal duty, and a warm understanding of Christian virtues – the Princess paid scrupulous attention to correctness in many of her dealings with people. She was always punctilious about such things as presents and thank-you letters. Although she disapproved of the sending of Christmas cards, she delighted, as she had as a child, in choosing, wrapping and giving Christmas presents. These were always practical. To the Queen, for instance, she might give powder puffs, appreciating that this was the sort of useful gift which no one else would ever think of giving. Her thank-you letters, on heavy writing-paper sporting a bold red M surmounted by a crown, were almost embarrassingly gushing.

Yet with those outside her little court, Princess Margaret could be frighteningly sharp. 'She can be unbelievably rude. Quite takes your breath away. I couldn't go along with her for very long,' admitted one of her escorts.[12] 'I have been at the same house parties as her,' claimed another observer, 'and her arrogance, her petulance, her rudeness and her plain bad manners were awful. . . .'[13] Her awareness of being royal, always strong, became even stronger with the passing years. After the publication of *Ask Sir James*, Michaela Reid's biography of Queen Victoria's doctor, Sir James Reid, the author's husband found himself sitting beside Princess Margaret at a lunch. Considering the book not to have been nearly deferential enough about her great-great-grandmother, the Princess subjected Sandy Reid 'to a tirade of vulgar abuse'.[14]

But if Her Royal Highness could be judgmental about what people did or had done, she was often less censorious about what they were. In his book *Answered Prayers*, the writer Truman Capote claims that she had once told him that she hated 'poofs'; in reply, he had warned her that she would, as a result, spend a very lonely old age. The Princess is unlikely to have said any such thing. She had a good many gay friends and acquaintances, and would certainly not have condemned them for their sexual orientation. On the other hand, she never became a gay icon, although it might have been thought that she was exactly the type of woman to have appealed to certain homosexuals. Perhaps she lacked the obvious vulnerability of other such icons, a Judy Garland, say, or a Marilyn Monroe. Her tongue was probably too sharp, her attitude too imperious. In short, she was too dauntingly regal.

In the summer of 1992 Princess Margaret saw Peter Townsend again. The two of them had not met for thirty-four years, when she had been twenty-seven and he forty-three; she was now sixty-one and he seventy-seven. The former equerry had come over to London from his home in France to attend a reunion of those who had travelled with King George VI and his family to South Africa in HMS *Vanguard* in 1947, and the Princess invited him to lunch at Kensington Palace.

Townsend's life, in the years since he had last seen Princess Margaret, had been both precarious and fulfilling. His marriage to Marie-Luce Jamagne, twenty-five years his junior, and by whom he had three children, had been very happy. Their homes were a small apartment in Paris, near the Eiffel Tower, and an eighteenth-century farmhouse outside the city. Although his wife's family had given him a certain amount of financial support, he had had to make a living in various ways: wine-dealing, public relations, film-making, journalism and writing. He had written on humanitarian subjects, as well as historical works and memoirs. His autobiography, *Time and Chance*, which appeared in 1978, had dealt discreetly with his affair with Princess Margaret.

The passing years, and a disenchantment with the country of his birth which, he felt, had rejected him, had turned Peter Townsend into a somewhat blimpish figure. Although he had retained his slender shape and his clear, blue-eyed gaze, his attitudes were now those of a disgruntled old man. He felt that Britain had betrayed what one witness calls his 'endearing Boy's Own ideals of British chivalry and valour, his remnants of patriotism, his fading love and loyalty for England, his war-survivor spirit full of the glory of British bravery and honour'. His conversation was peppered with complaints about falling standards, declining values, spreading vulgarity, and incorrectly spoken English. He had even managed to convince himself that, in agreeing to part, he and Princess Margaret had set a noble example. 'But the example it set seems to have been in vain,' he sighed.[15]

Feeling awkward about being alone with Townsend after all these years, the Princess had invited a few other friends to lunch that day. The conversation remained light and general, with the principal guest proving that he was no less the courtly, dignified, decent man he had always been. 'He hadn't really changed,' says one guest. 'He was a bit stooped. But it was the most amazing thing; he hadn't really changed at all. We just sat chatting on the sofa like old friends.'[16]

It is not possible to know what Princess Margaret's feelings were; or Townsend's. Her friends say that she was very nervous about seeing him again. During that lunch, did either of them imagine that, had events turned out differently, they might have been sitting together, one at each end of the table, as an old, happily married couple? It is unlikely. By now he would have realized how difficult marriage to her would have been, while she might well have considered him too staid for her taste. But one thing is certain: in the end, his life had been more resolved and satisfying than hers.

Peter Townsend died three years later, on 19 June 1995, at the age of eighty. Buckingham Palace issued a statement to the effect that Princess Margaret had been 'saddened by the news'.

'Tell her,' Princess Margaret once instructed a friend to say to a journalist who was writing an article about her, 'that everything I do is to support the Queen and to help her.'[17] In the light of her reputation it is easy to be cynical about this statement, but the Princess's loyalty to the Queen is unquestioned. Almost more than anything said of her, she resents criticism that she does not do enough to support the monarchy. Although it would be foolish to pretend that she is overworked, she does carry out a surprisingly large number of duties. These range from attending the State Opening of Parliament to inspecting supermarkets. In a single year she will undertake something like one hundred and fifty engagements: opening ceremonies, charity shows, lunches, dinners, banquets and receptions, Privy Council meetings, investitures and audiences. On tours abroad her schedule is even more crowded. Official visits to countries as disparate as Hungary and Swaziland go almost unnoticed by the British press and public. She is patron of over forty societies, associations and trusts, and president of a dozen more. She has been connected with some organizations for decades: the Guides Association, the Migraine Trust, the Sunshine Homes and Schools for Blind Children, the National Society for the Prevention of Cruelty to Children. A relatively recent involvement is with the London Lighthouse, the residential and support centre for people affected by AIDS. Long before the Princess of Wales was being so fulsomely praised for shaking hands with AIDS sufferers, Princess Margaret had been doing the same thing, but with almost no publicity. As to her capacity for work and effectiveness, all those who serve on committees with her describe her as knowledgeable, interested, efficient. 'When she does something,' says the Chairman of the Victoria League, 'she really does it properly.'[18] Her long Chancellorship of Keele University, although not without its upheavals (she was once banned from the annual ball and a motion proposed for her replacement as Chancellor), was surprisingly successful.

The Princess can usually be relied upon to bring a refreshingly unexpected touch to official functions. With a glass of whisky in one hand and a cigarette in the other, she made an unlikely looking President of the Girl Guide Association at a recent reception. 'But it soon became obvious,' noted one observer, 'that she knew as much about the association as any of the well-scrubbed ladies in navy suits and badges.'[19] At the opening of the restored Theatre Royal in Bath, she was delighted to see that a posse of photographers had been driven well back to allow her to pass. '*Crunched* into a corner,' she exclaimed loudly in her ginny, theatrical voice.

What she clearly enjoys most are her duties as President of the Royal Ballet. Not only does she love the ballet, but she feels thoroughly at home backstage. Before a recent Crush Bar party that followed a charity gala at Covent Garden, she sent a message to say that she wanted to see all the cast 'whatever you are wearing'. Joining them, she was obviously in her element. The stiff public smile had gone; she joked with the girls, presented her cheek to be kissed by the boys, listened to the gossip, and chatted with great animation and authority. 'She's a very nice woman,' said one of the dancers afterwards.[20]

Yet it is for her no less characteristic brusqueness in public that the Princess is more widely known. Unlike the other women of the family – with the exception of the Princess Royal – she never puts on a performance for the benefit of the public. The Queen, fighting down her natural reserve, will do her best to appear interested and responsive. The Queen Mother will treat every appearance like a gala occasion; as though, in the words of Harold Nicolson, 'she had just discovered a new and delightful way of spending an afternoon'.[21] At best, Princess Margaret will give a smile and wave and ask a series of questions. At worst, she will go glumly through the motions, demanding to know this or that and never bothering to stop and talk to the crowds that have waited, sometimes for hours, to get a glimpse of her. Her visits frequently end ahead of time. Her behaviour is all too often brisk, no-nonsense, even ungracious.

'I'm afraid we weren't very impressed,' says a member of one women's organization. 'We had all worked so hard and looked forward to her visit so much. But she just didn't seem interested. You felt that she was just getting through the whole business as quickly as she could. She only spoke to a couple of officials and that was that.'[22] Her opinion was echoed by one well-known national figure. 'I was furious,' he said, after the Princess had attended some public function. 'When I meet a princess, I expect her to behave like a princess. It's the least she can do.'[23]

Her tongue, especially when she is faced with pompous officials, can be extremely wounding. 'I'm in textiles,' explained one functionary, 'and I sit on the Bench.' 'You sit on the bench in textiles,' she replied sharply. 'How interesting, but uncomfortable.'[24] On other occasions she will often demonstrate an understandable world-weariness. 'All the town clerks are exactly the same,' she complains when discussing her half-century in public life, and 'all the students at Keele have just discovered Marx.'[25]

Not even at something like a charity concert can her much-vaunted bohemianism be taken for granted. At a gala performance in the Royal Albert Hall to raise funds for the Invalid Children's Aid Association, the singer Dusty Springfield, then busily reviving her career, was being wildly applauded by her many gay fans. 'It's nice to see royalty is not confined to the box,' announced the singer to the whooping 'queens'.[26] Princess Margaret was appalled. She not only snubbed Dusty Springfield after the show, but is said to have demanded a written apology.

Like many members of the royal family, Princess Margaret is inclined to lay the blame for the public perception of her on the misrepresentations of the press. Yet her complaints about misreporting are not always unfounded. She was once roundly attacked in the newspapers for not attending the annual ceremony at the Cenotaph in London on Remembrance Sunday. Why, it was demanded, had she not joined the other members of the royal family in paying tribute to those who had given their lives for their country? Because, explained Lord Napier in a statement to the press, the Princess had been fulfilling several engagements in Staffordshire at the time, and had therefore attended a Remembrance Day service in Lichfield Cathedral.

In 1992 Princess Margaret's annual Civil List allowance was withdrawn. This loss – which was also suffered by several other members of the royal family – marked the climax of an increasingly acrimonious public debate on the question of the royal finances. Two years earlier, Parliament had passed a substantial Civil List increase which was intended to last for a decade. Pushed through with the minimum of discussion, the bill was designed to put an end to the annual complaints in the press about 'royal pay rises'. By its terms, Princess Margaret's annuity was raised from £148,000 to £220,000. Although, in theory, the Princess was supposed to pay tax on this sum, in practice she received 100 per cent tax relief for expenses which were 'wholly, exclusively and necessarily incurred in the performance of the duties in respect of which the annuities are payable'.[27]

But no sooner had this Civil List increase been granted than the royal family became the object of intensely hostile criticism. Much of this was directed at the irresponsible behaviour of the younger members of the royal family, but an almost equal measure was directed at the cost of the monarchy. In June 1991, a *World in Action* television programme, based largely on the researches of Phillip Hall for his book *Royal Fortune*, which was published early the following year, examined the question of the Queen's exemption from income tax. In the face of mounting public pressure, the Palace began discussions with the Treasury on the subject. By the following spring, the Queen had agreed to pay tax on her private income and to remove all members of the royal family, with the exception of the Queen Mother and the Duke of Edinburgh – but including Princess Margaret – from the Civil List. (The Prince of Wales has his own income from the Duchy of Cornwall.) In future, the Queen would pay the annuities of five members of the family: the Princess Royal, the Duke of York, Prince Edward, Princess Margaret, and Princess Alice, Duchess of Gloucester.

The announcement of this important decision was badly mishandled by the Queen's advisers. Instead of issuing a statement in mid-1992, the Palace waited not only until after the Prime Minister, John Major, had paid his annual visit to Balmoral in September (thus making it look as though the Queen had merely responded to government pressure), but, worse still – though to be fair, no one could have predicted the disaster – until after Windsor Castle had been badly damaged by fire two months later. The impetuous, and almost immediate, pledge by a government minister that public funds would be used to pay for the damage to Windsor was very badly received. Why, asked even the fervently monarchist *Daily Mail*, should the recession-hit British public foot the bill when the immensely rich Queen pays no taxes? Thus, when, six days after the Windsor fire, the Prime Minister announced that Her Majesty would be paying taxes and cutting down the Civil List, it looked very much as though her hand had been forced.

Whether or not the matter had been badly handled was probably largely an irrelevance to those members of the royal family dropped from the Civil List. On Princess Margaret, these changes had a significant effect. From now on her annual allowance would be paid, not by the State, but by her sister. This annuity has been fixed until the year 2000; after that, it will have to be renegotiated.

The exact size of Princess Margaret's personal fortune – as is the case with the wealth of all the senior members of the royal family – remains a mystery. She is said to have inherited a considerable sum from her father. Astutely, King George VI's advisers had seen to it that, unlike his predecessors, he paid no tax on his private income whatsoever, something which would have added greatly to his private wealth. The Princess will no doubt inherit a further sum from her wealthy mother. The £20,000 bequeathed to her by Mrs Ronald Greville in 1942 (equivalent to almost half a million pounds today) would have been wisely invested and, during the course of half a century, will have appreciated considerably.

The Princess also owns – besides paintings, furniture and assorted *objets* – some valuable jewellery, including two diamond tiaras given to her by her mother, and the famous Poltimore tiara, which she bought before her wedding. She is very interested in jewellery design and has often had old pieces broken up and re-set by designers like John Donald and Andrew Grima. From time to time she has sold some of her jewellery; in 1979 Sotheby's sold seven pieces – five brooches, a pendant and a pair of earrings – for £11,000.

But Princess Margaret does not regard herself as rich. Her approved biographer talks of her 'relatively modest private funds'.[28] She is careful not to spend, or overspend, needlessly: her household, compared to the Queen Mother's, is small; for private holidays she travels economy class; she is always ready to accept the hospitality of wealthy friends. On once being asked, by some public body what she would like as a gift, she answered 'a cheque'.²⁹ When she is not using her house on Mustique (itself a gift from Lord Glenconner), she shrewdly lets it, fully staffed. She will even make those minor economies for which the royal family is renowned, such as having paper napkins on the lunch table. And, like all members of that family, the Princess is extremely sensitive to accusations of extravagance. 'Of course, I couldn't possibly have afforded that,' she will say.³⁰

If Peter Townsend's death had served as one reminder of Princess Margaret's chequered past, an even more controversial reminder surfaced in the spring of 1994. This came about with the publication of extracts from some of her love letters to Robin Douglas-Home, written almost thirty years before. They appeared in a book, *Margaret: The Untold Story*, by a journalist, Noel Botham, and were subsequently featured in newspapers throughout the world. The existence of these letters, graphically described as a time bomb waiting to go off, had been known about for years; they had once been withdrawn from auction in New York, and parts of them had earlier been published in Germany and Australia.

Their latest appearance is said to have distressed Princess Margaret considerably. No woman in her mid-sixties welcomes the reappearance of her old love letters, particularly when they are published for all the world to read. What could have been more humiliating than to see phrases like 'love me as I love you, know always that I want you', or 'our love has that passionate scent of new-mown grass and lilies about it' repeated out of their time and their context? And, as the tabloid press was quick to point out, these ardent letters were written at a time when the Princess was still married; her affair with Robin Douglas-Home had been adulterous.

There was, however, nothing she could do about it. An injunction against publication would be tantamount to an admission that the letters were genuine. Any action for breach of copyright (which, as the presumed writer of the letters, the Princess retained) would involve a potentially embarrassing court case. In the end, Princess Margaret did the only thing she could do: she kept a dignified silence. The Palace, making no attempt to deny the authenticity of the letters, dismissed the whole affair as 'an old story'. Robin Douglas-Home's eighty-eight-year-old mother, Lady Margaret Douglas-

Home, when sought out and approached by the press, confirmed that her late son had indeed been in love with the Princess, but added that it had all been 'a long time ago' and 'a very private thing'.[31]

In the end, far from exposing Princess Margaret to censure or ridicule, the publication of the letters, and the attendant publicity, resulted in her being engulfed in a wave of public sympathy. Her long-ago love affair was seen for what it had been: the desperate search for affection, understanding, comfort, of a deeply unhappy woman. It was described as part of 'her life's increasingly sad pilgrimage'. Even those columnists who took advantage of the publication to stress the Princess's many faults, admitted that the life of this attractive and intelligent woman had been ruined by the burdens of royal birth. 'For all the well-authenticated stories of her self-centred disregard for others,' pronounced the *Observer*, 'she is, in the end, a lonely woman whose years have been worn out in search of a spouse, of a role, of love. She has not been lucky on any score.'[32]

Whereas, thirty years before, the revelations of Princess Margaret's adulterous affair with Robin Douglas-Home would have caused an upheaval, it now proved little more than an overnight sensation. It was regarded as simply another, relatively minor, contribution to the troubles that were besetting the monarchy. For the truth was that, by the early 1990s, the royal family was falling apart. In a whirlwind of increasingly unsavoury scandal, the marriages of three of the Queen's four children collapsed (the fourth, Prince Edward, was still unmarried). In 1989 the Princess Royal separated from her husband Mark Phillips amid allegations that both had had extramarital affairs. In 1993, after the couple had divorced, Princess Anne married a Palace equerry, Commander Timothy Laurence. For Princess Margaret, the event must have been infused with might-have-beens. A generation before, the very idea of her marriage to a divorced equerry had caused a constitutional crisis; now the marriage of her divorced niece to an equerry raised hardly a ripple of public disapproval.

The break-up of the marriages of the Prince of Wales and the Duke of York was accompanied by much more lurid publicity. The entire world, it seems, was diverted by stories of infidelity, extravagance, vulgarity, fights, insults, media manipulation and, above all, the wholesale destruction of the aura of duty and decency with which Queen Elizabeth II had always striven to envelop the monarchy. Within half a dozen years, the carefully constructed edifice seemed to be on the point of crumbling to pieces. For Her Majesty, the only way of coping with the situation was to try to distance herself from the unedifying antics of the younger generation. From it she has managed to emerge, if not exactly unscathed, at least with her own reputation for dignity and dedication intact.

In a curious way, all this domestic and national turbulence worked to the advantage of Princess Margaret. The public began to look towards the older generation as exemplars, as reminders of the days when the royal family was generally more admired and respected, and could generally be relied upon to behave with greater decorum. Although Princess Margaret was hardly a shining example of royal respectability, she began to become associated in the public mind with the Queen, the Queen Mother and Prince Philip. It was true, too, that even in her most reckless days the Princess had never courted the limelight, had never publicly bared her soul or pleaded her cause. She had always suffered what she regarded as press intrusion in silence.

Her position was further strengthened by the contrast between the Queen's children and her own. Her son Lord Linley, although sometimes guilty of arrogance, had by now ceased to feature in adverse press reports. When, on one occasion, he was accused by a national newspaper of having behaved like a 'Hooray Henry' and an 'upper-class lager lout' in a Chelsea pub, the story was proved to be untrue. Linley sued the paper and was granted damages. In 1993 he contracted an eminently suitable marriage with the Hon. Serena Stanhope, daughter of a wealthy landowner, Viscount Petersham. In the following year Princess Margaret's daughter, Lady Sarah Armstrong-Jones, about whom not even the most intrusive tabloids had ever been able to unearth any scandal, made an equally acceptable match, marrying her long-standing boyfriend, a fellow artist, Daniel Chatto.

As she aged, so did Princess Margaret become increasingly grand. She also became more visible, more often on show. She began carrying out those ceremonial duties which would normally have fallen to the, by now, divorced and discredited Princess of Wales or Duchess of York. By the mid-1990s the three senior royal women – the Queen, the Queen Mother and Princess Margaret –

had become a powerful triumvirate; not only in the royal family, but also in the life of the nation. Their apparent indestructibility, their place in the national consciousness, were never more vividly illustrated than during the fiftieth anniversary celebrations of the ending of the Second World War in 1995. In these each, in her different ways, played her part, but it was the appearance of the three of them on the balcony of Buckingham Palace that most graphically symbolized the continuity of the royal family's role in British history.

But even here the Princess struck a highly individual note. While the Queen and the Queen Mother presented the conventional royal image in matching dresses, coats and hats, Princess Margaret wore a striking green satin coat, teamed with a towering and even more striking white hat. She looked, perhaps, as much *femme fatale* as royal princess.

'Battered by life,' wrote one journalist of Princess Margaret, 'but still a winner.'[33] And so, in many ways, she is. For while she is often depicted, by those who do not know her, as a deeply unhappy, pathetically lonely woman, a relic on the shores of life, the image is not altogether accurate. 'It's ridiculous to think that Princess Margaret sits all by herself in Kensington Palace, bemoaning her lost loves,' declares one member of her circle. 'She leads an extremely busy life and is surrounded by friends.'[34]

Although she has often been her own worst enemy, the Princess has emerged triumphant from the many turmoils of her life. At the very least, she has lived it to the full, and on her own terms. She is a survivor: defiant, unapologetic, armoured against the world.

And, if nothing else, the recent upheavals in the royal family have swung that once merciless media spotlight away from her. 'They leave me alone these days,' she says with her wry smile. 'They've got other fish to fry.'[35]

Chapter Notes

Prologue: The Last Real Princess

1 Godfrey Talbot, BBC interview
2 Bradford, *Elizabeth*, p. 200
3 Rose, *Kings, Crowns and Courtiers*, p. 191
4 Conversation with Princess Margaret
5 Bradford, op. cit., p. 200

1: Glamis Castle

1 Asquith, *Haply I May Remember*, p. 2
2 Longford, *Elizabeth R*, p. 34
3 Airlie, *Thatched with Gold*, pp. 183–6
4 Wheeler-Bennett, *King George VI*, p. 253
5 Airlie, op. cit., pp. 183–6
6 Clynes, *Memoirs*, II, p. 178
7 *London Gazette*, 22 August 1930
8 Wheeler-Bennett, op. cit., p. 253
9 Warwick, *Princess Margaret*, p. 9
10 Asquith, in *Weekly Illustrated*, 4 April 1953
11 Pope-Hennessy, *Queen Mary 1867–1953*, p. 196
12 Marie of Romania, *The Story of My Life*, II, p. 211
13 Conversation with Patricia, Lady Hambleden
14 Ibid.
15 Windsor, *A King's Story*, pp. 183–4
16 Ziegler, *Crown and People*, p. 47
17 Harewood, *The Tongs and the Bones*, p. 26

2: The Yorks

1 Pope-Hennessy, *Queen Mary 1867–1953*, p. 391
2 Wheeler-Bennett, *King George VI*, p. 60
3 Ibid., p. 220
4 Airlie, *Thatched with Gold*, p. 146
5 Pope-Hennessy, op. cit., p. 153
6 Ibid., p. 154
7 Bradford, *George VI*, p. 130
8 Conversation with Princess Alice, Duchess of Gloucester
9 Wheeler-Bennett, op. cit., pp. 150–1

10 Airlie, op. cit., p. 167
11 Wheeler-Bennett, op. cit., p. 150
12 Donaldson, *King George VI and Queen Elizabeth*, p. 32
13 Wheeler-Bennett, op. cit., p. 151
14 Airlie, op. cit., p. 167
15 Conversation with Patricia, Lady Hambleden
16 Cooper, *The Light of Common Day*, p. 73
17 Peter Townsend to the author
18 Windsor, *A King's Story*, p. 258
19 Wheeler-Bennett, op. cit., p. 230
20 Ibid., p. 209
21 Higham and Moseley, *Elizabeth and Philip*, p. 29

3: 'Golden Age'

1 Sheridan, *From Cabbages to Kings*, p. 66
2 Longford, *The Queen Mother*, p. 40
3 Wheeler-Bennett, *King George VI*, p. 263
4 Crawford, *The Little Princesses*, p. 25
5 Morrah, *The Work of the Queen*, pp. 16–17
6 Crawford, op. cit., p. 16
7 Astor Papers, MS/1416/1/4
8 Longford, *Elizabeth R*, p. 146
9 Warwick, *Princess Margaret*, p. 12
10 Private information
11 Crawford, op. cit., p. 20
12 Ibid., p. 21
13 Ibid., p. 26
14 Conversation with the Queen Mother
15 Warwick, op. cit., p. 15
16 Crawford, op. cit., p. 33
17 Ibid., p. 20
18 Longford, op. cit., p. 58
19 Crawford, op. cit., p. 26
20 Ibid., p. 33

4: The Dynasty

1 Conversation with Princess Margaret
2 Longford, *Elizabeth R*, p. 19
3 Ibid., p. 44

4 Gore, *King George V*, p. 375
5 Crawford, *The Little Princesses*, p. 16
6 Conversation with Princess Margaret
7 Warwick, *Princess Margaret*, p. 17
8 Longford, op. cit., p. 74
9 *Illustrated London News*, 26 January 1952
10 Conversation with Princess Margaret
11 Crawford, op. cit., p. 24
12 Chase and Chase, *Always in Vogue*, p. 238
13 Conversation with Princess Margaret
14 Channon, *Chips*, p. 32
15 Nicolson, *King George V*, p. 525
16 Bradford, *George VI*, p. 197
17 Frankland, *Prince Henry, Duke of Gloucester*, p. 125
18 Gore, op. cit., p. 435
19 Middlemass and Barnes, *Baldwin*, p. 976
20 Airlie, *Thatched with Gold*, p. 197
21 Crawford, op. cit., pp. 32–3
22 Crawford, *Margaret*, p. 20

5: *Love versus Duty*

1 Crawford, *The Little Princesses*, p. 36
2 Donaldson, *Edward VIII*, p. 184
3 Bradford, *George VI*, p. 211
4 Hardinge, *Loyal to Three Kings*, pp. 102–3
5 Windsor, *The Heart Has Its Reasons*, p. 225
6 Crawford, op. cit. (American edn), p. 72
7 Windsor, op. cit., p. 225
8 Crawford, op. cit., p. 36
9 Ibid., pp. 37–8
10 Windsor, *A King's Story*, p. 320
11 Wheeler-Bennett, *King George VI*, p. 277
12 Godfrey Talbot, BBC Radio, 1983
13 Wheeler-Bennett, op. cit., p. 284;
conversation with Princess Alice,
Countess of Athlone
14 Wheeler-Bennett, op. cit., p. 286
15 Crawford, op. cit., p. 39
16 Pope-Hennessy, *Queen Mary 1867–1953*, p. 574
17 Windsor, op. cit., p. 334
18 Crawford, op. cit., p. 39
19 Longford, *Elizabeth R*, p. 81
20 Asquith, *The King's Daughters*, p. 96
21 Crawford, op. cit., p. 39
22 Conversation with Princess Margaret

6: *A Family Life at Court*

1 Airlie, *Thatched with Gold*, p. 202
2 Wheeler-Bennett, *King George VI*, p. 310
3 Ibid., p. 293
4 Bradford, *George VI*, p. 380
5 Nicolson, *Diaries and Letters 1930–9*, p. 247
6 Warwick, *Princess Margaret*, p. 22
7 Crawford, *The Little Princesses*, p. 43
8 Wheeler-Bennett, op. cit., p. 393
9 Channon, *Chips*, pp. 126, 139
10 Pope-Hennessy, *Queen Mary 1867–1953*, p. 585
11 Crawford, op. cit., p. 44
12 Warwick, op. cit., p. 24
13 Longford, *Elizabeth R*, p. 92
14 Crawford, op. cit., p. 48
15 Lacey, *Majesty*, p. 143
16 Wheeler-Bennett, op. cit., p. 407
17 Conversation with the Queen Mother
18 Crawford, op. cit., p. 60

7: *Wartime Windsor*

1 Crawford, *The Little Princesses*, pp. 62–5
2 Conversation with the Queen Mother
3 Crawford, op. cit., p. 66
4 Ibid., p. 69
5 Conversation with Princess Margaret
6 Crawford, op. cit., pp. 71–2
7 Longford, *Elizabeth R*, p. 119
8 Queen Alexandra of Yugoslavia, *For a King's Love*, p. 111
9 Conversation with Princess Margaret
10 Crawford, op. cit., p. 84
11 Longford, op. cit., pp. 111–2
12 Longford, *The Queen Mother*, p. 83
13 Conversation with the Queen Mother
14 Conversation with Princess Margaret
15 Wheeler-Bennett, *King George VI*, p. 741
16 Edwards, *Royal Sisters*, pp. 105–6
17 Sheridan, *From Cabbages to Kings*, p. 113
18 Crawford, op. cit., pp. 79–80
19 Ibid., p. 81
20 Princess Alice, Countess of Athlone, *For My Grandchildren*, p. 260
21 Airlie, *Thatched with Gold*, p. 225
22 Longford, *Elizabeth R*, p. 122
23 Crawford, op. cit., p. 73
24 Barrymaine, *The Story of Peter Townsend*, p. 62
25 Crawford, op. cit., p. 82
26 Warwick, *Princess Margaret*, p. 42
27 Longford, *Elizabeth R*, pp. 121–2
28 Rosen, *The Goossens*, p. 257
29 Bradford, *Elizabeth*, p. 101
30 Glendinning, *Rebecca West*, p. 170
31 Wheeler-Bennett, op. cit., p. 749
32 Airlie, op. cit., p. 228
33 Townsend, *Time and Chance*, p. 121
34 Ibid., pp. 144–5
35 Ibid., p. 194
36 Ibid., p. 145
37 Wheeler-Bennett, op. cit., p. 622
38 Conversation with Princess Margaret
39 Ibid.

8: 'Enfant Terrible'

1 Crawford, *The Little Princesses*, p. 91
2 Townsend, *Time and Chance*, p. 157
3 Ibid., p. 156
4 Ibid., p. 146
5 Airlie, *Thatched with Gold*, p. 225
6 Conversation with Princess Margaret
7 Wheeler-Bennett, *King George VI*, p. 626
8 Ibid., p. 755
9 Townsend, op. cit., p. 146
10 van der Byl, *The Shadows Lengthen*, p. 127
11 Conversation with Princess Alice, Countess of Athlone
12 Longford, *Elizabeth R*, p. 134
13 Conversation with Princess Margaret
14 Conversation with the Queen Mother
15 Ibid.
16 Townsend, op. cit., p. 171
17 Ibid., p. 174
18 Conversation with Miriam Bloomberg
19 Warner, *History of the Kimberley Club*, p. 134
20 Conversation with Princess Margaret
21 van der Byl, op. cit., p. 134
22 Townsend, op. cit., p. 173
23 *Cape Times*, 25 April 1947
24 Wheeler-Bennett, op. cit., p. 692
25 Conversation with Princess Margaret
26 Edwards, *Royal Sisters*, p. 189
27 Crawford, op. cit., p. 108
28 Ibid., p. 99
29 Queen Alexandra of Yugolsavia, *Prince Philip*, p. 106
30 Townsend, op. cit., p. 181
31 Airlie, op. cit., p. 230
32 Crawford, op. cit., p. 116
33 Queen Alexandra of Yugoslavia, *For a King's Love*, p. 163
34 Crawford, op. cit., p. 118

9: The Glamour Princess

1 James, *Margaret*, p. 29
2 Lees-Milne, *Midway on the Waves*, p. 189
3 Conversation with Princess Margaret
4 Sissons and French, *Age of Austerity 1945–51*, pp. 148–152
5 Conversation with Princess Alice, Countess of Athlone
6 Townsend, *Time and Chance*, p. 180
7 Colville, *The Fringes of Power*, p. 621
8 Donaldson, *A Twentieth-Century Life*, p. 186
9 Private information
10 Spada, *Peter Lawford*, p. 126
11 Frischauer, *Margaret*, p. 57
12 Coward, *The Noël Coward Diaries*, p. 179
13 James, op. cit., p. 33
14 *Newsweek*, 27 July 1953

15 Crawford, *Margaret*, p. 26
16 Beaton and Strong, *The Royal Portraits*, p.34
17 Crawford, *The Little Princesses*, p. 120
18 Coward, op. cit., pp. 179, 136
19 Lees-Milne, op. cit., p. 186
20 Warwick, *Princess Margaret*, p. 48
21 Maychick, *Audrey*, p. 93
22 Conversation with Princess Alice, Countess of Athlone
23 Private information
24 Brough, *Margaret*, p. 137
25 Crawford, *Margaret*, p. 146
26 *Le Figaro*, 1 June 1949
27 Conversation with Princess Margaret
28 Crawford, *Margaret*, p. 37
29 Channon, *Chips*, p. 439
30 Townsend, op. cit., p. 187
31 Private information
32 Bardens, *Princess Margaret*, p. 111
33 Townsend, op. cit., p. 189
34 Ibid., p. 190
35 Pope-Hennessy, *A Lonely Business*, p. 242
36 Townsend, op. cit., p. 187
37 Ibid., p. 186
38 Ibid., p. 188
39 Ibid., p. 188
40 Dempster, *HRH The Princess Margaret*, p. 21
41 Brough, op. cit., p. 141

10: Peter Townsend

1 Bradford, *Elizabeth*, p. 171
2 Astor Papers, MS/1416/1/4/10
3 Crawford, *Margaret*, p. 19
4 Townsend, *Time and Chance*, p. 192
5 Frischauer, *Margaret*, p. 72
6 Townsend, op. cit., p. 194
7 Private information
8 Townsend, op. cit., p. 195
9 Ibid., p. 196
10 Ibid., p. 196
11 Ibid., p. 197
12 Warwick, *Princess Margaret*, p. 59
13 Bradford, op. cit., p. 197
14 Channon, *Chips*, p. 473
15 Conversation with Princess Margaret
16 Hartnell, *Silver and Gold*, p. 134
17 *Daily Express*, 3 June 1953
18 Conversation with Prince Charles
19 Clark, *Palace Diary*, p. 118
20 Channon, op. cit., p. 476
21 Townsend, op. cit., p. 199
22 *People*, 14 June 1953
23 Longford, *Elizabeth R*, p. 189
24 Townsend, op. cit., p. 201
25 Conversation with Lady Hambleden
26 *Sunday Times*, 12 July 1953; *The Times*, 13 July 1953

27 *Tribune*, 10 July 1953
28 Bardens, *Princess Margaret*, p. 140

11: The End of the Affair

1 Conversation with Princess Margaret
2 Bardens, *Princess Margaret*, p. 143
3 Coward, *The Noël Coward Diaries*, p. 236
4 Warwick, *Princess Margaret*, p. 69
5 Townsend, *Time and Chance*, p. 209
6 Ibid., p. 211
7 Warwick, op. cit., p. 69
8 Bardens, op. cit., p. 149
9 Frischauer, *Margaret*, p. 102
10 Ibid., p. 103
11 Coward, op. cit., p. 257
12 Bardens, op. cit., p. 146
13 Warwick, op. cit., p. 69
14 Coward, op. cit., p. 254
15 H. J. Ashwell to the author
16 Bardens, op. cit., p. 149
17 Bradford, *Elizabeth*, p. 209
18 Townsend, op. cit., p. 223
19 Ibid., p. 226
20 Barrymaine, *The Story of Peter Townsend*, p. 177
21 *The Times*, 23 October 1955
22 Townsend, op. cit., p. 232
23 Ibid., loc. cit., p. 232
24 Ibid., p. 237
25 *The Times*, 26 October 1955
26 *Spectator*, 23 May 1958
27 Purcell, *Fisher of Lambeth*, p. 244
28 Longford, *Elizabeth R*, p. 220
29 Townsend, op. cit., p. 236
30 *The Times*, 1 November 1955
31 Coward, op. cit., p. 290
32 Townsend, op. cit., p. 236
33 Ibid., pp. 229–30
34 Coward, op. cit., p. 289
35 Bradford, op. cit., p. 212
36 Ibid., p. 207
37 Private information
38 Rose, *Kings, Crowns and Courtiers*, p. 190

12: The Modern Princess

1 Barrow, *Gossip*, pp. 187–8
2 Frischauer, *Margaret*, p. 122
3 Bardens, *Princess Margaret*, p. 169
4 Murray, *Good Morning*, p. 321
5 Warwick, *Princess Margaret*, p. 82
6 Bardens, op. cit., p. 171
7 Whicker, *Within Whicker's World*, p. 87
8 Warwick, op. cit., p. 82
9 Frischauer, op. cit., p. 124
10 Dempster, *HRH The Princess Margaret*, p. 36

11 Warwick, op. cit., p. 80
12 Dempster, op. cit., p. 37
13 Bradford, *Elizabeth*, p. 402
14 *Sunday Times*, 5 October 1986
15 Gladwyn, *Diaries*, p. 238
16 Conversation with Lady Hambleden
17 Private information
18 Private information
19 Barrat, *With the Greatest Respect*, p. 99
20 Frischauer, op. cit., p. 131
21 Bardens, op. cit., p. 180
22 Townsend, *Time and Chance*, p. 278
23 Ibid., p. 279
24 Bardens, op. cit., p. 182
25 Townsend, op. cit., p. 280
26 *National and English Review*, August 1957
27 Longford, *The Royal House of Windsor*, p. 236
28 Longford, *Elizabeth R*, p. 225
29 Mitford, *The Letters of Nancy Mitford*, p. 374
30 Bradford, op. cit., p. 200
31 Dempster, op. cit., pp. 48–9

13: Antony Armstrong-Jones

1 Frischauer, *Margaret*, p. 147
2 Dempster, *HRH The Princess Margaret*, p. 45
3 Private information
4 Warwick, *Princess Margaret*, p. 87
5 Vickers, *Cecil Beaton*, pp. 435–6
6 Dempster, op. cit., pp. 46, 50
7 Ibid., p. 47
8 Ibid., p. 43, and Warwick, op. cit., p. 89
9 Vickers, op. cit., p. 436
10 Dempster, op. cit., p. 49
11 Amis, *Memoirs*, pp. 187–8
12 Warwick, op. cit., p. 93
13 Richardson, *A Long-Distance Runner*, p. 188
14 Dempster, op. cit., p. 50
15 Beaton, *Self-Portrait with Friends*, p.174
16 Warwick, op. cit., p. 95
17 Dempster, op. cit., p. 49
18 Warwick, op. cit., p. 95
19 Frischauer, op. cit., p. 10
20 *The Times*, 27 February 1960
21 *New Statesman*, 30 April 1960
22 Frischauer, op. cit., p. 152
23 Dempster, op. cit., pp. 48–9
24 Brough, *Margaret*, p. 184
25 Vickers, op. cit., p. 437
26 Coward, *The Noël Coward Diaries*, p. 431
27 Parker, *The Princess Royal*, p. 10
28 Botham, *Margaret*, p. 145
29 Warwick, op. cit., p. 99
30 Beaton, op. cit., pp. 336–8
31 Chester, Linklater, and May, *Jeremy Thorpe*, p. 31
32 Frischauer, op. cit., p. 155
33 Ibid.

34 *Sphere*, 14 May 1960
35 Coward, op. cit., p. 438

14: The Performing Dwarfs

1 Dempster, *HRH The Princess Margaret*, p. 51
2 Private information
3 Warwick, *Princess Margaret*, p. 80
4 Hoey, *The New Royal Court*, p. 53
5 *People*, 18 September 1960–9 October 1960
6 Frischauer, *Margaret*, p. 166
7 Hoey, op. cit., p. 53
8 Bardens, *Princess Margaret*, p. 202
9 *Ibid.*, p. 206
10 Hamilton, *My Queen and I*, p. 60
11 Conversation with Princess Margaret
12 *Private Eye*
13 *Sunday Dispatch*, 14 June 1960
14 *Observer*, 10 August 1980
15 Bradford, *Elizabeth*, p. 301
16 *Daily Express*, 4 September 1961
17 Warwick, op. cit., p. 111
18 *Ibid.*, p. 87
19 *People*, 7 October 1961
20 *Guardian*, 4 October 1961
21 Dempster, op. cit., p. 54
22 Glenton, *Tony's Room*, p.149
23 Frischauer, op. cit., p. 175
24 Bardens, op. cit., p. 207
25 Brough, *Margaret*, p. 195
26 Warwick, op. cit., p. 117
27 Seymour and Gardner, *Lynn*, p. 82
28 Warwick, op. cit., p. 117
29 Ibid., p. 110
30 Giuliano, *Dark Horse*, p. 64
31 Stark, *Remembering Peter Sellers*, pp. 120–1
32 La Rue, *From Drags to Riches*, pp. 119–20
33 Conversation with André Bothner
34 Delfont, *East End, West End*, p. 170
35 La Rue, op. cit., p. 119
36 Private information
37 Vickers, *Cecil Beaton*, p. 490
38 Glenton, op. cit., p. 95
39 Tynan, *The Life of Kenneth Tynan*, p. 270
40 Ibid., pp. 212–3
41 Dempster, op. cit., p. 60
42 Warwick, op. cit., p. 118
43 Botham, *Margaret*, p. 169
44 Glenton, op. cit., p. 146
45 Ibid., p. 94
46 Ibid., p. 180
47 Ibid., p. 182

15: Divisions

1 Dempster, *HRH The Princess Margaret*, p. 58
2 *Ibid.*, p. 53
3 Warwick, *Princess Margaret*, p. 122
4 Frischauer, *Margaret*, p. 183
5 Fisher, *Cyril Connolly*, p. 381
6 Dempster, op. cit., p. 59
7 Ibid., p. 62
8 Sinclair, *Snowdon*, p. 93
9 Ibid., p. 97
10 Warwick, op. cit., p. 124
11 Frischauer, op. cit., p. 186
12 Sinclair, op. cit., p. 98
13 Frischauer, op. cit., p. 184
14 Warwick, op. cit., p. 129
15 Dempster, op. cit., p. 67
16 Ibid., p. 68
17 Warwick, op. cit., p. 127
18 Walker, *Elizabeth*, p. 306
19 Edwards, *The Grimaldis of Monaco*, p. 294
20 Shipman, *Judy Garland*, p. 480
21 Brough, *Margaret*, p. 200
22 Hamilton, *My Queen and I*, p. 178
23 *New Statesman*, 26 November 1965
24 Brough, op. cit., p. 199
25 Ibid., p. 199
26 Private information
27 Dempster, op. cit., p. 67
28 Ibid., pp. 65–7

16: Affairs of the Heart

1 Private information
2 Botham, *Margaret*, p. 198
3 Warwick, *Princess Margaret*, p. 130
4 Dempster, *HRH The Princess Margaret*, p. 70
5 Botham. op. cit., pp. 218–27
6 *Ibid.*, p. 226
7 Dempster, op. cit., p. 72
8 Botham, op. cit., pp. 188–230
9 Dempster, op. cit., p. 88
10 Castle, *The Castle Diaries 1964–70*, pp. 47–8
11 Private information
12 Private information
13 Sinclair, *Snowdon*, p. 120
14 Williams, *The Kenneth Williams Letters*, p. 227
15 Sinclair, op. cit., p. 157
16 St Aubyn, *William of Gloucester*, p. 125
17 *Ibid.*, p. 186
18 *Ibid.*, p. 125
19 *Ibid.*, p. 128
20 Private information
21 Sinclair, op. cit., p. 108
22 Dempster, op. cit., p. 80
23 Ibid., pp. 77–83

17: *Goon Show*

1 Dempster, *HRH The Princess Margaret*, p. 92
2 Ibid., p. 87
3 Andersen, *Jagger Unauthorised*, p. 111
4 Lewis, *Peter Sellers*, p. 691
5 Ibid., p. 692
6 Ekland, *True Britt*, p. 227
7 Lewis, op. cit., p. 693
8 Ibid., p. 697
9 Evans, *The Mask Behind the Mask*, p. 132
10 Lewis, op. cit., p. 696
11 Ibid., p. 695
12 Ibid., p. 692
13 Ibid., p. 698
14 Ibid., p. 698
15 *Observer*, 17 April 1994
16 Dempster, op. cit., p. 127
17 Lewis, op. cit., p. 697
18 Private information
19 Brough, *Margaret*, p. 217; Bradford, *Elizabeth*, p. 404
20 *Private Eye*, 14 August 1970
21 Dempster, op. cit., p. 76
22 Ibid., p. 90
23 Warwick, *Princess Margaret*, p. 138
24 Dempster, op. cit., p. 84
25 Lees-Milne, *A Mingled Pleasure*, p. 244
26 Ibid., pp. 254–5
27 Graves, *Richard Hughes*, p. 406
28 Harewood, *The Tongs and the Bones*, p. 295
29 Warwick, op. cit., p. 138
30 *Report from the Select Committee on the Civil List, 1971–2*
31 Hamilton, *My Queen and I*, p. 60
32 Letter to the author
33 Conversation with Princess Alice, Countess of Athlone
34 Conversation with Princess Margaret
35 Conversation with Toby Barker
36 Laine, *Cleo*, pp. 303–4
37 Delfont, *East End, West End*, p. 170

18: *Toy Boy*

1 *News of the World*, 20 January 1980
2 Dempster, *HRH The Princess Margaret*, p. 101
3 Ibid., p. 119
4 Conversation with Stephen Birmingham
5 Conversation with Princess Margaret
6 Dempster, op. cit., p. 112
7 Ibid., p. 115
8 Ibid., p. 113
9 Ibid., p. 114
10 Warwick, *Princess Margaret*, p. 144
11 Bradford, *Elizabeth*, p. 405
12 Warwick, op. cit., p. 147
13 Dempster, op. cit., p. 124

14 Bradford, op. cit., p. 407
15 Ibid., p. 409
16 Dempster, op. cit., pp. 126–7

19: *Divorce*

1 Warwick, *Princess Margaret*, p. 148
2 Norman, *Elton*, p. 268
3 Ibid., pp. 274–5
4 Leonard, *Kathleen*, p. 208
5 Farson, *The Gilded Gutter Life of Francis Bacon*, p. 171
6 *Independent*, 2 March 1996
7 Private information
8 Benson, *No Regard for Money*, pp. 105–6
9 Hall, *Diaries*, entry for 6 June 1977
10 Bennett, *Writing Home*, pp. 320–1
11 *Sun*, 3 November 1977
12 Dempster, *HRH The Princess Margaret*, p. 143
13 Ibid., p. 144
14 Quoted in Dempster, op. cit., p. 145
15 Sinclair, *Snowdon*, pp. 169–70
16 Quoted in Dempster, op. cit., p. 146
17 Quoted in Sinclair, op. cit., p. 172
18 Quoted in Warwick, op. cit., p. 151
19 *People*, 26 March 1978
20 *Daily Telegraph*, 30 March 1978
21 *Evening Standard*, 7 April 1978
22 *The Times*, 30 March 1978
23 Warwick, op. cit., p. 153

20: *Tragic Princess*

1 Brough, *Margaret*, p. 242
2 Warwick, *Princess Margaret*, p. 158
3 Conversation with Princess Alice, Countess of Athlone
4 Bradford, *Elizabeth*, p. 409
5 Dempster, *HRH The Princess Margaret*, p. 176
6 *News of the World*, 20 January 1980
7 Dempster, op. cit., p. 176
8 Ibid., p. 169
9 Henderson, *Mandarin*, p. 300
10 *Daily Telegraph*, 18 October 1979
11 Caine, *What's It All About?*, p. 394
12 Henderson, op. cit., p. 405
13 *Observer*, 18 May 1980
14 Quoted in Warwick, op. cit., p. 162
15 *Observer*, loc. cit., 18 May 1980
16 Dempster, op. cit., p. 169
17 Ibid., pp. 185–6
18 Ibid., p. 188
19 Ibid., p. 191

21: *Aunt Margot*

1 Conversation with Princess Margaret
2 *Observer*, 17 April 1994
3 Dempster, *HRH The Princess Margaret*, p. 191
4 Private information
5 Private information
6 Barrat, *With the Greatest Respect*, p. 209
7 Rocco, *Independent on Sunday*, 3 October 1993
8 Vidal, *Palimpsest*, p. 194
9 James, *Margaret*, p. 142
10 Bradford, *Elizabeth*, p. 408
11 *Observer*, 14 September 1981
12 *Sunday Times*, 5 October 1986
13 James, op. cit., p. 166
14 Ibid., p. 69
15 Warwick, *Princess Margaret*, p. 167
16 James, op. cit., p. 163
17 Dempster, op. cit., p. 91
18 Larkin, *Selected Letters 1940–85*, 11 January 1985
19 Private information
20 Dempster, op. cit., p. 92
21 Private information
22 Jameson, *The Last of the Hot Metal Men*, p. 36
23 Norman, *Elton*, p. 268
24 Clark, *Diaries*, entry for 28 June 1990
25 Morton, *Diana: Her True Story*, p. 137
26 *Sunday Times*, 5 October 1986
27 Bradford, op. cit., p. 451
28 James, op. cit., p. 108
29 Courtney, *Princess Anne*, p. 105
30 Conversation with the Queen Mother and Princess Margaret
31 Vidal, op. cit., p. 372
32 Barrat, op. cit., p. 104
33 Bradford, op. cit., p. 442
34 Barry, *Royal Service*, p. 72
35 Ibid., p. 67

22: *The Survivor*

1 Peter Hillmore in the *Observer*, 21 April 1996
2 *The Times*, 7 May 1982
3 Conversation with Princess Margaret
4 Private information
5 Rocco, *Independent on Sunday*, 3 October 1993
6 Conversation with Jayne Fincher
7 James, *Margaret*, p. 156
8 Rocco, art. cit.
9 Private information
10 Idem
11 Idem
12 Rocco, art. cit.
13 Peter Hillmore, art. cit.
14 Thompson, *Ingrams*, p. 17
15 *The Times*, 15 April 1995
16 Rocco, art. cit.
17 Ibid.
18 *The Times*, 16 May 1991
19 Ibid., 11 October 1983
20 *Sunday Express*, 20 January 1983
21 Nicolson, *Diaries and Letters 1930–9*, p. 405
22 Private information
23 Idem
24 James, op. cit., p. 129
25 Conversation with Princess Margaret
26 *Daily Mirror*, 1 October 1989
27 Hall, *Royal Fortune*, p. 132
28 Warwick, *Princess Margaret*, p. 170
29 Private information
30 Idem
31 *Daily Mail*, 11 April 1994
32 *Observer*, 17 April 1994
33 Warwick, op. cit., p. 168
34 Private information
35 Conversation with Princess Margaret

$\mathcal{B}ibliography$

All books were published in London unless
otherwise specified

AIRLIE, MABELL, COUNTESS OF: *Thatched with Gold*, Hutchinson, 1962
ALEXANDRA OF YUGOSLAVIA, QUEEN: *For a King's Love*, Hodder and Stoughton, 1956
— : *Prince Philip: A Family Portrait*, Hodder and Stoughton, 1960
ALICE, PRINCESS, COUNTESS OF ATHLONE: *For My Grandchildren*, Evans, 1966
ALICE, PRINCESS, DUCHESS OF GLOUCESTER: *Memoirs*, Collins, 1983
AMIS, KINGSLEY: *Memoirs*, Hutchinson, 1991
ANDERSEN, CHRISTOPHER: *Jagger Unauthorised*, Simon and Schuster, 1993
ASQUITH, LADY CYNTHIA: *The Married Life of the Duchess of York*, Hutchinson, 1928
—: *The King's Daughters*, Hutchinson, 1937
—: *The Family Life of Her Majesty Queen Elizabeth*, Hutchinson, 1939
—: *Haply I May Remember*, James Barrie, 1950
—: article in *Weekly Illustrated*, 4 April 1953
BARDENS, DENNIS: *Princess Margaret*, Robert Hale, 1964
BARRAT, JOHN: *With the Greatest Respect*, Sidgwick and Jackson, 1991
BARROW, ANDREW: *Gossip 1920–1970*, Pan, 1978
BARRY, STEPHEN P.: *Royal Service*, Avon Books, New York, 1984
BARRYMAINE, NORMAN: *The Story of Peter Townsend*, Peter Davies, 1958
BEATON, CECIL: *Self-Portrait with Friends*, Weidenfeld and Nicolson, 1979
— and STRONG, ROY: *The Royal Portraits*, Thames and Hudson, 1988
BEHAN, DOMINIC: *Milligan: the Life and Times of Spike Milligan*, Methuen, 1988
BENNETT, ALAN: *Writing Home*, Faber and Faber, 1994
BENSON, CHARLES: *No Regard for Money: the Memoirs of a Racing Man*, Quartet, 1988
BOTHAM, NOEL: *Margaret: The Untold Story*, Blake, 1994
BRADFORD, SARAH: *George VI*, Weidenfeld and Nicolson, 1989

—: *Elizabeth*, Heinemann, 1996
BROUGH, JAMES: *Margaret: The Tragic Princess*, W.H. Allen, 1978
BRYAN, J., III, and MURPHY, J. V.: *The Windsor Story*, Granada, 1979
CAINE, MICHAEL: *What's It All About?*, Century, 1992
CAPOTE, TRUMAN: *Answered Prayers*, Penguin, 1993
CASTLE, BARBARA: *The Castle Diaries, 1964–70*, Weidenfeld and Nicolson, 1984
CHANNON, SIR HENRY: *Chips*, Weidenfeld and Nicolson, 1967
CHASE, EDNA WOOLMAN, and CHASE, ILKA: *Always in Vogue*, Gollancz, 1954
CHESTER, LEWIS, LINKLATER, MAGNUS, and MAY, DAVID: *Jeremy Thorpe: A Secret Life*, André Deutsch, 1979
CLARK, STANLEY: *Palace Diary*, Harrap, 1958
CLARK, ALAN: *Diaries*, Weidenfeld and Nicolson, 1993
CLYNES, J.R.: *Memoirs, Volume II*, 1924–37, Hutchinson, 1937
COLVILLE, JOHN: *The Fringes of Power*, Hodder and Stoughton, 1985
COOPER, DIANA: *The Light of Common Day*, Hart-Davis, 1959
COURTNEY, NICHOLAS: *Princess Anne*, Weidenfeld and Nicolson, 1986
COWARD, NOËL: *The Noël Coward Diaries*, Weidenfeld and Nicolson, 1982
CRAWFORD, MARION: *The Little Princesses*, Cassell, 1950
—: *Margaret: The Story of a Modern Princess*, Prentice-Hall, New York, n.d.
DE-LA-NOY, MICHAEL: *The Queen Behind the Throne*, Hutchinson, 1994
DELFONT, BERNARD: *East End, West End: An Autobiography*, Macmillan, 1990
DEMPSTER, NIGEL: *HRH The Princess Margaret: A Life Unfulfilled*, Quartet, 1981
DIMBLEBY, JONATHAN: *The Prince of Wales*, Little, Brown, 1994
DONALDSON, FRANCES: *Edward VIII*, Weidenfeld and Nicolson, 1974
—: *King George VI and Queen Elizabeth*,

Weidenfeld and Nicolson, 1977

—: *A Twentieth-Century Life*, Weidenfeld and Nicolson, 1992

DONALDSON, WILLIAM: *Great Disasters of the Stage*, Arthur Barker, 1984

EDWARDS, ANNE: *Royal Sisters*, Collins, 1990

—: *The Grimaldis of Monaco*, HarperCollins, 1992

EKLAND, BRITT: *True Britt*, Sphere, 1980

EVANS, PETER: *The Mask Behind the Mask*, Leslie Frewen, 1969

EVANS, WILLIAM: *My Mountbatten Years*, Headline, 1989

FARSON, DANIEL: *The Gilded Gutter Life of Francis Bacon*, Century, 1993

FISHER, CLIVE: *Cyril Connolly*, Macmillan, 1995

FRANKLAND, NOBLE: *Prince Henry, Duke of Gloucester*, Weidenfeld and Nicolson, 1980

FRISCHAUER, WILLI: *Margaret: Princess Without a Cause*, Michael Joseph, 1977

GIULIANO, GEOFFREY: *Dark Horse: The Secret Life of George Harrison*, Bloomsbury, 1989

GLADWYN, CYNTHIA: *The Diaries of Cynthia Gladwyn*, Constable, 1995

GLENDINNING, VICTORIA: *Rebecca West*, Weidenfeld and Nicolson, 1987

GLENTON, WILLIAM: *Tony's Room*, Bernard Geis Associates, New York, 1965

GORE, JOHN: *King George V: A Personal Memoir*, John Murray, 1941

GRAVES, RICHARD PERCEVAL: *Richard Hughes*, André Deutsch, 1994

HALL, PETER: *Diaries*, Hamish Hamilton, 1987

HALL, PHILLIP: *Royal Fortune*, Bloomsbury, 1992

HAMILTON, WILLIE: *My Queen and I*, Quartet, 1975

HARDINGE, HELEN: *Loyal to Three Kings*, Kimber, 1967

HAREWOOD, EARL OF: *The Tongs and the Bones*, Weidenfeld and Nicolson, 1981

HARTNELL, NORMAN: *Silver and Gold*, Evans, 1955

—: *Royal Courts of Fashion*, Cassell, 1971

HENDERSON, NICHOLAS: *Mandarin: The Diaries of an Ambassador*, Weidenfeld and Nicolson, 1994

HIGHAM, CHARLES, and MOSELEY, ROY: *Elizabeth and Philip: the Untold Story*, Pan, 1992

HOEY, BRIAN: *The Princess Anne: A Biography*, Country Life Books, 1984

—: *The New Royal Court*, Sidgwick and Jackson, 1990

HOPE, ALICE: *Princess Margaret*, Frederick Muller, 1960

INGHAM, BERNARD: *Kill the Messenger*, HarperCollins, 1991

JAMES, PAUL: *Margaret: A Woman of Conflict*, Sidgwick and Jackson, 1990

JAMESON, DEREK: *The Last of the Hot Metal Men*, Ebury Press, 1990

KING, STELLA: *Princess Marina*, Cassell, 1969

LACEY, ROBERT: *Majesty*, Hutchinson, 1977

LAINE, CLEO: *Cleo*, Simon and Schuster, 1994

LAIRD, DOROTHY: *Queen Elizabeth the Queen Mother*, Hodder and Stoughton, 1966

LANE, PETER: *Princess Michael of Kent*, Robert Hale, 1986

LARKIN, PHILIP: *Selected Letters 1940–85*, Faber and Faber, 1992

LA RUE, DANNY: *From Drags to Riches: My Autobiography*, Viking, 1987

LEE, PEGGY: *Miss Peggy Lee*, Bloomsbury, 1990

LEES-MILNE, JAMES: *Midway on the Waves*, Faber and Faber, 1985

—: *A Mingled Pleasure: Diaries*, John Murray, 1994

LEONARD, MAURICE: *Kathleen: The Life of Kathleen Ferrier*, Hutchinson, 1988

LESLEY, COLE: *Remembered Laughter: the Life of Noël Coward*, Knopf, New York, 1977

LEWIS, ROGER: *Peter Sellers*, Century, 1994

LONGFORD, ELIZABETH: *Elizabeth R*, Hodder and Stoughton, 1966

—: *The Royal House of Windsor*, Weidenfeld and Nicolson, 1974

—: *The Queen Mother*, Granada, 1981

MARIE OF ROMANIA, QUEEN: *The Story of My Life*, Cassell, 1934

MAYCHICK, DIANA: *Audrey: An Intimate Portrait*, Sidgwick and Jackson, 1993

MENKES, SUZY: *The Royal Jewels*, Grafton, 1985

MIDDLEMAS, K., and BARNES, J.: *Baldwin*, Weidenfeld and Nicolson, 1969

MITFORD, NANCY: *The Letters of Nancy Mitford*, Hodder and Stoughton, 1993

MORRAH, DERMOT: *The Work of the Queen*, William Kimber, 1958

MORTON, ANDREW: *The Wealth of the Windsors*, Michael O'Mara, 1989

—: *Diana: Her True Story*, Michael O'Mara, 1992

MURRAY, ALBERT: *Good Morning: The Autobiography of Count Basie*, Heinemann, 1986

NICOLSON, HAROLD: *King George V*, Constable, 1952

—: *Diaries and Letters*, 3 vols, Collins, 1966–8

NORMAN, PHILIP: *Elton*, Hutchinson, 1991

PARKER, JOHN: *The Princess Royal*, Hamish Hamilton, 1989

—: *The Queen*, Headline, 1991

PEACOCKE, M.D.: *The Story of Buckingham Palace*, Odhams, 1951

POPE-HENNESSY, JAMES: *Queen Mary 1867–1953*, George Allen and Unwin, 1959

—: *A Lonely Business*, Weidenfeld and Nicolson, 1981

Bibliography

PURCELL, WILLIAM: *Fisher of Lambeth*, Hodder and Stoughton, 1969

RICHARDSON, TONY: *A Long-Distance Runner: A Memoir*, Faber and Faber, 1993

ROCCO, FIAMMETTA: 'Duty Before Happiness', article in the *Independent on Sunday*, 3 October 1993

ROOSEVELT, ELEANOR: *This I Remember*, Hutchinson, 1950

ROSE, KENNETH: *Kings, Crowns and Courtiers*, Weidenfeld and Nicolson, 1985

ROSEN, CAROLE: *The Goossens: A Musical Century*, André Deutsch, 1993

ST AUBYN, GILES: *William of Gloucester*, Frederick Muller, 1977

SEYMOUR, LYNN, and GARDNER, PAUL: *Lynn: The Autobiography of Lynn Seymour*, Granada, 1984

SHERIDAN, LISA: *From Cabbages to Kings*, Odhams, 1955

SHEW, BETTY SPENCER: *Queen Elizabeth the Queen Mother*, MacDonald, 1955

SHIPMAN, DAVID: *Judy Garland*, Fourth Estate, 1992

SINCLAIR, DAVID: *Queen and Country*, Dent, 1979

—: *Snowdon*, Proteus Books, 1982

SISSONS, MICHAEL, and FRENCH, PHILIP: *Age of Austerity 1945–51*, Hodder and Stoughton, 1963

SITWELL, OSBERT: *Queen Mary and Others*, Michael Joseph, 1974

SPADA, JAMES: *Peter Lawford: The Man Who Kept the Secrets*, Bantam, 1991

STARK, GRAHAM: *Remembering Peter Sellers*, Robson Books, 1990

THOMPSON, HARRY: *Richard Ingrams, Lord of the Gnomes*, Heinemann, 1994

THORNTON, MICHAEL: *Royal Feud*, Michael Joseph, 1985

TOWNSEND, PETER: *Time and Chance*, Collins, 1978

TYNAN, KATHLEEN: *The Life of Kenneth Tynan*, Weidenfeld and Nicolson, 1987

VAN DER BYL, PIET: *The Shadows Lengthen*, Howard Timmins, Cape Town, 1973

VICKERS, HUGO: *Cecil Beaton*, Weidenfeld and Nicolson, 1985

VIDAL, GORE: *Palimpsest: A Memoir*, André Deutsch, 1995

WALKER, ALEXANDER, *Elizabeth*, Weidenfeld and Nicolson, 1994

WARHOL, ANDY: *The Andy Warhol Diaries*, Simon and Schuster, 1989

WARNER, CONSTANCE: *History of the Kimberley Club*, privately printed, Kimberley, 1965

WARWICK, CHRISTOPHER: *Princess Margaret*, Weidenfeld and Nicolson, 1983

—: *George and Marina*, Weidenfeld and Nicolson, 1988

WHEELER-BENNETT, JOHN: *King George VI*, Macmillan, 1958

WHICKER, ALAN: *Within Whicker's World*, Elm Tree Books, 1982

WILLIAMS, KENNETH: *The Kenneth Williams Letters*, HarperCollins, 1994

WINDSOR, DUCHESS OF: *The Heart Has Its Reasons*, Michael Joseph, 1956

WINDSOR, DUKE OF: *A King's Story*, Cassell, 1951

WYATT, WOODROW: *Confessions of an Optimist*, Collins, 1985

ZIEGLER, PHILIP: *Crown and People*, Collins, 1978

—: *Edward VIII*, Collins, 1990

NEWSPAPERS AND MAGAZINES

Daily Express, Daily Mail, Le Figaro, Guardian, Independent on Sunday, Illustrated London News, Mail on Sunday, Majesty, Daily Mirror, National and English Review, New Statesman, News of the World, Observer, People, Private Eye, Spectator, Sphere, Sun, Sunday Pictorial, Sunday Times, Daily Telegraph, The Times, Tribune

Index

Index

meets PM, 215; and Princess Margaretha, 216; marriage, 216; suicide, 220
Douglas-Home, Sholto, 216
Dudley, William Ward, 3rd Earl of, 110
Dudley, William Ward, 4th Earl of, 286
d'Urso, Mario, 293

Eastwood, Clint, 278
Eden, Sir Anthony, 133, 140–1, 145, 169
Eden, Clarissa, Lady, 141
Edward VII, King, 34, 69, 239, 295
Edward VIII, King *see* Windsor, Duke of
Edward, Prince, 201, 249, 267, 272, 296–7, 312
Ekland, Britt, 197–8, 230–2
Elizabeth II, Queen; *as Princess*: 9–10, 17, 22, 36, 38, 40, 42–7, 51–4, 58–63, 69–77, 78–92, 93–104, 105, 107, 112, 116, 120, 123; *as Queen*: 123, 126–9, 131, 134, 136, 140, 143–5, 148, 151, 155, 157–62, 169, 172, 175, 177, 181, 188, 192, 194–5, 199, 203, 206, 222, 230–1, 237–9, 243, 249, 252–3, 255–6, 261–2, 265–6, 272, 274–5, 279, 281, 283, 286–7, 296–7, 299–303, 307, 309–13, 315–7; birth, 34; death of George V, 53; on Abdication, 61; moved to Windsor, 80; becomes engaged, 96; turns 21, 100; marriage, 102–4; becomes Queen, 123; 'banishes' Townsend, 132; grants Snowdon permission to marry PM, 175; Silver Jubilee, 266; and Roddy at PM's birthday, 281
Elizabeth, Queen, the Queen Mother; *as Duchess of York*, 9, 30–4, 35–9, 41, 43–4, 46, 48, 51, 53, 55, 57, 59, 61; *as Queen*, 63, 67–80, 82–4, 88, 90–2, 95–101, 103–4, 106–8, 111–2, 115–6, 118, 120; *as Queen Mother*, 123–4, 126–7, 129–30, 132, 141–2, 154, 156–7, 172–3, 175, 177, 179, 181, 197, 199, 201, 205, 210, 230, 234, 237–8, 242, 250, 253–4, 257–8, 272, 274, 280–1, 290, 292, 296–9, 302–4, 310, 312, 314–7; birth, 30; marriage, 32; birth of PM, 15–22; becomes Queen, 63; death of George VI, 120; breaks news to PM of Townsend's 'banishment', 133
Elliot, Dominic, 110, 229, 281
Elphinstone, Mary, Lady, 37, 142
Epstein, Jacob, 151
Erleigh, Simon, Viscount, 227
Esterházy, Countess Marianne, 229
Everard, Dorothy, 208

Fagan, Michael, 304
Fabiola of the Belgians, Queen, 191
Fairbanks, Douglas (Junior), 136, 279

Farrer, Matthew, 268
Ferguson, Sarah *see* York
Ferner, Johan, 191
Ferrier, Kathleen, 258
Fincher, Jayne, 303
Fisher, Dr Geoffrey, Archbishop of Canterbury, 118, 145
Fitzgerald, Ella, 151
Fitzherbert, Maria, 57
Fleming, Ann, 206
Fleming, Ian, 40
Fleming, Peter, 40
Fonteyn, Margot, 197
Foot, Sir Hugh, 139
Foot, Michael, 133
Forbes, Bryan, 197, 257
Franz-Josef, Emperor of Austria-Hungary, 23
Frederick, Empress, of Germany, 21
Frederika of the Hellenes, Queen, 153, 179
Frost, David, 227
Fry, Jeremy, 178–9, 203, 266

Gandhi, Mahatma, 103
Garland, Judy, 211–2, 307
Gaulle, Gen. Charles de, French President, 192
George, Boy, 292
George III, King, 46, 69, 127, 271
George IV, King, 36, 57, 69, 72
George V, King, 16–7, 21–7, 29, 31, 45–6, 48–50, 52–4, 64, 67–9, 94, 127, 203, 237, 267, 295; PM's opinion of, 45; Silver Jubilee, 51; death, 53
George VI, King; *as Duke of York*: 16–8, 20–1, 26–34, 35–7, 42–4, 48, 51, 53, 55, 57, 59–62; *as King*: 67–80, 83–4, 86–101, 103, 106–7, 111, 115–20, 123, 127, 134, 143, 223, 238, 272, 296, 308, 313; birth, 26; marriage, 32; becomes King, 63–4; death, 120
George of Denmark, Prince, 153
Gershwin, George, 217
Gigli, Beniamino, 78
Gilliat, Dr Roger, 178
Glamis, Monster of, 16
Glenconner, Lord *see* Tennant
Glenton, Nellie, 194
Glenton, William, 171, 181, 200
Gloucester, Princess Alice, Duchess of, 31, 52, 107, 225, 299, 312
Gloucester, Birgetta, Duchess of, 304
Gloucester, Prince Henry, Duke of, 31, 52, 62, 107, 151, 225, 249
Gloucester, Prince Richard, Duke of, 304
Gloucester, Prince William of, 104, 225